# THE BUSINESS OF LUNCH

Portrait of Mavis Norrie by Raymund Rogers, 2007

# The Business of Lunch

## A Bookman's Life and Travels

**IAN NORRIE**

QUARTET

First published in 2009 by
Quartet Books Limited
A member of the Namara Group
27 Goodge Street, London W1T 2LD

A catalogue record for this book
is available from the British Library

ISBN    978 0 7043 7150 7

Typeset by Antony Gray
Printed and bound in Great Britain by
T J International Ltd, Padstow, Cornwall

This memoir is dedicated, in gratitude, to all those generous souls who subscribed sight unseen to *Mentors and Friends*, thus making its publication possible.

# Contents

# Preface

During the course of a long life it is not unusual to have known – as has been my good fortune – thousands, rather than hundreds, of people. Although, in this memoir, comparatively few of those encountered are mentioned, it should not be assumed that omission is due either to lack of regard and affection or to memory loss; the largest of W. P. Frith's narrative paintings could not include every single person at a railway terminal, on a beach or attending a race meeting.

Equally, it would be presumptuous of anyone writing autobiography to assume that those who are not mentioned might feel aggrieved. On a farewell tour the old-time actor, in his curtain speech, would declaim, 'I love you *all*!'; some in the audience may not have reciprocated the compliment.

# 1

## Childhood, War and Journalism

Rarely have I been unwilling to work – except at school – but I have always contrived to extend lunchtime far into the afternoon; he who cannot delegate may never achieve this.

My love affair with lunch began as a reaction to the nature of family meals. My father was not interested in food probably because he suffered from Scottish dentistry, having had all his teeth removed when a young man. Wearing a plate to support false replacements desensitised his palette causing him to yearn for a time when pills would provide all necessary sustenance. His taste buds reacted only to strong tea, whisky and preserved ginger. In consequence, my mother made a joke of seeing how quickly we could all get through a meal. I found this irksome and developed the habit of lunching on Sundays with an aunt and cousins who lived nearby. Edie, the aunt, loved to linger once the dishes had been removed, and to talk and smoke; I preferred adult company to that of my own age group.

Long lunches became a feature of my working life even before I had my own business. They and delegation must go hand-in-hand. The reason that neither Oscar Wilde nor any of the exalted epigrammatists of his time coined my maxim as an apothegm, an aside, or even as an old saw, is that none of them was required to leave an acolyte looking after the shop. They roamed the world dropping witticisms in their wake, only taking time off with a sigh of ennui to dash off the occasional masterpiece. They delegated nothing but their debts. Early on I learned to emulate them only in the manner of extending my lunchtime, a tendency reaching epic proportions when, in 1982, Mavis and I took a six-months sabbatical, on full pay, while my colleagues ran our company. I was truly fortunate that, in my case, while the cat was away the mice worked rather than played; in my innocence I trusted them and, for once, innocence triumphed.

Autobiography, I believe, should dwell on other people as much as on oneself. (I will try to remember that.) But how much does it matter what these people I encountered in my brief flutter on this planet were like in my estimation? Are they of any more consequence in the endless passage of time than a fossilised figure in a Pompeiian museum? Probably not; I am not; the reader is not. Despite which each of us can be uniquely fascinating. 'My' gallery features mostly, though not exclusively, literary and book trade folk. Some of the more celebrated I have previously written about in *Mentors and Friends* and they recur here only when it seems relevant to introduce them. Not all were stars; as on stage and screen, the bit parts in real life can prove little gems. Family do not necessarily fit either category.

My father, James Shepherd Norrie, from whom I inherited both impatience and scepticism, was born in Paisley in 1890. He was a retail pharmacist, who would prefer to have been a doctor or a surgeon and came from a seafaring Scottish family. James, his grandfather skippered a steamer, out of the Clyde; Robert, his father, was a ship's carpenter. By his time the family was in reduced circumstances so, although better educated than his English counterparts, there was no question of my father going to university or medical college. Instead he qualified as MPS, working first for Boots and coming south, like many Scots, to manage that chain's branch at Dover during WWI. Looking for digs, he spotted a boarding house on the sea front at Waterloo Crescent. The door was opened by two girls, daughters of the house. They told him that their mother let only to army and naval officers, never to civilians. He replied that his was a reserved occupation. Elsie, the younger of the girls remarked to her sister Hilda that there was 'that vacant little room in the next door attic'. Something about the caller made both reluctant to turn him away and they sought their mother's advice. She took one look at James Shepherd and decided that rules were made to be broken. He accepted the attic room and later married Elsie. My grandmother always insisted that she didn't have favourites but there is little doubt that my father was the son-in-law she most liked. When he predeceased her she, a simple devout Christian, wrote to Elsie, 'This letter is delayed. When I heard, I lost my faith for two days.'

My parents marriage was announced in the *Dover Express & East Kent News* for 18th April 1919. It appeared on the front page with other classified ads; on the back page over half a column was devoted to a description of the event including a list of 'many useful presents' received, along with the names of the donors. Readers of local papers expected it in those days, down to the humblest toast rack. Two years on my father opened his own pharmacy at Maidstone, remaining there until 1926 when the family – now numbering four – moved to Southborough, a small town adjoining Tunbridge Wells. There I was born one year later, on August 3rd.

The Norries were not practising Christians but conformed for the sake of christening, marriage and death. The only time I saw a clergyman in our house was in 1940, when my father, anxious to provide comforts for the troops of WWII stationed in Southborough, asked a local vicar for the use of his church hall as a canteen. Assisted by neighbours and family, for most of the war my parents spent several evenings a week running it. The canteen gave me my first experience of serving behind a counter which I was never required to do in the pharmacy.

Genealogy, I think, should be kept strictly within the family. I know little of my ancestry before 1873 when my maternal grandparents were born. (Untrue: family gossip has it that there was one poor devil who was hung, somewhere in Kent, for stealing a sheep.) Arthur Tapley first breathed in the city of Canterbury; Barbara Ellen Potts (Grandma – 'Nanna', to me) in the nearby village of Petham. I don't know what Grandpa (later known as Tom) was like as a child; his adult behaviour was affectionate but often eccentric. He frequently displayed a tendency to uttering what later were called catch phrases. These were of almost total irrelevance to the prevailing circumstances. Suddenly he would announce: 'Three ships went down that very day'. There was just no reply to that. As a child I giggled; later I thought, the old boy's at it again. Another of his observations was: 'Children coming home from school, looking in the open doorway . . . ' This at least had the beginning of a possible story but there was no development. There was also an instruction to a person named Marsh, 'to build your little 'ouse' which Marsh was apparently reluctant to do although we were never told why. Grandpa declaimed these street cries without embarrassment and took no offence when they fell flat. There was also an item of dialogue: 'You got back then, Tom?'

'Yessir.'

'Did 'e . . . er . . . pay yer?'

'Yessir.'

'Did 'e . . . er . . . say anything?'

' No, sir.'

(Pause.)

'Arrr! Ought to . . . er . . . charged 'im another shilling.'

I heard that routine, which provoked his daughter Babs to nick-name him Tom, a hundred times. It reflects a certain business acumen which Grandpa did not possess. By trade he was a carpenter which led in Edwardian times to his being 'the up and coming young builder in Dover', according to his son Donald who told me the enterprise foundered in 1915 because of the government contracts he held to service army barracks. Donald did not explain what went wrong, but in my mother's opinion, corroborated by her younger sister, he was too gullible to be a successful businessman. Following his bankruptcy Tom started a taxi service which became Tapley's Motors. Survival was helped by Nanna's role in providing for her large family by opening a dress shop and later a boarding house. For a simple country girl she proved commendably resourceful in an urban setting.

Donald's picture of the 'up and coming builder' does not quite fit with Grandpa's known wanderlust which took him away for long stretches to destinations not always disclosed in advance. Once he followed his brother Walter (who also filed for bankruptcy) to Canada; on another occasion Nanna thought of advertising for his whereabouts in the press, but he always returned and was at home sufficiently often to sire seven children, the last of them in 1913.

Tapley's Motors survived until the mid-thirties when Donald, who had forsaken a career in the merchant navy and studied commerce and bookkeeping, joined his father. Don, who along with his brothers and sisters had only an elementary education, was endowed with a keen financial brain and brought off a deal with Martin Walker, of Folke-stone, to absorb the family business. Later in life he recorded his appreciation of the head teacher responsible for it. He remained with Martin, Walker until the seventies when, as managing director, or maybe chairman, part of his retirement package was a new Rolls Royce. Don did well for himself and stood by his father and by Reg, an older brother who was a lame duck. (Reg was my godfather which brought me few benefits spiritual or otherwise; my sister's was Donald who gave her a twenty-first birthday gift of 78 rpm gramophone records including Beethoven's seventh symphony, a work which was an intense revelation to me and which I played whenever she was out of the house.)

For most of my childhood Grandpa addressed me as 'Boy'. He knew who I was but either couldn't or didn't remember my name. Once he took me to see a George Formby film during which he fell asleep and snored. He dozed frequently even on occasions at the wheel of his car. He was an appalling driver, one who never signalled or even looked before changing direction, especially when emerging from a side road, but he led a charmed life. None of his accidents was serious. Another of his characteristics was distinctly Chekhovian. Often when entering a room he would go instantly into golfing mode, practising shots with an imaginary club. At home he liked to be seated close to the coal fire, which effectively heated the chimney more than the living room. He would warm a newspaper in its glow, then place it on his cushion. He hankered after hot climates, often citing Egypt as a desirable place to dwell. He may have visited that country on one of his sudden journeys abroad which were resumed after Nanna's death. The last of these took him to Dublin where it was unlikely to have been excessively hot. He sent us a postcard written in the clear hand he had learned during his brief school-days. In those last two years, unprompted I think, he assumed Nanna's role of responsibility for Christmas gifts, concealing a one pound note in a card with his love to 'Ian and Linnet', as he called Mavis, whom he met only once. He had a hang-up about her name but knew it had a connection with either the thrush or the finch. I write of him at some length because I am conscious of a need to explore a deeper character than that of the buffoon I may seem to have depicted, and aware that my behaviour may sometimes appear odd to my four grandchildren.

Nanna was a saint. She adored her seven children, their wives and husbands, and her ten grandchildren. She went regularly to church, had a natural optimism, found amusement in many things, treasured her garden and grew plants from seeds. I spent spring and summer holidays wherever she happened to be living in Dover – she and grandpa moved many times – and she became a second mother. I loved her dearly.

My grandparents had four sons and three daughters. Of them, after my mother, I was most attached to her younger sister Babs (later she liked to be 'Barbara') and her brothers Donald and Aubrey. The latter and their brothers, Reg and Mark (known as Chum) all worked in Dover, three of them in the family motor business but Chum at Trinity House, the port authority.

Don's wife Edie was a practical, forthright former nurse and became a no-nonsense mother of three; she had no difficulty in matching her husband's style when they gravitated to a handsome four-storey house with large garden in Maison Dieu (pronounced 'due' by us) Road. They became the first of the family to take continental holidays although Edie, (later designated 'Edith' by Don) never grew to like either the French or wine. She became a particular favourite of mine especially after Don evacuated her with their three children to Southborough in 1940. She treated me conversationally as an adult which gratified me although I didn't realise at the time that she was desperately missing her husband whose work and civil defence duties kept him in Dover for most of each week. The meals and chats I regularly enjoyed with Edie were followed by walks in nearby country. (It was only recently that I learned from Diana, her daughter, that she found these occasions life-saving, which touches me greatly.)

Babs, and Bob Mortlock, her second husband, also talked to me as an equal during my many wartime holidays with them at a village in Hampshire. He, as a Bank of England official, was in a reserved occupation; she as a part time ambulance driver had a much tougher war when her duties saw her enduring the blitz on Southampton. They treated me as the son they never had and Babs, who as a kennel maid had acquired a semi-posh accent, mocked me into better speech by echoing my pronunciation of, for instance, 'nee-ow' when I should have said, 'now' (as in 'brown cow'). I was subsequently grateful. She also bullied me into eating what was set before me to counteract what she saw as my faddiness over food. To this day I detest soused pilchards.

Aubrey, beloved by us all, was an effortlessly humorous man, a rough diamond with a heart of gold, educated as rudimentarily as his brothers and sisters, but one who could write clearly expressed, pithy letters and who, like his mother, enjoyed reading. The dear man pur-chased, and perhaps even read, my first novel (the only other relative to earn me a royalty was Bob Mortlock). He always addressed me, after a famous journalist of the time, as 'Hannen' which was partly due to the length of my hair.

All of my relations in uniform survived the war; of the rest of us, only Nellie, Aubrey's first wife, did not. She died of cancer while he was overseas. I vividly remember her seated at our hearth in awful agony, her gaunt face dark grey. It was the first time I had seen anyone who was about to die. Nellie came from a tragic family all of whose young males became partially paralysed from polio while in their early twenties. After WWII Aubrey remarried, again happily, and became a prosperous bookie.

My mother undoubtedly spoilt me. 'Don't tell your father', was an oft-repeated command as she responded to my request for toys and books. 'Here's tuppence,' she would say as I objected to the meal on offer, 'Go along to Milly Young's and buy yourself a fish cake.' Fish cakes and home made fruit cake were my staple diet. It was only after I had married that I learned to relish fresh, cooked vegetables. Until then I had not realised that all taste and goodness does not need to be boiled out of them.

Following the outbreak of war in 1939 food rationing commenced, and my mother's protective instinct for her brood was aroused. She didn't mind going without but it wouldn't do for us. She bullied the grocer unmercifully, bartering saccharines from the pharmacy for 'a little extra, please' of whatever rationed commodity she needed. She was nine years younger than my father, had had little more education than her mother and was good at arithmetic, until it came to house-keeping. The constant request I heard throughout my youth, echoed her plea to the grocer, 'Jimmy, can you let me have a little extra, dear, please.' He had wisely budgeted for this.

Alice, as I came to call my mother, inherited Nanna's green fingers and coped lovingly with the garden. She was also an obsessive knitter, an activity she combined with reading. She was a perfectionist capable of following complicated patterns although when she failed to get one right she would unravel almost a whole garment and start again.

My brother Gordon was seven years my senior, my sister Peggy five. I regarded them, for much of my childhood, as regrettable adjuncts to my life and wished them far away. They didn't bully me but clearly thought our mother over-indulged me. They were closer to Bill, as I called my father once 'Daddy' was deemed inappropriate. (Why did I have a blockage about using 'Mum' and 'Dad'?). As an adult I became fond of Gordon after he had married; Peggy and I shared a passion for theatre and had a similar sense of humour. I never had a serious rift with either; for a long while we just made our separate ways.

I was brought up to believe that we were middle-class but in fact we were nearer to being lower middle. We had a living-in maid (ten shillings per week plus her keep, a candle to light her to her room at the top of the house) and a car. My father employed two assistants plus day- and evening-errand boys (their duties included pumping my bicycle tyres). He earned at least a thousand pounds per annum in 1939 and owned the property where we lived beside, behind and above the shop. (I still own one third share of it.) Every summer he employed a qualified chemist to deputise for him while we were taken on a fortnight's holiday to the seaside. One memorable year we toured Scotland. He loved driving, having bought his first car while still at Dover from my grandfather. When his brother-in-law delivered it intending to offer instruction he was told, 'Move over Reg, I'm the driver.' He taught himself and drove for thirty years without an accident.

When Bill, in 1936 or thereabouts, outlined the car holiday we were to take to Scotland the following summer I listened spellbound. My parents' friends, Reyn and Clare Martin, would be with us but not my brother and sister who had outgrown family vacations. The trip was one I relished before, after and at the time. I was intrigued by my first experience of hotels one highlight of which was being allowed ice cream for breakfast at Blackpool. We reached Scotland via Carter Bar, with one overnight stop at Harrogate. At Edinburgh we stayed on Princes' Street at a hotel which had a serious fire a few nights later but news of that was kept from me; I was said to be a nervous child. We stopped thereafter at Perth, Aberdeen (where we were supposed to rise early to watch the fishing fleet come in but we overslept), Inverness, Helensburgh and Dumfries. At Glasgow we visited my cousin Tommy's pharmacy which stayed open all night and met not only relations but also the Lord Provost. It was thought appropriate that he should receive my father, a native of nearby Paisley, and obligingly arranged a mock call-out of the fire brigade for my benefit. I hope I expressed thanks; my main memory was of his ill-fitting false teeth.

On the return trip, via Ambleside and Blackpool, I paid the first of many visits to Stratford-upon-Avon though there was no question of seeing a play at the Memorial Theatre. My parents and their friends were not into Shakespeare and I was considered too young. (Shakespeare was something you did at school. Nor did we do cathedrals, country houses or art galleries.) That holiday remained strongly in my memory; I did not return to Scotland for three decades.

The maid and the car indicates a certain status and prosperity, yet our house was not centrally heated, there were no fitted carpets, no fridge, no washing machine (instead we had a foul-smelling copper), no hot water boiler, only a dangerous gas geyser in the bathroom. My parents did not entertain, except at Christmas in years when we didn't go to Dover. This was not only due to Bill's indifference to meals but because we lived on the shop premises. In order to have freedom from dispensing prescriptions, he went to his club in the evenings to play billiards and meet his friends. This was reasonable. He could not be expected to be on duty for eighteen hours a day. As children we learned, while he was actually still at home, to answer the door and say he was out, which ought to have been confusing to children who had been brought up not to lie, steal, kill, or covet their neighbours' oxen and asses. I did not question it but realised there was a certain flirting with the truth of which Nanna would not have approved. Nor would she with my mother's habit of taking me out of school for a day to go Christmas shopping, by train or Green Line coach, to London, and subsequently writing a note to the Headmaster to say I had been ill. Is it surprising that I later played truant for at least two afternoons per week or sometimes treated the till float in my father's shop as petty cash?

That, for the present, is enough about family. What of those whose task it was to educate me? To a few of those teachers I owe a great debt, something I was not always willing to admit because I went through a long phase of believing I taught myself most of what I knew. This probably derived from having been able to read long before I was sent to my first school, Rosemead Kindergarten, where my strongest memory is of joyful mornings playing shops as a method of learning arithmetic. (As a result my mental arithmetic is still swift and accurate; I also played shops for forty years to earn a living.)

To make an outright boast may well be in the nature of auto-biography but it can also be an admission of failure . . . failure, in my case, to pass exams at a time when that condition was still tolerated in education. (Nowadays no one fails; they achieve lower grades, a situation which is at odds with a world obsessed by competitive sport where when there is a winner there must also be a loser, although even that status is being dumbed-down.)

On the first occasion I sat School Cert. (roughly analogous today, I think, with GCSE or O level) I failed by passing in only four subjects. On the second, taken at a time when Hitler commenced bombarding south-east England with flying bombs, I passed in the required five, even gaining a distinction in one and credits in two others. And none of these was 'Media Studies', 'Manicure Culture' or 'Pop Music'. My meagre triumphs were in English Language, English Literature, History, Geography and Maths; had Media Studies been on the curriculum in those days I might well have achieved a distinction because I listened to most programmes on the BBC Home Service and could imitate every comedian who appeared on Workers' Playtime and Tommy Handley's ITMA. The Third programme had not yet been invented but there was a channel broadcasting classical music and occasional plays and I had access to many newspapers and weeklies such as the incomparable *Picture Post*.

I scraped by in School Cert. because the examiners were lenient in the face of the doodlebugs (flying bombs); the only other exams I have ever passed were a trade test in the RAF, when we were openly assisted to the correct answers by the supervising sergeant, and the driving test, which I got through first time without any kind of a fiddle.

In consequence I cannot call myself an educated man. The only real target over which I triumphed was on my national service training course when, on the sole occasion I have ever fired a gun, I got four bulls out of five. (Against this achievement, when I threw a hand grenade my tin hat fell off. This was strictly contrary to orders but I was not placed on a charge because the supervising corporal was as relieved as I was that we both survived.) One way or another my life has been an unqualified success which has allowed me to manage a prosperous bookshop in Hampstead for thirty-two years and to retire at sixty-two. I had no official training in bookselling or publishing, in which I occasionally also dabbled, or in running an art gallery, which I did as a sideline for some years. During all this time I always wrote – reportage, newspaper features, revue sketches, plays, novels, local history, travelogues, book reviews – but without having a diploma in anything.

I grew up among library books. The only volumes we owned were a set of *Daily Express* encyclopaedias with a heavily thumbed (by me) map section. My parents belonged to libraries, my father to Boots, my mother to a small 2d one in the stationers next door. It seemed never to have occurred to either of them to use the public library service. My grandmother, who left school at ten, owned more books than either of them including a vast volume on Victoria RI, which I own. The first library in our house was mine. I was allowed to accumulate books and my father had no hesitation, although there was a shortage of wood, in commissioning a local carpenter to make shelves for my bedroom. I acquired books both new and second-hand in ever-growing numbers throughout my school-days but I never became accustomed to using the public library regularly; it never seemed to have what I wanted. I spent what money I was given starting a collection of plays and theatrical literature, much of it found in second-hand shops. For Christmas and birthdays I always asked for book tokens. Once I received one from a soldier who was courting my sister; naively he believed it would improve his chances if he was generous to me.

The shelves built for me were soon overflowing. I always preferred the look of new rather than used books but was never into serious collecting. (I was aggrieved fifty years on when I met, for the only time, Graham Greene, an author I read avidly, admiringly. His publisher, Max Reinhardt, introduced us. Greene asked, 'do you stock second-hand books?' When I replied, 'No', he lost interest in me instantly. That's where hero worship can lead you.)

I did not like school. I was good at English, History and Geography because they interested me and the teachers in those subjects were excellent. I was also competent at maths but loathed the teacher. He couldn't bear me because his other role was as officer in charge of the cadet corps which I had left at the height of the war when I had gone into a pacifist phase. My family remained silent in face of the shame I might bring on them. They didn't question the fact that I no longer donned uniform on two afternoons a week for cadet training but left the house, allegedly to study geometry exercises set by Vasey, the hated maths master. In fact, I played truant for two years on those afternoons. Vasey was so disgusted with me that he never asked to see my work and no one cared that I was not at school. Discipline was as lax as I was to find it when I was called-up into the RAF. The Head-master, as head of the local home guard, was preoccupied with military matters. He and Vasey had written me off.

Over the years I gave up Latin, French, Chemistry and Physics and was placed in class 5C to sit my school certificate. This was a gesture of disgrace but it did not deny me the attentions of Charles Preston, the senior English master, or of 'Percy' Taylor who taught history.

Mr Preston was a tall, gaunt Irishman, graduate of Dublin University, with a deep love of literature. He was also an accomplished actor which was how he overcame the horror of teaching the English classics to generations of mostly philistine boys. His lessons, in which he performed Shakespeare and Milton, were sheer theatre. He was a superbly funny Falstaff; in *Paradise Lost* he 'bellowed through the vast and boundless deep' whilst illustrating onomatopoeia. He would not tolerate pupils reading parts in *Henry IV Part I*, or have them mangling the sonorous verse of Milton. I lapped up his performances, so did one other boy in lowly 5C. Preston, a true thespian, played to us, for which I remain grateful. As I am to 'Percy' Taylor, the plump little histrionically-inclined history teacher. He was nowhere near as talented a performer as Charles Preston, nor did he take part in staff plays, but his impressions of 'Little Eric', unfortunate child of the industrial revolution, who was sent down the mines while father loafed on a street corner, and of Gabriel D'Annuzzio, as temporary ruler of Fiume, were funny and graphic. He brought history magnificently alive for whichever century he was teaching. And he was most helpful in anticipating which short questions we might be examined about in school cert because, even then, there was targeting. So we were well briefed in such recurring topics as the Agadir Crisis of 1911, the Jameson Raid and the Boston tea party. We also learned much 'modern' history from a book, 'Percy' persuaded the school to buy, *Europe Between the Wars*. I have not been able to trace its author. It was not specifically published as a textbook, nor was David Low's Penguin volume of cartoons, *Europe Since Versailles*, which I found for myself and still own. Both books taught me much about the era into which I was born.

Charles Preston had been at the school since 1910 and was deputy headmaster because of his longevity of service. He did not get on well with the Head and was sometimes heard disputing with him publicly. He smoked heavily and had fingers deeply stained with nicotine. At morning prayers he took no part in the service – presumably he was RC or an unbeliever -standing well to the right of the Head with hands clasped in his gown, blowing his cheeks in and out in time with the music. Next to him stood Norman Timmis, the art teacher (nickname Pansy; he did female impersonations for local concert parties), the only staff member without a gown. He was not a graduate, having only a diploma from Birmingham Art College. He was married, had three children, drove a Ford popular and was one of the very few approach-able teachers. In woodwork classes in the manual workshop he helped me to make a toy theatre and an egg holder (subsequently presented to an adoring grandmother) having recognised that my unaided efforts would lead to disaster.

For most of my life since 1944 when I left the Skinners' School, Tunbridge Wells I have fulminated against its shortcomings, allowing only that for English and History I had excellent teachers and that there were other masters who were at least human beings. I did not make any lasting friendships at school, I have never been back except to collect a form prize, I once stopped my car outside the entrance and exclaimed to my wife and daughters, 'that's the place! That was my dreadful school.' Now I feel I have been over-harsh. It was only the Head who was seriously objectionable; on that I do not withdraw so much as a syllable of invective but many of his staff, considered in the comparative calm of old age, were well equipped for their jobs. As well as Messrs Preston, Taylor and Timmis, Kenneth Phillips, Hugh Reynolds, Joey Mabbatt and Grace Haigh deserve at least a mention in despatches. (I wonder if they would think I do?)

Kenneth Phillips was a Quaker who lived to a large extent according to his principles. He was genuinely good. He was also friendly, caring, amusing (he had a penchant for terrible puns) and totally open. He was a conscientious objector or would have been had he not been exempted from military service because he taught maths. He applied to work on a mine sweeper but was turned down for the same reason. He, his wife and family lived frugally, giving much of what they earned to charity (I know this because after the war they were neighbours of my brother and sister-in-law); his clothing was shabby and patched, he rode an ancient pedal cycle. He was handsome, tall, dark-haired, a good cricketer and, much attracted to the theatre, a leaning which at one time would have been frowned upon by the Quaker elders. Once in the sixties we met again unexpectedly in my bookshop in Hampstead. This led to his sending me a play he had written asking for my opinion and because he thought, erroneously, I had influence with the Hampstead Theatre Club. I knew that, as a Quaker, he would expect an honest opinion and I gave one. I told him the play seemed several decades out of date, that dramatists didn't any more write three acts intended for a boxed set with French windows. I recommended him to see Hugh Whitemore's *Breaking the Code* which was then playing at the Haymarket in London. We had a friendly exchange of letters. I remember him also for understanding that it was fighting fearful odds to try to instruct me in physics; instead he permitted me to sit quietly reading at the back of his class. And, despite his goodness, he was not a saint. Very, very occasionally, when provoked by vile schoolboy behaviour, he briefly lost his temper. It was then apparent from his demeanour that he felt he had failed. His honesty was touching, something which I must have registered all those years ago. Or does memory, like a stew that improves in the pot, marinate to greater perception with experience? (Philosophy was not on the curriculum at Skinners'.)

Hugh Reynolds was even more involved in amateur theatricals than Kenneth. He taught French and Spanish and spoke umpteen languages. He was a bachelor with an apartment in a Regency terrace in Tunbridge Wells where he no doubt entertained local society. He was for decades very much a part of the social scene, a dominant figure in pageants, plays and musicals. He was a dandy and a swank, an ageing beau who dressed the part. He had more clothes than any woman I have known. He wore jackets in corduroy, leather, velvet, tweed and any material you care to mention (denim excepted), he had a wide variety of trousers, suits, shirts, waistcoats – usually in bold colours – and he wore a different tie every day of term. We counted them. He had a resonant, deeply pitched voice and could turn on the charm in an imperious manner. He would put on immaculate whites for the annual cricket fixture between masters and boys; when his House team was playing rugger against another he deployed himself conspicuously on the touch line, storming up and down bellowing exhortations of the rah-rah variety, thus diverting attention from the game itself. My sister and her friends in the local operatic society thought him pompous and patronising. When they put-on *The Mikado* he played Pooh Bah, which was typecasting. He was a one-off, larger than life. Had we known each other as adults I am sure we would have got on; it was a shame I had little aptitude for languages.

Reynolds was unmarried but there was gossip when he was observed in the countryside cycling with Grace Haigh, who had succeeded Norman Timmis as art teacher when the latter was called up. Probably they were just culturally kindred spirits. Miss Haigh was a tall, willowy woman of uncertain age who unintentionally shocked me. She encouraged some of us to go with her to an exhibition of the works of Feliks Topolski who was familiar to me from his illustrations for the Penguin edition of *Pygmalion*. As we walked there I asked her opinion of the artist and she replied, after some consideration, 'I am not sure I would like to live with him.' When she realised I was not familiar with the non-sexual meaning of this phrase she blushed and hastily explained. The dear lady was the first person who encouraged me to appreciate painting and drawing even though I had no talent for them myself. What she set in motion in art, Joey Mabbatt, who took us for singing, did for music. My family were more or less indifferent to both although they did not actively oppose such slight awakenings as I felt at this time. Mr Mabbatt played the organ each morning at assembly, seated in a tiny loft above the dais at one end of the high ceilinged hall. There he also, later in the day, held singing lessons which for most of their duration, must have been torture to him. He faced the task with brave optimism and no lowering of his high standards. It would not be his fault if we failed to appreciate Schubert Lieder; one or two of us came to do so. Well, one for certain. And it was not his way to compromise. Having introduced the class via *Heidenroslein* (in English, *Rose Among the Heather*) which it was not too difficult for most of us to sing in tune, he embarked on *Der Erl-König* (*The Erl King*) which is not easy for even a great singer to interpret. Joey, splendid man, had conviction. He sang it; we should sing it. And the secret of his success was that *he* enjoyed it, sitting there at the piano, the tails of his gown flapping around him, as his whole body gave credence to that powerfully dramatic Schubert song which thunders superbly to its tragic conclusion. I did not then realise just how imaginative Joey's teaching was. On another occasion he interrupted a lesson to convey his enthusiasm for the Proms, describing how on the previous evening he had listened on radio to Sir Henry Wood being called back for ovation after ovation. How could I not come to love music in the face of such adulation?

I knew 'Joey' also as the dumpy, rather genial pedagogue who once chastised me good-humouredly for accidentally knocking against him on the outside steps of the school. This collision caused him to spit out a dog-end, down almost to its last grain of tobacco, clinging to his lips. Once he was free of classroom and organ loft, Schubert and nicotine went hand in hand. I do not doubt that he genuinely loved both. He also directed the school's 1938 Gilbert & Sullivan offering, *HMS Pinafore* in which Alec McCowen, who subsequently had a distinguished West End career, played Little Buttercup. Although I was only eleven at the time I recognised that his performance was in a different league from others in the cast.

There was another 'teacher' who flitted briefly across the screen, a young man who presided over a few lessons while he was awaiting call-up. He was Eric Wright, former head-boy, captain of cricket and rugger, mace bearer for the Officers Training Corps, scholar who had won an exhibition to Oxbridge, lead in the annual G & S opera and a talented jazz pianist. He had been a revered figure when I entered the school in 1935, aged eight, and I would never have dared to address him had we ever come in contact. He was a veritable polymath of whom parents of other boys spoke in hushed awe. His university studies were curtailed because of the war but before enlisting in the Fleet Air Arm there was a period when he was at a loose end. Lt Col Bye, the Headmaster, whose favourite he had been, invited him to help out during a teacher shortage. Even class 5C was inflicted upon him.

Eric Wright's approach to teaching was relaxed, informal. He sat on the edge of his table facing us, legs swinging gently, and talked, asking questions, encouraging our participation. I wish I could remember some of what he said but it's only his presence that I recall vividly after more than sixty years. A schoolboy crush? No. He had charisma. It was as simple as that.

Some while later my brother, on leave, came in for lunch, downcast and angry. 'You won't see Eric Wright again,' he told us. He had been killed in an air attack on the German battleships *Scharnhorst* and *Gneisenau* escaping to base through the Channel. This brought home to me more than any other single incident the appalling waste that war inflicts.

Nor was it a crush I had on Adrian Bristow who came to Skinners' late in the war when his family moved to Tunbridge Wells. He was older and more scholastic than I but we clicked because we were drawn towards theatre and acting. He introduced me to Shaw and Ibsen and was witty. Although we were in different classes we always met at break and spent the time chatting. This came to the notice of the prefects so I was hauled before Harris, the head-boy, and *warned*. It had little effect because I hadn't the faintest idea where his innuendo was leading. I stood bemused before him and endeavoured to look serious.

'You know what I'm talking about, Norrie, don't you?'

'Yes, Harris,' I lied.

'Watch it, then', he ordered, and looked daggers at me.

I said, again, 'Yes, Harris;' and left the room.

I didn't tell Adrian or anyone else about this. What Harris was unaware of was that Adrian was greatly taken with one whom we knew as 'the Girl in the White Mac' who cycled the streets to another school. Observing that she lived somewhere in Southborough beyond my father's pharmacy, he insisted on coming home with me to watch her, from my bedroom window, riding her bike along London Road. I don't believe they ever met and I only came to understand, much later in life, what Harris had been hinting at. (Like so many of my generation I did not receive any sex education at home or at school. I learned about sexual deviance from a Pelican book called *The Physiology of Sex* which I read when I was nineteen).

Lt Col W. R. G. Bye, the headmaster, was a first world war veteran with an MC and DSO, and probably a very brave man. I detested him. His nickname was 'Creeper' from his habit of roaming the school in softly soled and heeled shoes and spying on us all. He weekly subjected us to half-hourly lessons of abstruse Christianity which were mind-bogglingly tedious but probably helpful in permanently alienating me from religion. He also taught calculus to clever sixth formers, among whom I never ranked. I played a trick on him on the day I left school.

On the previous afternoon, immediately before the final period of the day, which was English with Charles Preston, I suggested to one Alan Maynard, 'Let's skip it and go into town. It's our last opportunity to play truant.' I was flexing my wings for freedom. Next morning Mr Preston asked where we had been. Did he look a little hurt? Had there been something special he had planned for the last lesson? I didn't attempt to lie to him, nor did Maynard. Preston said we must report to the Headmaster even though it was the last day of our final term. It was a salutary lesson in discipline. Or was it? We did go to see Bye who was, I think, expecting us. As we walked into his study I said, 'We've come to say goodbye, Sir.' This wrong-footed him but he should have rebuked us. Instead, giving us a very old-fashioned look, he asked us what we were planning to do in adult life but without displaying much interest. The interview quickly ended.

Maynard and I laughed to one another after this episode. I didn't much mind having turned the scales on the Head but I have since felt shame about the way I treated Charles Preston whom I never met again. I once tried to make amends for my guilt by sending a letter to the *Kent & Sussex Courier* when I heard that Preston had retired, saying what a fine English teacher he had been and what a great off-stage Falstaff. I don't think it was printed. And it wasn't only Falstaff. Actually on stage, he played Balmy Walters in the staff production of

Shaw's *You Never Can Tell*. It was the first straight play I ever saw, and he was very funny indeed in a part in which I have since seen Ralph Richardson, Michael Hordern, Harcourt Williams and Edward Fox. Like Polonius, played by a natural actor, Balmy Walters is a role that is almost proof against failure.

Despite living in that part of the UK which after the fall of France in 1940 was closest to the enemy most of us in Kent and Sussex endured a comparatively quiet war. Few, away from the coast and the capital, suffered much from the hostilities. The Battle of Britain was fought in the skies above us, the Luftwaffe could be seen and heard making its way towards London yet towns such as Tunbridge Wells, Maidstone, Sevenoaks, Lewes, Horsham, bore little brunt from bombing.

Dover was an exception. When a German shell destroyed a terrace opposite to my grandparents' house by good fortune they were staying with us in Southborough and were unharmed by the dressing table mirror which was blasted across their marital bed. Donald's family had moved to a village behind Dover out of range of the great guns on Cap Gris Nez, although Don himself was in charge of the ARP post nearest to the enemy. There were supposedly close seasons for shelling during which I heard *The Messiah* in the town hall at Easter '42 or '43 and, attended the wedding of my uncle 'Chum' Tapley and Eileen.

We, as a family, had a lucky war. The single most extraordinary instance I recall, apart from my brother's return from Dunkirk, was in August 1940 when, with invasion expected at any moment, my father drove my mother and I from Southborough to Bournemouth for two week's holiday. He believed we all needed a break and he wasn't allowing the war to upset his plans. Even more amazing was the fact that my sister, who worked in the Ministry of Pensions at Tunbridge Wells, remained at home while we travelled on roads swarming with military vehicles, across Surrey and into Hampshire. At Bournemouth we watched while the central sections of two piers were blown out to frustrate easy landing by enemy troops and, on the sands, I immersed myself in reading the *Penguin Dictionary of Politics* and biographies of cricketers. Later in the year, this time accompanied by Peggy, we drove north to Bawtry in Yorkshire where Gordon was stationed, to spend a week close to his camp. We skirted London to avoid the bombers; in our behaviour there was an element of Drake playing bowls while the Armada sailed up the Channel.

My father did not envisage a career for me in books. Regarding me as academically fifth-rate and an unlikely starter for any career in commerce he had one solution for my immediate future when I left school in 1944 . . . the civil service. This was rich coming from one who, for as long as I could remember, had poured scorn on all bureaucrats and especially on government and municipal workers. Despite which, when my sister left school in 1939 she, who had wished to become a dancing teacher, was packed off into the Ministry of Pensions, 'until you get married.' (Which, in 1945, Peggy was and has never had a paid job since.)

Bill thought I was idle because I got bad reports each term and was rarely seen to be doing homework. Instead I used the blissful hours away from school for reading and writing plays. Once in our garden I was seen staring fascinated at ants busying about the lawn. Bill said, 'Why don't you do something, instead of just sitting there.' I replied, 'I am doing something. I'm watching ants at work.'

After being informed I was to become a civil servant I ignored my father for a whole week. Totally ignored him. I didn't bid him, 'good-morning' or 'good-night'. I avoided any situation where I would have felt compelled to say, 'thank you'. I sulked, prodigiously. The entire house was pervaded by my sulks. It wouldn't surprise me if they didn't have an effect on trade in the pharmacy. No one could get a word out of me. I ate only as much as I needed to prevent starvation and stayed in my room when I wasn't at school or playing truant.

At the end of a week Bill confronted me and said that at his weekly Rotary Club lunch he had spoken with the Editor of the *Kent and Sussex Courier* and ascertained that journalists could lead relatively normal, respectable, well-remunerated lives. By then he had conceded that I could write. I had left a three-act play around in the hope that he would look at it. He did and commented about it to Donald Tapley with the words, 'It's absolute rubbish. Fancy spending his time doing that,' Donald, bless him, replied, 'It may be rubbish, Jimmy, but just think of the effort involved in filling all those pages and inventing it all.'

I had an interview with Mr Webster, the Editor of the *Courier*, who invited me to submit a crit of the play being performed that week at the Assembly Hall, Tunbridge Wells. I did and he approved it, then wrote to my father that he thought I might well have a successful career as a journalist. Bill relented and arranged for me to become an articled pupil with the *Eastbourne Gazette* (published on Wednesdays) and *Eastbourne Herald* (published on Saturdays). He paid the proprietors a hundred pounds. I would not receive a wage but would be allowed modest expenses. I was to live with friends in Eastbourne, the benevolently inclined Sybil and George Gillham, parents of, Peter, a childhood friend. (I soon learned how to make expenses less than modest.)

It was late 1944, the war in Europe was in its last phase but could have continued in the Far East for many years. There was every prospect that I might be destined for a grisly death in the Burmese jungle in a regiment of infantry. Bill began teaching me to drive so that I might join the RASC and perhaps escape the front line. He was a good driver; I was a poor learner. I enjoyed being at the wheel but would keep querying his commands. When he called for me to make an emergency stop I asked why because I couldn't understand the need for it. He was unusually forbearing and gradually I understood the sense of the discipline he was trying to instil on me. Petrol was rationed, the driving test had been suspended, so my lessons were confined to weekends when I came home from Eastbourne. I readily took to the wheel and had visions of borrowing the car once I was deemed qualified. I felt confident in charge of the family Vauxhall saloon until the day when, approaching home under the supervision of my Uncle Aubrey, I miscalculated in trying to avoid a pony and trap and hit a brick wall. No one was harmed but sufficient damage was done to take the car off the road, and there was no other vehicle available to send me out with for the sake of restoring my nerve. I didn't drive again for twenty years.

This incident took place early in 1945 before my sister's wedding, to William Harry (known as 'Peter') Scott, in March of that year. The wedding was a gathering of the clans, a term which is permissible because along with battalions of the bride's relations and of the groom's, all solidly pre-Norman in origin and possibly, on Peter's side, Icenian, there was a twosome from north of the border, my father's sister Kate and her daughter Cathie Watson.

Bill found his sister's company irksome but adored his niece; so did we all and not just from pity because she was married to the original mean Scot. Once, decades later, while Jim waited for me at a Glasgow hotel I suggested he should leave the car and have a drink at the bar while I made myself ready. No way! He remained in it until I called him, then allowed me to buy the only two rounds. On their honeymoon he and Cathie had stayed for free with my parents; they would not have left Glasgow had not Jim, as an employee of the railway company, been entitled to travel without paying. But he was not with us at the 1945 festivity for which the bridegroom himself had returned on leave from active service in France and the low countries, having been transported across the Channel to the Normandy beaches soon after D day. (He never talked to me of his experiences any more than Gordon ever mentioned Dunkirk.)

Precisely how the clothes rationing regulations were circumvented to allow my sister and her bridesmaids to be decked out in traditional wedding gear I cannot remember, although there were traders in Southborough (as everywhere) who dealt in the black market. Aubrey Tapley's contribution did not come exactly into that category. He, having returned to Britain on the *Queen Mary* from Cape Town, where he had been convalescing after the desert campaign in north Africa, was a quartermaster sergeant, RASC. This enabled him to arrive for the wedding breakfast with provisions which included a whole ham the like of which had been seen in few wartime larders. I listened to him explaining in his genial way how it was possible to 'milk' the sacks of sugar and other commodities in the stores. Somehow or other it was deemed correct to appropriate army property because it all, theoretically, belonged to us.

Thus, in March 1945, with VE day only two months ahead, there was this almost old style wedding in the parish church on Southborough Common (I had not been there since my christening, nor had my parents) followed by a lavish-for-the-time reception in the Victoria Hall, which faced our home. At this same venue Peggy had appeared in pantomimes written and produced by Christopher Fry, who had also staged a pageant there, in aid of Dr Barnado's Homes, in which I made my first brief stage appearance.

All that was missing from the fare was Champagne. Even though by then most of France had been cleared of Germans, it was only available in some London restaurants and hotels and was not on sale at our local off licence. The substitute was a lethal concoction made from gin and champagne cider on which I and many others got drunk. I returned next day to Eastbourne nursing the first major hangover of my life, made tolerable only by a pick-me-up dispensed by Bill who said I had behaved disgracefully, *and* in front of his sister. By the following weekend, when we all gathered to relive the occasion, he had forgiven me, having learned that Aubrey, flat out in the corridor of the train he had taken to Charing Cross, was woken by the guard in time to prevent his immediate return to Tunbridge Wells. Also, on arrival back at Dover, my ten-year-old cousin Diana had been proclaimed to be the worse for wear, by Donald, her father. It was as though we were all celebrating victory in Europe which was proclaimed about eight weeks later.

Being a newspaper reporter brought out the worst in me. I was a cocky seventeen year old, an embryo angry young man with a streak of idealism, a callow, would-be intellectual with little application for study in depth. I was a teenager at a time when that category had, like television, been proscribed by the war. At eighteen you were deemed old enough to die in battle or to work in the pits but it was well nigh impossible to express the rebelliousness of youth except during a brief period between school and call-up. Between 1944–5 were the golden ten months for me. The *Gazette and Herald*, in an Eastbourne no longer in the front line, regained some prosperity as its partly evacuated readership returned to the prospect of a peaceful life. The Editor, Mr T. S. Palmer – I never called him 'Tom'; he addressed me as 'Norrie' – was desperate for another pair of hands and found me promising material. Because I was an articled pupil he felt duty bound to send me to the County and Police Court sessions, alongside a senior reporter, so that I could practice my shorthand and submit my version, for his eyes only, of the proceedings, but he also sent me alone to cover stories ranging from funerals to school sports. At church doors I had to take the names of all mourners and list them in alphabetical order (I learned to check spellings – readers resented appearing in print as 'Stevens' when they were actually 'Stephens', or as 'John' if they were 'Jon'). On school playing fields I watched relay racing, high jumping and other deeply yawn-worthy tests of athleticism which never inspired my writing. I was more responsive to the many theatrical performances, amateur and professional, which I witnessed while, after VE and VJ days, my accounts of victory tea-parties, held on every street, gave me scope for the odd if not purple, at least pale violet, patch of prose. I also took over the Young Eastbourne column under the inherited pseudonym of 'Juvens' when a woman colleague left to have a baby. Let loose with little interference from Mr Palmer I soon offended local youth workers when I attacked them for lacking enthusiasm and foresight. I quickly learned the basics of being a typically unpleasant, muck-raking journalist and in retrospect I am grateful that I was called-up. This gave me nearly three years of respite in which to consider an alternative career but in 1945 I bitterly resented the prospect of military service interrupting a life I was relishing. I made friends with Raymond Andrews, the paper's photographer, who had somehow wangled release from being a Bevin Boy, and we went out on many stories together. There was an Australian army unit stationed in East-bourne which included several test cricketers including Lindsay Hassett, a post war captain. We celebrated VE night in their sergeant's mess and later, on the beach, we met the cast of the play showing that week at Devonshire Park Theatre. I felt I was hobnobbing with history when I chatted with two members of the Forbes-Robertson family and when, having missed the last bus, Raymond and I spent the night in the newspaper office, on former firewatchers' beds, I began to feel I was roughing it in war-correspondent style.

My shortcomings as a reporter were made obvious when I was despatched to cover a football match. It is the only one I have ever seen. I neither understood nor wished to understand the offside rule. I abhorred the noise and the mud – both reminded me of the even more distasteful game of rugger, endured at Skinners' – and I filed very brief, dull copy. This upset many of the printing staff who, for pleasure, read only the sporting pages of the paper. On another occasion I was assigned up on to the Downs where a farmer was demonstrating a new combine harvester. Technical know-how has never come easily to me. This time my copy was not accepted and to make amends a colleague was sent to report on a second demonstration. Had I not been an articled pupil I would have been fired but Mr Palmer didn't even rebuke me. Instead he became more circumspect in assigning stories to me. What I loved best was going to the local theatres although I was not permitted to make adverse criticism except to a very minor degree. The theatres and cinemas were regular advertisers so honest appraisal was out. This also applied, though less rigorously, to amateur productions. One of them featured an ageing soprano excruciatingly deficient in musical talent. I decided not to mention her. On the day the paper was published she came to the office and berated me for failing to recognise the exceptionally high quality of her singing. She demanded that I attend a repeat performance of the same show the following week. I duly reported on it, writing that 'she had one of the most remarkable voices ever heard in Eastbourne'. It was true . . . but she took the double entendre as praise. I learned to insert other small digs when I didn't care for what I had seen. I longed to be a dramatic critic on a London paper. That, I decided, was my ambition. I read James Agate and Ivor Brown, the two leading critics of the time and had fantasies about being invited to take over from them when they fell suddenly ill or dropped dead. I never met Agate but fifteen years on Ivor Brown, a customer at my Hampstead bookshop, generously agreed (for a ludicrously small fee) to write for three of the symposia about London which I published and edited.

Such ambitions became irrelevant when I was summoned to report to RAF, Padgate, in Lancashire, on 26 September, 1945. I travelled by slow train from St Pancras, latterly through the beautiful Derbyshire Peaks, on a glorious, sunny autumn day, feeling intensely sorry for myself, deliberately arriving at the latest authorised hour. In a station buffet at Manchester, where I changed trains, I had what I thought of as my last pint of beer before personal liberty was obliterated, probably for years. One hour later I was swapping life stories with other rookies as we prepared for Lights Out; three nights on and I was listening to Louis Kentner playing Beethoven sonatas at a recital on camp. The ticket cost me 3*d.* The new life promised to have its moments.

The immediate future, however, was not all that agreeable. Eight weeks training included running one mile in full pack and constant square bashing. I have never since been so fit but I pined for the *Gazette & Herald* and hated wearing uniform. (I also thought how Captain Vasey, of Skinners', would approve of what I was enduring.)

# 2

## From Airman to Bookman

When asked, 'what did you do in the air force?', my customary reply is: 'nothing'. This is a partial truth, relating only to the so-called working day. I was mustered as a Clerk General Duties, Shorthand & Typing, for which I was paid 4s. 3d. per day (21.25p). Had I been a mere Clerk GD I would have received only 3s. (15p). My shorthand was dodgy but I took the risk for the sake of an extra 8s. 9d. per week. In that role for much of the next two and a half years I truly did 'nothing' and very boring it was. Occasionally there was a variation when that which I did could have been described as 'nothing any sane person would have considered of importance.' The war had ended. There wasn't, in our sphere, anything urgent which needed to be done. From the orderly room or office where we 'worked' we sent signals to other orderly rooms and offices where they were filed appropriately, just as we filed the replies. The actual content of these signals was invariably trivial.

Why was it necessary to send so many of us to the Indian sub-continent to do nothing? In order, so it was said, to release those who had been there for much of the war but who were now due for demobilisation. Even so, why in India? Couldn't we have done 'nothing' equally unproductively in the UK? The answer was, to over-see the peaceful transition of power from Britain to the indigenous population. When this had formally taken place, in August 1947, the Hindus and Muslims set about slaughtering each other which was no concern of ours so we were shipped home. In Bombay (now Mumbai), where I was stationed most of the time, and in Karachi, where we embarked for the UK, we witnessed none of the riots we read about in the press and were free to roam about unharmed. Earlier in the year when there were said to be civilian disturbances in Bombay we had been confined to camp. To relieve the boredom some of us volunteered to take the rations in armed trucks to outlying units. I spent many a late evening speeding through the deserted streets of the city holding a loaded sten gun which I had no idea how to fire. It was a another way of doing nothing.

When I was first flown to India it was actually proposed that I should do something. I had already been alerted to stand by to fly first to Washington, later to West Africa, because someone in authority in those places had signalled that they needed a Clerk GD, S & T. Presumably the need passed because I never went to either place but I did make it to Bombay where I was sent at considerable public expense to practise my skills at a court martial of airmen said to have mutinied. I found this posting tiresome because I had settled to a rewarding routine on a camp in inner Hertfordshire from which I was able, without an official pass, to journey into London twice a week to see plays. Provided one had the nous to avoid mainline stations there was little likelihood of being apprehended by the air force police. I got away with it for weeks and naturally felt peeved when drafted to Bombay, a city not within commuter distance of the West End theatre.

I travelled by flying boat to Karachi, which was then still in India, in the company of army officers and civilians. When I reported to the BOAC terminal at Victoria I was asked for my name by a clerk who did not glance up at me, 'A. C. Norrie', I said.

The clerk studied his list. 'Air Commodore Norrie. Thank you, Sir.'

'No,' I told him. 'Aircraftsman.' He registered surprise.

My fellow passengers of superior rank overlooked my lowly status, particularly one army captain with whom I chatted and took meals for the next three days.

My parents did not take foreign holidays, so as a child I had not been abroad. On my first night ever out of the British Isles, aged nearly nineteen, I stayed in Marseille at the Hôtel Splendide. A pleasant major kindly invited me to join others from the flying boat for dinner.

It was the first of thousands of meals since consumed in France but I cannot remember what I ate or drank. It was followed by a rowdy night which is firmly impinged on my memory. I became certain that part of what I thought of as a mob, seemingly laying siege to the city, was encamped on the balcony of my bedroom. I could only hear it carrying on, shouting incomprehensibly, behind the shutters but became convinced that it would batter its way in and bludgeon me to death. If this were so, I ought to have been ready to defend myself for the sake of the honour of the RAF. I did not see it like that. I was in Abroad for the very first time, alone and terrified. Also, unarmed.

What was the Air Ministry thinking of in endangering my life thus? I rang for room service. Then I fell asleep. I was woken by a banging on the door. What did Monsieur need? I pretended I hadn't been able to open the window, felt ashamed and sent the caller away, pondering what I would have done if I'd ever been sent into action.

Next day we flew from the Étang de Berre, familiar forty years on when, in retirement, I lived in Provence and often collected visitors from Marignane Airport. It did not register deeply; the next stop, Augusta in Sicily, did. I thought it the most enchantingly beautiful place I had ever visited. The launch from the flying boat landed us near a beach where we lunched alfresco on olives and little else. On to Cairo, where the Captain and I strolled around murky streets, peopled by shadowy figures, close to the houseboat where we slept briefly before many hours of flight over middle-eastern deserts. I have never wished to repeat the experience. I found the landscape utterly un-lovable and sinister. In the middle of another night we reached Karachi where my time as a VIP ended abruptly with the arrival of a lorry to take me to the RAF transit camp at Mauripur. I was stranded there, on the edge of another desert, for three weeks. This gave me time to get acclimatised. There were no daily parades, no supervision, no lights out. After a long while I enquired of a corporal, the one to whom I had reported on arrival, when I was to be despatched to Bombay to work on the court martial. 'You went a fortnight ago,' he replied. 'They needed you urgently.'

Once in Bombay, at BHQ, I was relieved to learn that the court martial was proceeding apace without me. Local shorthand typists had been commandeered and John Harris, the other airman who had been flown separately from UK for the job, had been demoted to Court Orderly. So already there I was, halfway round the world, doing nothing. For the next eighteen months I was a pillar of compulsory inactivity in one of the more agreeable neighbourhoods of a huge city.

To a teenager who had spent the previous seven years confined to south-east England, Bombay was a widening experience socially and architecturally. The gently concave shoreline between Colaba Cause-way and the affluent suburban peninsular of Malabar Hill jutting into the Arabian Sea was lined by western-style blocks of flats (which occasionally collapsed) facing a wide road used by makes of American cars totally unfamiliar to European eyes. Behind them lay the sprawling metropolis, the centre of which was partly Indianised Victorian-Gothic with a cathedral, cinemas, coffee houses and busy shopping streets, where an occasional sacred cow might be exercising its ruminant right of way as it searched for pastures new.

When John Harris and I met up at last, we strolled one evening along Marine Drive, which had the familiarity of a seaside resort back home until we turned up a filter road to make our way back by an inland route. At once we were into bizarre bazaar territory flowing with people wearing dhotis and saris, arguing, bargaining, trading, exchanging banter. Many of them regarded us with a mixture of surprise and suspicion. Young whites, obviously servicemen in mufti, were not a common sight in this seemingly endless street. We realised we were probably out of bounds, wondered were we in danger, then fell silent, each looking hopefully for other filter roads to take us back to Bombay-on-Sea. There was none. No one approached us even to offer goods for sale but we were watched. There could be good reasons why this area might be out of bounds. The experience was similar to one I had in a village pub in Northamptonshire, when I had walked into the public bar and asked if it would be possible to have a sandwich. The landlord, watched by his silent regulars staring at me over their pint pots, said, 'No.' I got the message. John and I would like to have left that long, unfriendly thoroughfare as simply as I had got away from the pub. On and on we walked, fearful of running, until we emerged, of course unscathed, close to Churchgate Station, facing the art deco Eros Cinema, a few blocks away from Marine Drive Camp, our barracks. It was the only time in eighteen months on the sub-continent that I felt ill-at-ease with the indigenous population (by which I would mean 'the natives' if, as a native of Britain, it were politically correct for me to use those words).

Later I made friends among Indians, took leaves in the Himalayas and at Bangalore and 'served the air force' for about six hours a day five days a week. Occasionally I was detailed for guard duty. Then, having lost mine, I had to borrow a forage cap. Most of the time we wore civvies – meaning a shirt and slacks – and had we been more generously paid it would have been a truly ideal existence. Even on our meagre wage it was possible to take afternoon tea at the Taj Mahal Hotel by the Gateway to India, visit air conditioned cinemas, go occasionally to the 'whites only' private swimming pool at Breach Candy and employ a bearer. Mine, named Babu, brought morning tea and *The Times of India* to my bedside, one of at least sixty in a standard basha (or hut) where there was no privacy except within a mosquito net. Babu was always good for a loan until pay day; he didn't charge interest. We were the masters. He had dignity, but did I?

Going on leave was economically possible because we had free rail travel. At Naini Tal, beside a Himalayan lake, we stayed with an English widow who fed us lavishly. We walked rather than climbed in the wooded hills and were hurled to and from the rail head by a wild driver who constantly turned his head to indicate vehicles which had gone over the side. We broke the return journey at Agra to see the Taj Mahal shimmering magically like a giant toy. I suffered heat stroke on the non-air conditioned train. Uncharacteristically, I didn't keep a journal.

Back in Bombay, in my spare time I assisted in the writing of a camp magazine and became secretary of the Allied Air Forces Club, a civilised feature of service life with membership restricted to other ranks. The officers enjoyed our weekly dance so much that they made it clear we should invite them as paying guests. My Saturday evenings were spent sitting in the balmy air, welcoming Indian ladies and selling tickets to them and to officers, a task for which I was rewarded with endless pints of free beer. It instilled in me a lifelong habit of sitting in the night air, talking and drinking.

Infrequently, the overall inertia of camp life was disturbed. Once there was a mild mutiny about the food in the airmen's mess. Suddenly a message circulated verbally, 'Will you be taking tiffin (lunch) in the mess on Sunday?' The answer was an unenthusiastic, 'I suppose so,' which provoked the comment, 'Well, I won't. Or dinner either.' It soon became apparent that there would be a general exodus from camp for both meals. Not in the form of a demonstration but in an orderly, casual manner, in small groups or individually. No one knew whose idea it was, no pressure was exerted on anyone, there were no gatherings or meetings. No protest was ever officially made but it worked. On that Sunday not more than a handful attended the mess for either meal.

On Monday the base Group Captain made a rare visit to Marine Drive Camp to hold an enquiry. Individually, fifty or so of us were called before him and asked why we hadn't eaten in the mess the previous day. I told him that camp food was so unappetising that I ate elsewhere as often as I could afford to. The Group Captain said we were on the same basic rations endured by the British population during WWII. I replied that I had lived through that period and felt adequately nourished. (I didn't tell him of my mother's barter system with the grocer.)

Following the enquiry it was said that *agents-provocateurs* were placed in the huts to discover who had initiated the walkout. Those responsible were never found. Nor, I regret to record, did the food in the mess noticeably improve.

When we moved from Marine Drive to Sassoon Docks Camp I was identifiably implicated in another protest against food. This concerned the manager of the camp canteen and the Indian Camp Commandant who was a high caste Brahmin. Often of an evening we chose to eat at the canteen and pay for egg and chips. Gradually it became apparent that the precise number of chips served could be assessed at a glance. When it was reduced to no more than six we complained to the manager, a pleasant Goan, who increasingly showed signs of stress. One evening he broke down and told us that he couldn't afford to serve larger meals because Flying Officer W—, the Camp Commandant, kept raising his personal levy on all transactions. We persuaded him to inform BHQ and told him he could name us as dissatisfied customers. Very soon the Camp Commandant was removed and said to be facing court martial. I was posted to another camp at Worli, up the coast from Bombay. None of us was called upon to give evidence at his trial, if it ever took place. I encountered F/O W . . . some weeks later at Worli when he greeted me affably. The person who suffered most was the Goan manager who lost his job.

My particular racket concerned cigarettes. Each airman had a free weekly issue of fifty Players' in a tin. The Station Warrant Officer's clerk – my job after I had been flung out of the orderly room at BHQ for failing to take my non-existent duties seriously – was responsible for the weekly order, which was based on the ration strength supplied to the cookhouse. I kept the tins in a locked cupboard. There was always a surplus because the ration strength was overestimated and I never had to buy a cigarette during that time, nor did my friends. When I was posted, the SWO felt sorry for me and gave me several tins to see me on my way.

It was in Bombay that I enjoyed my first real experience of French cuisine. On Churchgate Street there was a restaurant named Gourdon's where on birthdays and other occasions I was introduced to the classic dishes of France – but without wine, although India was not then 'dry'.

Either imports had not re-started since the war, it didn't travel or we simply couldn't afford it.

There were other excellent places to eat in Bombay. To one I was taken by English civilians who introduced me to Indian residents. Ibrahim Alkazi, known as 'Elk', was a handsome man of Arab origin married to Roshan, a Hindu. I attended a celebration for their first born and was given the freedom of their flat on Colaba Causeway. Elk ran a drama group and was also an art student. He was about to complete a self-imposed task of illustrating *Ulysses*. To emphasise the book's universality the drawings were in contrasting styles; I was deeply impressed. Learning of my interest in drama he gave me his copy of Allardyce Nicoll's *The Development of the Theatre*; he also introduced me to Nissim Ezekiel, a teacher of English at Bombay University who took me on a tour of slums in the notorious Grant Road brothel district which was probably out of bounds to British servicemen. There I saw tiny rooms with upwards of a dozen people living in them. Both men – and Roshan – subsequently came to London, Elk to take a course at the RADA, Nissim to study for advanced academic qualifications. He was already a Professor of English but was humiliated to discover he couldn't understand what London bus conductors were saying. Elk kept in touch for many years and commissioned me to contribute articles about theatre for a magazine he was publishing. I have sometimes wondered what its readers made of my analysis of West End intimate revue. By the late fifties we had lost touch which I regret. I wonder what may have happened to them all in the religion-troubled sub-continent. The child whose birth I celebrated is half-Hindu, half-Muslim although its parents were not practising either religion. I hope they have survived without persecution.

In my time in India I learned that Eurasians, Anglo-Indians as we dubbed them, were looked down upon by all races, which was grossly unfair on them. Connie, a delightful woman who assisted in doing nothing in our orderly room, pretended she had been raised in England where, she said, they had lived in Northampton and moved to Southampton in the winter. (Or did she just say that because others did?)

In November 1947, after a month of perfect post-monsoon weather when the almost habitual humidity was much diminished, we were flown to Mauripur to await embarkation from Karachi. There I suffered humiliation by haircut.

I have intimated that discipline was lax. Relations between officers, NCOs and other ranks were easygoing. The brave new democratic world in which vile totalitarian regimes had been toppled, well some had, made all of us equal. Everyone had had enough of issuing and taking orders. But not quite everyone.

Unusually, we were called on parade. There was a desperate rush to don uniform, to find one's mislaid cap. Raggedly, we formed into ranks. It was good news. A date for embarkation was announced. It seemed natural to cheer but not to the corporal facing our motley crew. Suddenly, we were being inspected. The wretched man took it out on all of us with long hair. Time and again we were ordered to visit the camp barber. Three times I was sent back until I was virtually shaven headed. At no time in my life have I felt greater hatred towards anyone than for that corporal. Fortunately I controlled myself. Despite my rage I was determined not to miss the boat. I took to wearing a cap to hide my shame; it was three months before my hair regained its natural length; at eighty, I still have appreciable amounts.

We sailed on the *Empire Trooper*. It was a three-week voyage which remains a highlight of my life. We slept in hammocks, we had no duties, we did not even have to pretend to do nothing. We spent the time reading and talking, setting the world to rights. We enjoyed one day ashore at Port Sudan, soon after which the formation of a concert party was announced. George Simpson – a close friend to this day – and I were accepted as cast and for the latter part of the voyage we rehearsed and gave nine performances of *Homeward Bound*. On reaching Southampton there was a nasty moment for me when I was ordered to join the baggage party, an unpleasant humping operation which was considered a fatigue. I complained to the officer who had been in charge of *Homeward Bound*. He registered outrage. 'We can't have that, Norrie. You were in the concert party.' I was restored to indolence and passed the day gazing, through a light, winter mist, at Southampton before being sent home on leave for 28 days.

The last months of my national service were spent at the Air Ministry, Bush House, Aldwych, WC2. I lived out with Babs and Bob in Banstead, Surrey and donned uniform once a fortnight to collect my pay. It was a vintage theatre-going time for me, three nights a week for four months, usually seated in the gallery which would now be declared unfit for humans by the Health and Safety Authority. Today there are actual seats, whereas we sat on long benches without arm rests. But these were red letter nights and one could hear every word because actors' voices had not then been ruined by mumbling roles on television. The Old Vic company was at the New Theatre (later the Albery, later still the Coward). It was the season that Alec Guinness came to fruition, playing the Dauphin in *Saint Joan*, Menenius Agrippa in *Coriolanus* (I saw both three times) as well as a thoughtful Richard II – 'Here, cousin, seize the crown ' was a gentle throwaway – and a patchy Government Inspector. Occasionally I went to operas – twice to *Peter Grimes* to have a restricted view from the gallery slips and once to a thrilling performance of Gounod's *Faust* at Sadler's Wells – but it never became a habit as the theatre had been from childhood. I couldn't afford tickets on other evenings which I often spent walking about London with a friend, talking and observing, sustained by at the most two coffees. Beer was too expensive.

Only the days were tedious because although the office to which I was detailed was allegedly planning the post-war air force there was less than nothing to do. The Wing Commander and Squadron Leader in charge of this solemn project spent much of their time folding paper aeroplanes and sending them out of the window and up Kingsway, which must have seemed tame after piloting Spitfires. When my demob became due the Wing Commander had to provide a character reference for me. 'Superior', he kindly wrote on my documents. On this note I returned to civilian life far from eager to re-embrace provincial journalism. I had benefited, considering travel and the lifelong friendships made, rather more than the RAF had from my two years and eight months 'in uniform'. I had even escaped being placed on a charge despite an incident in 'the black hangar' at Blackpool, where we were first marshalled for export in 1946.

Hundreds of us sat idly in a vast auditorium. Suddenly I was called.
'206 AC Norrie! I stood. 'Sergeant?'
'What's your bleeding religion, airman?'
'Agnostic, Sergeant.'
A titter ran round the hangar. He glared at me.
'What's that bleeding mean?'
'It means, "I don't know", Sergeant.'
Another, louder titter. Wait for it, I thought; he'll have me for insolence.
Instead he scratched his head and went on to something else.

Months later, in India, a stranger addressed me: 'You're the bleeding agnostic.'

I could have replied, 'Would you like to see my stigmata?'

Neither in 1945 nor when I returned to the Eastbourne newspapers did any offers come my way from Fleet Street. My Wing Commander's superior assessment had fallen on fallow ground. In August, 1948, I resumed my interrupted articled-pupilship at the *G & H*, with the management offering to pay me three guineas a week as well as expenses. I lived at home rent free. But my heart was not in it and I developed a nervous illness which led to my release from the apprenticeship. That was when I became a bookseller.

In the spring I had taken a week off theatre-going to spend a leave at Hastings, to which my parents had moved, accompanied by George Simpson who from that time became a part of the family. On our first morning we took the inevitable walk along the front, in a vile wind, towards St Leonard's (the posh end, to which my parents were to make another move later in the year). The most notable feature of St Leonard's is a 1930s semi-skyscraper built to resemble a vast ocean liner. The impression is probably more convincing from some way out in the Channel; close up it joined an old terrace of buildings with shops beneath an arcade. In the newer part, above the Plimsoll line, at no. 15 a young man had daringly opened a distinctly modern bookshop. The windows were open to the street, the shelves were painted a gleaming white and were boldly signed, Fiction, History, Sport, and in one instance which caused more than a few residents' eyebrows to rise, Sex. The display tables were low; the entire shop was visible at a glance from outside; no hidden corners or crannies so beloved by those seeking something unusual, and by shoplifters. As we entered a dark-haired, bespectacled man emerged from the office at the rear and bade us, 'Good-morning.' Nothing more. He wished only for us to know he was there in case help was needed. He didn't go into a hard sell but busied himself at a desk, giving instructions to his boyish assistant until I asked how long he had been open, adding that I admired his shop. We became instantly friendly. When, soon after being demobbed, my twenty-first birthday loomed I put it about that books or book tokens would be highly acceptable and that Martyn Goff, the bookshop owner, had 'my list'. This was heavily influenced by his taste and I naughtily believed that some titles on it may have been ones he was finding difficult to sell; he was very new to his occupation and in those days publishers did not readily accept returns of slow-selling titles. If that uncharitable thought was true Martyn would have first convinced himself that it was something I would like or desperately needed. His own gift to me was *A Portrait of Edith Wharton* (an author of whom I was in total ignorance) by Percy Lubbock. He told me it had been the subject of a two-page spread in the *TLS*. I was duly impressed and kept reminding myself of this fact as I read it. And I did finish it – it was part of the lingering Protestant ethic – but I have never been attracted to the work of Mrs Wharton apart from the account of an early motoring holiday in France. Even that is not compulsive reading; she did not wear her learning lightly.

Martyn played a significant role in my book trade career. His bookshop excited me, his company was stimulating, he hinted he might have a job for me. I already had doubts about continuing in journalism if I couldn't fairly quickly move from reporting to feature writing; nor was there any pressure from the *Gazette & Herald* for me to return before the end of my long demob leave. Mr Palmer was absent indefinitely, having succumbed to stomach ulcers, his place being temporarily filled by the same Mr Webster who had interviewed me at the *Courier* years before. I didn't let on to my parents that I was reluctant to complete my apprenticeship, especially as I realised my father didn't like Martyn. To him he was a swank, conceited, talked too much and worst of all, was Jewish. Whether or not he realised that he was homosexual I am unaware; in those days the subject was not much discussed publicly and in ordinary family circles not at all. My mother, on the contrary, found Martyn a breath of fresh air. He amused her. She hated living in Hastings-St Leonard's, missed her large circle of friends in Southborough and felt cut off from her daughter and grandson in Essex. My father's health was already deteriorating so they had little social life. Martyn's occasional visits when she would be flattered outrageously for a brief spell and entertained with gossip about the famous were a welcome relief. Neither of them knew that Martyn had actually offered me a job.

When I suffered my minor breakdown and was diagnosed (wrongly) as a 'neurasthenic' I spent a month at home or staying with Babs and Bob in Surrey. I couldn't face Bill to tell him that returning to the *Gazette & Herald* hadn't worked. I did so only after a visit to London and a matinee of *Twelfth Night*, at the New Theatre, during which I gripped the side of my seat, stifling a constant need to push past other people in the row and get out – *just get out*! To where, I didn't know. But I stayed and quivered, the top of my head seeming to come off, until the lights went up. Then I made my way to Charing Cross and a train which took an age to reach St Leonard's. On arrival at home, I broke down and it all came out. Bill took it very well. I was not rebuked for having wasted my training. (In the long term I hadn't.) He even accepted the fact that I wished to work for Martyn and encouraged me to start at the St Leonard's shop straightaway to learn as much as possible before going along the coast to Seaford where I was to manage Goff's first branch. I spent a preliminary month at Marine Court where the first book I sold was to my future wife.

I had met Mavis Matthews early during my demob leave at a friend's in St Leonard's, where she gave French lessons to the daughter of the house. The following day at her home nearby her mother joined us in the drawing room. 'This is Ian, Mummy,' said Mavis. 'He came to talk about world government and has stayed to talk about John Gielgud.' Her mother was even shorter than Mavis; both had soft speaking voices with good elocution. Mavis was thin, rather than sleight, with brown hair to match her eyes and perfect, slightly prominent teeth. We saw a lot of each other that summer of 1948. She came to my twenty-first birthday party, presenting me with 78 rpm discs of Mozart's Hunt Quartet. (On my seventieth she gave me a CD of the same work.)

Immediately after Christmas I moved into digs at Seaford where the Martyn Goff Book & Music Shop was the penultimate unit in a short row of emporia far from the town centre, on a road which led across a desolate patch of waste ground down to the bleak promenade. Here were a few small hotels and guesthouses lying to the east of a sea wall broken in many places. The economy of Seaford depended more on its many private schools than on its merits as a holiday resort. When Bill saw the location of the shop he exploded. 'The man must be mad,' he fumed, 'to buy one in such a position, especially as there is an established bookseller in the main street.' I tried to justify it by pointing out that Martyn's shop was in the same complex as the Ritz cinema. Soon I was to spend sombre evenings in the empty café above the Ritz lamenting, along with its lessee, the day we had ever come to Seaford.

I stayed for seven months during which time trade never 'picked up', even with the arrival of summer. We took so little cash that I often only had to bank it once a week, although we were selling gramophone records as well as books and sheet music. I wrote to all the schools to solicit their business; either they ignored my letter or pointed out that they were well satisfied by their present supplier. I suggested we hold a party to prove that our service would be better but on what grounds I cannot remember. Wisely, Martyn vetoed the idea. The Net Book Agreement, in operation for all of my bookselling life, prevented price cutting. I was not a natural salesman. I did not know what to do apart from trying to immerse myself in the life of the dreary little town. I joined the amateur dramatic society in time to be assistant stage manager (a.s.m.) of the current production. Later I got a fool-proof supporting part in *Young Mrs Barrington*, as the teenage son of the family. I had all the best entrance and exit lines but didn't have to sustain a character for more than a few minutes. It was a cinch. I was quite a success in the role, but it did nothing to improve sales at the shop. George and Eddie Wheeler (also ex-RAF, Bombay) each came to stay a weekend, regaling me with tales of the Mountview Theatre Club in Crouch End, North London, where they belonged to a company which put on fifteen plays a year for ten night runs. I yearned to belong to it.

The weekend when Eddie visited, Mavis invited us to nearby Lewes on the Sunday to meet her friend Joan Aiken, then married to a journalist, Ron Brown. Mavis and Joan had met as teenagers at a secretarial college at Gerrards Cross. Joan, daughter of the American poet Conrad Aiken and his English wife, was embarking on a highly successful life as a writer, which was temporarily interrupted by the recent arrival of her first child. The Browns lived above Lewes High Street in a flat which, memory insists, was principally furnished with books, as was true of all Joan's subsequent homes. She was small and round with a short-sighted frown; Ron, tall and slightly stooping, was going through an intensely communist phase and harangued us fiercely.

Martyn was very good tempered about the failure of the shop. He drove over from St Leonard's each week and took me out to lunch where we discussed endlessly what we should do. He acquired a partner, Don Berry, whom he had known in the RAF. Don was highly critical of me and of my literary opinions. I got the message and began to read the Situations Vacant column in *The Bookseller*, looking for work in London. At Foyles in Charing Cross Road which I had haunted as a boy I was offered a job to start in ten days time; I felt I was returning home and left Seaford with great relief. After some time Martyn managed to sell the shop. When he returned to pay a friendly call on the new owner that person bellowed, 'There's the man who sold me this damned place. Get out!'

During this unfortunate episode Martyn and I never quarrelled; we are close friends to this day. Subsequently I worked with rather than for him, serving on the Executive of the National Book League (later the Book Trust) during his directorship and was introduced by him to voluntary work with the Booker Prize and the Book Trade Lives Project of the National Life Story Collection. He also advised me at Hampstead when I opened a department for LPs in my bookshop. Our paths have crossed constantly and we have corresponded for more than fifty years. I have three bulging box files of his letters to me, commenting – pertinently, humorously, speculatively and at times scandalously – on books, bookmen, paintings, music and above all people. They are a monument of informed (occasionally misinformed) gossip. I believe that we are two of the world's last prolific letter writers.

Martyn has written several novels, manuals about collecting LPs, and other books on subjects as diverse as social care for adolescents, the county of Surrey, in which he lived for many years, and the Brighton Pavilion. He was a fiction reviewer for the *Daily Telegraph* and became a pundit about book trade matters generally, his utterances gaining regular attention in the media, especially when, as administrator of Man Booker, he dropped judicious leaks about the prize and its judges in order to gain maximum publicity at just the appropriate moment. He was for a while *persona non grata* in the higher realms of the book trade. In his early years, after he had sold St Leonard's and moved to Banstead, Surrey, he over-exposed himself in the correspondence columns of *The Bookseller*. His letters, complaining shrilly of the short-comings of publishers were justified in most instances but his business transactions with them were so small that he was derided. Who, they demanded, was this Martyn Goff with his piddling little shop to tell them what to do? Understandably, that became the attitude of many. I was amused and often took him to task on small points, just to keep the correspondence going. It brought us together again after the Seaford fiasco when for a spell we kept in touch only at Christmas. Then, one evening, in a queue with two friends at the Curzon Cinema, hoping for tickets to see *La Ronde* (the version with Anton Walbrook) I was suddenly aware of a man in evening dress hailing me. Martyn was temporarily working for his tycoon brother-in-law Harry Wingate, while Don Berry ran the shop in Banstead, and was doing a stint as front of house manager. We were taken from the queue and ushered into best seats at the back of the auditorium.

Not all publishers were anti-Martyn. Some saw sense in his criticism while others offered him contracts, notably, Roger Lubbock, at Putnam, who bought his first novel *The Plaster Fabric*. This had a homosexual theme which ensured a certain sale because at that time gays, as they were beginning to be called – thus forever spoiling the former meaning of the word – kept a low profile. The law still forbade sex between consenting males. Martyn 'came out' long before most. When I first knew him he talked of a fiancee who never seemed to be in evidence and he liked to relate anecdotes about Stephen Spender and the ménage à trois the poet enjoyed with his wife and boyfriend, to illustrate how broad minded enlightened people could be. Later he ceased to refer to the fiancee, making his sexual orientation known to all whilst maintaining friendships with men who were not gay, and with women. This has remained a feature of his life.

In 1948 Martyn was already passionately supportive of the National Book League, formerly the National Book Council, which was enjoying a rare period of trade popularity under its new director, the writer and editor, John Hadfield. On entering the book trade I was rightly brainwashed into believing the League was a good deed in a naughty world and I spent much time over the years in promoting its interests, often against heavily loaded antagonism or apathy from publishers and booksellers. By 1970, when Martyn succeeded Jack Morpurgo as Director, among the publishers who had come around to the view that he was not to be dismissed as a show off and windbag was Michael Turner, of Methuen, who lobbied successfully for his appointment. I will write in a later chapter about Martyn's often tempestuous eighteen years in office and of his thirty-five as Administrator of the 'Booker'.

# 3

# London Bookselling

In 1949–52, in what were deemed the post-war austerity years I loved living in London. There was no hardship to be endured, no blackout or threat of bombing. The capital was not *all* in ruins. Most theatres had survived intact and the same went for hotels, department stores, bookshops, galleries, railway termini, palaces, churches and schools. Thousands of homes remained habitable and many shops had lost little more than glass windows. Some parts, notably the city, dockland, and other areas close to the Thames, suffered appallingly but many districts were little more than scarred. As a whole, London was not as devastated as pre-Haussmann Paris had been in the early nineteenth century when wholesale destruction was imposed for the sake of redesigning a city of which the centre, give or take Les Halles and the Pompidou Centre, has scarcely changed in two hundred years.

My wage-earning life for almost forty years was spent in London. I played various roles mainly as a bookseller but also as occasional publisher, author, editor, reviewer, trade journalist and general book-man, throwing and attending parties and stirring it up on the letters page of *The Bookseller*. I doubt if any other milieu could have brought me into contact with so many way out characters or offered greater friendship. I was helped by being granted for more than three decades a view of contemporary life from Hampstead High Street, where the pavements jostled with the just, the unjust, the holier-than-thou, seething with discontent, fulminating against the government, the opposition, the establishment, the workers, the lack of 'real' shops and the parking problem. And, bless them, all buying books.

Martyn Goff was my first book trade employer. There were three others before I became my own boss . . . Christina Foyle, Frederick Joiner and Hubert Wilson. Of Christina I have written at length else-where and will have little to add here. Joiner was the subject of a long

*Bookseller* article in the seventies but it is realistic to suppose that those who read it may not recall all, or even any, of my words. Hubert Wilson, sometime President of the B.A., was more loveable and if anything even more eccentric than Joiner. I have not written of him before.

The Foyles of my youth and early manhood was the best-known privately owned bookshop in Britain. It was not revered as were Blackwell's and Heffer's, where students at the two major universities bought, 'borrowed' or simply read the texts they needed; nor did it have the kudos of Hatchard's which was under royal patronage or Bumpus, in Oxford Street, where the legendary John Wilson personally formed the tastes of many of his clientele. Foyles, larger than any of them, was scruffy, badly-signed, a veritable muck-heap of a shop where would be customers foraged among books lying as much on floors as on shelves or hidden in badly-lit recesses. Christina, daughter of one of the founding brothers, had become well-known as the organiser of literary luncheons at Park Lane hotels. She tyrannised over the shop and its staff of more than one hundred, drove her brother to drink and an early death, bought myriads of second hand books at next to nothing and sold them at up to a thousand per cent profit, perhaps more. This ongoing process mitigated the loss sustained on huge overstocks of 'newly' published books, some of which had been languishing on undusted shelves for decades. The shop attracted vast numbers of customers who, with or without help, usually the latter, often found what they needed. It was believed by some that the family had its own method of banking part of the takings; it was bound by its own rules. Trades unions were not recognised, there were no pensions, no contracts of employment and few members of staff remained for sufficient time to qualify for a paid holiday. As Christina remarked to me grandly, many years later, 'I like them to feel free to go when they choose', which might have been amended to, 'when *I* choose.'

I related many Foyles stories in *Mentors and Friends*. I will repeat one of them. A customer enquired, 'Please, will I find *Ulysses* in this department?', and was told, 'Sorry, he's gone to lunch.'

When I escaped Christina's clutches I accepted a lower salary to work for a man who had as few scruples as herself and was only marginally more civilised as an employer. I studied the Situations Vacant columns in *The Bookseller* and applied for jobs. I phoned Mowbray's, who claimed to be general as well as theological booksellers, and was asked, 'Are you Church of England?' 'I'm not even Christian,' I replied, so no interview was offered. That was the only blank I drew. I was invited to attend at William Jackson (Books) Ltd, Southampton Row, Bloomsbury. There I met an elderly coarse character wearing a grubby, food-stained suit. In another environment I might have mistaken him for a dustman or a tramp. Here, seated at a desk in a passage between the bookshop and the export packing department, I was interviewed, the ruffian, observing me from his one good eye behind a thick lens. He asked me about Foyles and how it was doing. I admitted to not having been shown any actual figures by Christina but said it seemed to be fairly busy. I wished to make a change because there was a total lack of security in working for the lady. This instantly made me vulnerable because the old man, messily smoking loosely-packed Gold Flakes, asked me what I was earning. I should have said, seven pounds per week; stupidly, I told the truth. (Six pounds fifty.) He made no comment, instead telling me that the vacancy was for an assistant in the shop who would spend at least half the working day in the much larger wholesale export section. That I could type was greatly in my favour because orders were received daily from all parts of the world and no one on the staff except the export manager could hit a keyboard with any degree of accuracy. Confirmation of this came several days later when the old boy's henchman appeared at Foyles, to hand me a letter heading with a period engraving of ships steaming into and out of 102 Southampton Row. Beneath this impressive logo was scrawled an offer to join the crew at six pounds per week. I accepted.

   Thus began a sojourn of more than five years which led to many lifelong friendships, although that was certainly not the intention of Frederick C. Joiner, the one-eyed man in the grubby suit, who did not care for his staff to become pally with one another. As with the dread Patsy, Christina's assistant chief terroriser at Foyles, he frowned upon the use of first names. The shop manager when I joined Jackson's was a colleague for much of my working life but in Joiner's presence we were Mr Ford and Mr Norrie, just as the owner's henchman, Bill, who doubled as night watchman at a factory, was Mr Hunter, the export manager was Mr Stern and the miserably paid elderly packer was Mr Dimmock (I never learned the latter two's first names.) In addition, there was a Dickensian rag-bag of a man, who was our collector, known plainly as Warren, a wretch who was not permitted to aspire to misterdom. Warren was paid fifty shillings a week (two pounds fifty) but Joiner assumed he made as much again by a system known as doubling up, operated by the collectors' in unison. This depended on cash payments to publishers who gave less discount for single copies than on multiple orders. So if two or more collectors needed a single copy of the same book a harmless racket, worth the price of a few cups of tea and a sandwich, operated. It had when Joiner trod the streets with a bag early in the century; he assumed it still prevailed. And Warren was the lowest of the low whereas he, Fred Joiner, had had the wit to become his own boss through the time-honoured practice of pinching his employer's customers. He was a product of Forster's 1870 Education Act, numerate but barely literate and possessing cockney awareness. He was nobody's fool. At William Dawson's, exporters to Europe and the United States, he cottoned on to the fact that many American booksellers wanted English editions of books which, the rights having been sold, were not supposed to cross the Atlantic. Publishers often turned a blind eye to this practice until there were complaints from the American publisher to whom they had sold them. Then angry phone calls or letters ensued and Joiner, who was by now trading in his own right, as William Jackson (Books), of Took's Court, Cursitor Street, off Chancery Lane, would apologise, maintain he'd made a mistake or simply swear that the books had not been obtained through him.

He moved, soon after WWII ended to Southampton Row, into solid Edwardian premises still standing today with shops at street level and four floors of apartments above. Below are basements to the depths of which we had to descend to lavatories. We, the staff did, but not Joiner; he had a pail under a sink off the packing room; little Mr Dimmock was required to empty it daily.

Beside the small oblong shop, formerly a jeweller's, was a passage bounded by large areas of window for display, suggestive of a huge interior. Joiner had not previously had a retail shop and settled for using the jeweller's fixtures and fittings, although he may have had no option because building materials, like so much else, were in desperately short supply. He could have removed the glass-fronted doors to the upright cases, which had once held watches, bracelets and other valuable items but he did not trust customers, who were not only forbidden access to the books behind glass, they weren't allowed into the shop by the street door. Moreover, when they gained some sort of admittance by the passage, a counter barred them from getting at the actual stock. They had to ask for what they wanted and have it handed to them. The first shop manager accepted this restrictive arrangement, the next succeeded in persuading Joiner that an open street door would lead to increased custom. When she left, her successor, John Ford, was allowed to have the glass fronts of the bookcases removed. He was also given leave to put up 'new' shelving made of any scraps of suitable wood he could find in the basement. By the year of my arrival, if the interior didn't resemble a purpose designed bookshop it could at least be likened to a makeshift library. Brash new neon strips illuminated the basic gloom over most of the area and the Gollancz yellow jackets helped to add colour.

There was early morning trade (we opened at half past eight) in postcards bought by foreign visitors staying at the Bonnington Hotel just along the block and business was brisk around lunchtime when office girls came to collect reserved copies of *Woman* and *Woman's Own*, then rationed to retailers. Most of the trade was in books, but usually we did not specialise or have promotions. An exception was Christopher Fry whose newest play, *Venus Observed*, was in great demand from both retail and export customers. He is not much performed now but before the renaissance of British playwriting, centred on the Royal Court Theatre, Fry was, for a period, our leading new dramatist, expressing himself in exuberant, fanciful and witty free verse which made up for thinness of plot. John Ford allowed me to mount a large window display in the passage of all his plays, which Joiner sent illegally to the States.

In the early fifties a problem for exporters was obtaining sufficient strawboard for packing. I usually composed Joiner's letters for him once he had outlined what he wished to impart. He invariably approved and added his sprawling signature, which resembled a Rorschach personality test, but one letter to a supplier pleading for more strawboard only partially passed muster. When he'd read it, he said, 'Put at the end, "surely you will help a Brother?" I was shocked. I was not a Freemason but my father was. Moreover he was one who was not in it for business benefits and I had often heard him say it was wrong to use membership for personal gain.

'You don't really want me to put that, do you, Mr Joiner?'

'Yes. You put that, Loll. It might help.' It did.

'Loll' is the closest I can get phonetically to how Joiner addressed me. It was quite a breakthrough; I was court favourite; everyone else was 'Mr', apart from the wretched Warren and henchman Hunter, who was 'Beell'. He couldn't have managed 'Ian' – too strange for his

Cockney tongue – but how Norrie became Loll I shall never know.

Other letters I was asked to write, of less vital importance to the welfare of the business than that sent to the strawboard supplier, were addressed to Buckingham Palace and Downing Street. Joiner and Ethel, his repellent gnome of a wife, had become obsessed with acquiring a knighthood or at least achieving elevated status in the fast disappearing British Empire. Once I had to inform the sovereign of his prowess in exporting British books and enclosed the cleared cheque, paid to the Book Centre, showing Jackson's quarterly purchases had amounted to more than two thousand pounds. Some Palace minion sent a formal acknowledgment; Joiner said, hopefully, 'I suppose She saw the letter, Loll?'

The 'Misters' on the pay roll were frequently replaced. Mr Stern was succeeded by Mr Crabbe who fell foul of Joiner when he accepted an estimate for the repair of the shop blind which had been vandalised by marauding football fans down for the cup. They were a menace to local traders and inhabitants, booking into local boarding houses and, in popular belief, never going anywhere near Wembley. Poor Ernie Crabbe agreed to pay more than Joiner thought reasonable for the damage they wrought. Next, it was John Ford's turn.

John habitually took his annual fortnight's holiday during the last two weeks of July. This coincided with the arrival of American tourists at the Bonnington and other hotels. Whilst he was away I took charge of the shop. Trade was brisk, cash rolled into the till, it was a pleasant change from typing orders. At the end of the day Joiner would look in en route to the pub and ask, 'done any good, Loll?'

Invariably I would reply, 'yes', and quote a figure.

'My friend!' Joiner would cry. It was one of his catch phrases.

The following year John and Sylvia, his wife, were off again at the same time and business was even brisker.

'Done any good, Loll?'

'Very well indeed.'

'Funny,' remarked Joiner. 'Funny you doing so well', adding, with typical subtlety, '*and Mr Ford away.*' He gave me a wicked wink; we were to be conspirators if he had his way. 'Why d'you reckon we're doing so much better?'

'It's because the American tourists have arrived, Mr Joiner.'

It was not the answer he wanted. Ethel had decided to take against John; it was his turn. 'They' all got too big for their boots.

When John returned from his inevitably wet two weeks on a Cornish coast, I suggested it would be diplomatic to take an earlier holiday next year, and told him why.

He thanked me and instantly began to look for another job. By then our working lives had a new pattern because we were also doing the bookkeeping for an extra thirty shillings (one pound fifty) a week each which, even in those days, was cheaper for Joiner than employing a qualified clerk. I have always felt grateful for this experience which later allowed me to talk to my accountants with understanding. I learned the value, also, of having up-to-date figures and of being able to calculate in advance of the annual audit what would be my company's likely gross and net profit. (I retained that advantage but ceased in later decades to be able to understand a balance sheet because the expertise of chartered accountants, combined with the deliberate obscurity built into every Finance Act, made them incomprehensible to anyone who, though numerate, did not have a twisted mathematical brain.)

When John left, in 1952, to manage John Seager's shop in East India Dock Road I was not considered as his replacement because Joiner preferred me to take on all the bookkeeping as well as the export ordering. I was also willing, for a tax free 'dropsy', to take orders home to write up when we were particularly busy, although I would have preferred to manage the shop. I had especially cherished the freedom which doing the collecting for the retail side gave me. It allowed me to lunch with my friends and to book theatre seats or put down stools for places in the gallery, as was then the practice.

Actual lunch in those primitive times was a quick meat-and-two-veg, plus a sweet and coffee costing not more than one shilling (five pence). Following that I learned the intimate geography of west central London, with incursions into west and south-west, entering alleys and narrow passages leading usually to the nether parts of publishing offices, sometimes down area steps, occasionally across grubby yards littered with rubbish. At Gollancz in Maiden Lane, almost next to Rule's (not then one of my luncheon venues) there was the hazard of being struck in the rear, while waiting at the trade counter, by the great VG himself after he had thundered down the bare, back wooden stairs on business of his own. At Collins, in Bow Street, next to the Opera House, a lugubrious character named Arthur glowered and grunted, revelling in declaring the items required as 'out of stock'. At Macmillan's, near the National Gallery, the premises were more up market. I doubt there was actual carpeting but it was clean and orderly, with a servants' entrance at the back. Only the directors and authors went through the grand front portals. Macmillan's was a hierarchical company, its owners consciously upper class, a status still comparatively new to them. At Chatto's in William IV Street, close to Charing Cross Hospital, a charming, former professional musician, operated methodically but slowly. Whatever sighs of impatience might be heard from collectors anxious to book their next theatre seats, his pace never varied. (Perhaps that was why he was no longer in an orchestra; he couldn't accept a change in tempo.) The Bodley Head trade counter was in a mews in Bloomsbury in a building which, although it had survived the blitz, seemed dangerously close to collapse. Inside, crazily leaning stacks of books looked certain to fall at any moment. I seldom met other collectors which precluded me from inclusion in 'Warren's racket.'

Most publishers maintained counters through the fifties, many into the sixties, a few into the seventies. At a time when delivery from warehouses could take weeks it provided a way of keeping some individual customers satisfied. Prior to WWII, they had been known to wait in a central London bookshop for what they required whilst a runner fetched it from a nearby publisher.

Sales reps were permitted to call at William Jackson's on most mornings without making appointments, presenting themselves at a barrier close to the table where I sat, usually in a draught, dealing with orders and invoices. They made an interesting cross-section of men (there was only one woman) with little in common. The fortunate ones, who were not necessarily the least sensitive, had learned to grow a protective skin against the hazards of their calling. Almost all smiled and were polite. Some had strong enough nerves to take the active antagonism provoked by the sight of what they had to sell; some were natural salesmen, keeping their cool, resigned to taking both rough and smooth. A few arrived looking defeated or seething in anticipation of rebuffs. They often fared ill; a tiny minority argued and suffered even more. Most braced themselves for the unexpected, calling out, 'Good-morning, Mr Joiner' but usually receiving no reply. In due course, dread Fred would slouch towards them to collect their samples which he dealt with at his bench, referring to standing orders from overseas libraries and booksellers. A few shops in the States allowed him to buy speculatively on their behalf but the main function of the rep was to pick-up orders already placed with us. Time and labour could have been saved if in the first place Jackson's had posted them on to the publishers.

If he was in a good mood Joiner would return with the books and exchange badinage with the rep; if he was not, he tended to throw them one by one, saying – 'don't want that bloody thing', 'don't want that bleeder' etc. On one occasion, at least, a book was thrown back at him. Mostly, his uncouth behaviour was tolerated and he was labelled, 'a character', 'an eccentric' and 'difficult'. What else was the rep to do?

Some who I first encountered while they stood awaiting Joiner's attention became friends for life, foremost among them Ronald Whiting, then of Allen & Unwin. Our relationship has even withstood him becoming my publisher on two occasions. The others, all dead, were Norman Askew, Ronald Cortie and David Harrison. Norman, an ex-officer who had served in the Burma campaign, combined the duties of rep and sales manager for Jonathan Cape without being given a salary commensurate with the latter role. It is not possible to overlook the parsimony of many of our most distinguished publishers (and booksellers) during much of the twentieth century. Norman's worth to Cape was not materially recognised until Graham C. Greene became part owner of the company a decade later. In my Jackson days Graham was still at Eton; later the three of us worked together on the publishing history he commissioned from me with Norman, unusually for him, playing the role of Special Editor.

Ronald Cortie, of Chatto & Windus, took over from Gilbert Hart (one who certainly threw a book back at Joiner). They, along with Tommy, the imprint's trade Manager, had been soldiers together in France, in 1940, all escaping 'on the last boat out', all remaining friends. One by one, they were recruited to Chatto. Given the Chatto and Hogarth Press lists of the time it was a prosperous arrangement for the two who went on the road and who were paid mostly on commission. Gilbert was not a literary person; Ron, who was, not only read the Chatto books, he enthused about them, even to Joiner. It made no difference to the order he received.

David Harrison, of Heinemann, something of a dandy in his attire, was a fair-haired handsome man with a laugh in his voice. He was a graduate of LSE, a confirmed theatre goer and a cricket fan. We clicked at once. All four had charming wives, who also became family friends.

Charles Pick, a future chairman and managing director of Heinemann, called in his capacity as export manager for Michael Joseph. I suspect he knew for which country the large quantities of Joyce Cary novels we ordered were destined; Cary was more popular in the States, where the rights had been sold, than in Britain. This writer's work was an enthusiasm I shared with Charles and Joiner did not ball me out for chatting to him about it. (In fact, Joiner never took against me on any point until our final disagreement.)

At midday Monday, on the dot, Harry Smith of Hutchinson, an enormous man with huge horse-like teeth, arrived. The Hutchinson Group, comprised of no one knew just how many imprints, published numerous titles every week, all of them undated. If he had with him a new Dennis Wheatley and Joiner ordered fewer copies than of the previous title (because our customers had ordered fewer) Harry became semi-hysterical. 'What am I going to tell them back at the office?' He would complain. 'They're not going to like this, Mr Joiner.' Fear caused him to behave this childishly; Walter Hutchinson was a tyrant to his staff of the same dimension as Christina Foyle's. When he died Edmond Segrave, then Editor of *The Bookseller*, despatched him with the most derogatory obituary I have ever read. Given such an employer it is understandable why poor Harry Smith was incapable of treating reality phlegmatically. He and his bachelor brother took their holiday every year in Norfolk with their widowed mother. A sad, amiable man.

The rep from scholarly Routledge & Kegan Paul (I forget his name) was a major purveyor of dirty jokes. As soon as Joiner had taken his samples away he would call me to hear his latest, relating it with a great many giggles and snuffles. In complete contrast was John Mugliston of Evans Brothers who dressed like a stockbroker and wore a bowler. His Oxford accent came naturally; he was never less than impeccably polite, letting Joiner's uncouth behaviour wash over him. In due course he seconded my membership proposal for the MCC. Some years after, I learned that he was politically to the left. A surprising and charming man, he had much in common with Howard Gibberd who travelled the entire British Isles for Zwemmer, art publishers and booksellers. Howard was a short man, inclined to plumpness, who sported a tidy, small officer's moustache which went with his Guards tie and wore a brown trilby hat. Desmond Zwemmer, younger son of the founder, was at that time building the architectural side of the list which had also acquired the agency for Skira art books. Selling them, especially in the provinces, was a soul-destroying task and, ten years on, it literally killed Howard who died from a heart attack whilst visiting a library supplier in the north. He approached his job with dedication, despaired of what he saw as the philistinism of many booksellers, but was eager to spread interest in art books. He worked dedicatedly for Zwemmer's and should have been rewarded by a mention in the company history, *More Than a Bookshop*, by Nigel Halliday.

The noisiest traveller who came to the Jackson counter was Reg Dignum, of Gollancz, who affected a brash, hail-fellow-well-met approach to his job, treating each call as though he were a stand-up comic going on in front of a thin house. Patter fell from him in rapid flow as he came bursting through the door, pipe at the ready, and continued throughout his greetings and presentation. He prattled on about his books, the weather, the state of the nation, of incidents that had happened to him and to others. He never actually ceased to talk throughout his visit yet, somewhere along the line, he contrived to register who everyone was and what they had said. Beneath all the banter, and behind the heavy black spectacle frames, there was a classical music lover who was also attuned to the social pretensions of his firm's publications. (At his retirement lunch, in the seventies, I met his charming wife. She must have been a delight to come home to after a bad day visiting booksellers.)

A representative whom Joiner never abused was Roger Hutchinson, of Heinemann, David Harrison's predecessor. Roger had the bearing of a magistrate, was always correctly dressed, neatly moustached and carried a perfectly rolled umbrella. He, an old style bachelor who lived alone in a large house overlooking Streatham Common, exuded rectitude; it was easy to imagine him doing the *Daily Telegraph* cross-word over a cold supper with pickles. He carried a good list and if it included a title which, although it made no instinctive appeal to him, he recognised as a potential winner, he took professional pride in selling it. He subscribed Aneurin Bevan's *In Place of Fear*. Of all ministers in the Attlee Labour Government Bevan was the most hated by Tories, who believed him to have designated them 'vermin'. When Joiner saw the book he vented a crescendo of barrack room epithets against the man he saw as standing between himself and gentrification. When his wrath had subsided Roger said quietly, addressing him, as it were, from the bench, 'I think there's a lot of common sense in this book, Mr Joiner.'

Of a much older generation was Alfred Boon, of Methuen, a member of the Boon family of romantic-fiction publishers. He had been on the road all his working life and was proud of the fact that he had earned five pounds a week before WWI. I felt honoured when he invited me to call him, 'Alfred' and presented me with a copy of Hesketh Pearson's biography of Oscar Wilde which Methuen published.

And there was Mr H. F. Johns who had once been a lowly paid assistant at W. H. Smith. He had an entrepreneurial air, introducing his list with a twinkle in his eyes, declaring, 'Batsford don't have customers; they have friends,' and expressing a bland belief that every shopkeeper had at least one hand in the till most of the time. It was not possible for him to make precise appointments with Joiner but when I knew him later he did so, as much in the interests of conserving his own time as mine. He was a good friend to booksellers, introducing his own system of exchanging slow-moving titles for quick sellers long before this became trade practice. Friendly he was but also formal. Right up until the eighties, he remained, 'Mr Johns'; never revealing what 'H. F.' might hide. I never knew, but at his retirement lunch I learned his office nickname was 'Bonzo.' This certainly didn't suit him, 'Mister Johns', cheerily intoned, did.

Among the more colourful characters was the author and balleto-mane, C. W. Beaumont who had a bookshop in Charing Cross Road where he printed and published his own works. He also delivered orders and insisted on cash which did not please Joiner. Another C.O.D. publisher was R. C. Caton, owner of the Fortune Press, a 'one-man band' who published over 600 titles, including several editions of Dylan Thomas's early poems. He had pronounced personality problems which, at one stage, led to his refusal to service orders or answer callers. At this time he still ventured out, appearing at the counter, screwing his face in pain at the sight of Joiner and insisting on down payment for what he was delivering.

Then there was shabby Ron Russell, tall and stooping, with a pain-lined face and withdrawn personality. He was the original down-trodden bagman who hated his occupation and endured I believe an unsatisfactory domestic life. Years later in Hampstead I got to know him better. He unbent to the extent of making ritual jokes about some of the backlist titles I took. He reacted to gentle treatment. I could be fierce with reps but not to those who were incapable of standing up to me, and Ron Russell was like an old sheep dog. It is, however, astonishing that he represented one of the smartest and most successful of independent publishers, Faber & Faber, whose list epitomised the necessary commercial balance between high and low-brow literature. It was strong in practical subjects such as gardening, cookery, crafts, sports and pastimes and was esteemed for its poetry. T. S. Eliot was a working director and selected outstanding poets published by the company. So who chose Ron Russell to sell them? And why was he offered this job? Probably, because he was cheap. Only publishers such as Billy Collins, who believed in selling, deliberately employed reps trained and motivated by sales. I don't know how it happened but probably Ron Russell was pulled off an office stool, perhaps in the accounts department (I can imagine him on a high perch pouring over an old fashioned ledger) and offered another five bob a week to go out on the road. Yet the other Faber rep in London, named Strudwick, was of an entirely different character. He believed books could be sold like baked beans (which they cannot) and had a positive, turn-this-one-down-at-your-peril, approach.

In contrast, Charles Roth, was an intellectual, a deeply convinced socialist of the old school who, with Secker & Warburg, found the list he could believe in both politically and culturally. Fred Warburg, in both volumes of his engaging memoirs, pays tribute to Charles who read all of his books, never over sold but was utterly reliable in assessing their potential with his customers. He did his best for Fred Warburg and for his bookseller customers. Charles was thoughtful, gentle and charming in his approach (he looked like a don) but he had his bad days. Not with Joiner, who seemed to respect him, but perhaps from brasher, younger buyers. On those occasions his remedy was to go to the Civil Service Stores, on the Strand, where he would find Audrey Graham-Jones, who was always Mother to reps.

Probably the most eccentric of all the reps who called was Herbert Joseph, known as 'John', a second cousin of the more famous Michael. John was exceptionally loquacious and his accent belonged to a bygone age, not as affectedly 'Oxford' as Anthony Eden's but close to what Kenneth Tynan called, when referring to the actress Hermione Gingold, 'an extension of all that is worst in South Kensington vowel sounds.' John had a Proustian talent for telling an anecdote of such complexity that I found it fascinating to listen to him tying up the ends. Some thought him boring, but much of what he said was amusing, instructive and often fantastical. While he addressed you, occasionally demanding a comment or answer, he gestured so that if you faced him beside the bar he would gradually move you from one end of it to the other. Once we even turned a corner.

When I first knew John, he had long ceased to have his own imprint. Herbert Joseph Ltd had gone into liquidation during the war but in its time it had had a best-seller or two, notably the cookery books of the Countess Morphy. In my Jackson days he was representing Neville Spearman and selling remainders. I learned from him one useful lesson of publishing, of which more anon.

It was not only reps who called at the counter. Joiner was also a publisher, dating back to the twenties when he had a young partner, Alan Steele – hence, Joiner & Steele. Steele had long since moved on and with his departure the literary side of the list died. Now all titles in print were concerned with contract bridge. Co-author of one, *The Acol System*, was Ben Cohen who called periodically to collect his royalties. How Joiner came to take on the book from anyone as astute as Cohen or as well-known as Terence Reese, the joint author, I don't know but it became his foremost seller. There didn't seem to be a written contract and I don't recall that Reese was ever sent a cheque but perhaps Cohen paid him out of what he managed to extract from Joiner.

There was a ritual pattern to Cohen's visits. He drove down from the north, parked outside the shop, came to the counter and hailed Joiner who quickly turned away.

'Hallo, Mr Joiner! How are you?'

'I'm busy. Can't see you.'

Cohen would then exchange a few words with me and wait patiently while Joiner seethed. 'I've told you. I can't see you.'

'It won't take long. I wondered if you could let me have something on *Acol*. Is it still going well?'

'I'm not giving you any bleeding money.'

'I'm only looking for fifty.'

'Fifty!' roared Joiner. 'I don't owe you fifty. Anyhow, I'm busy.'

'I'll hang on. No hurry.'

'There's no point in waiting. I'm not giving you a penny.'

So it went on with Joiner cursing and shouting and Cohen keeping his cool. He was always utterly polite. He knew Joiner would eventually write a cheque, and that it would be for £25. He never left empty handed.

Finally Joiner paid the price for not having a contract. One day the Allen & Unwin rep who succeeded Ron Whiting subscribed a new edition of *The Acol System of Contract Bridge* by Cohen and Reese. Loud were Joiner's lamentations against Cohen, Stanley Unwin and the entire world of publishing. He had no redress and Cohen's visits ceased.

An *Evening Standard* journalist, Ewart Kempson, compiled *Bridge Quiz* for the Joiner & Steele list and it was this that contributed to my first publishing blunder. *Bridge Quiz* sold moderately well so I decided to bring out a companion volume on cricket. I invited a colleague, Maurice Jones, to assist me. Leslie Compton, brother of Denis, wrote a foreword, an artist friend designed the cover. I toyed with a first printing of five thousand but that was not viable at my proposed selling price of two shillings and sixpence (twelve and a half pence). It was then that I unwisely heeded 'John' Joseph who advised, 'double the print run and halve the cover price.' I did and was no longer working in Southampton Row by the time the booklet was pulped. (A revised edition published by Constable also fared badly.)

Other visitors to Jackson's were American customers who were not in the 'trade' but academics. Leon Edel was the most distinguished. He had edited the plays of Henry James but was still at work on the multi-volume biography. The plays, published by Hart-Davis, flopped as badly in print as they had in the theatre. When reissued as a cheap edition their stout binding made the cost of postage exceed the cover price. Yet Joiner let Edel buy them post free. I think my employer had an innate awe of anyone he met who had written a book; had he traded in Hampstead he would have got over it.

Another academic who visited was a Professor Hannay who was collecting material for a life of William Cowper. He was a tall, stooping man, almost the prototype professor, and tedious to match. He seemed totally unaware that the subject which switched him on was of minimal interest to most others. He would come into Jackson's mumbling about a letter which had turned up to radically alter his assessment of the poet. We all pretended to show an interest as he dickered on. Whether or not his Great Work ever got off the press I don't know but I recall the same subject being treated by Lord David Cecil, and that didn't set the literary world afire.

James Hanley, the highly talented, but on the whole unsaleable, novelist who had been published by Eric Partridge, in the twenties, and by Joiner & Steele, also called. Hanley had written 'hot' books by the standards of inter-war decades. He was a rough diamond, a primitive from whom words poured naturally, an ex-sailor with a touch of literary genius, a powerful writer who received immense critical acclaim. Several publishers, including Faber, persevered with him because they recognised the quality of his prose and storytelling but he never appealed to a large public and his last books were assisted by Arts Council grants. One day he came to Southampton Row to sign a novel published by Jonathan Cape which he had written under a pseudonym. Why the signed copies should have been thought an attraction since the books under his own name didn't sell I don't know, but perhaps Joiner had tipped off someone in the States who thought it worth having a few. It didn't do James, who I came to know in Hampstead, any good. There was no breakthrough but nothing could stop him from writing.

The most significant figure, from a personal viewpoint, who visited Jackson's, was the one who gave his name to the publishing imprint – Alan Steele.

About twice a year a man of medium height, bespectacled, well but quietly dressed in a blue or grey suit and wearing a brown trilby, would walk up to the counter, open it, enter the Joiner area and greet the old rogue affably. This was reciprocated, after which visitor and Joiner disappeared to the pub for a modest session. (Modest was apparent from the fact that Joiner did not return shouting, 'My friend! My friend!' as he lurched up the passage.) The degree of forgiveness present in this relationship was almost entirely on the side of the man in the trilby. Alan Steele was big enough to dismiss the slights he had endured pre-war when Ethel Joiner had persecuted him. He, as junior partner in both William Jackson and Joiner & Steele, had been deemed 'too big for his boots' and consigned to a windowless, partitioned interior at the Took's Court premises. (See *Mentors & Friends*.) Meeting him at Jackson's later turned out to be of crucial importance to me. Meanwhile bookselling was of secondary importance in my life to the theatre.

# 4

## The Mountview Theatre and Playwrights' Clubs

The trade counter I most frequented was that of the specialist play-publisher Samuel French down area steps in Southampton Street, off the Strand. The reason I did so much business there on behalf of Jackson's lay with the Mountview Theatre Club, Crouch End, where I had joined my ex-RAF friends George Simpson and Eddie Wheeler. I became part of it on arrival in London. George helped me with my audition, a Cassius speech from *Julius Caesar* and a short scene out of *Private Lives* (I read Elyot and he read Amanda). I was accepted with a marked lack of enthusiasm to become a member of the student group. Peter Coxhead, Director of Mountview and his fellow auditioners, had not heard of my amazing success in *Young Mrs Barrington* at Seaford and I believe I got in mainly because *Macbeth* was scheduled for December and there was a shortage of spear carriers, lords at the banquet and bit-part players. I was duly cast as Angus, a role in which few if any have made their name, and also allocated as a.s.m. to the autumn season's second production, Lionel Hale's comedy *She Passed Through Lorraine*. It was due to the latter that I became, for a few years, part of the establishment at Mountview. Having tried the patience of producer Milton Krever for the lacklustre manner in which I read the parts of those absent from rehearsal, he then had to endure my replacing one who defected permanently. He worked on me with the ability of a true teacher when at short notice I stepped into the secondary role of a dirty old priest. There was general relief that I was not as awful as anticipated.

Mountview, for the next three years, was the centre of my life. I spent five nights a week there and most of my weekends. I acted, produced, wrote for revues and served on committees for play selection, casting and general management. I took time off only to go to the West End theatre or to spend time in my digs writing. When it became known that I worked in a bookshop my fellow thespians (as we did not refer to ourselves; we thought we were a cut above that) found it convenient to order copies of play scripts through me. Samuel French published most of them.

The club had begun in 1945 in Colombo where Peter Coxhead and his friend Ralph Nossek were serving in the Royal Navy. As 'other ranks' they were not eligible to act alongside their officers who put on plays so they formed a drama group to entertain fellow sailors, with Peter directing and Ralph playing leading roles. One of their colleagues was John Hughes who re-emerged at Crouch End about the time I joined, having graduated from Cambridge in English. (In one of the many coincidences of life he was to become managing director of Samuel French long after my trips to its trade counter had ceased.)

After demob, Peter attended drama school and then re-established the Colombo enterprise at sundry addresses before being offered a semi-derelict hall and basement, part of a four storey house on Crouch Hill, Hornsey. The first production there – *The Importance of Being Earnest* – opened on a cold, foggy night to an audience of thirteen. Twenty years later, The Theatre Club, Mountview (President, Sir Ralph Richardson) had become the Mountview Arts Centre Ltd, with a school which was a registered charity and had an associated film theatre.

Peter Coxhead was short, inclined to tubbiness, had a deep, clear speaking voice with a cutting edge, a fat round face, eyes that were often reproachful and a long, loud, affected laugh which could deteriorate into a pig-like squeal. He was straight-haired, later bearded, unhandsome but not without presence. He was utterly single-minded and adept at using people, from elderly spinsters and prosperous businessmen, to gifted young actresses and untalented, aspiring actors whom he fancied, to carry out his vision – and he did have one. There was a genuine spark there although it could get obscured by his crude behaviour. A small part of him wished to act but he soon got over that in favour of direction, teaching and wielding power.

He was determined to have, first, an amateur theatre which included student classes and, later, a grant-aided theatre school supplying 'the profession', offering scholarships and exhibitions to applicants from all parts of the world. He became affluent, with a town house and another, grander one, in the country. He had a genuine love of theatre and an ability to recognise and nurture talent but he was vulgar. He liked to make large effects. Theatrically everything must be bigger, ever bigger, even though his theatre was tiny. He was essentially a showman; he had little intellect.

Peter tolerated the seeming democracy of Mountview. There were contested elections to the general management committee but he alone appointed members to the play selection and casting committee, nominated other directors, oversaw the upkeep of the property, and employed canteen staff (the only people connected with the club who were paid). He encouraged those creatively inclined to get involved and delegated jobs such as designing and painting scenery, helping backstage, managing the box office and the wardrobe, looking after membership records, organising programme printing and coping with the press. He had prodigious energy, moved swiftly about his small empire issuing commands, listening to petitions, coping with some crises (creating others), taking rehearsals and student classes, emitting his hyena-laugh; or sitting cooped in his airless office beneath the stairs planning productions, arguing with members of the casting committee, whilst stamping his personality on almost everything.

It was foolish of those of us with democratic tendencies to believe we could alter the way the Theatre Club was run. Without Peter it wouldn't have survived. Like some Byzantine mogul or Medici he contrived to make it work in *his* way at the same time as allowing many of us to express our own aspirations provided they did not conflict with his overall policy. He succeeded because Mountview was fun and exciting and gave its members an illusion of being part of the alluring world of the theatre. It attracted former professionals, would-be professionals and art students, but the bulk were amateurs and some had genuine talent.

We complained endlessly to one another about Coxhead, quoting instances of his most recent monstrous behaviour yet none of us seriously doubted that, by and large, Mountview was 'his' thing. Of course he couldn't do without us but for each one who walked away exasperated there was always an eager replacement. Just before I became an active member Peter had dealt with a major insurrection by one of the leading ladies and her husband, a producer, as we then called directors. Their bid to topple his rule had little support and it was they who went, subsequently forming their own company to give occasional performances in the town hall.

From the start Peter had engaged the help and backing of George

Norman, an estate agent who served on Hornsey Council and later became Mayor. Norman admired Coxhead's ambitions and ability, found him the semi-derelict property on Crouch Hill (rent twenty-five pounds a year) and became the club's first president. The two men had seemingly little in common except that both were short and industrious. Peter had no better friend. 'Mr Norman', as most of us addressed him, came regularly to performances and knew us all by name, as did Ruth, his charming wife. There was a touch of grace and favour in their attitude but perhaps they also were acting a little. Their daughter Valerie was a fellow student. Surprisingly she was not given all the plum parts; there was no pressure from the president and his lady. She composed music for a cabaret number I wrote for Eddie Wheeler.

The Theatre Club attracted goodwill from other councillors (although the one whose daughter fell for Eddie dealt summarily with our friend, hounding him out of the ancestral home with Victorian vigour) and from *The Hornsey Journal* which reviewed one production on its front page. Number 104 Crouch Hill became our social centre, at least for that vital minority making up the majority of the audience. These at times long-suffering folk were the counterparts of that section of the public which still supported weekly rep in the provinces and suburbs. Television, reintroduced soon after the end of the war, was restricted to BBC on one channel and transmitted live from Alexandra Palace which was just up the road from Crouch End. The 'telly' had not yet altered the lifestyle of the entire nation. Live theatre beyond the West End was yet viable for professionals and amateurs.

In London N8, from the ranks of well-to-do residents came Hugh and Winifred Gamlen who were a major blessing to the Club. Hugh ('Mr Gamlen', to all of us except, again, Peter Coxhead) was a silversmith in the City. He lived across Crouch Hill in a filter road, in a similarly large Edwardian house to that occupied by the club though it was in rather better nick. He was married to Winifred ('Mrs Gamlen', again to most of us – 'Winnie' to Peter) who was severely lame, bespectacled and spherically shaped, an amateur musician with a talent for composition at precisely the level the club needed for its pantomimes and revues. Mrs Gamlen's score for *Cinderella*, the first Mountview panto, was memorably tuneful. (Over forty years on, Doreen Barnett, an a.s.m. on the show, who emigrated to the States, came home on holiday and sang it all from memory at a private party.) They were performed originally by a principal boy and a girl with smashing legs and thighs, by two of the campest ever ugly sisters and by a roguish Buttons who made it to the professional stage. There was no orchestra – there wasn't room for even a small one. We had two pianos, one played by Winnie Eamlen and the other by Arthur Parsons, with the latter so smitten by the principal girl that he sometimes had to be prompted back into active key board service by his composer partner.

I became an assistant stage manager on this production and vividly remember one performance for that crucial moment when Cinderella was about to be summoned home from the ball. The chimes were being sounded by my colleague Lydia Nossek using, for some extraordinary reason, a china cup against a metal cylinder. Midnight had proclaimed itself only seven times when it became plain to me (I was holding the cylinder) that Lydia was not going to make it. The cup was fast disintegrating, the whole historic plot of *Cinderella* was in the balance. The final stroke came thinly from my key ring, after which Lydia and I collapsed into the garden in hysterics.

'Into the garden' is correct. There was no easy access to or from the stage at Mountview. Despite immediate post war restrictions and shortages, somehow Coxhead had got his theatre into shape with an auditorium, at first unraked, fitted with discarded cinema seats, and an adequately equipped stage. There was no sheltered route from what were hilariously called the dressing rooms, only a path through bushes leading to steep steps up to the stage door, which would often slam in the wind, thus shaking the scenery. (For some productions, those entering stage left had to make their way past brambles and foliage around the back of the theatre to an entrance through another outside wall.)

There was more winter snow and rain in the mid-twentieth century than nowadays. The pantomime was performed in early January when it was remarkable that we escaped serious outbreaks of illness among the scantily clad cast. What was more extraordinary was the apparent adequacy of the single, all-sexes lavatory used for both cast and audience. At least the door had a lock. This was permissible under Health & Safety rules only because Mountview was a club. There is a curious law still, so far as I know, operative that allows private theatre clubs to ignore the rigorous fire and other precautions taken in public buildings. In my years at Mountview there was available just that one loo which during any interval of a performance could theoretically have been needed by at least a hundred and fifty people at the same time.

Winnie Gamlen's involvement in our rather squalid premises is explicable only because she was a composer and musician ready to take part and overlook the less desirable features of the property. How did Hugh Gamlen see it? He was a well to do city trader, respectable tax and rate payer, genial, tolerant and possibly a hidden backer of Coxhead and Mountview. He enjoyed crossing Crouch Hill, entering the canteen and observing us all apeing what we supposed were theatrical manners. As for Winnie, who also smiled upon us while aware of her own contribution, she could be firm about having her own way. When she wished to introduce a number into a revue which didn't quite fit with my overall perception of what was required, she always prevailed. It was never mentioned that she enjoyed this right, possibly because she kept open house (and garden) for Mountview rehearsals. There was no resentment; she never abused the privilege. Coxhead was treated like a favoured stepson and the rest of us as his extended family.

Peter wooed theatrical stars such as Margaret Rutherford and Bobby Howes – later Ralph Richardson and Judi Dench – to offer their patronage and it was largely through his dynamism that audiences were found to keep the theatre live for about a hundred and sixty nights each year, including two whole weeks, with matinees, for the annual pantomime. When serious minded young members, of whom I was one, dared to challenge his authority on the management committee he played his trump card. The mortgage on the property was in his name. He guaranteed payment to the building society which had granted it. At this period in the early 1950s he displayed a superhuman quality of endurance. He had no money of his own and had to work as a sales assistant in a West End men's outfitters for five and a half days a week. Into the remaining one hundred plus hours he poured massive energy to keep Mountview afloat, while personally directing at least one, probably two, plays per season, teaching his students and reading hundreds of playscripts. He was maddening and impossible. I and others constantly disagreed and quarrelled with him but the show went on. And it was he who insisted on a wide repertoire ranging from Shakespeare, Ibsen, Wilde, Chekhov and O'Neill to popular farce, comedy and thrillers. Some of it taxed our regular, on the whole loyal, audience.

It was regrettable that when we presented Shaw Peter, with no intellectual appreciation of GBS whom he found boring, insisted on directing *Saint Joan* and *Pygmalion*. George, Eddie and I had to plead with him not to cut the epilogue to the former, when all the characters return to earth to praise Joan. Into it the playwright brings an English soldier who had handed Joan a makeshift cross as she was about to burn. Peter, who couldn't see the point of this additional scene, for once allowed himself to be overruled but in another, between Warwick, Cauchon and the Chaplain, he introduced an unnamed character who suddenly glared in upon them, said nothing and walked away. 'What ', I asked him, 'is that supposed to imply?'

'The scene is too static. The audience needs a diversion.'

'But he doesn't say anything, or do anything. It has no dramatic meaning.'

Peter had no answer but remained convinced that Shaw was at fault.

*Macbeth* was both a triumph and a disaster. It was daring to envisage the great tragedy on our small stage and to make it the December offering to an audience which had enjoyed *Gaslight*, *She Passed Through Lorraine* and *Miranda* (a popular comedy about a mermaid). Peter approached the task with typical zest. He had formidable leading players, a boy wonder to take the tiny part of Macduff's son, Milton Krever to make a gem of the Porter and one of the club husbands, a trained fencer, to arrange a thrilling fight between Macbeth and Macduff. He researched early Gaelic, or some such language, to provide the walk-on soldiers with strange battle cries – 'Gracchan!' and 'Ayeez-to-ayeez!' and overcame illness and accidents to himself and others. (He conducted most rehearsals from a chair because he had a broken foot.) Also on the debit side was a supporting cast rabble of tattily dressed, extremely amateurish actors with little or no ability to speak the marvellous verse – surely the finest in all Shakespeare? The basic set was simple but there were many scenes played in front of a drop curtain with small contingents of other ranks storming on stage left and passing across to exit stage right, uttering incomprehensible cries. It was several nights into the run before I understood the reason for the titter when I appeared in one of these. My sword just about passed muster but my scabbard was the size of a small saucer. The lights were too low in the banquet scene for the audience to perceive that some of the lords were young female members of the company wearing unlikely moustaches and with their hair mostly concealed beneath Viking-style helmets.

*Macbeth* is the shortest of the major plays and rattles along at a fine pace provided the actors allow it to do so. Peter Williams, who played the title role, was professional material and promising, but chose a city career over the theatre. His diction was fast and clear; so was Ralph Nossek's (Macduff). Both understood the rhythm of the verse. Brenda Morriston, who played Lady Macbeth, was said to have been a pro although one was never given any detail. She was a large lady with large features to match and a resounding voice. She towered over Macbeth which was in character but her performance was probably too overwhelming for our theatre and, as with almost anything Brenda did, on or off stage, there was an element of hysteria not far from the surface. Even so these two individuals transmitted some genuine Shakespearean magic.

It was a happy touch to cast Milton Krever as the Porter. Milton, a generation older than most of us, and at least a generation wiser, was the club's senior producer after Peter. He had a serious stutter which he was plagued with all his life, but not on stage. The stage, was in a way, a therapy to him. The porter is a small part but essentially the only comic relief in the entire play, which is sadly lost on a contemporary audience ignorant of early seventeenth-century allusions. It provides an important cathartic interlude between the actual murder of Duncan and its discovery. Milton staggered drunkenly about the stage, only slightly overdoing it, making the most of those lines fantasising about the identity of the person responsible for 'here's a-knocking indeed'.

Milton, in faintly joking manner, often reminded us that he was an American citizen. We had no evidence of his father, only of his Jewish momma with whom he lived in Canonbury and who had a junk shop in Muswell Hill. He was employed in the fur trade and occasionally wrote philosophical pieces for a house magazine. He was deeply thoughtful and had a bubbling sense of humour often expressed by a richly appreciative chuckle. As a producer he cared passionately that actors should essay truthful interpretations. He understood that sincerity in amateur players could make up for lack of technique.

Milton remained single until after his mother's death. Then he married Betty Corkhill who was not Jewish. They enjoyed many years together. When Betty died he married Velma, a friend of theirs, and moved to Bexhill-on-Sea where George and I attended his funeral in 1998. Milton was one of a dozen or so who, first encountered at

Mountview, remained friends for life. He had humility, a touch of gravitas, plus an affectionate and generous awareness of others.

It was Milton who, for *Macbeth*, introduced Gawn Grainger to the club. The twelve-year-old invested astonishing power into his one brief scene between Lady Macduff, her son and their murderers, his vivid dark eyes carrying absolute conviction. He and Ralph Nossek were both to become National Theatre players; Gawn married Zoe Wanamaker and was once an amanuensis to Laurence Olivier. (There was some reflected glory in being in that *Macbeth*.)

Although I learned much about books, authors and publishers in my years at Jacksons, the work became automatic, leaving time whilst engaged upon it to be thinking of the revue scripts and plays I was writing. During my first year at Mountview, Peter Coxhead permitted me to stage a students' revue, much of which I wrote myself and also appeared in. There was a number in which Eileen Toby, a charming and talented teenager, and I sat on stools borrowed from the canteen to be bitchy about the personalities and characteristics of the older members. This idea I had filched from Alan Melville's wildly successful *Sweet and Low* series when Hermione Gingold and Henry Kendall had behaved similarly, pretending that they were dining at the Ivy.

There were further student revues. Then, in the following year, the committee agreed, that there should be a main production revue to run for ten nights. I was to be one of the cast and principal writer but, during the early rehearsal period, I took over as producer. In retrospect this was a mistake – I should have concentrated on revising my material. All the same, *Mixed Grill*, as it was named, was my Mountview high spot. Winnie Gamlen wrote music for ensemble numbers, providing her own, rather tame lyrics, although hitting a topical note in one which closed the first half with, 'Summer was on a Wednesday afternoon in 1951'. It was regrettable that we were not able to collaborate as lyricist and composer but I think to have done so would have been foreign to both our natures. Not being able to compose was certainly a major shortcoming for me. Arthur Parsons, the other pianist, could write both words and music. It was Festival of Britain year, bravely marking the beginning of the end of wartime austerity. A dominant feature of London's South Bank Exhibition was a high, semi-elliptical, somewhat phallic construction of no practical use called the Skylon. What was its purpose? Was it merely decorative or was it a symbol of the times, heralding a new, hopeful era when rationing would become a thing of the past? No one knew. The Skylon didn't do anything. It wasn't climbable, it didn't move, light up, bear signs or messages. It just was. Arthur's lyric raised the question – 'What shall we do with the Skylon when the South Bank Exhibition closes down?' I don't remember it arrived at a conclusion, even a rude one, but it was lightly ironic and in keeping with the carefree air of the exhibition itself. I do not have a copy; I believe it is lost, along with Winnie Gamlen's music.

Eddie Wheeler, who had already established himself as a comedian at the club with numbers and routines he wrote and invented himself for occasional Sunday night revels, was prominent in my cast. Getting him to rehearse his own numbers was tricky. He insisted they would not work without an audience; I said he must go through the motions so that we could at least time his acts and gain some idea of their content. This tortured him and he pleaded to be let off, although he was not opposed to rehearsing sketches or other numbers in which he appeared. One of them, 'the cinema sketch', was the hit of the show. The original idea was, I think, his but I wrote the dialogue after we had worked out the business together. It was a simple situation of two people snogging in a cinema and impeding the view of the person in the row behind them, whose feelings were further incensed when the man, played by Eddie, lit a pipe. Inane comments on the film were made incessantly by the female snogger and there were regular interruptions by the loud voiced usherette who wielded a bright torch to show other patrons to their seats. Thanks to Eddie's inspired clowning, plus Don Cregor's low-key performance as the put-upon film-goer in the row behind, it worked uproariously. Except, on the Monday night when it played to almost total silence. This was of special concern to me because, following the cinema sketch, I filled in with a short solo number, taking the mickey out of Stanislavsky, while the cast changed rapidly for the first half finale. That Monday I died the death in a big way. Such experiences were salutary and taught us not to take any audience for granted. It was perhaps the nearest many of us came to tasting the reality of the professional theatre.

Rereading some of the material we wrote and used, I blush. We should have been more self-critical. Bob Beckley, the permanent stage director, who never performed himself, was a help. After the first night

of *Mixed Grill* he phoned me at work, was mildly complimentary –
Bobby never allowed himself to be carried away about anyone or anything apart from the women he chased – and said we must cut two
numbers to keep the momentum going. I asked which two. He had
thought it out, right down to considering how long it would take for
costume changes. One weak sketch was to be axed and one straight
song. Shirley, the singer, had been brought in from the local operatic
society solely on the strength of her voice. Her presence irritated me
because her acting was wooden and she had no sense of comedy. Also
she was used to being a leading lady in musicals such as *The Maid of the
Mountains* and to receiving bouquets at curtain call, a ritual we didn't
encourage. Coxhead had insisted we include Shirley in the cast; it was
his only interference. He wasn't consulted about the cuts. Shirley
sulked momentarily but recovered. I seem to remember we cut
another of her numbers later in the run. There were others with
which we should have been equally ruthless but on the whole *Mixed
Grill* was well received. It included one item which would not be
tolerated today even in a private club theatre. This was a solo I wrote
called *A Few Veiled Remarks*. It was performed by a girl wearing what
we then called a yashmak who announced herself as one of a sultan's
harem. The opening lines were – 'Being in purdah / Is murder',
followed by a general lament concerning the difficulties of smoking,
going to the dentist and taking breakfast ('Shovelling cereal/Through
this material'). There was not a murmur of protest from cast or
audience and one local press critic praised it as the best number in the
show. (In contrast to my reporting experience at Eastbourne, the
'Mountview' local press was permitted to write candidly – and did).

Amateur acting can be dire to watch. Thanks partly to an element of
embryo and ex-professionals, what was staged at Mountview was often
tolerable. The standard was not as high as at the Tavistock, in
Canonbury, or at the Questor's, in Ealing, but there were frequent,
genuinely theatrical moments. One was Milton Krever's production of
*Uncle Vanya* in which George Simpson played the title role, proving,
perhaps, that RADA had been wrong to reject him. I saw it on a cold,
wet, windy February evening when I was one of an audience of about
twenty. Miraculously, Chekhov came through; there was true sus-
pension of disbelief. I went round after, as one does, and found George
and others silent in their dressing room. Initially they suspected I was
being unnaturally lenient and uncritical when I said I had really

enjoyed the play. Then they knew I meant it because the truth of that particular performance had also been their experience.

Although Mountview occupied most of my non-working hours holidays were not totally bypassed. In theory by 1952 I was sufficiently affluent to plan a holiday in Paris; in fact I was able to amass only twenty-two pounds of the permitted travel allowance of £25. Six of us – the others were Mavis and George, Lydia Nossek, Margaret Pope and 'Shorty' Sheen – took the Folkestone-Boulogne ferry. Shorty, who was christened Leonard, was another ex-RAF friend; Lydia and Margaret were active at Mountview. Only Mavis, whose sensible parents had sent her to live with a family near Bordeaux for three months in 1946, was fluent in French which through much of her life she taught at schools and evening classes. George was extremely proficient in the language but refused to speak it in case he made mistakes. I remembered very little from my school-days but tried it out which led to numerous gaffes and much mockery. Shorty knew only a few words.

We were a very proper sextet; the men slept in one room, the women in another. Mavis and I went to a night club in Montmartre and drank expensive vinegary plonk before walking back as dawn broke to our hotel near the Étoile. Otherwise erotic delights were confined to a visit to the Folies Bérgères. We also saw Maurice Chevalier in a revue and an evening of Marcel Marceau and his mime company which included a masterful version of Gogol's *Dead Souls*. Mavis, already well acquainted with Paris, had friends living on the left bank. One invited us to a rehearsal of the play he was directing. I couldn't understand a word but was fascinated by this glimpse into French theatre behind the scenes.

We did many of the correct first time things – Notre Dame, the Louvre, the Jeu de Paume, the Rodin Museum but did not take a bateau mouche trip because we couldn't afford it and only some of the party ascended the Eiffel Tower. We traipsed the boulevards, climbed to Sacré Coeur, had drinks on the Boul' Mich and often used taxis because Mavis worked out it was cheaper for six to travel in that way than by bus. In the cafes we were constantly approached by Africans carrying huge carpets for sale. We dismissed them by pleading poverty and declaring, 'Nous ne sommes pas américains,' which was received with delight.

In Bombay I had discovered French cuisine; now I had my first experience of wine every lunch and dinner time. I doubt if I would tolerate today what we drank then but we couldn't afford to be choosy. We afforded regular meals by one of us ordering a main dish, another some vegetables, a third, a starter, and so on; then sharing the more than ample portions. We also learned to sip our aperitifs, to make them last. We were into cinzano, byrrh, suze and other often sickly potions which I never see anyone drinking nowadays. It was only when the heatwave struck that we desisted a little. The rail journey home via Boulogne reminded me of returning to Bombay from the Himalayas. Only Margaret bore it well. She was a very relaxed lady, always correctly and smartly dressed. She sat in a corner of the compartment wearing a neat little hat and showed no sign of being in the least uncomfortable or hot. The rest of us were parched, running with sweat, longing for the sea breeze to come.

That was the end of travel abroad for another three years during which I went no further than Stratford-upon-Avon. On this first visit since passing through in childhood the theatre was the attraction. Four of us from Mountview, George included, chose a vintage year, one when not only were the plays produced in period costume but were performed by well-trained players who knew how to enunciate and throw their voices. And what players! Led by Peggy Ashcroft (Cleopatra and Portia), Michael Redgrave (Lear, Antony, Shylock), Marius Goring (Richard III, Petruchio, etc) and Yvonne Mitchell (Katherine etc), they were supported by Harry Andrews, Rachel Kempson, Tony Britton and others. Over fifty years later it remains the outstanding Shakespearean experience of my life. And not only did we watch these fabulous beings on stage, on one of the Sundays of our eight-day treat they were to be seen in the nets limbering up for a cricket match against the town. Robert Shaw was bowling to Peggy Ashcroft, duly padded-up, while Harry Andrews looked-on. He did not participate, having broken a wrist in an earlier match which meant he acted every performance with one lower arm in plaster of Paris. And we got to know the not too tourist-ruined, historic town with its exquisite Clopton bridge and its Tudor and mock-Tudor architecture; we rowed on the Avon and, when there was a day off – we saw five plays over eight nights – we drove to Worcester, Kenilworth, Henley in Arden. I enjoyed many subsequent trips to Stratford but none as much as this one. I wrote an ecstatic account of all five productions for Elk's Bombay magazine.

Stratford has an enduring appeal for me. I love being there and until recently invariably took joy from my visits to the Memorial Theatre on the banks of the Avon. It was sheer delight to approach it across a stretch of not too municipalised public garden, to have a drink on the balcony overlooking the river and, above all, to be in the auditorium where I was always able to see and hear from any seat in the stalls or circle. Now it is being revamped to make it a more interesting playground for over-obtrusive directors and to provide better dressing rooms for the actors. Yet already the stage had been extended by several acres. (In one production of *Hamlet* the Prince, surveying Claudius praying from metres away in outer Worcestershire, muttered, 'Now might I do it pat.' I knew what he was saying but he couldn't actually be heard.) Temporarily the plays are being performed in the Courtyard Theatre where an apron stage deprives part of the audience at any one time from an overall view of the action. I'm all for actors having decent working conditions but those who pay to watch them also deserve consideration.

The moderate success of *Mixed Grill* and other Mountview shows led me to attempt breaking into the professional world of late night revues then fashionable in even smaller club theatres in the West End, notably the Watergate and the Irving. Why I did not use the obvious opportunities at Crouch End to write plays for the company I knew and belonged to I cannot now remember. I was still spawning one annually but I never submitted any for consideration even though I had been on a panel which read several hundred typescripts sent in for a competition we promoted in an effort to find new work. There was only one which any of us thought worthy of production and that we rejected with some reluctance because its subject matter – the supposed relationships between Ibsen and the women who had inspired his heroines – seemed too literary and way out. A prize was not awarded. Why that did not lead me to offer my own work indicates a contrariness in my nature. Perhaps I could not face the possibility of being turned down? Some of it was shown elsewhere tentatively and one three-act tragedy, originally composed in blank verse but rewritten in prose, had an airing at the Playwrights' Club.

The Playwrights' Club met monthly at the Round House, a pub on the corner of Garrick Street and New Row, to read and discuss a member's work. Most members had actually written plays, or were trying to, apart from Ray Stanley, the secretary and driving force. His motivation seemed entirely on behalf of others. Soon after joining I enquired why the club did not have a production unit since a play could not really be called a play until it had been acted. Ray thought this a sensible suggestion; other members were dubious. If a play were actually staged whose work would it be and who would choose it? Wouldn't this lead to dissension within the club? Wasn't it more comfy to keep the boat steady and just *read* one another's work? Somehow the committee was convinced that this was the only way forward and that I was the person who should choose, direct and cast the play, which provoked no little hostility. I chose *Typewriter on the Sand* by one John Parry which led to a long, valued friendship with both the author and Linda, his wife. Also, in the short term, to a mediocre production, burdened by a leading man who was able to face an audience only when half cut, and to the demise of the Playwrights' Club. John never had another play produced anywhere; all I had achieved was the spoliation of a few mildly egotistic people's innocent pastime of reading and criticising one another's work.

About this time I attended lectures on the art of the dramatist given by Stephen Joseph, devotee of theatre-in-the-round, the man who 'discovered' Alan Ayckbourn, and son of Michael Joseph and Hermione Gingold. I showed him the play that had been read at the Playwrights' Club. Kindly, objectively, he told me, 'you describe the characters carefully but the words you give them do not bear out your assessments'. I took the hint and didn't write another play although many years later I showed the same script to Jimmie Roose-Evans, the founder of the Hampstead Theatre Club. He made different objections from Stephen's but said he would consider staging it if I re-wrote the last act. I said I would do so if he guaranteed a production. There the matter ended.

*Typewriter on the Sand*, a revue I directed for the Royal Marsden Hospital (because one of its physicists was a Mountview friend) and, of all unlikely diversions, a gang show I organised for Crouch End boy scouts, indicated a tendency to withdraw from the Theatre Club. I came off various committees and ceased baiting Coxhead. I moved from Harringay into a small back room in Bloomsbury, within a few minutes walk of my work, and attempted to concentrate on writing.

The back room was in Coram Street in a nineteenth-century terrace later obliterated by the Brunswick Square development. On the site of where I lived happily for over two years there is no trace of what I knew. Cities must change; the terrace was a poor item of run of the mill Georgian-style domesticity. The interior of the house I lived in would not today actually be condemned as unfit for human habitation but it offered little in the way of home comforts. It was on five floors, including basement, with a common staircase for the top four. This destroyed privacy because the kitchens, bathrooms and living quarters were on different split levels, all opening directly on to the stairs. There was insufficient space to eat in the kitchen; meals had to be carried 'in public' to the living room. If you needed the lavatory at night you reached it down unheated, uncarpeted stairs. In the basement there was a prostitute whose clients entered via the area steps off the pavement; there was no rear access. On the ground floor lived an attendant at the Turkish baths in Russell Square. From both, at night, noises suggesting violent sex emanated. On the first floor dwelt Harold Elvin, estranged husband of the dancer Violetta who took his name to escape from Soviet Russia where he had been employed at the British embassy in Moscow; on the top floor was a family of three, husband, wife and slightly retarded adult daughter, who were mostly unemployed and often drunk; on the second floor was my landlady, the widowed Connie Cowan, who let her marital bedroom (with the most comfortable divan on which I have ever slept) to me. She occupied a tiny bedroom with two doors, one into her living room, the other on to the public landing. We shared the tiny kitchen and bathroom. There was neither garden nor lift, nor central heating. Windows rattled with a gust of wind and vicious draughts ensured there was no danger of death from suffocation. Mrs Cowan was lame and had no option but to use the staircase, which had sharp curves at each main landing. She distracted herself by mothering me, cooking supper whenever I chose to stay in and allowing me the use of her rooms for an occasional party in return for having a seat booked at a theatre of her choice. She talked often of Ellis, her late husband – 'he was a gentleman; *you* too are a gentleman.' Their name had been changed from Cohen. Ellis had been in leather goods but his heart was not in business. There were no children. She was devoted to his memory but interested in others. She was a good soul but when I had flu I was rebuked for permitting Mavis to look after me. ('Tell your girl friends, *I'll* take care of you'); on my wedding morning she broke down in tears in my brother's arms.

From Coram Street I could walk to the Irving Theatre in Irving Street, now a paved way between Charing Cross Road and Leicester Square. The Irving was owned by a plump Indian named Chaudhuri, who dressed in a loud check suit and seemed to enjoy a liaison with a spirited, capricious Irishwoman called Kathie. The tiny theatre, with club room above, acquired fame for a while by staging witty revues written by Peter Myers, Alec Grahame and David Climie, produced by Ronnie Stevens and performed by Joan Sims, Vivian Pickles, Kenneth Connor and others. When these talented folks moved on to public theatres and fame Mr Chaudhuri sought, 'the new materials – we must have the new materials, isn't it?' – and new writers. Ian Carmichael, then appearing in *The Globe Revue* on Shaftesbury Avenue, was engaged as producer and accepted several numbers of mine. By the opening night of *In The Picture*, I was left with one-and-a-half, the other half having been rewritten, without any consultation, by David Climie who had been persuaded to help knock the new show into shape. The one – still mostly mine – and another by fellow newcomer, Ken Hoare, were the only items to get approval from the critics, who slated the show. On the opening night, Noël Coward and Cicely Courtneidge sat together in the front row. Rosaline Haddon, that lady's niece, was one of the company. After the final curtain, Coward and Courtneidge rose in front of the audience, embraced each other extravagantly as though in long farewell, then walked upstairs together to say, 'Darling, you were marvellous!' to Rosaline Haddon. Why didn't I make a point of meeting Coward and saying, 'I wrote that solo number of Ros's, Mr Coward'? It might have drawn a terrible put down but it is just possible he had found some merit in it. And wasn't that the way you got on in the glittering world of showbiz? It was how I had behaved as a cub reporter, bursting into the dressing room of Benno Moisiewitsch, the great pianist, and subjecting him to puerile questions about how he liked playing in Eastbourne.

Fortunately, I had grown up a little since then. I never met Noel Coward and spoke only once to Rosaline Haddon. Instead I hung about the Irving bar during the run of *In The Picture*, and for the following twelve months, believing I was rubbing shoulders with the near great. There I met Tony Hayes, soon to star in *The Boy Friend* for several years. He wanted cabaret numbers which sounded sophisticated but weren't full of clever quips, as they were in Irving revues. That was the first dead end. Then there was a man who believed that the much heralded independent television would mean jobs for all would-be comedians. He required even more dumbed-down material than Tony Hayes, the kind which studio audiences would laugh at when ordered to do so. Dead end number two. A delightful chap named Paddy Ward, who was in one of the subsequent revues, got summer work at the Mowlem Theatre, Swanage and urgently needed solos. Nothing that mentioned religion, politics, sex or anything remotely controversial would be admissible. I got away with one about cricket which Paddy maintained provoked hearty laughter on the Dorset promenade. It even earned me a pound or two. Slightly more rewarding was the half sketch with David Climie which was filmed in performance at the Nuffield Centre, Charing Cross, by BBC television – LIVE! Then Ken Hoare and I decided to pool our materials and offer them as jointly written numbers. Several went into a revue at the Bolton's, South Kensington, where we so disliked the staging of them that we demanded their withdrawal. This was pre-empted when the show suddenly folded. Ian Carmichael was friendly to us both and accepted numbers for another revue. Ronnie Stevens, by now appearing with Ian and Cyril Ritchard in *High Spirits*, one of the last old style revues, was also helpful, tactfully suggesting revisions to scripts but I soon found that being in the theatre world, as I supposed myself to be, was largely a matter of buying people drinks at the Irving bar. Dead end number three.

By then I had come to an arrangement with Joiner to work only from Tuesdays to Fridays. The shop manager who succeeded John Ford had his own assistant in the shop and my work was all in the outback. I convinced Joiner that I could complete it adequately in four days and offered to accept a lower wage. He, for once magnanimous, said there would be no reduction, so for twelve months I was free on three days each week to write in my little back room in Bloomsbury. But it wasn't leading anywhere and what was it I really wished to write? I was hampered with revue because what I needed was a composer rather than another writer like Ken. I wrote a play and part of a novel but there was little to show for twelve months work. Ken took a job with ITV and our business relationship, such as it was, ended.

Another activity with a small, literary magazine named *Grub Street* came about through meeting the founding editor, Ron Hosie, at the Irving. He engaged me to be his dramatic critic but *Grub Street* was not, of course, on any theatre's free list so I had to buy my own tickets; nor was I paid for what I wrote because Hosie didn't have any money. Indeed, such was his lack of it that he couldn't pay his printer's bills which was when the Parrys stepped in and took over, thereafter financing it for the next three issues. I was made features editor (again unpaid) and appointed Martyn Goff, music critic, and another friend, Martin Worth, film critic (they received a small fee each). I also became distribution and sales manager, which meant that I filled a grip with copies and touted them round the London bookshops and station bookstalls. Reluctantly, many shops and stalls took copies on sale or return; only Lou Simmonds, in his unkempt Fleet Street shop, took a realistic, charitable view, saying he would buy six copies and paying me on the spot. Trying to sell *Grub Street* was a dispiriting experience, especially returning with the subsequent issue to find very few copies of its predecessor had found customers. There were a small number of subscribers – mostly friends and acquaintances and would-be con-tributors – but virtually no advertisers. Despite this we did publish a few worthwhile stories and poems. One story which John and I liked came from an unknown named Leon Townsend. Linda also read it but didn't take part in discussing it until she had heard that we thought we should accept it. Then she revealed it was her work. This was to lead to a novel which, a year or so later, I mentioned to Norman Askew, of Cape, who showed it to their reader and editor, Daniel George, who accepted it at once. Linda altered her pseudonym to Leo Townsend but wouldn't use her maiden name, Linda Carmen, which was how she signed her paintings. She enjoyed some success with *The Young Life* which took the then unfashionable line of siding with the victim rather than the perpetrator of a crime, an attitude that was not at all approved by some Hampstead intellectuals. It was translated into several languages and sold to Corgi as a paperback.

*Grub Street* gave me the opportunity of interviewing Kenneth Tynan who had shot to fame as drama critic of the *Evening Standard* soon after his predecessor had mocked his performance as the Player King in Alec Guinness's disastrous *Hamlet*. Beverley Baxter, the reviewer, said that Tynan waved his hands at friends in the audience. Very soon after, with the short run of *Hamlet* ended, Tynan replaced Baxter and became instantly loathed by one half of the theatre-going public and the acting fraternity and all but idolised by the other. He had a wide vocabulary and showed off on all occasions, was very witty and also knew his theatre, as he had previously shown in a slim volume named *He That Plays the King*. He campaigned for a national theatre and demanded very high standards from playwrights and actors. I was thrilled to meet him at his flat in the Holland Park area where I was served coffee by his first wife. Tynan was extremely friendly and forthcoming. His almost obsessive admiration of Laurence Olivier led him to rate Vivien Leigh at rather less than her true value. She was certainly not in the same class as Olivier but she was a talented actress on stage and screen and a beautiful woman. Tynan thought that she held Olivier back from the heights he should scale. (I privately thought that he had already reached the summit several times in *Oedipus*, *Henry V*, etc., but didn't say so.) The young drama critic – two years my junior – grew savage as he talked of Vivien Leigh. 'I wish she would drop dead!', he spat out with great venom. The stammer which sometimes afflicted him was not much in evidence that morning. He told me confidentially that he would shortly be leaving the *Standard* to succeed Ivor Brown on *The Observer* and I had to promise I would not reveal this information. (When my copy was sent to the printers in Bristol it drew a faintly disparaging query, 'Doesn't Ian Norrie know that Mr Tynan has been appointed to *The Observer*?')

*Grub Street* came to an abrupt end when the flat above the Parry's house in Chalk Farm caught fire and forced them to move into temporary accommodation. There was no alternative but for publication to cease, which, as with so many small literary magazines, was a mercy. Few people had read it; fewer missed it.

Early in 1954 the sight of Joiner's good eye was failing and he underwent operations at Moorfields. He appointed me to the board of William Jackson and I became, in effect, managing director, working a five-and-a-half-day week for twelve pounds. And I had to forego a holiday because it worried him to think of my being away. As compensation I was invited to accompany the Joiners on a weekend visit to friends of theirs at Stony Stratford in Buckinghamshire. There I was expected to stay for two nights listening to wild little Ethel yacking on about whatever came into her tiny mind, in addition to leading poor, blind Fred down to the local at regular intervals. It was the most excruciatingly boring weekend of my life. I cut it short by making a pretext for returning to London at Sunday midday.

For a year I ran Jackson's, reporting to Joiner on Monday evenings at his home in Walthamstow. Having admitted me into her house, Ethel mercifully kept to the kitchen. On the sitting room table stood a bottle of port and two glasses. This had to be emptied before I was permitted to leave. I cheated by pouring Fred larger measures than I took. One evening as Ethel showed me out I told her shyly that I had become engaged and would be marrying in the spring. Her puffed little face registered a twinge of malice as she emitted a strangled Eliza Doolittle-sound which might have said either, 'congratulations' or 'I'll get you.'

Get me she did, her triumph coinciding almost exactly with my nuptials. She had two things in for me. One, I had made soundings about the possibility of buying the business; two, I had endangered its viability by becoming honest with publishers about destinations for export orders. The first need not have worried her because the Joiners, with her brother Bert, owned all the voting shares but Ethel may have supposed that my intention was to float a new company and pinch Jacksons's customers as Fred himself had done in 1918 when he left Dawson's. In fact, in league with Alan Steele and others, our intentions were honourable. We simply proposed to make an offer for the business with capital supplied by Alan and Roger Hutchinson.

The Joiners got wind of what we were planning through their retired accountant, Leonard Ruskin Sextus Pope, who was, like Fred, a Freemason. David Jennings, his successor, warned me that I was accused of showing the company accounts to 'outsiders'. The Joiners were outraged, so was brother-in-law Bert Flemming.

More crucial was my naïve behaviour to our American customers. My final undoing came about through Jonathan Cape and the un-expurgated edition of T. E. Lawrence's *The Mint*. Cape had been waiting for years for the right moment to publish what was considered to be 'a hot property'. There had been eager interest in it, especially from America, and Jackson's had booked many orders. It was Jonathan himself, always antagonistic to booksellers, who wrote to demand that I give an undertaking, on behalf of Jackson's, that I would not export any copies of *The Mint* to the States. I told Joiner I felt obliged to agree. He said, 'all right, Loll', automatically assuming that I would not honour my word. I saw it differently.

The axe fell quickly. A board meeting was called for three days after my wedding. Bert Flemming, debenture holder and director, took the chair. It was at once proposed, seconded and passed that my salary should be halved. Only one vote against.

'You're earning too much for a young man,' said Bert whose previous advice to me had been: 'never trust anyone in business.' I wrote my resignation and again began consulting Situations Vacant in *The Bookseller*.

# 5

## Alfred Wilson, Marriage and Hampstead

It was not a propitious start to married life. Mavis and I had a brief honeymoon – two nights only – at the Lygon Arms, Broadway, because I was required to return for the directors' meeting at which I was effectively sacked. She had a job at Galeries Lafayette in Regent Street though soon she was to become a sub with the short story magazine *Argosy*, on which Joan Aiken worked. We had known each other for seven years and had spent much time together. She had trailed over to Seaford to see me in *Young Mrs Barrington;* she was briefly at the Mountview Theatre Club, appearing as a hamadryad in a pantomime of Wagnerian length in which I played a lemon seller, but she did not have acting aspirations. We came and went out of one another's lives, aware that we had much in common but neither of us *sure*, although one friend at the Club said baldly, 'I've never known two people who were so much the same.' When we at last made up our minds I was riding high at Jackson's and Pop, my father-in-law to be, was impressed when he learned I was earning a thousand a year. Within one month of our marriage I was out of work.

Alan Steele who felt he had inadvertently contributed to my fall from grace concerned himself in helping to find me a new perch. As a book printer he knew everyone in the trade. Publishers were his customers. He also knew the leading booksellers because he was hon. treasurer of the Society of Bookmen, a limited membership dining club which met monthly at Kettner's, in Soho, to discuss matters of moment in the trade. In its heyday it was an important sounding board for ideas; even in the fifties and sixties it was still a club to which most people in publishing, bookselling and printing especially, were proud to be elected. In 1955, one of the bookseller members was Hubert Wilson, who at Alan's prompting, became interested in exploring the possibilities of developing a wholesale export side to his business. He offered me a job at seven hundred pounds per annum to succeed a lady who was about to go into publishing. At the same time, André Deutsch offered me the position of trade manager at six hundred pounds. I would love to have gone to Deutsch. I admired his list but doubted if my talents were right for him. André said he wanted me 'mind, body and soul', so common sense dictated that I accept Wilson's offer. Within a month I was sounding out Deutsch to see if his job was still going. It wasn't.

The day I arrived at Alfred Wilson's headquarters in Ship Tavern Passage, a typical City of London alley between a main thoroughfare, Gracechurch Street, and a filter road, Lime Street, with other openings on to Leadenhall Market, I knew I'd made a mistake. The so-called office I was allocated, a partitioned cubicle in which four of us had desks, was just one of many centres of dissension in the firm, where morale was at a low ebb.

During my first morning I learned that supplies from various publishers had been stopped because accounts had not been paid. When I took Barbara Wilding, whose department I was taking over, out to coffee, I heard her forthright opinion of Hubert as managing director. He was all blather, she said. There was no coherent policy and the manageress of the shop at Ship Tavern Passage bought wildly. So, to a lesser extent, did the managers of the other two retail outlets in Victoria Street and Hampstead High Street. Then there were the crafts and stationery departments, at all branches, which were horrendously overstocked. All around there was waste and in-efficiency and business with the Crown Agents for the Colonies, a major account in her department, was unprofitable and riddled with bureaucracy. In addition, said Barbara, there was her assistant, dear old Peter, who dealt with ships' libraries and who was secretive about how these accounts were serviced. Peter had been with Wilson's since the early 1940s, had firewatched with Hubert, on the roof, during the blitz, was underpaid (like everyone else) and a law unto himself. Once when he had found the cost of living rising intolerably he had gone to see 'H. M. W' (Hubert Marten Wilson), berated him for grinding the faces of the poor and demanded an increase of five shillings (twenty five pence) per week. Hubert offered him ten shillings. Peter insisted on five shillings. I'm glad to say Peter Beckingham and I became good friends (it's wonderful what a drink after work can do) and I felt almost honoured when he explained to me how to look after the ships' libraries. I was the first to be instructed into the mystery. Prior to that, when Peter went on holiday, the accounts had not been serviced.

It was Hubert's practice, when staff feelings were particularly ruffled, to call heads of departments together at nearby tearooms and open a discussion on what should be done. He was a believer in democratic procedure, everyone was allowed to say what they thought. He prided himself on listening to complaints and suggestions. Fifteen, or more, of us would descend upon a café, causing minor chaos as tables were moved together and extra chairs fetched. Hubert took our orders for tea or coffee, then discussion began. No holds were barred. Hubert professed himself, 'very interested'. An hour or so later we returned to Ship Tavern Passage. No action resulted. When this became apparent someone went to Hubert's office and blew his/her top and the whole procedure was re-enacted.

It was not a happy ship. There was friction between most of the departments, all of whom accused the packers and the collectors, who serviced all of us, of giving priority to individual departments. I took over what was known as Town Department which was a misnomer because we dealt almost exclusively with the Crown Agents and shipping companies. At the other end of our floor was the Export Department dealing with individual customers all over the world. Between us was a passage occupied by the packing bench ruled over by the bloody-minded Bill Rice, assisted by the amenable Robert. Ernie Taylor, manager of export, Bill Rice and others supplemented their low wages by 'working nights on the papers' for far more than they earned at Wilson's. What if anything they actually did on the papers was obscure; they were part of the intense overmanning on which the unions insisted until the eighties. Probably they slept to remain fresh for the daily conflict at Wilson's.

Ernie Taylor regarded my appointment with deep suspicion and assured me the wholesale project was doomed to failure because we were 'on stop' with so many publishers. 'I can't get the books my customers order because we can't pay for them.' I had little time to test the water for the few accounts I gained, some as a result of Martyn Goff acting as a commission agent for us when he went to the States on holiday, because it was soon obvious that the company was on the verge of collapse. In any case Hubert Wilson, as a pillar of the Booksellers' Association, was unwilling to send books to the States on which the rights had been sold. I found it difficult to put my heart into the task for which I had been engaged but, by the autumn, I had found another role.

Alan Steele accepted Hubert's invitation to join the board of Alfred

Wilson. The company's auditor recommended the appointment of efficiency experts to get the business on an even keel. For several months two poker-faced men in black suits interviewed the staff and probed into the organisation causing resentment because of what it was rumoured they were being paid. I forget now their actual fees but they demanded and received daily settlement. I thought their presence a waste of money as it was obvious that the solution lay in pensioning off Hubert to his large house in the Surrey countryside, where he successfully grew mushrooms. He was the root cause of the mismanagement. A man of intellect, personal charm, ideas and humour, Hubert might have been a don or a politician but by the accident of birth he succeeded his father as head of a thriving business. It took him almost thirty years to ruin it.

Many, including Alan Steele, believed Hubert had spent too much time engaged on Booksellers' Association affairs and in writing his pseudonymous column for *The Bookseller*. In retrospect, I think he did much less harm when he was away from the business than when he was there. Apart from procrastinating about decisions there was his eccentricity. He would take bets with Ella Nye, manageress of the shop at Ship Tavern Passage, about how many copies of a new book she might sell instead of insisting on a smaller initial order. Ella (Susan to me, for some reason) was a lady much beloved by reps though not always by their sales managers, the wiser ones of whom cut some of the orders taken because the account was behind in payment. At the annual stocktaking, in which all staff participated over a weekend, the results of the over-buying put many of us into a state of shock. Even after the Receiver had been called in Ella Nye came to me one morning and said, 'did you know the snack bar next door is for sale? It would make a marvellous extension to the shop.' I looked at her in disbelief. 'Don't you understand, Susan, that we're broke? We can't afford to buy anything. Even your salary is at risk'. She shrugged her shoulders and said it was a pity; she'd had her eyes on that property for a long while. She was a charming, attractive lady with a great love of books but she lacked any real business sense. You could say she was made for Hubert.

But the Receiver had not been appointed in the autumn of 1955 when I, out of sheer frustration and believing I had nothing to lose, offered my services to save the company. The bookkeeper, like everyone else, was inadequately paid and had resigned. This was a wise move on his part because it was discovered after his departure that he had failed to apply the correct code to his personal PAYE and the company was liable for his uncollected tax. My experience at Jackson's had made me familiar with bookkeeping so I reckoned I could administer the financial running of Wilson's without difficulty. I was unduly optimistic but Hubert was impressed both by my zeal and by the fact that I didn't demand an increase in salary. Inevitably he set up a meeting – not at a tea-shop but at the Bishopsgate Institute – attended by all senior and middle-ranking staff. He told them I was now Assistant General Manager and that my colleagues could expect me to manage and resolve the problems that were arising on a daily basis. Little did any of us know that matters had already gone far beyond our control and that it was only months to go before crunch day.

Now that I had official ranking Alan urged Hubert to make me better known in the trade for the sake of giving Alfred Wilson's what we would now call an improved image. As a start Alan invited me as his guest to the next Society of Bookmen meeting where I was impressed to find myself dining with the cream of the trade under the chairmanship of Rupert Hart-Davis, a publisher I much admired. It was less agreeable to be greeted by George Kamm, of Pan Books, the hon. secretary of the Society, who took me aside and asked when the Wilson account would be settled. I assured him I would look into it and felt a pang of guilt, as if I personally owed him money. However encountering James MacGibbon, still an independent publisher at the time, was different. He enthused about a forthcoming book on hydrography; 'was thirty pounds too high a price?' I wasn't quite certain what hydrography was but James seemed such an easily companionable person that I dared to ask. We remained friends and, decades later, I found myself at the tiller of his small boat on the River Dart, while he went below to investigate a fire. I preferred knowing James on dry land.

Such was my induction into the inner world of the British Book trade. I longed to be part of it in my own right, not in the shadow of Fred Joiner or Hubert Wilson, and certainly not as the emissary of a company which wasn't paying its bills. At that time publishers were still licking their wounds following the collapse of the wholesaler, Simpkin Marshall, owned in its latter days by Robert Maxwell. Rumblings of financial insecurity at Alfred Wilson, coming so soon after, had them rattled although the hierarchy at Bedford Square, where the Publishers' Association had its offices, was unaware that Hubert was already probably technically guilty of embezzlement. Nearly one third of the Wilson business was in magazine subscriptions for which, traditionally, subscribers paid annually in advance. Wilson's accepted these payments but to ease the overall cash flow placed the orders with magazine wholesalers on a monthly credit basis. This worked all the while the wholesaler's accounts could be met but, given a Receivership, the subscribers became creditors rather than customers.

In the gloom and extreme cold of January 1956 this situation had not been revealed to me. I was only aware of an increasing shortage of cash. We lurched through the spring while I became ever more familiar with the inadequate infrastructure of the business. I began to feel I was not up to the task but Alan Steele and others seemed to have faith in me. Hubert took me on a trip to Oxford to inspect Blackwell's accounting system. There I met the Gaffer (Basil Blackwell) for the first time, an impressive and kindly man who combined qualities of scholarship and business acumen to become the century's outstanding bookman – he was a bookseller, new and antiquarian, publisher, printer and binder. I valued the introduction to him. Apart from this encounter my visit to Oxford served little purpose. It was doubtful that we could afford a new accounting system.

Next, at Alan's suggestion, I accompanied Hubert to Thurlestone, on a tip of the South Devon coast, for the annual Booksellers' Association Conference. It would be an opportunity for me to bolster confidence in Wilson's among the publishers attending. I encountered much goodwill and met many well-known figures in the trade including Edmond Segrave, editor of *The Bookseller*, who had just published an article by me. Norman Askew and Ronald Whiting were also first-timers, so was Gerry Davies, newly appointed secretary of the Booksellers' Association (BA). I enjoyed the weekend, apart from the business sessions which were dominated by trade 'politicians', mainly department store managers for whom being President was a necessary part of their career structures. They were able to devote time to the Association without, like Hubert, ruining their businesses in the process. In the years ahead they were tolerant of me when I blasted off about the establishment of the BA but that didn't happen at Thurlestone where my duty was to spread the word that Wilson's was on the mend.

It wasn't. Yet publishers were genuine in their desire to save it. We represented a market for the sale of £100,000 of books per year, which was a substantial sum at that time. The publishers had a vested interest in preserving us but Hubert didn't see it that way; they were the enemy. I went with him to Bedford Square to meetings in the fine first floor PA, council room. He wandered in, scruffily dressed, dandruff falling, holding his battered, small attache case bulging with loose pages of statistics that were meaningless to anyone but him. The publishers wanted official figures from our accountants. Hubert kept promising them but they didn't materialise. One meeting began with stern words from Kenneth Potter, then head of Longman, 'Mr Wilson, have you got the figures you promised us. If you haven't I shall advise this meeting there is no further point in trying to help you.'

Hubert cackled goonishly, peered over his half-moon specs, and opened the shabby case, in which vegetables from his garden shared space with papers. Yes, indeed, he had figures. He always had figures. Thin, spidery figures in tiny writing. I cringed inwardly as he waffled on about modernisation and the possibility of taking this action and that. No one believed him, so in midsummer of that year one publisher – Eyre & Spotiswoode, I think it was – called in the Receiver.

I felt a great relief. Alan had already resigned under some pressure from his Chairman at Butler & Tanner. He could not afford to be associated any more with Wilson's, although, behind the scenes, he continued to take an interest in what was happening. William Balleny, the city accountant appointed Receiver, was to be another important figure in my life. He was already auditor to the PA and the hon. treasurer of the National Book League, an austere, much trusted Ulsterman, an infantry officer who had survived the horrors of the Western Front. He had shining, deep-set eyes, a receding forehead and tended to hold his body forward, not so much as though advancing upon the enemy, more to get a clear view of the nature of the situation. He spoke succinctly, to the point, but he listened. He had the profound common sense which I associated, through my father, with a Scottish heritage; if he was an Ulsterman, as I believe, that could still have applied.

Hubert fought the receivership doggedly, and in so doing made an enemy of Balleny's chief lieutenant, Freddy Caine, the tallest, thinnest man I have ever known. Hubert could not, would not, understand that he was no longer in charge of his father's business; Freddy brought it home to him. Balleny soon contrived a sale of The Ship Tavern Passage shop to Tony Godwin, of Better Books, who gutted it and renamed it

The City Bookshop. The Victoria Street lease was sold, the Rainham Pottery was disposed of, so was the crafts department at Hampstead. Then the ticklish problem of subscriptions and the creditor status of many customers was solved by Hubert persuading his uncle, Charles Chitty, who owned flour mills in Kent, to purchase the export division from the Receiver. It was a clever move which led to the formation of Hubert Wilson Ltd (employing several ex-Alfred Wilson employees) operating from the Borough High Street, near Southwark Cathedral, and left only the Hampstead High Street shop in Balleny's charge.

During the elongated death throes of Alfred Wilson Mavis did her best to divert my preoccupation with Hubert's shortcomings. I retained a slender connection with Mountview, producing and writing for a Christmas revue in 1955, but she introduced a new factor that gave us and many of our friends huge delight for years to come.

1955 was a heatwave summer from May into the early autumn. I spent many Saturday afternoons at Lord's which made Mavis enquire why I didn't play cricket myself. She was not satisfied with the explanation that I just was not good enough so she bought for my birthday, a bat, ball and set of stumps. Unfortunately she got them at Hamley's which catered exclusively for children but I got the message. I arranged a match between a team made up from Mountview and another chosen by Tony Marriott, an actor friend whom I often met at Lord's. The enclosed pitch on Parliament Hill Fields, on the southern edge of Hampstead Heath, not far from where we lived was booked for the last Sunday in August. Tony invited Robert Shaw, then playing small parts at Stratford and the Old Vic, to play for him which was a move that all but won him the match. Bob Shaw, a forceful personality in all he did, used my undersized bat to make over sixty. After the game, which my team won by five runs, we returned to our first floor apartment in Heath Hurst Road for a bottle party. Mavis cooked huge amounts of cabbage, potatoes and other sustaining foods; we couldn't afford much else. The day was reckoned a success and led us to call a meeting to form a Sunday club. This was attended by all of four people including myself. My former colleague John Ford proposed we should name the club The Pretenders because of the acting connections. In 1956 we played several matches and enjoyed the first of a series of boisterous annual dinners. The team was a motley collection of mostly incompetent players led by me (I wore whites but had no boots) although there were two or three who might well have found places in regular club sides.

Mavis and I spent most of our first year of marriage in Hampstead living in expensive furnished accommodation. By the time Balleny and Freddy Caine entered our lives we had moved to a cheap, family-owned flat on Highbury Hill paying a controlled rent of twenty-five shillings (£1.25) per week. I had hated working in the City and had not liked Victoria Street where I had moved my office to get away from Hubert. Once the Receiver had been appointed I had my eyes on the Hampstead shop where I had already, before the collapse, organised a publicity evening, chaired by James MacGibbon, and addressed by novelists E. Arnot Robertson and Ernest Raymond, on the subject: 'What Sort of Bookshop Does Hampstead Want?' (This led to my first article for *The Bookseller*.) Although we had moved out of NW3 it was easily accessible from Highbury and I gained Freddy Caine's permission to manage the shop which Balleny needed to keep open for reasons not then clear to me.

By then Mavis had borne the severe disappointment of losing her editorial job on *Argosy*, a short story magazine designed 'for men to read on trains'. It was good middle-brow literature meticulously compiled and edited by a team of dedicated women. (Anyone subbing copy was expected to check everything – even down to the spelling of London.) When ownership changed hands cuts were inevitable and the last to join was the first to go. Mavis found a job with a much more down-market publication, *Mirabelle*, intended for teenage girls and leaning towards the pop music world. For a while she quite enjoyed the novelty of interviewing the likes of Lonnie Donegan and inventing gossip about emergent celebrities, but her heart was not in it.

Mavis, throughout her working life, was usually an active member of the Labour Party. At Transport House during the time of the Attlee government she had worked with Peggy Bowyer and Barbara Hosking who today are still valued friends of mine. In 1956 Mavis made contact with the East Islington Labour Party (EILP), which I also joined after the Suez debacle. Suez divided the nation but the Tories who were in government survived it with a change of prime minister. Mavis and I marched down Whitehall shouting, 'Eden Must Go'. He did because he was ill but the Tories went on for another eight years. The invasion coincided with an attempted revolution in Hungary which was suppressed by Soviet tanks and led to many long term supporters leaving the British Communist Party.

These grave issues made little impact on the general management committee (GMC) of the EILP of which I became a part within weeks of joining. Those in seemingly perpetual power on the GMC were also councillors of the Borough of Islington as a whole. They ruled it from the town hall in Upper Street which I had visited only once when Mavis was covering, for *Mirabelle*, a concert given by a flabby-faced Dickie Valentine who, as the fans swooned and raved, moaned good-naturedly into a mike.

My fellow members of the GMC went to the town hall not for pop music but to attend group meetings of the three Labour parties existing in the borough, helping to formulate policy which was later presented for rubber stamping at statutory monthly public council meetings. There was no opposition so no pretence of debate. This was their version of democracy in action. It was not until a few of those elected on the Labour ticket resigned the whip and sat as independents that the actual machinations of the ruling junta were heard openly. Our GMC met in dowdy premises in St Paul's Road, Highbury Corner and it was there that I became associated with the dismal process of party politics at local level. It was a dispiriting experience, exacerbated by editing a monthly newsletter named *Progress*. I had wanted to call it *Inside Left* because of our close proximity to the Arsenal football stadium but this was frowned upon. 'Left', I was informed by an Islington alderman, 'has a certain *connotation* . . . ' We quarrelled with that constituency party when it objected to an influx of new members who were suspected of being supporters of the Campaign for Nuclear Disarmament (CND). For Mavis defection was temporary because we and Amanda, our first born, moved, with Jessica imminent, to Finchley where on the next few general election days we had committee rooms in our house. There we both were active for some years until I grew disillusioned with the Wilson administration.

Early on in my engagement at Foyles, during another extremely hot summer, I had left Charing Cross Road at lunchtime on my half-day and made for Hampstead Heath, which I had read about long before. Memory suggests I travelled there by trolley bus from Tottenham Court Road but it may have been by tram or double decker. I can't be sure. Certainly the terminus was, as it still is, at South End Green in the shadow of the Royal Free Hospital, close to the corner site café which had been Westrope's Bookshop where George Orwell once lodged and worked. (Some twenty years on I would be partly responsible for the placing of a plaque to him on its frontage.)

I walked on to that glorious swathe of hillside which forms the Heath, saved for the enjoyment of all by publicly spirited folk of the nineteenth century who prevailed against the wishes of the Lord of the Manor. His intention had been to turn it into a vast housing estate and a few incursions on to it still stand. At the halfway point of East Heath Road, there are two large apartment blocks, six storeys high, built as late as 1903, encroaching upon the blessed land while beyond, in that dip known as The Vale of Health, there had long been a community with a pub and fairground. There Leigh Hunt had lived and I was to publish the first book about it by a formidable lady who also dwelt there. Bordering the Heath's southern ponds were cul-de-sacs, one of them named Parliament Hill, with rows of terraced and semi-detached houses all brimming with literary and artistic associations. From their nether ends, paths led on to the Hill itself where Boudicca, then still known as Boadicea, may or may not have been buried in a barrow. Magnificently situated, at the northern end of the ridge, along which Spaniards Road runs into Hampstead Lane, is Kenwood, an elegant Adam house, with attendant stables, kitchen, dairy and a fine collection of paintings.

In July 1949 Hampstead was virgin territory for me; by 1956 I had been a resident and wished to work there. I was deliberately not rushing into my next employment. Tony Godwin, who had taken Wilson's Hampstead manager to run the Ship Tavern Passage, recommended me to Paul Hamlyn and was cross when I turned down an offer from the young entrepreneur. Humphrey Tenby, Director of Book Tokens, invited me to join that organisation. I declined. The Hampstead shop was what I wanted and I was single-minded about it. Balleny allowed me my head, trusted me not to over order, increased my salary to one thousand pounds a year and seemed sympathetic to my attempts to raise capital to buy the shop. Martyn Goff and Alan Steele were both interested but what could not be revealed to us at that stage was that Balleny was seeking someone concerned in paying substantially for a tax loss.

You could say it was chance and the effect of a long, hot summer, which in 1949 had led me to Hampstead; you could also say it was destiny or just natural good taste. Where else would one wish to live and work in Greater London? Which is precisely the type of comment that riles detractors of Hampstead, who are not few in number. Chelsea residents are particularly suspicious of Hampstead, even those who actually know where it is, and superior about their own location. *They* 'have the river', they tell you. Hampsteadians reply, '*We* have the Heath.' The Chelsea dweller retorts that they have closer access to the West End and are then told, 'our hill site overlooks it.' And so on, a not too serious affectation on both sides. It is strange though that people are either Hampstead or Chelsea and that those who live in one seldom migrate to the other.

There are also lesser areas of distinction such as Dulwich, Blackheath, Highgate, although Highgate is a sort of honorary Hampstead, custodian of the Heath at its north eastern Gate where once there was a toll house, nowadays replaced by a good pub incorporating a theatre.

Hampstead, by the time I traded there had long been a healthily sited dormitory favoured by the affluent and by egalitarians of all social classes. It attracted actors and actresses by the score, writers – novelists, poets, biographers; historians – social historians, art historians, architectural historians, 'pastorall/comicall/tragicall' historians; compilers of recipe books, knitting books, flower-arranging manuals (though not car-repair manuals, they didn't do that sort of thing in NW3); authors of children's books, animal books, bird books. Not to mention, philosophers, psychoanalysts, dramatists, political commentators, education pundits, painters, sculptors, architects, composers, musicians, reformed (and unreformed) convicts, journalists . . . even compilers of crosswords. Plus business moguls, academics, media personalities, including immigrants from Hitler's Germany, liberal Jewish South Africans, refugees from McCarthyism in the States, escapees from African countries awaiting the right moment to return home to become despots – all these . . . and even a couple of literate England cricketers. Not all residents were celebrities. The pavements, in fact, were thronged by the ordinary man and woman (Hampstead version), accepting or maybe politely declining offers of literature from well-behaved, well-heeled protesters against almost everything. I came to love the neighbourhood and the people (most of them) who made it .

It surprised me, in 1956, that Hampstead had not had, at least within living memory, a better bookshop. Wilson's had its origins in the early nineteenth century and under various names there had been a bookshop on or close to its site ever since. Hubert bought it in 1936 when it occupied a high-windowed double-fronted Victorian addition to the early nineteenth-century house backing on to a spacious garden. Though its fabric had been seriously neglected, literally to the point of near collapse, it was still functioning as shop and flats twenty years later. It had never contributed anything but overheads to the city based company apart possibly from the small controlled rents paid by the domestic tenants. Its book turnover was around ten thousand pounds per year in a good year which left a gap yawning to be filled. Less than a quarter of a mile away at the upper end of Heath Street competition came in the fifties from a small, smart bookshop energetically owned and managed by one John Moore but it was off centre. Had he bought Wilson's he probably would have been the successful manager-proprietor that Hubert never was. Wilson had employed a series of poorly paid managers who had not been encouraged to use initiative. Turnover had fallen to just under eight thousand pounds a year; the field was wide open for anyone who took it on. The shop also sold greetings cards, stationery, pens and art materials, had a picture-framing service and was temporarily lumbered with the stock from another company-owned Hampstead shop which traded in pottery, ceramics and craftware. This had closed following suspected embezzlement by a former manageress. Hubert related a wry anecdote about being on the brink of obtaining a confession of guilt when her infant child had rushed between them demanding, 'Potty Mummy! Potty, Mummy!'

I removed the ceramics and crafts to be part of a grand closing down sale of the Victoria Street branch. Then I was permitted to concentrate on reviving book sales at Hampstead in time for an encouragingly busy Christmas during which I discovered that, in NW3, I could sell titles I cared about such as Rose Macaulay's just published *The Towers of Trebizond* to a public which I understood. A sale seemed to be within my grasp but, in the New Year, it eluded me. There was no progress with our tentative bid. John Moore came to look over the premises and assured me, in a patronising way, the shop would soon be his. I need have had no fears. Balleny was dealing with a much bigger fish. In the spring of 1957, having sold the tax loss of Alfred Wilson to 'Lloyd's Banks' Nominees', he informed me that the business was to continue indefinitely and invited me to remain manager. I would be working for 'Mr X' whose identity was not, and would not be, revealed. This turned out to be a recipe for success because while my new employer wished to remain anonymous he/she could not be seen to be interfering. All communication between us had to pass through Freddy Caine and Balleny's office. For seven years I was given every encouragement to expand, even into publishing; for seven years I was allowed to treat the business almost as though it were my own. When Mr X. insisted on selling the decrepit freehold property in which we operated, new premises were found further down the High Street. Meanwhile we had become the 'High Hill Bookshop' and were already well known in the trade.

When, also in 1957, Mavis became pregnant I did not have to worry about having paternity leave forced upon me. It had not yet been invented but could have been disastrous during the time I was engaged in building a business which provided us a good living and an even better pension. Mavis shared my belief that the place of the young mother is in the home but I understood her need to continue exercising her excellent mind. Joan Aiken, once again, helped by arranging for *Argosy* to send Mavis a weekly typescript for a reader's report on serialisation material. This helped our finances to the tune of five guineas a week and when she was too busy to cope I read it for her. As the children grew less demanding she embarked on obtaining the university degree which had eluded her wartime childhood. I admired enormously her self-discipline in studying for this at home on an extension course from Cambridge and was very proud of her when she achieved a French honours degree, having taken as a special subject, Proust's *A la recherche du temps perdu*. (This amused us both because, in the early sixties, when I was enthusing about Proust – in English – she had thought this rather affected of me.)

In 1957 I concentrated on making the bookshop more appealing to the local residents, ninety per cent of whom not only knew the difference between a book and a magazine, but were already book-buyers. I do not believe it was outstandingly clever of me to discover that they were eager and willing to enlarge their personal libraries and might find it convenient to do so locally. The publishers among them were delighted to join in, both as suppliers of their own, and purchasers of their competitor's books. Not least Jock Murray – a member of the sixth generation of that family in publishing – and a proud resident – who told Alan Steele, 'this bookshop must be saved. My children need it.' Jock (see *Mentors and Friends)* became an exemplary supporter and friend over many decades; so did many of his neighbouring publishers.

# 6

## The High Hill Bookshop – Press, Gallery & Colleagues

Once the business was trading profitably my thoughts turned to filling the demand for a new book about Hampstead. From 1814 onwards there had been one at irregular intervals, but by 1957 the only two in print were a hardback by a former Keats Grove librarian and a pamphlet by a man preoccupied about the incidence of Bagshot sand on the Heath. Mr X, through, Balleny and Freddy Caine, authorised me to publish a volume under the imprint High Hill Books. Mavis and I were to be the editors of an illustrated symposium with chapters by upwards of a dozen resident Hampstead authors. For me this was a quantum leap from *Cricket Quiz*. I was told that the authors could expect little remuneration, only an outright fee of ten guineas (£10.50). I tried this sum on Ernest Raymond, who had made his living as a novelist for thirty years. He said his literary agent would certainly advise him to refuse but that he would write me a piece on serving in 'Dad's Army' on the Heath during WWII, and I could have it with his blessing. He would not accept payment. It was to be seen as a return for my displaying his books in the shop window. Another novelist, E. Arnot Robertson, accepted the ten guineas without comment, so did the biographer Joanna Richardson, who was not to become an enemy for at least another two decades (she quarreled with almost everyone), while ancient Eleanor Farjeon, despite being committed to a multi-volume autobiography, sent for me, made it clear she would not be excluded and submitted a perfect item of nostalgia.

Thus encouraged, Mavis said I should next approach Donald Ogden Stewart, the American humorist and Oscar-winning script writer of *The Philadelphia Story*. He was an exile from McCarthyism and had had his passport withdrawn. He was living in Frognal, one of Hampstead's choicer addresses, in the house that had belonged to the first ever Labour prime minister, Ramsay MacDonald. There, when we first lived in NW3, Mavis had been a secretary to him, and to Ella Winter, his occasionally charming, more often rude and always eccentric wife. Don wrote us a gentle essay on the welcome and happiness accorded them locally.

We had made friends, through High Hill, of Joan O'Donovan, a teacher whose first volume of short stories was about to be published by Gollancz. She said she would adore to contribute. What she wrote had little to do with Hampstead, being mostly concerned with hilarious goings-on on the west coast of Ireland but I could hardly, in view of the fee offered, turn it down. (It was a different story forty years on when a whole book was in dispute.)

For an account of the famous Everyman Cinema in its days as a theatre I turned to actor Walter Hudd, a customer who had remained loyal throughout the difficult Wilson years. 'Dickie' Hudd was an accomplished actor who was rarely out of work. He played mainly secondary roles in the West End and at the Old Vic, taught at the New College of Speech and Drama and regularly visited Iceland to instruct and direct drama students at Reykjavik.

Oswell Blakeston, sometime avant garde writer and artist, as much a figure in Soho as in Hampstead, was recommended by Anthony Blond, a new, bright young publisher who would have done the book if I had agreed to his terms. He knowingly suggested 'pubs' as Oswell's subject. I offered architecture to Michael Floyd, another customer who became a close friend, institutions to John Parry and painters to Linda. My colleague Monica Carolan undertook the history, Mavis and Ken Hoare were allotted light-hearted subjects, I indulged myself with a piece on 'the air and the people'. Several resident photographers were enrolled and drawings were commissioned from an artist who did not live in Hampstead but was recommended by a friend of a friend.

Mavis and I read all the previous books about Hampstead and were lucky to find two cheap sets of Barratt's three volume *Annals*, first published in 1910. I paid less than a tenner for each set, one of which I kept at home, the other at High Hill. Within a few years Barratt was fetching at least £100 per set and is now regarded as a collector's item; it was an invaluable source of reference. Thanks to Mavis's experience at *Argosy*, I received instruction in efficient subbing and copy editing, despite which errors crept into the text. There would have been more if I had not had a working knowledge of most of the Hampstead pubs. Oswell wrote a delightful essay but in the first draft he included an inn which was four miles away in Finchley. He tended to merge features of one into descriptions of others in a splendid spirit of artistic and bibulous licence.

Any literate person is capable of editing a book; producing one to an acceptable standard is more difficult. Anthony Blond was much derided within the trade when on starting his list he admitted to lacking technical knowledge and sent typescripts to the printer with the instruction, 'Make it look like a Cape book.' In fact, in his situation, unable as yet to afford a production manager, this made sense. As I was not planning to publish more than one book and I didn't wish it to look amateurish I went to Alan Steele, the only printer I knew. He took me through the whole process carefully. Butler & Tanner bought the paper and also bound the book. Alan showed me typefaces, suggested layouts, enquired if I would like a coloured top, headbands, produced sample bindings, giving me alternative quotes, talked me out of galley proofs and generally taught me a lot. To arrive at a selling price, at that time publishers were customarily multiplying by around three-and-three quarters on unit cost, I was able to lower this to three on the assumption that most copies would be sold through our own retail outlet. Nevertheless, it was necessary to make provision for a trade discount, which was as well, because the book actually sold nearly as many through other outlets as over our own counter.

I became a self-appointed rep for my book. This may have provoked a chortle or two among the professional purveyors of publishers' outpourings, some of whom had suffered my inherent impatience on being invited to purchase their offerings. 'Now he'll get his comeuppance', would have been a justifiable response.

I forget why I began my trade subscription at the demure, prestigious premises of Heywood Hill's Bookshop in Curzon Street, Mayfair but there it was I went first to present *The Book of Hampstead*, about which I was quietly pleased and unapologetic, to the buyer (and partner) Handasyde Buchanan. He was a man of strongly expressed views and waspish characteristics, who made a good living out of the all pervading gentry who were his clients. (I don't think, at Heywood Hill, they had anything as commonplace as *customers*.)

Buchanan greeted me graciously, as neither acolyte nor equal, and handled the inspection copy presented to him as though it were some precious plant species of a suspiciously hardy nature. Its stout binding did not give under pressure and no tendrils erupted when it was squeezed. He opened and surveyed the contents page, flicked gently through the book, then pronounced, 'I should like to represent this in my stock. Please send one copy.'

Out into Curzon Street I went as one who had entered the kingdom of heaven. Braced by the experience, I walked to Harrods where David Leck, presiding over almost the last of the private subscription libraries, ordered twenty-five. I managed to restrain an urge to embrace him; his colleague Geoff van Danzig, manager of the Book Department, took twelve.

At that point I went home, by tube to Finchley, to apologise to Mavis because we were heading for Parnassus; I knew she would not wish to move there because it was unlikely to become a marginal seat for Labour to win.

I cannot recall meeting Handasyde Buchanan subsequently which is odd because the book trade was almost incestuously gregarious but there were two other notably individualistic London booksellers, encountered on that errand, whom I knew until their deaths. On my subscription round in Bloomsbury I was cordially received by Ivan Chambers, at Bryce's, Museum Street. His corner shop had decorously dressed windows with the backs of them built up to exclude a view of the interior. Nor was it possible to see much through the small door-way which was hung with magazines and notices. When I called, Ivan, dressed in a corduroy jacket and flannel trousers and wearing, of course, a tie, introduced me to Mrs Rothenstein, a middle-aged dragon who bought art books for stock. Ivan was a highly respected, literate, witty man, who had overcome, while still a boy, the misfortune of losing the use of one arm from polio. This did not deter him from becoming a cyclist and riding across Europe, nor from becoming a bookseller and holding piles of books single-handedly. He was a short, thin, bespectacled man with a prominent, pointed chin and jaw. He had shining, merry eyes and had cultivated a didactic form of speech, employing epigrams, Socratic argument and Wildean turns of phrase, all spoken dead pan; he was capable of verbally slaying any adversary. His bleak countenance whilst delivering his orations could be terrifying but it was usually followed by a disarming smile. He was a man who overcame grave physical disability to become a master of his chosen profession. He read books, knew books, sold books, sufficiently to make a living, and asked for no more. He became happily married late in life and had one child, a daughter. He was loved throughout the trade except, possibly, by some publishers' reps, who found him intimidating. His business was eventually bought by W. H. Smith and he became one of their pensioners.

On his retirement in 1971, the Society of Bookmen gave him a subscription lunch at the Criterion Restaurant, Piccadilly, at which the novelist Angus Wilson delivered one panegyric; I gave the other. Some of what I said I repeated at his memorial service (a secular occasion) in the parish church of Axminster, Devon, in February 1998. In the intervening years his numerous friends in the trade had kept in touch, many visiting him in the converted pub which became his home and where, eccentric man, he slept on a mattress in a cupboard under the eaves. Ivan wrote for the parish magazine, although he was not a believer, and enjoyed sending totally inappropriate Christmas cards, such as reproductions of *The Rape of the Daughters of Leucippus*, after Rubens.

Louis Simmonds, Ivan's friend, already mentioned here in relation to *Grub Street* traded in Fleet Street, next door to the listed Prince Henry's Room. His shop was a visual disgrace: dusty, dirty, untidy and with an ancient form of central heating below shelving which Lou had bought, probably on the black market, when he set up immediately after WWII. He operated on four or five narrow floors, incorporating shop, library supply and export, on the verge of both the Temple and Gray's Inn. Lawyers and their clerks were his clients, as were journalists. Lou was a softly spoken man and so diminutive, that at publishers' parties, one could seldom hear what he was saying – he was below the sound barrier. He was a midget yet he had driven an ambulance during the blitz. He was much loved by his customers and his family but refused to modernise the shop, or to hand it over to the next generation. He lived in the Hampstead Garden Suburb where, he confided to me, he refused to be an official bookseller to his synagogue because, 'they would expect a discount.' When he died, in the late nineties, Lou had two obituaries in *The Guardian*.

Once launched, *The Book of Hampstead* had satisfactory sales in bookshops throughout the country and even beyond our borders. It was favourably reviewed in *The Daily Telegraph* and *The Sunday Times*, received gratifyingly large space in *The Evening News* and *The Spectator*, John Mortimer in the latter ending a by no means enthusiastic notice with the eminently quotable words, 'Those who like Hampstead will like it very much.' The feature writer who tore it up for the *Evening*

*News* was allowed half a page in which to vent his spite. Bob Chris, bookseller of Cecil Court, phoned me to say, 'Ian, you've got a wonderful review in *The Evening News*'. It certainly did us little, if any, harm. And I was interviewed by the BBC on radio and television. The first thousand copies I had cautiously had bound were gone in a week; the other thousand went by the end of the summer by which time I had ordered a reprint.

The most effective non-review came from the soon to be defunct *News Chronicle*. David Holloway, its last literary editor, devoted most of his book page in the week of publication to reproducing an illustration, a gem of a photograph showing a heavily pregnant woman exhibiting her paintings at the open air exhibition held annually at the top of Heath Street.

To the launch party at The King of Bohemia, the pub next door to us, came the MP, Henry Brooke and his wife, town clerk Brian Wilson, and other local dignitaries. Publication did much to establish High Hill as a community bookshop, a term possibly suggestive of greater significance than might be warranted. If a bookshop doesn't serve its community then presumably it is geared towards custom from mail order or export, or it may have some specialist nature, drawing customers from afar to inspect its stock of books about birds, militaria or whatever. So is not W. H. Smith a community bookseller? Its branches frequently have more customers than many neighbouring shops. Although they may be buying stationery, cards, DVDs, magazines, newspapers and lottery tickets more than books, in my day publishers usually regarded W. H. Smith as a major outlet and in my brief experience of managing an imprint I welcomed its custom. Like Boots, the chemist, it is one of the lasting names on fascia boards across the country; it has endured for nearly two hundred years. Yet I doubt if any W. H. Smith manager considers himself a community bookseller. Certainly the downcast creature in charge of the branch on Rosslyn Hill, Hampstead, two hundred yards down the main thoroughfare from High Hill, kept the lowest of profiles, even to the extent of switching off lights to save electricity when there were no customers. He was highly embarrassed when I took a sample of *The Book of Hampstead* to show him, offering copies on a sale or return basis. The poor man exhibited agonies of indecision before handing it back to me, saying he didn't believe there would be any demand. Soon after, Smith's closed that branch about the same time as they closed another, in

Banstead High Street where Martyn Goff traded. Prior to this it had
been company policy never to close an outlet.

I got a different reaction at W. H. Smith, Golders Green, two miles
away over the heath to the north. There an ebullient manager said he
would certainly 'give it a go' and went on to engage me in chat about
his 'sidelines', as he put it. 'I do a bit in property,' he confided, 'I expect
you're the same.' He had the makings of a community bookseller if, by
that, I mean, someone who takes part in local activities, knows his
customers and expresses views on issues that are engaging them. To
justify applying the term to myself, I worked voluntarily for the Hampstead Theatre Club, wrote for the *Ham & High*, took an active part in
the High Street Improvement Scheme, (an environmental project),
supported charities such as the Burgh House Trust (preserving an
eighteenth century building with historical connections, to make it a
centre of cultural activity) and published books about what we liked to
call 'the village'. All of which, admittedly, were in my commercial
interests, as was becoming supplier to various schools in the neighbourhood and frequenting many a local pub and restaurant.

What I did was not always approved by my peers or my superiors.
Some did not think it proper for me to wear a CND badge (traders
should not be political, apart from backing the Tories), some took
exception to views I expressed as a book reviewer (I provoked one
minor uproar when I referred to Christianity as having been 'a colossal
flop'), others were outraged when I displayed a large notice in the shop
window exhorting one and all to save the Greenhill lavatory (a small
men's urinal in a roadside wall greatly appreciated by passing lorry
drivers), still more by my insistence that children should be well-
behaved on our premises and unburdened by ice creams and sticky
cakes. Hampstead mums were mostly devotees of free expression. But
by my behaviour, for better or for worse, I became a part of the
community, contributing this, taking that. I think that is all I mean.

The launch at The King of Bohemia coincided roughly with the
start of the Hampstead Theatre Club by Jimmie Roose-Evans who had
briefly, as an out of work actor, had a temporary job with us. Like many
theatrical people while they are 'resting', Jimmy came to a decision to
give up the stage, making comments such as, 'It's just not on. I must
have a regular income.' In his case he felt a calling to enter book
publishing. Would I make introductions? He came to a party at the
shop where he met Alan Steele who was sympathetic, arranging for

him to meet Roland Gant, a senior editor at Michael Joseph. But, all the time, he was planning the Hampstead Theatre Club, eliciting help from everyone he knew. Stage folk are like that, they can't help it. Soon he dropped all pretence of wishing to work with books and brought us into his confidence. He would take the Moreland Hall, adjoining the Everyman Cinema where he would mount his first productions while a theatre was being purpose-built for him as part of the new Swiss Cottage library complex. The Council, he said, would definitely back him. I was cajoled into becoming a member of his Appeals Committee which was to be chaired by Dame Barbara Brooke, wife of the MP. We met at their house in Redington Road. Once, had I been a terrorist, I could have assassinated our member when I was permitted unchecked access and went in error into the room where he was dining. Brooke hated having the police guarding his property which, for home secretaries, was the norm but, in his case, the officer so deployed appeared to be encouraged not to harass innocent looking visitors. It must have been difficult for the cop. Suppose I had been an assassin?

Walter Hudd, along with the novelist Kay Dick also joined the committee. Eleanor Farjeon hosted a reception in her garden to launch the venture. When Jimmy took something to heart he became relentless. Utterly relentless, charming everyone into accepting that there was no more profound purpose in life than establishing The Hampstead Theatre Club.

The first play, a period drama in verse by a Welsh dramatist, starring Sian Phillips, was followed by a Harold Pinter double bill and a new piece by an unknown dramatist friend of Jimmy's. And the Box office, until more convenient arrangements were made, was at the High Hill Bookshop during our opening hours. Jimmy graciously conceded that we need not remain open later than our usual time, or on a Thursday afternoon, which was then still early closing day. In return for this concession I must permit him to employ Leslie Martin, my new junior assistant, as an extra. Leslie would not be paid for his services and his presence might be required occasionally during shop hours. Jimmy was incredibly adept at barn-storming his way through other people's lives without giving offence. Leslie had no acting aspirations whatsoever and was highly amused. I was less enthusiastic about taking on the box office.

The season at the Moreland Hall was brief and not markedly

successful but it got the venture underway and the Pinter plays attracted some attention. The Roose-Evans charm had been applied successfully to Hampstead Council and the Theatre Club was established beside the new library, opening on one freezing winter's night with a production of Chekhov's *The Seagull*. This was not a hit but its successor, a revival of Coward's *Private Lives* was. I complained that we had not all striven to support Jimmy's enterprise for the sake of putting on yet again one of the century's most enduring comedies. Jimmy was more realistic, pursuing a policy adopted by publishers who I admired, in recognising that you can only afford the icing on the cake if you are earning your bread and butter. *Private Lives* transferred to the West End. The Hampstead Theatre was established and still exists in newer, larger premises.

Leslie Martin joined us at a time when finding suitable staff for book-shops was at its most difficult. Unemployment was low, shop assistants were badly paid compared with office workers and most were required to work on Saturdays. I tired of advertising in *The Bookseller* because it resulted in applications from the same people I had been turning down at William Jackson's a decade before. I turned to the *Evening Standard* which led to a phone call from a cheerful sounding young man who I invited for an interview. Next day he rang again to say he did not wish to waste my time because he would be due for call-up within a year. (He was in the very last age group to do National Service.) Thinking that he probably wouldn't last a year I said he should keep the appointment.

   A lightly built, medium-height, boyish figure appeared. He had a ready smile, bright eyes, quick movements, an engaging manner. He read books but had little formal education and was working for a wholesale potato merchant at Edgware, who told me, 'He's a serious chap. Works well. In his lunch break he reads the Bible; he's absolutely honest.' I confirmed the offer of a job and Leslie started the following week, instantly making himself agreeable to colleagues and customers. He was quick and willing to learn. After a few weeks, he didn't come in one morning. When I phoned his digs his landlady said he had a tummy upset and was in bed. She didn't think it was serious. He didn't appear the next day either. I phoned again and received the same message, although the landlady added that she thought it was mostly depression. I decided to visit him and was shown to his room where he lay on his bed looking withdrawn and gloomy. I told him I didn't think there was much wrong with him, that he would probably feel a lot better if he got up, had something to eat and then came to work. He promised he would.

For much of the next eleven years he worked for us, before and after army service, becoming a capable bookseller and close friend, not only of mine and others at the shop, but of Mavis and our daughters. When his digs proved unsatisfactory we rented him a spare room. But bookselling was not for Leslie who, like Shaw's Joan of Arc, was in love with religion. He moved around various nonconformist Christian sects finally reaching, in late middle age, the Church of England. He would like to have been a minister but was rejected probably because of his lack of formal education (he had played truant for much of his schooldays). The church authorities may have made a mistake because Leslie was an essentially good person who more than most people I have known genuinely tried to follow Christian precepts. He helped others out of a simple belief that he should do so. He acquired hundreds of friends and acquaintances in many parts of the world. He travelled extensively on all the continents apart from Africa. He enjoyed discovering new places but he was also searching for himself. He came reluctantly to admit, in his mid-twenties, that he was homosexual. There had been girls he wished to marry and there were others who attracted him. He told Mavis and I about it one evening over supper because he couldn't bear to live a lie. He never found a permanent partner but remained a believing Christian until his death from lymphatic cancer soon after his sixty-fifth birthday. Almost the last time I saw him in hospital, before he lost his sight and hearing, he had a wry look on his honest countenance. He said little but I had the distinct impression that he was following a thought that his God had not played quite fairly by him.

Leslie exemplified my belief that bookselling is best learned on the job. There is no mystique about it. It does not, like medicine, electrical engineering or making furniture, require specific training but it does demand intelligence, application, a degree of literacy and numeracy and a capacity for tolerance in the face of the public. Leslie had all these qualifications which were lacking in so many of those who, egged on by their misguided relatives, suppose that being in a bookshop is of a therapeutic benefit to social misfits and high-powered neurotics. It borders on the bizarre that I, who possessed few of the attributes mentioned above, should have made it successfully through four decades of bookselling. What, in the early years in Hampstead, drove me close to breakdown was having too few colleagues who were competent. Fortunately there were some, in addition to Leslie. Monica Carolan, one who was, had been employed by Alfred Wilson's before my arrival. She liked to give the impression that she was a New Zealander. In fact, she had been born in Portsmouth naval barracks and was taken to the southern hemisphere as a babe. She was a librarian whose NZ qualifications were not recognised in Britain, a devout RC, a spinster with an astonishing knowledge of children's literature and a passion for travel. She had a wide general knowledge and an agreeable manner with those customers whom she liked. She was short, inclined to fat, with swept-back red hair, wore spectacles and liked to wield a lengthy cigarette holder. She had an unnerving habit of eschewing formal greetings and launching straight into an account of whatever subject, usually genealogical, was uppermost in her mind. She was so absorbed in her family history that she tended to assume that everyone else was equally fascinated by it. She suffered from sore feet, excess weight and had a rasping voice tinged with a New Zeal accent. For long, she gave us valuable service, buying for and managing the children's department, rigorously banning Enid Blyton and exercising other prejudices with which Hampstead seemed in sympathy.

When Ralph Abercrombie (see below) was going through his booziest phases Monica was helpful, tolerant and loyal. Herself, following a few glasses of wine, could raise an eyebrow as when, at a directors' lunch, she referred to Henry the *Ninth*. At our parties she bored anyone willing to listen with interminable stories about relatives. I learned to switch her off which is why she was justified in sometimes accusing me of not having absorbed some vital item of information she had passed on.

Monica was elected to the High Hill board, which was my mistake. I had failed to understand the difference between a good and loyal employee and one who could effectively administrate. Monica, although she could be bossy, was unable to assume authority. Eventually we lost the ability to communicate; a distance grew between us and between her and other colleagues. Increasingly she lived in a world of her own, retiring from the shop floor, partly because of the condition of her feet, to look after the accounts in an upstairs office. She was efficient at this and, when invoices were found to be missing, she would storm around accusing members of staff of throwing them away. A few old established customers asked permission to visit her. One sold her cosmetics, another conducted a wine tasting for her benefit.

While she remained on the shop floor Monica had a circle of cronies who warmed to her idiosyncrasies but if any dared to enquire the names or status of those about whom she was discoursing, she would contemptuously enlighten them. One was supposed to know everything Monica knew; those who fell short were ignorant. She had a curious way, when asked, from normal courtesy, 'How are you?', of responding not with the conventional, 'Well, thank you', but of striking a pose and saying, in a drawl, 'I don't really know', followed by some spiel about an ancestor, or even the Earl of Leicester – who turned out to have been a family cat.

At home she accumulated a large library. She read not only children's books but detective novels, history and travel. She turned in a learned, well-researched account of the history of Hampstead for our first publication but it made dull reading. It had no flow. When I attempted to enliven it by throwing in some phrases of my own, she did not complain. She also assisted the late Emily Anderson in the compilation of *Beethoven's Letters*, and in the revision of Mozart's. She would often mystify customers by oblique references, such as, 'another of old B's letters has turned up' or, 'Alec is worried about the authenticity of dear M's letter from Prague.' Alec was the musicologist, A. Hyatt King, who was a resident and a chum of Miss Anderson.

Monica was part of the success of High Hill in those early years and I believe she was treated well when she took early retirement, with pension, but I wish we had enjoyed a more friendly relationship. Instead we became a little like those married couples who stay together 'because of the children.'

One of several customers who became colleague and friend was Liz Cooper. She was the wife of Jack, a *Times* journalist who were in those days as badly paid as booksellers, which was why he had been lax in settling his account with Alfred Wilson's. He was a most genial person, in no way a con man; just hard-up. A messenger boy at Printing House Square before being called-up, he had done well in the war, been commissioned into the RAF Regiment and served in India and Burma. When he was de-mobbed it was an embarrassment for *The Times* to find Jack a job appropriate to his new status. Former Flight Lieutenant Cooper was not going to ease its problem by conveniently looking for an alternative employer; he was ambitious to be in the news room, for which he had no qualifications, and by perseverance he achieved it. Jack was above medium height, had dark, penetrative, gleaming eyes, sported a Van Dyck beard and stood out in a crowd. He was a life-enhancer. He paid off his account in instalments, continued to buy books and was invited, along with Liz, to our first Christmas party at the shop. There, I told him about The Pretenders' Cricket Club and he instantly honed in and took charge of it. A strong link was formed at personal and business levels; it lasted forty years.

Liz was then a part time assistant at a local Montessori school and a familiar figure in what I learned to call 'the village'. Between them Liz and Jack, who were pillars of Town Ward sector of the Hampstead Labour party, seemed to know half the inhabitants of NW3. Jack wrote also for a journal named *Eastern World* and broadcast regularly on the BBC World Service. They had met during the war when both were serving with the RAF, from which Liz was soon after demobbed because she had become pregnant. They had four children and lived in a terraced house on the hillside, close to the High Street, with her mother who was the widow of the poet and academic Lascelles Abercrombie. The Abercrombies had also had four children to the same pattern as the Coopers, three boys and a girl, and it was the youngest of these sons who became a highly valued colleague of mine. Our acquaintance was heralded one autumn day when Liz, dressed in the anorak-of-many-colours from which she was inseparable for years, breezed into the shop crying, 'Darling! You need some Christmas help, don't you?' I agreed. 'Well, darling, you can help me. My brother Ralph. He's been a bookseller. He was with David Archer and with Tony Godwin, at Better Books, and he's an absolute sweetie. You'll love him. He needs a job. He's been ill. Wants to get back on his feet.'

She did not mention that Ralph had a history of mental depression, had been in and out of Napsbury, Shenley, and other psychiatric hospitals, had a drink problem and also a stammer. She just flew straight at her target. I needed an extra assistant for Christmas and one who knew about books. She could provide one.

So I came to interview the lean-faced, partly-bald caricature of a thirties intellectual, with spectacles slipping down his nose, who was Liz's brother. He was medium height, extremely thin, almost ghoul-like, but I was immediately struck by his intellect and knowledge. He confirmed he had worked for Tony Godwin and I thought, if Tony, who was notoriously impatient, tolerated this wreck, there must be something about him. Ralph told me about the disaster of working for David Archer when the shop, with its attendant coffee bar, had been closed because of a typhoid outbreak. An element of black humour was evident at once. Beneath the harrowed face, indicative of much suffering, there was a discernible human being. But was this the person I wanted for the hectic Christmas rush? I took a chance.

I didn't regret it, even years later, when I had gone through the agonies of knowing and employing Ralph during periods of alcoholism and mental distress, involving not only him but also Julien, his wife, Liz, Mavis, Monica, Leslie, other staff and even some customers. While Ralph could contain the wild spasms of his nervous system and limit his drinking, he was, at both a social and literary level, the best colleague I ever had. He knew even more than Martyn Goff. He was steeped in English literature, with an encyclopedic appreciation of poetry, and possessed a gift for sopping up amorphous knowledge He knew about sport, science, nature, medicine, economics, philosophy, religion, ancient history, modern history, geography and politics. He had served in the army pay corps for four years after he was due for demob because the discipline appealed to him. How he ever came to be called-up is a mystery but indicates that his neuroses must once have been under control, as does the fact that, in his best years, he had contributed to the *Times Literary Supplement*, even being entrusted to write the central feature. (This, of course, was when *TLS* articles were all printed unsigned.)

Ralph accumulated gossip about writers, actors, booksellers, publishers; he recalled what people had actually said; his brain was like a computer. We turned to him frequently with our shop-floor queries. At home, Mavis and I, discussing something and failing to find an answer, would say, 'Ring Ralph. He'll know.' He was a formidable asset to the business who, on our behalf, interested himself especially in egg-head paperbacks which were coming on to the market, mostly from the States. Thanks to Ralph we ordered stock of Ann Arbor and Grove Press paperbacks. He had a nose for what would be right for Hampstead, playing an invaluable role in helping our expansion and in satisfying the demands of that part of the resident population which was on his wavelength. I think it was entirely due to him that Colin MacInnes, writing in *Encounter*, singled out High Hill as the only London bookshop, apart from Dillon's, which should be taken seriously. Never mind the exaggeration, it was a marvellous statement to have printed about one's business in a prestigious journal.

There was another side to Ralph, apart from alcohol and neuroses. He was not an organised person. His vast intellect did not embrace business efficiency, or even the practical common sense of a corner-shop proprietor. When, during our many sessions together in the shop, or next door, at The King of Bohemia, I would refer to the danger of over buying or under buying that which did not appeal to us personally, he would reply, 'Oh, sure, sure.' He was with me, he agreed, but I knew that really he considered that was my problem, not his. In fact, it did not present a major difficulty because paperback publishers were already falling over sideways to look after us. We were the only outlet of our type in the whole of north London and they were only too willing to take back what we could not sell. They needed our presence to sell all those titles thought to be 'Hampstead'.

There was a long period when having Ralph at my side worked wonderfully. We had a true rapport. Mavis and I, Julien and he, wined and dined each other as couples do. There was also the companionship which Ralph and I enjoyed with our neighbourly high street butchers, Frank and Geoff, who we met on Saturdays in The King after we had closed our shops. Frank and Geoff talked of war experiences in Burma and Bulgaria, also about books they had read. Frank liked 'a rattling good story' so I passed proofs to him from time to time and occasionally gave him books for his grandchildren. He was a generous man who sold me the Saturday evening steak and the Sunday joint at very favourable prices. One Hampstead friend who heard of these meetings, a white collar trades union leader who sent a chauffeur driven car to collect books he bought for foreign delegations to Britain, made patronising remarks about drinking with the hoi polloi. He was unable to appreciate that the four of us relished our weekly meeting. Long after they had ceased I met Frank, by now retired, with George Gates, my jobbing builder, for drinks in Barnet or Mill Hill.

I seriously disturbed my relationship with Ralph by making him manager of The Belsize Bookshop, as we renamed the branch of Collet's which we bought in 1961. I thought it would be good for his self-esteem because this brilliant man was too much under my shadow at High Hill. It soon became apparent that the appointment was a disaster. Ralph who could sell books, recommend books, talk about books and, without arrogance, share his vast knowledge of them with customers and colleagues, could not manage a small bookshop. He was incapable of mastering the mundane but necessary routine of writing up the daily sales book, doing the banking, controlling the staff, writing letters or any of the other run of the mill duties that are a part of management. I tried to make amends. I told him we were missing his expertise at High Hill (which was true) and that we needed him back. He was far too intelligent not to realise I was soft-soaping but he returned, knowing he was not up to the responsibilities that had been forced upon him. He felt the failure deeply and resumed drinking heavily.

Following another long stay at Napsbury he returned to High Hill for one final period. By then he had left Julien to live in an apartment above a restaurant in Heath Street, before finding sanctuary with Liz and Jack in the former family home. He died in 1967, aged about fifty. There were rumours of poems he had written but suppressed. Probably they would not have met his exacting standards.

Not quite equally into poetry was Bunty Sharp, a customer, like Liz, who later became a colleague. Bunty was the diminutive wife of a distinguished ear, nose and throat surgeon with whom she lived in constant domestic conflict in the Garden Suburb. She trolled into the shop one morning in 1957, leading a small rodent-like dog, to enquire if the book she had ordered was in. I regretted that it was not. 'Oh, fuck,' she exclaimed, which was surprising language to hear at that time from a middle-class lady. Although educated at private schools, and coming from a semi-county background, Bunty could not refrain from using 'language', although once she had come to work for me, she didn't swear in front of customers – unless they were her friends. She had two young sons, regularly overspent her allowance and because she adored buying books supplemented the housekeeping by delivering orders for Forster's, the High Street grocers. She was a kind soul. When she learned that our washing machine had crashed and that Mavis, with two small daughters, was desperate for essential linen, she drove over to Finchley, collected the soiled goods and returned them clean. That was the sort of service I could expect from some customers.

It was sometimes difficult to maintain friendship with Bunty, who seemed to have a deep felt need to quarrel, at some stage of her acquaintance, with almost everyone. I was unaware that I had offended her until I received a note and cheque settling and closing her account on the grounds that I 'couldn't take a joke.' I reached for the phone, got through instantly, and said, 'What the fucking hell is this all about?' We soon sorted it out. (I bet I would never have learned that kind of solution to a problem on a training course.)

It was when Bunty fell out with Forster's that I invited her to join us. I knew her wide knowledge of literature would be an asset and foresaw that her old Ford car could become the High Hill 'van'.

She tended to act the lady in front of customers and was always extremely obliging to them until they had departed when she sometimes went through an elaborate simulated retching routine. She was enormous fun to work alongside, made a pretence ogre figure out of me always referring to 'Sir' ('Sir said . . . Sir demanded,' and so forth) and making false accusations about the deprivations suffered by all who worked for me. 'No one ever tells you anything,' she would lament. 'When you come here, you fall in at the deep end and learn to float. Then Sir goes off for his Saturday booze-up and comes back reeking of Guinness and feet . . . ' She was hilarious; she was also hardworking and efficient.

After buying Bunty's small Ford Escort I paid for her to drive us and Peg Bowyer to Italy on holiday. The following year she went to live in the Thames valley and found work in a Reading bookshop, one that was rather more sedately managed than High Hill. She found the contrast painful and soon found a backer for a shop of her own in Henley-on-Thames, the finance coming from Dan Brunner, of the banking family. There, as Bunty McNeil (she reverted to her maiden name), she had a ball, building a good business, making weekly trips to London trade counters with which she had established chi-iking relationships while working for me. She regarded every special order as a priority to be obtained, so far as was possible, direct from the publisher by making a personal visit. A member of the Oxford Branch of the Booksellers' Association, she invited me as her guest to the annual dinner held at a pub somewhere in the countryside. The actor Robert Morley was the guest of honour. He was good value as speaker, having made a second name for himself as a professional rude man, possibly originating from his famous WWII role in *The Man Who Came to Dinner*. He began his speech in fine style, literally throwing his ample weight around, as he insulted first, booksellers in general, then W. H. Smith in particular.

'I live near Henley,' He proclaimed. 'There is nowhere to buy a book in Henley.'

'Nonsense,' I cried.

He glowered at me, all bushy eyebrows, delighted to have audience reaction.

'My hostess, Bunty McNeil,' I said, 'has an excellent bookshop in Henley.'

'Where's your bookshop, darling?' asked Morley.

She told him and, thereafter, he and someone who Bunty supposed to be either a frightened acolyte or an indulgent friend, frequently visited the Bell Bookshop, with the actor bullying the lady into buying many books and making purchases himself.

Then Bunty, being Bunty, relations with Dan Brunner deteriorated. He began to complain about her management. She showed me audited figures indicating she was doing very well but the rift was already too deep. She swept out, in true Bunty style, abandoning her living accommodation, along with the shop, and moved down river to Marlow where she acquired a new backer and another shop, also with a flat above. While operating here she moved her actual living quarters to a house in nearby Medmenham so that, when the next contretemps occurred, she lost only her job. Subsequently, she surfaced elsewhere in the Thames valley, with a mail order company, and finally at Hammick's, in Windsor.

Wherever Bunty went sparks flew but books were sold. This unpredictable and memorable lady moved to Shropshire, worked briefly again at a bookshop and died, probably still smoking, in hospital. She was unfair, outrageous, lovable and hugely stimulating.

## 7

## Mainly Authors and Painters

Christina Foyle once wrote to me, 'I cannot understand how you could employ friends.' I forget my reply but the short answer should have been, 'because it nearly always worked.' The longer answer would have pointed out that she regarded ninety nine per cent of those working for her as incipient criminals and potential enemies. It never occurred to her that by treating staff fairly and paying them what she could afford instead of as little as she could get away with, she might have encouraged loyalty, honesty, respect, affection even. She was tyrannical, suspicious, selfish and a spoilt child. Despite all of which I came to enjoy her company.

Friends I employed identified with High Hill's 'corporate image' as did many of those I hadn't previously known. Undoubtedly, I could be classed as difficult but has there ever been a boss who didn't fit that category? Certainly, *they* displayed faults but that is true of all employees. There were occasional scenes between 'us', or between 'them', or between 'them' and 'us', and when one of those who had been, 'them' became 'us', that could lead to some of those who were still 'them' feeling resentment, but major schisms were avoided.

Other 'mums' who worked for me included two wives of Labour MPs whom I met through Jack and Liz: Ann Swingler and Kerrie Baird. Ann's husband Stephen was one of the far left *Tribune* group. They made an interesting couple in that he, who was the son of an archdeacon of the Anglican church, had cultivated a regional, lower class accent while she, who was of humbler origin, had learned to speak posh. They let part of their large Victorian house in Belsize Park Gardens to Jack and Kerrie Baird. Jack, a dentist by profession, had the doubtful distinction of being the first Labour MP not to be re-adopted by his constituency party. He drank heavily and became incapable of carrying out his political duties, let alone his dentistry. Kerrie stood by him while he died of cirrhosis of the liver. Both ladies were comely blondes whom I picture as always smiling; neither was especially bookish. Kerrie who stayed with us for much longer than Ann did not retire until she was eighty. She was totally reliable and invariably available in a crisis if phoned to undertake an extra lunch-time or afternoon. She worked in the children's department where she was extremely fierce with any brat who misbehaved or dared to touch a book while eating. She had a delightful lowland Scots accent with very precise diction. In 2008, one hundred and two years old, she died at Wadebridge, Cornwall, where for many years I lunched with her annually at a tavern near to her sheltered accommodation.

Another Labour Party connection was Bridget, granddaughter of Ramsey MacDonald and wife of Dick Clements, editor of *Tribune*, who had known Mavis at Transport House. She was part-time in the early years but worked a full week once her sons were old enough. Bridget, who had had a varied career before marrying Dick, having studied for the stage and trained as a nurse, befriended many customers, amongst them the actor, Alastair Sim, and Elias Canetti, our only Nobel-Prize-winning author. Both liked to be served by her.

Elias Canetti lived mostly in Hampstead but part of the year in Zurich where his wife was resident. He was dumpy, bespectacled, untidy and had a flabby face with a slightly unkempt moustache. He wore baggy clothes and usually carried a brief case, making him a caricature of a typical Jewish bagman. He was unfailingly polite with-out a touch of arrogance but I read that he held a low opinion of the English because his books were not more widely known here. On the only occasion I attended the Frankfurt Book fair I was astonished by the publicity accorded to him by his Austrian publishers. Tom Maschler, who published his *Auto-da-Fé* here, pronounced him the greatest genius living in Hampstead. I reviewed this densely written book without ever being on its wavelength.

Once, knowing that Canetti was the dedicatee of Iris Murdoch's second novel, *Flight from the Enchanter*, and baffled by a later book of hers, I asked him what he thought of her current style of writing. He said she was trying to emulate George Eliot, without committing him-self to saying whether he thought she was succeeding. He made the comment with deep conviction and I let it go. What I did not know until both were dead was that Iris Murdoch visited him in Hampstead because they were lovers.

Another highly valued female member of staff was Barbara Scott, also a friend of the Coopers and of Joan O'Donovan. She came to us when she felt the need for release from the classroom. Highly efficient and widely read, she also had self-sacrificial tendencies which made her eager to take on everyone else's tasks as well as her own. Jack Cooper once said of her, 'She'd like to be a door mat so that you could tread on her' – unkind but partly true. Regrettably the holidays we could give her did not match up to those that Don (a Pretender and a teacher) enjoyed, so for the sake of domestic tranquillity, Barbara returned to school, becoming a remedial head in the troubled Borough of Brent where she gallantly visited grotty housing estates to demand of parents why their offspring were playing truant. She was not mugged.

A task which unexpectedly fell to Barbara was to legalise me while I took up driving again. Very soon the shop was being directed on auto pilot. For three months, when I wasn't paying for driving lessons from an authorised instructor, I was bullying friends into sitting beside me while I had further practice. Even Liz Cooper fell into this category once I had convinced her that under no circumstances would she be required to drive the vehicle herself. She had qualified while serving in the Women's Auxiliary Air Force (WAAF) but was terrified of getting behind a wheel again; in any case, she maintained, she had only ever been completely in control while she was reversing. Barbara's mastery of the car was of a higher order. She was careful, competent and law-abiding with a born teacher's ability to instil confidence. Shortly before I was due to take my test I was out with her one day when I became convinced I'd fail. Calmly but with a sharp edge to her voice, she said, 'Just think of all those little Indian women you see behind a wheel . . .' I passed first time and instantly took the passenger seat beside Mavis to assist her. In due course I returned to bookselling, for which I never passed any kind of examination or test.

What sort of books did Hampstead buy? Contrary to received opinion customers' tastes were not especially highbrow. Middle to upper-middlebrow, yes, low brow, on the whole, no. They were aware of the latest trends and responsive in those early years to almost any title praised in the *Sunday Times* and the *Observer* on the same day; also to 'Books of the Year' mentioned in those same 'heavies'. The two comparable, serious dailies (*The Times* and *Telegraph*) could also have an appreciable effect on sales. Between them they reflected a standard of literary taste and acted as a rough guide to the best that was being published. The weeklies, the *TLS*, *New Statesman* and *Spectator*, were also regarded as reliable barometers, plus two revered provincial news sheets, the *Manchester Guardian* and the *Yorkshire Post*. A practising bookseller did not need to read all of them but was made aware of some of what they had reviewed by his customers and colleagues; in addition the weekly *Bookseller* ran a column of comment about what the critics had written. Another advantage of trading half-a-century ago was that there were tens of thousands fewer new titles published.

We were general booksellers, strong in fiction, verse, history, travel, biography, the classics, with sections on art, cookery, gardening, works of reference, children's literature; weak on science, economics, technology, religion (apparently the worst Bible territory in Britain, according to one rep at Oxford University Press), sport, sociology and DIY. Only to a small extent did this reflect my preferences. Customers did not use the shop to be instructed by me in what they should read but to obtain the books they thought they wanted. Our success depended largely in anticipating what those would be and in reacting swiftly to demand.

There were other factors which assisted the integration of the book-shop into the community. Throwing occasional parties for resident authors was not then a regular feature of national bookselling activity. At that time writers were not expected to tour the country to publicise their books. Promotional activity in actual shops was at nothing like the level it was to reach by the nineties. The only nationwide chains were W. H. Smith, where 'other goods' predominated and, to a lesser extent along the same lines, Wymans. Numerous provincial towns and suburbs of great cities catered only minimally for book-buyers; there was a huge, untapped market which on one level Paul Hamlyn, entrepreneurial publisher of mass market literature, was just beginning to exploit; Hammick's, Dillon's and Waterstone's were far into the future although the needs of students in the new universities were beginning to be catered for more effectively by Blackwell's and Bowes and Bowes (recently purchased by W. H. Smith).

In North London, the catchment area for anyone attempting to run a larger than single unit bookshop was nearly fifty square miles. For years High Hill had little competition and drew custom from all over the north and north west post codes. One way in which we became known was the publicity from our parties. The first, held in September 1958 on a night when few of those invited were repelled by an almost monsoon-type downpour, was for the novelist E. Arnot Robertson who lived in Heath Street. Miss Robertson, wife of Sir Henry Turner, a senior colonial civil servant, had achieved popularity pre-war with several novels, particularly *Ordinary Families*. She was a tall, untidily dressed lady who often forgot to apply make-up and who could be seen trailing around Hampstead with a shopping trolley, seldom recognising friends or acquaintances. Her relationship with Sir Henry was so close that when, in 1961, he drowned while making a repair to their small boat on the Thames, she never recovered, taking her own life a few months later. In happier days she occasionally graced the panel of the Hampstead Subscription Library brains trust. An earnest member of the audience once asked what was being done to stop vital stocks of custard powder being sent out of the country. She replied that it must surely be seen as a benefit if, having rashly manufactured this commodity, we were enabled by some twist of commerce to export it.

It is likely that the party for *Justice of the Heart* conferred more benefit on High Hill than on the author and the publisher. In my experience launches do not boost sales except during the actual celebration. Launches though supportive of the image of books play little part in the establishment of a best-seller which is often due to word of mouth or an apposite comment by a media celebrity.

Arnot Robertson, who never became a regular customer or a friend, wrote an enigmatic and seemingly irrelevant inscription in the copy of her book which she – or to be accurate, her publisher – gave me:

> Lord, let monogamy
> Not make a hog of me,
> The way that polygamy
> Once made a pig of me.

Authors are often in despair about what to write in copies of their books; probably it is better to just sign – 'with good wishes'.

Parties, which may or may not help sales, are held because they are fun and supposedly provide evidence to authors, agents and others concerned that the publisher is doing something to attempt to promote the book. In my first decade in Hampstead High Street we held one or two every year but dropped them when too many publishers and authors became eager to launch books on our premises. I always resisted holding signings during opening hours when the normal trade of the business would have been disrupted and the novelty of parties wore off as an ever increasing public came to us with its welcome patronage. Then we began holding evening book sales in schools. Following the Arnot Robertson party there were others for Robert Shaw, Kathleen Farrell and Ernest Raymond, for Penguin Books' silver jubilee, our own publications and the official opening of our new premises in 1961.

Robert Shaw, I thought, was more gifted as a novelist than as an actor. He lived in Belsize Park and I knew him slightly through that first Pretenders' cricket match. *The Hiding Place* was his first novel concerning two captured British airmen who were kept imprisoned by an insane German long after WWII had ended. It was published by Chatto & Windus with whom I had excellent relations stemming from Ian Parsons, its charismatic managing director, to Ron Cortie, its sales rep who was a regular lunching companion and also a Pretender. The Chatto list ranged from Richard Hoggart's *The Uses of Literacy* – a big seller in Hampstead – to *Little Black Sambo*, my favourite book when a small child. And it did not make me racist. I knew it by heart and until political correctness drove it out of print it sold thousands of copies every year. Max Reinhardt gallantly reprinted it in the nineties. After I had retired, I bought copies at Harrods for my grandchildren but the gift was frowned upon by my daughters.

The bookshop's status in the community was possibly affected when I became the first regular book reviewer for the *Ham & High*, then a broadsheet edited, since the thirties, by John Parkhurst who accepted me as a contributor after I had suggested myself to the owner, Arthur Goss. Goss, a Quaker, supporter of CND and a descendant of the founder, was personable in a quiet way and notably stingy. When I asked what fee he would pay he had said it would be good publicity for High Hill and that I would get books free for review which I could later sell over my counter, so there would not be one. I went along with this in order to have a foot in the door but felt like a black leg, which was what H. D. Ziman, literary editor of the *Daily Telegraph* and resident of Belsize Park, made it clear that he thought I was. When I accepted Goss's conditions I insisted I must feel free to give honest opinions of books I reviewed, most of which would be by Hampstead authors who must not expect to be praised just because they were probably regular readers. This was agreed by both Goss and Parkhurst.

My first column, Best Books of the Year, 1959, did not raise problems; the next, a novel by a friend and CND colleague of Goss's, did when the latter read my adverse comments. Goss said publication would create a difficult situation for him and put it to me that, although not a masterpiece, it wasn't such a bad book. Would I reconsider my verdict? I refused. He then suggested that I select an alternative book. I said there wasn't time before press day to read and review a new one and it would be a shame if the column failed to appear on only its second week. We reached a compromise. I chose an anthology by another Hampstead citizen (a publisher!) and wrote a hack piece based on a quick perusal of the contents page. I thought it was a poor way of embarking on my regular feature but Goss didn't interfere again. John Parkhurst never influenced my selection and was an agreeable editor whom I came to know better over lunchtime drinks in the King of Bohemia. When I hadn't had time to read anything appropriate, he accepted satirical pieces about invented titles.

Despite the almost ceaseless output of books by residents there were weeks when I chose one without local affiliations. This suited the developing image of the paper under John's successor, Gerry Isaaman, who visualised Hampstead and environs as a microcosm of not just London but the UK publishers' publicity managers, ever desperate to find new outlets for review copies, sent in far more volumes that I could cope with so Arthur Goss, had a point. Some went into our stock, but I never returned unsold items to the publishers for credit.

One of the first semi-local authors, who lived in St John's Wood, was Olivia Manning whose Balkan Trilogy began to appear in 1960. I became an instant fan and praised them in the *Ham & High* and in *Books and Bookman*, a monthly magazine for which I was also writing. Olivia soon introduced herself, coming to the shop accompanied by Dr Jerry Slattery whose minor mission in life was to befriend female novelists. I felt very flattered that she had taken this trouble, not understanding at that time that she was paranoid about being reviewed. When the second volume, *The Spoilt City*, was published two years later I again wrote two notices (using different copy). By then she had reviewed my first novel generously in *The Sunday Times*, for which I was grateful. I saw her often at this time. On one occasion I mentioned I was doing a fiction review for *London Magazine*. Instantly she said, 'They haven't done *The Spoilt City*.' 'You should worry,' I told her.

'You've had notices in all the nationals.' She gave me a very old fashioned look; no stone must be left unturned. 'My copy is already filed, Olivia, and I have done you twice already.' Next day I got a phone call from Charles Osborne, assistant editor of *L. M.*, saying he had heard from Olivia. 'I've just got room for a short par. Could you add it to the end of your piece?'

Olivia was married to BBC producer, Reggie Smith, a well-known Communist sympathiser, cricket fanatic and third programme pundit. She incorporated him into all her novels. Indeed, many people supposed that the only reason she remained married to him was because he was essential copy. Whenever I mct them together she nagged him constantly and complained about almost everything he said. Reggie was impervious. He was indeed a maddening man, heavily built, short-sighted, stooping, untidily dressed in food and booze-stained garments but extremely affable to almost everyone and a nicer human being than Olivia. According to Ralph Abercrombie, he got away with his pronounced pro-Soviet views because the BBC liked to know where it stood with its employees. Reggie never deviated, nor did he deal with political programmes. He was responsible for classical literature and maintained high standards. There was no question of dumbing down in his day. Occasionally I met him at Lord's where he stood close to the Tavern holding a regularly replenished pint beer glass. Once, during one of those rare compulsively watchable moments of a test match, he tried to divert my attention by giving me advice on how to write for radio. I kept saying, 'Not now, Reggie . . . yes, thanks very much, Reggie, very nice of you but *Reggie!* Look! The game could go either way! It might be a tie!' He was reproachful; he was trying to help me. At such moments I identified with Olivia.

On a summer evening Olivia drove me to the Theatre Royal, Stratford East where Reggie wanted to see a play by James Hanley which he thought might be dramatised for radio. Hanley was as doomed to relative failure in the theatre as with his novels. It was a powerful play, held my attention throughout but it did not have that quality which sends word-of-mouth recommendation around the country. After, in the bar, Reggie lectured us all about it, with frequent references to miscasting, as he sank Guinness after Guinness while Olivia nagged him to drink up because she wanted to go. At nearly midnight they dropped me on the Finchley Road to catch the last bus which I nearly missed because Reggie was once again urging me to write for radio. I thought how unsuited as a couple they were but he was good copy indeed; I used him myself in a book thirty years later.

Olivia was a highly gifted novelist, a true page turner. She deserved greater success than she achieved in her lifetime. This made her envious of other writers, especially women novelists, who became bestsellers or icons – Iris Murdoch, Muriel Spark, Edna O'Brien, Ivy Compton-Burnett. Their names were bandied around by Olivia and others, such as Kay Dick, whose works did not get snapped up for paperback editions. They liked to mention their intimacy with these favoured ladies at the same time as conveying the view that they were overrated; within the circle there was often mutual denigration and bitchiness. When Kay Dick's relationship with Kathleen Farrell had ended and she found it difficult to get credit, Olivia commented, 'I said to her, "why don't you get a job as an international telephone operator?" Well, her French is very good . . . '

Kay had been a character for so long that it had ceased to be an act. She was tall, slim, played with a monocle and owned a totally untrained, constantly yapping dachshund. She had been employed in publishing and journalism before she lived with Kathleen, who had private means and a house in, first Heath Street, later in Flask Walk. Kathleen wrote slight but perceptive novels in a minor key and also children's books. She was witty and friendly and once charmed me into allowing her publisher to host a party in the shop for her latest book. Kay also wrote novels which didn't sell widely and a learned book about the *commedia dell'arte*. After the break-up with Kathleen she took rooms in a nearby friend's house, where she attempted suicide, then moved into a first floor flat in the High Street. Here she recovered her poise and made some sort of living mostly from reviewing. She had a cruel tongue but didn't use it to lash me, at any rate not in my hearing. She liked to confide, regarding me as a kindred spirit because she had been in the trade. When she left Hampstead, curiously following Kathleen to Brighton, news of quarrelsome scenes were fed back to those who remained. (In fact, Kathleen was generous in her will to her former partner but Kay dismissed the bequest as mean.) I heard about these from Elizabeth Divine, not a writer herself, but married to one. David was *The Sunday Times* defence correspondent and had written at least one memorable book: *Boy on a Dolphin*. He was also the first historian of the Dunkirk evacuation. They lived in Keats Grove in a delightful, large detached cottage next to St John's Church, Downshire Hill. It was Elizabeth's business to know everyone, especially the residents of Hampstead and persons in the book trade.

When we were first married we had a furnished flat in Heath Hurst Road, which runs from Keats Grove to South End Green. Harold Elvin whom I had known at Coram Street, adored Elizabeth; he adored all beautiful women and Elizabeth was one who remained strikingly handsome even into old age. He told her erroneously that we had become neighbours of hers which must have driven her frantic because no one dared to move house in Keats Grove without first informing Elizabeth. Once tracked down, we were invited to coffee and grilled. She was a scout in London for Macmillan New York, publishers, and was deep into book trade gossip. She took to Mavis and I must also have passed muster because she and David, who was usually too engrossed in creative thought to pay much attention to visitors apart from liberally pouring them drinks, accepted a return engagement. We also invited John and Linda Parry. They had known Elizabeth whilst on wartime ARP duties, when there had been little love lost between them. The reunion did not improve relations.

We saw little more of Elizabeth until I was installed as her neighbourhood bookseller. She regularly frequented the High Street, walking upright and elegant, taking in all that was happening, never missing a trick. After many years she joined my staff as an invigorating though not especially efficient part-timer.

Another Manning, Rosemary, no relation to Olivia, was also a novelist and highly acclaimed children's writer. The latter occupation was something of a bus woman's holiday because she was Principal of St Christopher's, Belsize Park, a school highly esteemed by local parents. She closed it almost without warning to concentrate on her writing which came to include a frank memoir revealing her lesbian nature. She wrote an excellent account of Belsize Park for my *Heathside Book* which was republished in the revised *Book of Hampstead*. Rosemary, on the page and in person, brimmed with stimulatingly perceptive comments and energy, having a disconcerting vigour which suggested she might have come straight from a hockey pitch.

One Hampstead author who lived much of his life beside the Heath, in an apartment block which a century later would not have got planning permission, was Ernest Raymond who despite writing two major best-sellers between the wars did not enjoy the financial rewards which many novelists of a later generation would have earned.

Ernest (born 1888) was a clergyman who served at Gallipoli in WWI and renounced his cloth a year after his first novel, *Tell, England*, was published in 1923. The book was turned down twelve times before Newman Flower, head of Cassell's, had the perception to realise its potential. It became a bestseller, was advertised on the London tube and presaged, or complemented, much that was offered to the public in verse, play-form, fiction and memoirs about the excruciating ordeal endured by the often mud-bound warriors of the Great War.

In the thirties, Ernest wrote another acclaimed novel, *We, the Accused*, which was partly inspired by a passionate conviction that capital punishment should be abolished. There was no paperback deal because there were no paperbacks, as we know them. (Penguins started in 1935.) The TV rights were not sold for half a century, nor was there a large-screen film; *Tell, England* a silent movie had sunk without trace. Ernest settled to become a widely read novelist but his public increasingly resorted to borrowing his books from circulating and public libraries, so he never became a rich man. He earned enough to live sufficiently from his writing and had no other occupation. He did little reviewing and did not become a media personality because, until after WWII, the media was restricted to the BBC and it could not accommodate more than a handful of writers, of whom J. B. Priestley, much admired by Ernest, was one.

Although born into an era long before the orange juice generation, Ernest was well over six-feet tall, and had a natural air of authority. As he strode about he looked benignly down upon the world around him. Had he remained in the church perhaps he would have become a bishop. He often looked intently at those he addressed, almost as though studying a portrait painting. I never saw him produce a notebook to record what he saw but I can vividly recall him, on several occasions, registering 'copy' as he sat in a pub or a restaurant. He was a born story teller who noticed how people behaved and what they looked like. Towards the end of his life (he died in 1974), thanks to *A Georgian Love Story*, he needed to register for VAT because the American rights were sold. In jocular mood, he greeted me in the High Street one day, raising his walking stick to hail me with the glad news. When I said I had read the book in one sitting he regarded me quizzically because he knew I found his prose style too flowery for my taste. He could have been wondering if I was trying to be kind to an old man and of thinking, why does he find it necessary to say anything?

That is not unlikely because he once remarked, 'If you don't like the look of someone's new baby you don't tell them so. Why do readers find it obligatory to volunteer an opinion of one's new book?' But I wasn't pretending. This particular book had grabbed me and I was pleased because he was someone I liked.

There were occasions when I felt sorry for Ernest. When he was already into his seventies, I heard him remark, 'what shall I write about next?' He knew he must produce another novel. It was needed for income. Which was why, understandably, he was keen on public lending right at a time when I still felt ambivalent about it.

Ernest's bluff was called one year at the local council elections for Hampstead. He, Pamela Frankau, his wife's cousin, and a friend, had for decades stood every three years in the Liberal interest. They had never expected to be elected but suddenly, one year, the Tories in Town Ward were in such disarray that the voters rejected them.

'Serve you right,' I told Ernest.

'Now I'll have to write a novel about it,' he replied.

Ernest was a scrupulously disciplined writer, keeping his annual deadline with Cassell's, occasionally slipping in an extra book for them, or for another publisher. He was a member of the Garrick, where he went after his morning session of writing, to lunch and, in the afternoon, to write further, while Diana, also his secretary, typed his morning's work and then attended to her own, because she too was a novelist. I always mounted a display of their new books. Ernest's seldom sold more than a few copies but he was too polite and under-standing ever to enquire 'How is it going?' Diana's often did better. It wasn't an issue. They introduced me to Diana's cousin Pamela Frankau who came to live with her partner, the theatrical, director, Margaret Webster (daughter of actress Dame May Whitty) in Christchurch Hill, NW3. Pam was enormous fun, bubbling over with enthusiasm about this and that. Once, at a party in John and Marganita Howard's charming house, Capo di Monte, she confided in a moment of intense feminism, that she thought Diana should not be Ernest's secretary. 'She has her own work, ' she said, 'it's awful of him.' I said it might be a matter of economics. Pamela exploded and maintained that Diana ought not to be the victim. Next morning, Pam burst into the shop and asked me to forget all she had said about Ernest. 'He's a dear . . . ' and so on. Of course I have not forgotten but nor did I blame Ernest or Diana. It was a matter for them alone. I now have the wry recollection that Diana, long after Pamela's death from cancer, was commissioned to write her biography for Virago. She worked on it for three years, giving up fiction temporarily to concentrate on it (thus losing out on her PLR payments), only to have it rejected. Hilary Rubinstein, her agent, got compensation for her from Virago but the incident hurt.

Ernest died, virtually in harness, published by Cassell to the end. His sales declined but his standing with the company was such that everything he submitted was published by them even after the Flowers and the Gentrys, who had long owned the list, sold to Collier-Macmillan, New York. His many books included three volumes of autobiography, the first of which we celebrated with a party at High Hill. Unfolding like a detective story it told the story of his search for identity as the illegitimate son of a high-ranking army officer. He unravelled his past in a masterly non-fictional story. In later volumes he described his return to the church, to which Diana by then belonged. A close friend to them both was the eccentric clergyman, Joseph McCulloch who wore a device on one index finger which saved it from being discoloured by nicotine. Another priest in evidence at Raymond parties at The Pryors was the young Richard Harries, then curate of Hampstead parish church, later Bishop of Oxford, a friendly, learned man, one of the many clergy I have found disarming. Graham Dowell, also to be found at The Pryors with Sue, his militant feminist wife, actually conducted my elder daughter's first marriage service. She wed Simon Clark, son of two practising believers. Graham was strongly CND, accepted the permissive society, did not object to Simon and Amanda living together before marriage and was, in every respect, modern and left wing. (He was also wealthy from an inheritance, a fact he disclosed to few.)

Because I didn't wish to risk giving Ernest an unfavourable notice I funked reviewing his novels for the *Ham & High*. I once handed over my weekly book column to Mavis who wrote with honest enthusiasm about his *Mr Olim*, a novel based on a teacher at St Paul's. (It also had a good notice from Compton Mackenzie, another former pupil, in a Sunday heavy.) I liked many of Diana's novels and was able, long after Ernest's death, to contribute to the success of one of them. In 1982, she was part of our house party on the Aegean island of Aegina. This was thanks to a television film of *We, the Accused*, in which Ian Holm gave a memorable performance as the murderer acting, in close-up, with every fibre of himself down to the eyelashes. Ernest had never taken Diana to Greece but he had urged her to go, after his death, when finances allowed. She joined us for two to three weeks and, wrote a story which grew out of the experience. It was enthusiastically reviewed, particularly by Martyn Goff in the *Daily Telegraph*, and the American rights were sold.

On Aegina Diana was the best of companions, as she was years later in Provence, during our retirement, and didn't require looking after every minute of the day. When outings and entertainment were not provided she contented herself with reading and writing. (Her stepson, Patrick, whose career was with the RAF also wrote novels.)

Asking journalists to write for the anthologies which followed *The Book of Hampstead* required a degree of cheek. National newspapermen have always been paid more highly than the majority of authors. Mostly they were gracious about accepting the low fee offered perhaps because, in several instances, no one had previously published them in book form. This was not so with Ivor Brown who had written a distinguished life of Shakespeare, much criticism and books about etymology. As recorded earlier I had, as a youthful reporter, admired him from afar. He was a gruff old thing, inclined to potter about Hampstead wearing plimsolls but beneath the shabby raincoat, which placed him in a certain era of journalism, and the crusty exterior, was a kindly, scholarly person who brought dignity and learning to a profession increasingly bereft of it. He contributed to three of my books.

The High Hill symposia kept my taste for publishing alive. My then anonymous employers made no objection to *The Book of the City* for which I had the benefit of Edwin Smith as photographer. He was the husband of Olive Cook, who had reviewed *The Book of Hampstead* ecstatically in *The Sunday Times*. Edwin was a master of black-and-white photography, a short, bearded man of equable temperament who was a joy to work with and complained not a jot when my printer failed to reproduce his halftones as well as they deserved. He also was paid a derisory fee which he fixed himself.

For this volume I went outside Hampstead for many of the essayists. David Holloway, soon to succeed Ziman as literary editor of the *Daily Telegraph*, the novelist Colin MacInnes, Martyn Goff, who wrote about the fur trade in which his family had long been concerned, Desmond Heap, the City Solicitor who conducted me personally around the

Mansion House, Derek Hudson, an editor at OUP, then in offices at Amen Court, near St Paul's, Canon John Collins, of actual St Paul's, a priest heavily committed to CND and other left-wing causes, Ian Peebles, former captain of Middlesex, urbane cricket correspondent and wine merchant, and Naomi Lewis, an exquisite writer whom I had met at parties and who pleased me by the observation, 'it's always Sunday afternoon at the *Observer*', the newspaper for which she most frequently wrote.

Ian Peebles, recommended to me by publisher and Pretender Ernest Hecht, invited me to meet him at his offices near Finsbury Circus where, for elevenses, we drank white wines and talked cricket. As Joan O'Donovan had for *The Book of Hampstead*, he wrote a piece which had almost nothing to do with the City.

Naomi Lewis's subject was Liverpool Street station about which she rhapsodised in words that made me look afresh at what I had always the thought the filthiest and most depressing of all the London rail termini. I had much difficulty in getting final copy from her. I nagged, implored, by phone and letter, when 'the last possible date' was missed once again. I offered to go to her flat in Red Lion Square to collect it. No, she must not be disturbed. Or she might not be in. Finally, she rang to say it was ready but . . . 'How am I to get it to you?'

'The post?' I dared to suggest.

Out of the question. 'I could bring it to you on my bike,' She announced. It was worth waiting for. Both her book, and Olivia Manning's evocation of Highgate Cemetery for *The Heathside Book*, were a privilege to publish. Lena Jeger on Trafalgar Square and Mary Murry on the City as wasteland, were on a par. Women, pre-eminent as novelists, make admirable essayists too. In fact in literary terms there was no necessity for Virago. With the pen, woman has been as mighty as man for at least two centuries. In the nineteenth century no two writers in English excelled George Eliot and Jane Austen. And, late in the twentieth century, it was another woman novelist, Lettice Cooper, customer and resident of West Hampstead, who asked on a television programme, 'Why don't we have a 'Macho Press' for forgotten male novelists?' I passed on the idea to Hilary Rubinstein who failed to sell it to various publishers.

The final anthology, *The Book of Westminster*, was a commercial flop. It had many reviews, all favourable, more stunning photographs from Edwin Smith, plus Ronald Saxby's masterly drawings – but it did not sell. Mr 'Batsford' Johns may have put his finger on it when he commented, 'It's not popular enough. You ought to do books like ours.' I think its failure had to do more with people not identifying with Westminster, whereas they might have connected with Soho, Victoria or Mayfair. Sales did not even reach one thousand.

Despite *The Book of Westminster* being a financial failure it enabled me to rank Joan Aiken among 'my' authors; she contributed an amusing piece about working in an advertising agency. By then Joan had become a friend of all the family. My daughters acted in her play *Winterthing* presented by the Puffin Club at the Young Vic one Sunday afternoon, and adored Joan's so-called children's books, those marvellous fantasies starting with *The Wolves of Willoughby Chase*, in which there is no hint of writing down. (Olivia Manning reviewed them in *The Spectator* as adult novels.)

Joan was a prolific writer, a fact perhaps reflected in the near-slum-like ambience of her home in a converted pub at Petworth. Separated, later widowed, she was the main support of her two children but she could have written under any circumstances; she was naturally creative. There were not only the fantasies (which became successful Puffin publications), but also Jane Austen reconstructions, thrillers for Gollancz, radio plays and much else. When Liz and John had become adult she moved to an enchanting former hermitage, also in Petworth, overlooking a valley of quintessentially lovely countryside. When we stayed there the bedroom in which Mavis and I slept doubled as a warehouse for multiple copies of Joan's books. She lamented that the publisher sent them unasked and she couldn't bring herself to dispose of them. She was by then married to Julius Goldstein, New Yorker, teacher of art history, himself an accomplished watercolourist. For decades they alternated between his apartment in a downtown Man-hattan block without a lift and her tranquil West Sussex home. Julius suffered from chronic stomach ulcers but this did not disturb his genial nature. When later I stayed with them alone, after Joan had made her habitual early retirement to bed, we would watch old movies together in the spacious drawing room strewn with books overflowing from shelves on to tables and chairs. In the adjoining kitchen-diner, with an annexe hung with Julius' paintings, diminutive Joan cooked slightly abstractedly at a huge Aga, serving us at an enormous, rectangular, unpolished, wooden table at which a typewriter lay at one end poised for instant use. She enjoyed book and literary gossip. When her comments were barbed they were spoken in her throw away, soft manner, devoid of malice. She was not a reluctant cook but accepted with a beaming smile any suggestion that her guests might bring in a take away Chinese meal.

One reason why we did not see more of Joan and Julius was that Mavis thought her talented friend should not be disturbed in her work. Time and again when I suggested we invited them for dinner and to stay overnight she would say it wouldn't be fair to distract Joan from writing the old imperishable. But Joan, despite an air of seeming detachment, did not live in an ivory tower. She dispelled a need for protection by writing to us, 'Please come to see me. I think I am going deaf and would love to chat while I can still hear you.' She cherished her friends, did not regard them just as copy. She was a very special person.

Another sideline which rarely proved profitable was the picture gallery I had for a few years. This came about when Sydney Arrobus, an artist from whom we bought (and sold copiously) hand-painted greetings cards of Hampstead, put pressure upon me to make more frequent use of a room at the back of the semi-basement. Sydney accustomed to seeing his paintings regularly displayed at the Everyman Cinema and on the walls of many local restaurants, visualised them on ours too. He priced his work modestly and sold it swiftly. He specialised in scenes of Hampstead in which the topography was more or less accurate and the colours always cheerful. When he gave himself time he drew superbly and I own an enchanting watercolour of the old Wilson shop which hangs on my staircase. (It has also been used as the cover illustration for this book.) He was a cheery, dapper little man who usually wore a pork pie hat, had a neat officer-style moustache and walked around NW3 at a quick trot, his drawing board under one arm.

'What are you doing with your Christmas card room?' Sydney asked one day and, before I could answer, added, 'May I have an exhibition of my paintings there?' I promised to consider it. Over the next few weeks he persisted and I acquiesced. At our first private view we sold many of his attractive canvases which encouraged me to think of the card room as a gallery. It also provoked other local artists to submit their work. Oswell Blakeston was also a painter; he even had a work in the Tate. How could I refuse him?

Oswell I liked; it was his friends who were the problem. They came in hordes from Soho to the private view and sat with their backs to the paintings until the wine ran out, then retired to the King of Bohemia next door. I don't think we sold one. This was hardly surprising because most of his friends were unemployed, scraping by on a living made from the advances on failed books.

A tall, formidable lady with a firm look in her eyes bore down upon me one morning. 'I would like an exhibition in your gallery,' she said. 'Come and see my work. I live in Parliament Hill.' I obeyed and, after being shown many mediocre paintings, I was hypnotised – you could say, intimidated – into agreeing she could have a show. She was Maeve de Markiewicz, daughter of the first woman elected to the House of Commons. The Countess de Markiewicz, who never took her seat, had been condemned to death for her part in 'the troubles' across the Irish Sea but was reprieved. The exhibition was a success, attended by all manner of Gore-Booths and other Irish gentry, also the Irish Ambassador who arrived half an hour late to formally open it. He announced disarmingly that he couldn't stay long because he was already two hours overdue for an earlier appointment. The guests drank merrily and red stickers soon started to appear below the paintings. The profit we made paid the overheads.

When we moved our premises down the High Street we opened the High Hill Gallery at the rear of a shop selling artists materials and running a picture framing service. There we had many exhibitions until, for economic reasons, we could no longer afford them. The first was for Edwin Smith and Olive Cook; she sold one, he none. More successful was a retrospective of Gerard Hoffnung's witty cartoons of the musical world.

It was through Ronald Whiting that the cartoonist came all too briefly into my life. The Hoffnung books were published by either Putnam or Dobson, sometimes both. Gerard, an endearing eccentric, looked much older than he was. Short, rotund, almost bald, he wore wire-framed Schubert-style spectacles and drove an ancient car (I think a Citroen). He and his lovely wife, Annette, lived in the Hampstead Garden Suburb from where they planned his unique Royal Festival Hall concerts at which fellow musicians willingly let their hair down to perform the antics Gerard wished upon them.

Notwithstanding his teetotal status, Hoffnung drew the cover for the first anthology of *The Compleat Imbiber*, published by Putnam, showing a degenerate character receiving alcoholic drinks through a multi-topped funnel. 'Look at it,' he moaned. 'It's disgusting!' His more serious side was shown when he asked me to interview a released criminal and give advice on getting him a job in the book trade. Gerard was a prison visitor and the man in question had worked in the gaol library. I did not have a vacancy, nor did I know what the man's offence had been. I invited him to the shop. He was depressed and unhopeful. He had come because Mr Hoffnung had asked him to. He expected nothing from me but accepted a loan which we both tacitly knew would not be repaid.

Once Hoffnung allowed me to borrow his famous tuba for a window display. He parked his vintage vehicle opposite the shop and came in clutching with a grubby handkerchief the instrument. It was not, so far as I knew, covered by insurance while it lay, for a few weeks, in my window, attracting much attention.

Hoffnung died, shockingly young, in his thirties, from a cerebral haemorrhage. We were all stunned. Annette, with two young children, rallied, saw to their education and eventually came to live close to the shop. She suggested the exhibition of Gerard's drawings of which we sold a great many, and she subsequently managed worldwide tours of Hoffnung concerts.

Another exhibition which particularly pleased me was the one instance when I displayed entrepreneurship as a gallery owner. We had employed an assistant in our Belsize Bookshop who was a struggling artist but showed little sign of becoming a competent bookseller. She nervously informed me that she was having an exhibition in a branch public library in Finchley. Did I think I might possibly find time on my day off . . . ? I did and admired the quality of her architectural drawings which prompted me to suggest that if she were to paint a series of Hampstead houses we could invite their owners to see them at our Gallery. It is gratifying when a simple notion works. Not only did many who lived in those houses buy Eileen Smith's work but it had a snowball effect. Decades later I would come across her around Hampstead carrying out yet another commission. If I had been a true professional in the art world I would have placed Eileen under contract and taken a cut forever and a day but it is only in the retailing of books that I obeyed the instinct to make money.

Our removal, in 1961, to new premises was due more to my unknown employers' sensible decision to sell a valuable site than to seeking larger accommodation for an expanding business. I welcomed the latter but was sad to abandon the dignified high Victorian double frontage of the former Wilson building with its two massive plate glass windows. It was true that the flat roof extension over the former front garden still leaked frequently, that the residential accommodation on the upper floors should long since have been condemned as unfit for human occupation and the basement area verged on the primeval, but it was here that High Hill Bookshop had been established. I loved every draughty crack in its walls, every mouse hole.

We were lucky to move into only marginally superior premises where a company specialising in industrial design had offices and a small factory rambling over the equivalent of several units. To visualise it as a bookshop required imagination. Freddy Caine, as my go-between with Mr X, had just that, and soon enthused me, although I was to fall out with the architect he engaged who had never designed a shop in his life. There was a considerable advantage in acquiring a long lease at fixed rent and paying the landlord less annually than we received from subletting those parts we didn't need, a happy state of affairs for some years.

The new premises were officially opened by the founder of Penguin Books, Sir Allen Lane, who 'cut the ribbon', observed by Sir Stanley Unwin, doyen of publishers resident in Hampstead. It was a great party, also celebrating publication of *The Book of the City*, attended by publishers, other booksellers, printers, authors and readers.

Within two years I had itchy feet. I longed to be both a publisher and my own boss. The capital needed to become an independent general publisher was far beyond what I could have expected to raise and I didn't wish to saddle myself with huge debt. Becoming an independent bookseller proved easier. I informed Freddy Caine that I was looking around. He asked Balleny to persuade me to stay. Balleny instead went to Mr X who said I could buy the business for ten thousand pounds. Freddy, furious, said, I would be buying my own goodwill but Balleny and Mr X understood that High Hill was what I wanted more than anything else and that the price was reasonable. There was still some tax loss to be absorbed and it would be several years before a rent increase could be imposed. I confided in Alan Steele, who took only half an hour to return my call and say, 'Joan and I will back you for less than fifty per cent; you must have a majority shareholding.' I remarked to Mavis, 'I'm sure your parents will help.' She replied that I was not to think of asking them, it was too great a risk and might alienate her brother. I insisted there was no risk and she finally gave in. Her father agreed on condition that we should have sixty per cent of the shares (£6,000), but not pay him any interest.

I was born lucky. (My parents-in-law were repaid within three years; the Steeles earned sixteen per cent on their investment over the next twenty five years). Mr X – later revealed as Christina Foyle – commented, 'I think we did you a good turn.' I agreed.

# 8

## Customers and Characters

It was a comfortable perch in Hampstead, serving a literate community and protected by the Net Book Agreement which meant, give or take the odd glitch, that booksellers mostly observed prices fixed by publishers and there was no 'three for the price of two' nonsense. But that will do for trade politics of which I have written all too often. The people who bought and sold the books are more interesting.

I am sceptical about statistics even though they have fascinated me since boyhood. This first came about when, aged eleven, a sudden enthusiasm for cricket led to my immersion in *Wisden* for all too many of my leisure hours. My head is still crammed with useless statistics picked-up by obsessive study during WWII of the edition covering the last season before hostilities. When I found gaps in the copious records I added my own; at High Hill one of my customers was the man who compiled the official ones.

There is a further admission. I count things. Almost all things . . . the daffodils in bloom in my garden; the towns, cities and villages in which I have stayed in each country I have visited; the number of times I have seen each Shakespeare play . . . and so on. It is compulsive. It can bore me to distraction. But some calculations have been beyond me, such as a tally of customers entering through High Hill's doorways, each day, week, month, year, a statistic which might have been of value. Nor do I know the total of how many could have been accommodated in the shop at any one time, or the percentage of those who browsed without buying or the average amount each one spent. But I remember many of the actual people, some well-known, others of little or no fame; all fascinating human beings.

Why does Dave Mindline come first to mind? He was an industrial photographer of working class origin from London's East End who had prospered sufficiently to buy a modest house in Hampstead. He claimed to be, or to have been, a communist and he always addressed me, satirically, as 'Comrade', expecting me to respond the same way. He adopted a world-weary slouch, physically and mentally, but his innate intelligence and curiosity was easily aroused so he seldom sustained the act for long. He was one of the prime movers, in the late fifties, in founding the New Hampstead Society. This came into being largely because the post-war generation found the long established Heath and Old Hampstead Society, which had survived it, fuddy-duddy. One enterprise it promoted was the High Street Improvement Scheme in which I participated. There was both cooperation and resistance. Some resented the well-intentioned dictates of a woman architect with distinctly Thatcherite characteristics who told yeoman-type shopkeepers what they must do. They retaliated by telling her where she should go. The amorphous nature of the street defied any overall enhancement but a small element of civic pride prevailed.

Dave was in the shop once when I told him we were planning a holiday in the Dordogne. He lost his world weariness instantly, his eyes lighting up. He had stayed there at our mutual friends, Michael and Pat Floyd's, second home. 'You must go to Perigoo,' he said 'The cathedral's marvellous.' He enthused further, then left with his customary 'Cheeroh Comrade.'

A woman who had been browsing and eavesdropping remarked, 'I would never take advice from someone who pronounced Perigueux like that.' I gave her one of my looks; she never returned.

Dave was a natural addict of the written word and bought avidly. He was not above seeking recommendations, aware that his education had been rudimentary. I took a chance one day and put him on to Anthony Powell's *A Dance to the Music of Time* which was not an obvious choice for him. He was hooked at once and subsequently impatient for each new instalment of this twelve-part sequence, some of which were three years or more a'coming. Along with other aficionados, on the appearance of each volume we would exchange our views on what Kenneth Widmerpool, the unexpected star character of the whole epic, had latterly got up to.

Geoffrey Drain, general secretary of the black-coated trades union NALGO, was another Powell fan. He also featured in my life as umpire for the Pretenders, a role he took sufficiently seriously to purchase and wear a correct white linen jacket. Politically he was, at least in theory, on the far left of the Labour Party but also a member of MCC. One afternoon seated in front of the long room at Lord's he declared loudly 'Peter May' (then captain of the national team) 'is the Gaitskell of English cricket'. Nearby elderly members looked in danger of having apoplectic seizures; years later Geoffrey too became corrupted by the establishment when he clearly basked in invitations to dine at Buck House.

One morning a man parked opposite the shop by the site of the urinal which I had failed to save and entered bearing a long, typed list of titles in haphazard order, some with the names of the publisher added. It featured art books, histories, biographies, travel manuals with no particular emphasis on any one subject. He handed it to Ralph Abercrombie, saying 'I doubt if you'll have many of these in stock. Would you like to order them for me?' Ralph, impressed by the list, thanked the man, chatted with him and promised to let him know when the books were available. Then he came to me, looking worried and said, 'Do you think he's all right? Should I have asked him for a deposit?' This was not our policy but there was a lot of money involved. I decided we should take a risk.

For the next few years Robert Ottaway, a journalist who lived in mansions off the wrong side of the Finchley Road, ordered hundreds of books from us, around a thousand pounds worth annually, which was an impressive sum for any individual customer, in Hampstead during the early sixties. He was the easiest of customers to satisfy, never in a hurry for titles which were reprinting or couldn't be traced. He wrote his cheque for whatever books were to hand and carried them off in the boot of his car. Occasionally I gave him lunch (when the Wilson government legislated that there should no longer be tax relief for entertaining British citizens Bob, on petty cash dockets, became Herr Ottomann) and I also invited him to address a Society of Bookmen meeting, at which members were overawed by his statement that he reckoned to spend ten per cent of his net income on books. He was likeable, sociable and knowledgeable. After being commissioned by Macdonald's to compile a multi-volume story of art for which he needed quantities of reference works he continued to purchase from us.

I lunched with Bob at the Cresta, a Polish restaurant owned by one Captain Mario Czaplicki, who resembled an eccentric English aristocrat as depicted by Osbert Lancaster. He was imposing, noisy, choleric and wore a monocle; if he didn't it was there in spirit. He was a Pole, with a distinguished war record as a parachutist, now married to an Englishwoman who may or may not have assisted with running the excellent restaurant on the corner of Heath Street and New End. There traditional Polish dishes – presumably authentically cooked – were served. I found them delicious. In the evenings, after he had imbibed, Captain Czaplicki, now looking a little like the comic Fred Emney, would seat himself at a harmonium-type instrument of the sort associated with nonconformist chapels, and entertain the diners with cabaret songs in a Viennese genre. He sang and played with splendid elan.

In nearby Flask Walk, at a slightly later date, was Mr Eddie's Restaurant. It appeared too small to be economically viable unless serving to capacity which was one reason why it operated on a staff of three, Eddie, a German, Pino, his Italian wife and Carlos, the South American waiter. The other reason was that most people would have found Eddie utterly impossible to work beside. Savage roars emanated periodically from the kitchen where he cooked every dish himself. This caused long delays on busy days, with Pino and Carlos soothing any customer showing signs of impatience. Eddie had been a chef at the House of Lords; he was not by temperament suited to be his own boss. Outside the restaurant he dressed soberly in a severe, unbelted navy blue raincoat over dark trousers, giving him the appearance of a plain clothes man. Neither he nor Czaplicki were regular book buyers although Eddie occasionally ordered titles about freemasonry; I was more often to be found in their establishments, entertaining customers or publishers.

One Saturday morning, at the old Wilson shop, there burst into my life a man with a gaunt, dissipated face partly hidden by a badly-trimmed beard. His appearance suggested both insomnia and chronic consumption but he was too old for Louis Dubedat or Chopin and too spunky for Lytton Strachey. His eyes were bright, his bones taut beneath the skin; he had a challenging smile and a Franz Hals manner. His name was Georg Rapp, he lived in Lower Terrace in a house where John Constable had once resided and he dealt successfully in scrap metals. He asked me for a book we did not have.

'When can you get it for me?'

'I'll order it tonight. The publisher doesn't have a London trade counter so I can't promise it by Tuesday or Wednesday. I can't give you a firm date, I'm sorry.'

'Young man,' proclaimed Rapp, mouth and eyes laughing together, probing me with an imaginary sword, 'if you wish to succeed in this world, you'll get me that book *today*.'

I leaned back against a bookcase, smiled and said, 'Let's assume I don't wish to get on.' He grinned and indicated he was prepared to listen. 'No publisher,' I told him, 'works on a Saturday. I would love to sell you the book today but it's beyond my powers.'

This diminished me further in Rapp's estimation. 'Right,' he said, 'do you know Bryce's, of Museum street?'

'Indeed, I do. Ivan Chambers is a friend of mine.'

'Phone him and ask if he has the book.'

I said I would be delighted to do so. I had begun to like this character who further demanded, with great disdain directed at me, 'if he doesn't have one ask him to order it for me, and I will collect it next week.'

'Certainly.' I did so. Ivan was amused to take the order.

Subsequently, Georg Rapp bought books from both of us. He was Hungarian, an educated, cultured man and friends with various Hampstead intellectuals. He desperately wished to be part of the publishing scene – he was always to remain sensitive about his connection with scrap metals – and first formed a partnership with Donald Carroll, a minor, minor poet. This didn't last long and while he was looking for a new partner with experience of publishing I introduced him to Ronald Whiting. They clicked and Rapp & Carroll was quickly replaced by Rapp & Whiting and the two proved good foils for each other. Georg, now George, gave the list a certain cachet, bringing to it the beat poets; Ron supplied the bread-and-butter, SF for instance, also the publishing know-how. He had been in the trade for more than twenty years, he knew all the booksellers, he understood modern concepts of marketing and had experience of working for single-minded tycoons. George, a workaholic as well as a womaniser, was not a crook. He loved socialising, enjoyed his food and wine and burnt the candle, as Ronald liked to say, not only at both ends but in the middle too.

Rapp & Whiting was developing reasonably well with George absorbing Ronald's know-how and learning fast when he suffered a severe cardiac arrest which heralded the end of both the company and of himself.

Until well into the eighties few booksellers opened on a Sunday. This made Saturday the climax of our week, usually a very busy day when both customers and money rolled in. Among the former were several Labour MPs who were greater in number among local residents

than their chief rivals. Hugh Gaitskell, a leader who never became
prime minister, lived in Frognal Way. (Harold Wilson, who did, lived
in the Suburb.) Frank Soskice was in elegant Church Row; Tony
Greenwood in equally handsome Downshire Hill; Steve Swingler in
Belsize Park Gardens; Douglas Jay and Eirene White (married to
Oxford University Press publicity manager, John White) in Well Walk.
Soskice, Greenwood, Jay and Swingler were all members of Wilson's
1964 administration.

There were far fewer Tory MPs. One was Henry Brooke, the local
member who actually lost the seat to Labour. He was a near neighbour
of Gaitskell's. Tony Greenwood was a particular friend and regular
customer. On the Saturday afternoon following the 1964 election,
when Wilson was forming his government, he parked opposite the
shop to call with the news that he had been made Colonial Secretary
(he had hoped for something more prestigious) with a place in the
cabinet. His visit made me feel at the hub of things. A few years later
he was responsible for Jack Cooper being appointed press officer for
his ministry (by then redesignated Overseas Development, because
colonies were no longer politically correct). This enabled Jack, who
had only narrowly lost Hampstead for Labour, to leave *The Times* and
earn an adequate salary for the first time in his life. He had decided not
to contest the seat again – Liz was relieved because she did not wish to
be wife of an MP – and was later to serve Ben Whitaker, the man who
won it in 1966, and who succeeded Tony in a reshuffle.

Into a different political category, as exiles from McCarthyism, came
Donald Ogden Stewart, who contributed to *The Book of Hampstead*, and
Ella Winter, his wife, for whom Mavis had worked in 1955. She spent
(see p. 102) several happy and enlightening months working as secretary
to one or other – she was never certain which. Sometimes she would
be with Ella, in her sitting room, translating Brecht, the next moment
Ella would be in the garden dead-heading roses and Mavis would be
taking down the next act of Don's play. Then all three would be having
coffee and discussing Marxism, the Hampstead shops or *The Mentality
of Apes*, the Pelican book which Ella had translated.

We were sent a typescript of Don's play, *The Kidders*, with a request
for our comments. I found it puzzling on the page but liked it when we
saw it at the Arts Theatre, from which it was transferred to the St
Martin's for a short West End run.

Don was a remarkable American. Not only did he enjoy watching cricket, he understood it. I sometimes met him at the pavilion at Lord's and found him more engrossed in what was – or was not – happening than any native. Occasionally we were invited to 103, Frognal for drinks. Once, Ella, a small bombshell of a woman, who fired on all cylinders at once, was supposedly ill with flu, so drinks were served at her sick-bed. Periodically she leapt from it to empty a waste paper basket or disappear to harangue kitchen staff, afterwards returning to lie beneath the sheets, hectoring us about this and that.

She acquired the habit of coming to the shop to bully me about books she had ordered but not received, stating loudly how much more efficient 'Noo Yark' booksellers were until I pointed out that the titles she had ordered weren't yet actually published. So she bullied my staff instead until I intervened when she would leave to buy groceries at the next door mini-market. Twenty minutes later she would reappear, give me a dazzling smile, and say, 'Ian, would you deliver what I've bought next door, on your way home, please?'

On one occasion Don came staggering into High Hill, very late on a mid week afternoon, clutching a wine bottle. 'Ian,' he said, 'I've got this Hock. I want you to taste it. Can we go some place?' I took him to my office where he slumped into a chair. By then I was thinking in terms of tea but he insisted we drank the Liebfraumilch. It was as though he had heard the name for the first time in his long life. Then, as folk do when they become plastered, he turned antagonistic. He suddenly seemed displeased with me but didn't hint why. I got him down to the shop and sent him on his way home. Not long after, he queried his account, alleging he had been charged for goods not supplied. I had a clear memory of handing over the actual books but he (Ella?) wouldn't have it. The account was never settled. I didn't see either of them again except to catch a glimpse of an old, bent-over couple, one behind the other, rounding the foot of Branch Hill and making intently for the Everyman Cinema as though their lives depended on it. Soon after they died, only a few days apart. Mavis commented, 'That's how it should be. They were so close.' I am just sorry there was no reconciliation.

The Stewarts became permanent residents. Other Americans stayed for shorter periods yet identified themselves intimately with Hampstead. Al Levinson was a New York teacher who became so besotted with the place and its people that he wrote, and published, a long poem which included references to many of us. He also attached himself to

Michael Palin, who lived in Gospel Oak, on the unpoliced border with Kentish Town, and somehow inveigled himself on to film locations with the Monty Python team. Al was so likeable that he was welcomed everywhere. Jack Cooper came across him with his family wandering the streets looking for temporary digs and they became instant friends. In the course of time we supplied Al's New York school with sets of copies of Chekhov short stories which he insisted he was unable to buy on his side of the Atlantic.

Mrs Hotson, wife of an American academic who periodically dwelt among us to pursue his Shakespeare studies, was into Bible commentaries and regularly ordered unfamiliar religious texts for her study class way out in the mid-west. Her orders were always accompanied by friendly, appreciative letters, usually with a digression extolling the virtues of the Republican president of the time. The books had to be obtained from obscure tiny presses in the provinces. This added to my knowledge of the breadth of publishing activity I later attempted to record in the revision of *Mumby's History*.

Numerous luminaries of the entertainment world were among our customers; some behaved off stage as normal citizens, others carried with them an air of hoping to be recognised at the same time as being embarrassed when they were. I learned from them of the transient nature of fame. In the mid-fifties Anton Walbrook was, for my generation, still a name with which to conjure. He had an apartment in Hampstead and often bought books and LPs from us, invariably cadging a cigarette from me when he called. During WWII he had made *Dangerous Moonlight*, a hugely successful romantic film in which he played the 'Warsaw Concerto' in a bombed house in the Polish capital. The manager at the Classic Cinema, Eastbourne told me they often reverted to showing it when business was lagging. Post-war he starred in the first make of *La Ronde*. By 1960, when I asked a junior assistant to deliver a book to Walbrook's flat, the boy didn't know who he was.

Peter Cook did not suffer such an eclipse, perhaps because he died too young. He was not prone to ask for cigarettes – and by his time we had stopped smoking on the shop floor – preferring to use our phone although he was only a five-minute walk from his house in Church Row. To compensate he bought piles of books – usually hyped novels or showbiz biographies. Often he seemed slightly drugged and was invariably distrait; sometimes he had dyed his hair pink. Although according to his biographer he was a compulsive comedian forever trying out witticisms, I don't think any of us heard him make an even mildly amusing remark. On stage and screen he was certainly one of the funniest performers I ever saw, especially in TV sketches with Dudley Moore, who also lived in Hampstead. I don't recall the latter ever being in the shop although the other two of the prodigiously talented *Beyond the Fringe* team occasionally were. Alan Bennett and Jonathan Miller were resident, I think, in Regent's Park or Camden Town, but I didn't get to know them. Once I was unwittingly rude to Dr Miller when he asked for a copy of Racine's *Andromaque* which I handed him commenting involuntarily, 'I suppose that's the next classic you're going to mess about with.' At the time I was resentful of the style he had chosen to apply to his production of *The Merchant of Venice* which he set it in the late nineteenth century. It was the only time we were able to take our young daughters to see Laurence Olivier and the anachronisms marred the performance not least when the clean-shaven Shylock spoke the line, 'Pluck my white beard'. We had a happier experience at the Royal Court watching Paul Scofield's impeccable *Uncle Vanya*. Cast beside him in a minor role was Denis Carey whom I met regularly in the shop and at The Rosslyn Arms. Denis directed more than he acted and always enjoyed discussing the play on which he was working. He was a short, stocky, Irishman and could be extremely temperamental or just plain drunk. There was a tiresome period when he decided he must write his memoirs and that I should help him. Fortunately he forgot about this when he was sober.

The actress and former dancer with Sadler's Wells, Moyra Fraser remains to this day a friend. She was married to the publisher Roger Lubbock and lived in Well Walk. When she came to High Hill we tended to go into a routine that amused customers who were present. Elegant, smiling, tall, beautifully poised, Moyra would appear at the doorway and exclaim, 'Ee-yarn'. I would respond, 'Moyra, light of my life!', move forward and peck her gently on the cheek. No flirtation could ever have been more innocent. One of the highlights of Moyra's career was in the Royal Court revue *Airs on a Shoestring* when she used her beautifully flowing auburn hair in a delicately comic solo number.

Another former ballet dancer was the lady I knew as 'Mrs Balyuzi', mother of five sons, one of whom, Robert, remains working in Hampstead sixty years after his birth there. 'Mrs Balyuzi', who when I knew her was both plump and petite, had been Molly Brown, one of Ninette de Valois original Sadlers Wells company in 1931. In 1935 she was in *Façade* with its choreographer Frederick Ashton; Moyra described her to Robert in her crisp, precise diction as 'a *character* dancer'. I introduced them over dinner in 2007 when for the first time Robert met someone who had danced with his mother. Molly Brown was one of the company who escaped from Holland in 1940 when the Germans invaded that country without warning. Later during the war she married a Persian-born broadcaster Hasan Balyuzi, the most naturally charming of men, who expressed his peaceful Baha'i faith in books which he never pestered me to stock. Robert, after an unexpected start as a sorter and deliverer of newspapers became High Hill's personal estate agent helping many of us to find or manage our properties. After our closure he asked my permission to name the offices he occupied above what had been our bookshop, High Hill House. I felt –alliteratively – honoured.

The most distinguished of all patrons was Peggy Ashcroft, the greatest actress I ever saw on stage or television, an enchanting lady who was a customer for more than thirty years. She was graceful of manner and speech, commanding attention because she radiated charm. She did not act off stage; she had natural star quality.

Dame Peggy, as I always addressed her despite my aversion to titles, was friendly and considerate. Once she came quickly into the shop in a semi-panic; was it her handbag or her purse she had lost? I forget. But there was a crisis. We were unable to help. She flew off. Ten minutes later she returned, smiling, relaxed. She had found what she had lost at the chemist a few blocks up the High Street; we were not on her way home but she wanted us to know. She liked to chat about new novels although our tastes rarely converged; she was always willing to talk theatre and expressed quiet pleasure in a little adulation. When she took to a particular book she bought numerous copies to give away. This might be a volume of Leonard Woolf's autobiography, *Sowing*, the one which is predominantly about Ceylon; or the wryly amusing Bill Humphrey's fishing yarn, *A Spawning Run*; or it might be the Souvenir Press stocking-filler, *Le Petomane*, about a French vaudeville performer of the late nineteenth century whose act consisted basically of farting. If I was on the floor when she came to the shop it quite simply made my day. Mavis said I was in love with her; I suppose I was. She was the only goddess I have met. Her successor as leading actress, Judi Dench, was also an occasional customer. I did not get to know her but have great admiration for her on stage and screen. She starred in the witty, up-market TV soap, *As Time Goes By*, in which Moyra also made occasional – too few for my liking – appearances.

Soon after I arrived at Hampstead, Wendy Trewin, a pretty, shy woman, in early middle age, who dropped her eyes bashfully on greeting, called one day to tell me how much she thought I had improved the old Alfred Wilson bookshop. She had, I suspect, to make an effort to face me, although I came to discern in her the same underlying toughness beneath an innate reserve, characterising John, her husband, and their son Ion.

John and Wendy Trewin, hailing from Cornwall, were Hampstead residents since the thirties. Known professionally as J. C. Trewin, deputy drama critic to Ivor Brown on the *Observer* until the advent of Kenneth Tynan. He had made his way to London from a local news-paper, determined to write about theatre. And what a good critic he became, never cynical, never tiring of his vocation. He had a deep knowledge of the drama and a patience which saw him through many tedious performances. Once, on the second or third night of Derek Jacobi's *Hamlet* at the Old Vic (by then he was writing for *The Lady)* I noticed him, with Wendy, sitting close to us in the stalls. I went over to greet them. They acknowledged me politely and, instantly, I realised my mistake. It was the umpteenth time John had seen the play (he wrote a book, *Five and Eighty Hamlets*); I was interrupting his and Wendy's preparation for an experience which they took every bit as seriously as the actors who were about to perform. That some players felt this was borne out at a party in Highgate one Sunday at Ion Trewin's house when Donald Sinden proposed John's health on his seventieth birthday. John could be critical but not unkind. He never scored points off actors. He walked about Hampstead, often clad in a grey overcoat and black beret; he and Wendy worshipped at the parish church and edited a book of recipes in aid of the restoration fund. They also knocked into shape a book about Norman MacDermott's years of running The Everyman as a theatre. MacDermott, long retired and living in Scotland, had submitted it to High Hill Press but finding it no more than a collection of scribbled notes I rejected it. It was typical of the Trewins that they volunteered to make it publishable. They were workaholics. John wrote many books; Wendy compiled fewer but did much social work. Soon after John's death (in the early nineties) she took over his duties at *The Lady* and attended first or second nights journeying from Hampstead to theatreland by tube and returning late, often unaccompanied, a practise she maintained until almost the end of the century.

The Trewins featured in both the exhibition and the book of *Writers and Hampstead*. There is a touching photograph of them, standing bravely facing a world with which in some respects they were increasingly out of sympathy. Once, in the nineties, at a lunch at Christopher Wade's, their alienation from what they dubbed 'Royal Courtism' was apparent when Mavis and I were enthusing about the night we saw *Look Back in Anger*, John Osborne's play which ushered in the modern movement. I said how the intervals were agonisingly long because we had been aware we were in on the start of a new epoch and couldn't wait for the next act. Wendy looked puzzled. 'We didn't see it that way at all.' Then, briskly, she said she must go and tend a sick friend. All this sitting about lunching and discussing past plays would not do for her. She was a dear; so was he. Their son Ion, one of the few genuine editors still extant in publishing, is their worthy successor.

In strongly contrasting mould, was Arthur Marwick, Professor at the Open University, and author of the many times reprinted, *The Nature of History*. Arthur was not part of a literary or academic circle in Hampstead, or anywhere else. He was a loner, an iconoclast who lived in a flat on Fitzjohn's Avenue. On first acquaintance he and I did not seem destined for a warm relationship. Invited to the opening of the High Hill (University) Bookshop and plied with wine, he responded by mocking me during my brief speech. Subsequently, in the Flask Tavern, when he had joined me unasked, then excused himself for a pee, I walked out in his absence. This did not improve relations. Then he wrote a letter, identifying ourselves as, if you please, 'the two most distinguished persons in Hampstead' and saying we ought to be friends. I try never to refuse an olive branch, so we made it up and thereafter often boozed together on Saturdays at The Horse and Groom in Heath Street, joined by Trevor Moore, a publisher's salesman whose friendship interlaced with occasional bouts of fierce dispute, I have long enjoyed, and two deep-dyed Tory customers of mine who Arthur regularly needled. Sometimes, if there were only ourselves, we would have intelligent, unprovocative conversation which led to his putting my name forward to the Open University for an honorary doctorship, on the grounds of my revision of *Mumby*. Flattered, I agreed. Soon after, on our sabbatical, somewhere, deep in Europe, I remembered his suggestion and felt false. My wife and daughters had worked and studied for their degrees. Why should I get one for writing a book for which I was paid? And wouldn't I have to dress up in all that regalia and look an ass? How could I get out of it? I didn't have to. About a year later Arthur wrote to me, genuinely embarrassed, to say I had been turned down. I was relieved.

Not long before we closed High Hill Arthur wrote *Beauty in History* for Thames & Hudson, a book we often discussed while it was a work in progress. When it was published Gerry Isaaman sent it to me for review and I found it intolerably wordy and obtuse. Arthur had attempted a subject too broad to pin down. I was unable to read more than half of it. I didn't pan it too heavily. He questioned me about it but never resolved whether I had liked or hated it. What I did learn from Simon Huntley, then Thames & Hudson sales director, was that at a conference in some grand country hotel, Arthur had rubbished his book in front of the entire sales force. Arthur was like that but he was great company. That is if you weren't a far right Tory, a practising C of E, or an academic who had taken against him – and there were not a few of those.

John Hillaby was another who tended towards confrontationalism, in or out of the pub, on or off the Heath. John, a Yorkshire-born journalist, was one of the world's great walkers. I think the best of his books was *Journey Through Britain* which I read when I was suffering from mental exhaustion. I subsequently recommended it to many, many customers who were similarly afflicted, and also to those who were not. It was one of the few books, in all my bookselling years, which I plugged confidently. It was intelligently, slightly crossly written, describing self-inflicted hardship combined with a true spirit of adventure. It made you care about the environment, the shortcomings of government, national and local, and about people.

John lived in West Hampstead and began his day by striding towards the Heath for exercise and to observe nature. Often on my way to work I saw him cross the traffic jam as my car crawled up North End Road. Later in the day he might be at the Flask where he would be arguing with Jack Cooper, Gerry Isaaman and others, and probably making rude comments about Peggy Jay, of the Greater London Council which at one time administered the Heath. This was somewhat unfair on Peggy who also cared about the environment, but John needed aunt Sally's. His third wife, Kate, was tough, and she had to be to cope with him, but when he was showing only average levels of irascibility, they were stimulating to meet in the local taverns. He didn't listen too much to what others said but cottoned on sufficiently to make intelligent responses. He cared passionately about disappearing species of plants and the destruction of the countryside. I was not too surprised to learn, at his funeral, that he was a practising Christian. Correction . . . a *believing* Christian. On one of the last occasions I met him he was seated beside Lettice Cooper, at Burgh House, during a party I was throwing for the *Writers and Hampstead* exhibition (see the poster on page 334), in which they were both represented.

For the Hampstead millennium celebrations in 1982 I undertook, for Burgh House, to record some of the observations made down the ages about the borough and it residents. I wrote a commentary and invited George Simpson, by then a professional calligrapher, and Keith Wynn, a local photographer, to turn the material into a visually attractive exhibition. George was endlessly patient as I extended the range of quotes chosen from twenty-five to fifty, then sixty, finally to '101 from Domesday to Drabble', while Keith took time off from his Heath Street shop to tour around NW3 taking shots of where some of the writers had lived. The exhibition was well supported so it seemed a good idea to turn it into a book, especially as it cost nothing in typesetting; the printer just photographed George's calligraphy. In fact, the book did not sell well, except among students at George's various evening classes and weekend courses. He sold more copies than we did at the bookshop to all the adoring ladies he taught.

John Hillaby and Lettice Cooper both hailed from Yorkshire and lived in West Hampstead; that apart they might not have been thought of as natural buddies. Miss Cooper, when first encountered in the old High Street shop, represented to me a typical, on the verge of upper-middle, English matron with a dash of the Lady Bracknell about her. She was always accompanied by her shorter, plumper sister Barbara who might have been taken for her companion. The impression was utterly false. Lettice, from a well-to-do county family, was socially deeply aware and had written at least one outstanding novel, *Fenny*. She was a generous, liberal-minded soul who understood from many viewpoints what the industrial revolution had done to the Ridings. Her work was reprinted by Virago and it deserves to endure the test of time, being in the great tradition of storytelling. She and Barbara were spinsters with a passion for lieder and the Wigmore Hall. I know nothing of Barbara's private life but I believe Lettice had a long affair with a writer or broadcaster. Barbara was an editor for John Lehmann at *London Magazine*, from which office, according to Charles Osborne, she was periodically ordered out by the proprietor when he flew into a paddy. Barbara Cooper would go quietly then reappear a day or two later and resume her work.

The Cooper sisters' niece by marriage was Jilly, a hugely successful authoress of romantic novels and sometime columnist for *The Sunday Times*. She is a lady who oozes sex appeal and laughter. I have met her several times and appeared on a Melvyn Bragg programme with her. Leo, her husband was an editor and publicity manager with Longmans and Hamish Hamilton, before founding his own imprint devoted to military books. He is not noted for industriousness and has a certain cavalier attitude to employment. He has written a very funny account of his publishing life entitled *All My Friends Will Buy It*. That branch of the Coopers was never part of Hampstead; John le Carré and Kingsley Amis were.

Le Carré's books we would have sold anyway whether or not he had come to live locally. It was Jane, his wife, who made sure that I was kept up to the mark. Even after they had gone into paperback she gently but firmly pressurised me to stock the hardbacks as well. Sometimes she was proved right, which was slightly maddening, but they were good customers in Hampstead. I first met him when he addressed a Society of Bookmen meeting while I was Secretary and Alan Hill was Chairman. Having read, sold and admired *The Spy Who Came In from the Cold* and *The Looking-Glass War*, I asked what he intended to write next. Something, he replied which truly took the lid off the entire espionage world; it was a theme of which he never tired, nor did his public.

When he addressed the meeting he was the kind of speaker who brought relief to both Chairman and Secretary. He was witty, personable, knew how to time his laughs and how to engage his audience. He had the natural authority, urbanity and charm of a star performer. In Hampstead he lived first in Gayton Crescent, around the corner from the shop in a comparatively modest four-storey terrace residence, later in exclusive Gainsborough Gardens, close to the Heath but hidden from the prying gaze of Bank Holiday trippers. He became extremely famous and needed a protective aura, assuming a certain detachment but never becoming arrogant. My colleague Derek

Johns knew him better that I did. Derek has a way with celebrities; he
has since become a literary agent.

Kingsley Amis and Elizabeth Jane Howard, his second wife, came to
reside in Hampstead at Gardnor House, near the end of Flask Walk, in
the 1970s, having previously lived on Hadley Common. He was a very
occasional customer and did not become a friend; I invited him to
contribute an essay on his school-days at the City of London School to
*The Book of the City* but he declined, politely and in beautifully legible
handwriting. His elegant Hampstead home was almost opposite Burgh
House, an institution then always in need of funds. This was why, one
day, when I was paying my bill at the Garrick, with Amis beside me, I
asked if he would 'do' a book signing of his latest book for the Burgh
House Trust. He agreed.

On the appointed Saturday morning he arrived on time, neatly
dressed and groomed, as always, and was set down beside a bottle of
whisky. David Roy, sales director of Hutchinson, and Brian Perman,
the editorial director, were also there. There was a poor turnout, with
few readers queuing for copies of what proved to be one of Kingsley's
least successful novels. David went to the piano and strummed a
Mozart sonata. Brian and I conversed. Kingsley was content with his
scotch. Eventually George Malcolm Thomson, distinguished Beaverbrook journalist and High Hill customer, appeared and bought a copy,
exchanging good-humoured chat with the author; Tom Rosenthal,
publisher, foothill resident of Hampstead down in the Regent's Park
area, bought another. My regular, excellent customer Ed Woolf, a
nursery gardener of repute, came in nervously, made his purchase and
asked Kingsley for advice on the best six twentieth-century novels.
The author treated him patronizingly, particularly recommending
*Lucky Jim* (I seethed silently). Few others came. Brian suggested we go
for lunch at Mr Eddie's. Amis said he would prefer to finish the bottle
of whisky first. We then went to the restaurant where we drank wine
and brandy. Around four o'clock Brian abandoned me – David had
long since shuffled off to visit his sister who lived nearby – leaving me
alone with the writer. I said I ought to get back to the shop.

'Why?' he asked. 'You're the boss,'

I watched him down another brandy while he related, maliciously,
with a cruel laugh, that Elizabeth Jane had got 'writer's block'.

What astonished me about Kingsley was the clarity of his mind at
a stage of his life when he had been boozing heavily for decades.

Whenever I read any critical or non-fiction piece of his I am impressed by his command of argument and content, and the coherence of his thoughts. He must have been one of those who woke early with a clear head and wrote rapidly until lunchtime. But by two o'clock he was often plastered and, at the Garrick, came down to eat only because the bar closes at that hour. Then he would partake of the smallest of omelettes, possibly made with a mere quail's egg.

Many other authors lived in Hampstead. Unregimented phalanxes of them crossed my path but, where there are no specific stories to tell, it is better to treat them like autumn leaves and sweep them gently aside, however illustrious their names. The same goes for the vast majority of customers who were not household names, who did not behave eccentrically, criminally or in any way unpleasantly. They were neither saints nor sinners to any discernible degree and therefore recording them all individually would be tedious.

There were few Saturdays when I didn't have a visit from one or both of the Gorbs. Peter, a marketing executive, was blessedly a chronic book-buyer who enjoyed discussing his purchases and recommending his enthusiasms to me; Ruth embarked on a late journalistic career when she began to contribute pieces to the *Ham & High* on resident's gardens. Gerry Isaaman, realising her potential, later employed her to write the woman's page at which she became indispensable to the degree that he insisted on her providing copy for weeks when she was on holiday. Ruth had that happy knack of being compulsively readable without giving offence. Gerry was often an inspired editor who raised the prestige of the paper to national level.

And there was Stephen Wilson, Keeper of the Public Record Office. He and Patsy, his north American wife, lived in one of the Erno Goldfinger 1930s houses in Willow Road. One day Stephen was browsing and asked, 'What's that new Paul Gallico, *Flowers for Mrs 'Arris*, like?'

'Repellent', I pronounced.

'I'll take a copy.'

With such customers how could I go wrong? And it was Stephen who loaned me maps and guides for our first Provençal holiday.

At each end of the short, slightly curved, at one point bulging, High Street there operated two formidable personages who were dominant figures in the community. Neither displayed literary or artistic characteristics, both stood, or sat, indefatigably plying their wares in wind, rain, sleet, snow or occasional heat waves.

Flower-seller Maggie Richardson, who might have been Eliza Doolittle's daughter although she had not achieved, or probably aspired to, refinement of diction. Her pitch was at moveable sites above the southern junction of the street with Willoughby Road, into which at some periods it overflowed (there is a plaque). In the mid-fifties when I first encountered her, Maggie was already weather-beaten and had been setting up her stall for decades. Her son delivered her with her stock of a morning and collected her in the early evening. They dwelt, I think, in the Euston area.

Residents who had forgotten the imminence of an anniversary or who needed a bouquet for whatever reason were attracted by the flowers Maggie had to sell. Once she had carefully wrapped their purchase in old newspaper and handed it over she would invariably state, with a slight stammer, 'ter-two-and-six to you, my love' or 'fer-five bob, that's all', proclaiming the transaction a bargain such as others would not receive. In repose she was not a welcoming figure; she was, after all, ignored by hundreds, thousands even, of passers-by each day. She could not be expected to maintain a constant, glittering, theatrical demeanour welcoming the entire world but, immediately any person faltered in their quick ascent or descent of the High Street and cast the merest glance at her flowers, Maggie's shrewd eyes gleamed in anticipation. This was her livelihood; she was seldom, if ever, absent due to illness.

Her pitch was not always close to my bookshop but once when she lost her permanent space lower down, she arrived in a nearby, temporarily unused doorway. There, one Christmas Eve as I returned from depositing a wallet of banknotes in the night safe, I saw her crouching in the bitter cold, awaiting her son, yet eager to sell all that remained of her semi-frozen goods. I took pity and brought her a tot of scotch, which she gratefully accepted. Thereafter, every yuletide, she commented, 'We always 'ave a drink together at Christmas – don't we my love?' Maggie was a human version of what became known as 'street furniture'.

Bob Brady, at the top end of the thoroughfare, on the steps of the tube station, enjoyed a more protected perch but had to endure the crosswinds blowing up or down Heath Street. He also needed to keep his wares dry because he owned a news stand serving, strictly for cash, everyone from cabinet ministers upwards.

Bob was a sturdy six-footer, had a permanent fag end at one corner of his mouth and wore a flat, peaked cap. At morning and evening rush hours the pounds and pence poured into his pouch or on to a tray from which he selected change. At less busy periods he left an assistant in charge and went for a cuppa or just for a stroll. Once, in lower Heath Street, he swaggered up behind a traffic warden and tweaked one of her buttocks. The woman turned in a rage and hailed a nearby policeman. The two glowered at Bob who said, defensively, 'I fought she was Pearl. I always pinch Pearl's bott'm.'

Common sense prevailed. The copper put away his notebook and gave Bob a caution.

When I passed Bob's stand I was not molested but sometimes he would shout out, 'Got any more of them maps?' This meant he had sold out of the Hampstead plan published by my company. He always solicited a new consignment as though I was doing him a great favour in allowing him to sell it. He paid for them on the spot, in cash, and didn't require an invoice or receipt. I would thank him and say, 'I won't ask you for it twice, Bob.'

'If you did, you wouldn't bleedin' get it.'

Probably Maggie and Bob, over a long period of the mid-to-late twentieth century, were more familiar figures to the greater part of the local population than any of the many celebrated residents of Hampstead Village.

Less well known to them was Sylvester, a Norweigan-born former whaler who was a night watchman at the Medical Research Council's premises above Holly Hill. During the day Sylvester frequented The Rosslyn Arms. He bore some resemblance to Ernest Hemingway, constructed model ships as a hobby and was an entirely congenial drinking companion most of whose utterances were unintelligible. He spoke in a series of 'whoops', expressing amused surprise at almost anything one said. He regularly became quietly and unaggressively drunk, usually on cider. On one occasion he found it necessary to take off his trousers before staggering home. For this he was arrested and brought to court where a magistrate, peering down from the bench, enquired in patrician tones 'Ever been up before me?'

Sylvester, coherent for once, replied, 'I don't know what time you get up, my lord.'

(Laughter in court). 'Order!'

'Case dismissed.'

# 9

## Family, Travel and Mumby

There was life beyond the book trade. The family circle was smaller than the one I had known as a child which was mainly due to dispersal over wider areas but there was benefit in that because it ruled out the unspeakable habit of dropping in. We exchanged cards at Christmas, met occasionally, mostly at weddings or funerals and, yes, on the whole we were closer to our friends. I dare say this was not unusual.

Alice, my mother, who was widowed in 1951, aged only fifty two, remained in St Leonard's where she had lived with Bill. She was untrained in any job or profession but Bill had left her well provided for. She resolved not to impose herself on her elder son and Joan, his new wife, at Tunbridge wells although Gordon had promised his father he would look after her. Alice knew this would place an unfair strain on a new relationship and insisted on returning to the Sussex coast.

Mavis and Alice enjoyed an easy relationship unlike that of many daughters-in-laws with their respective mothers-in-law. My mother had known my wife for almost as long as I had, while Bill and Wilfred Matthews, had met as Freemasons so there was little ice to be broken there. The main difference between the two families was that the Matthewses were practising Christians; the Norries were not. This did not spoil friendship between them although Louise, my mother-in-law, a lady of innately charitable inclinations towards all except for one of her nephews, tended to pity Alice and believed she needed assistance. Louise's main motivation in life, one endlessly proclaimed, was to help others – ''tis better to give than to receive'. I pointed out that there was a fatal flaw in this philosophy because it was bound to render those on the receiving end selfish. On that occasion she used her severe deafness not to hear what I had said.

It was strangely uncharacteristic of Pop to have become a Freemason. It must have come about when he was forced to move from Enfield to St Leonard's to manage the family property business.

My maternal grandparents, Arthur & Barbara Tapley

Waterloo Crescent, Dover, where Nanna ran a boarding house at which my parents met.

My parents: 'Alice' and 'Bill' Norrie

**Aunts and uncles**
Edie and Babs (sisters-in-law); Robert and Donald (brothers-in-law)

Diana, my cousin, and Alice; Tapleys to a T

Aubrey, brother of Babs & Donald

Gordon and Joan *née* Sild (1951–83)

**Alice & Bill's children**

Peggy, Ian and Gordon (*c.*1931), who between
them enjoyed 129 years of marriage.

Peggy & Peter Scott (1945–99) and (*right*)
Mavis *née* Matthews and the author (1955–98)

Wilfred and Ivy 'Louise' Matthews, parents of Mavis

Their grandchildren,
Jessica and Amanda
Norrie, in 1976

Jessica; her children
Robert and Rosalyn;
Amanda with her sons
Jonathan and Michael

**My book-trade employers**

Martyn Goff, 1948–9

Frederick Joiner, 1950–55

Christina Foyle, 1949–50, 1957–64

And one I turned down. Sir Allen Lane at the opening of the new High Hill Bookshop, September 1961

**Book-trade members of the Pretenders' Cricket Club**

John Ford  (Wm Jackson, High Hill)

Ernest Hecht (Souvenir Press)

David Harrison (MacGibbon & Kee, Wildwood)

Ronald Cortie (Chatto)

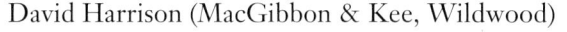

**Mountview Theatre Club members who became my lifelong friends**

Founder, Peter Coxhead (*above*)

Scene from *Mixed Grill:* Skit on actor-managers: 'Here's Hamlet! Will you please put back the ham.' (*left to right*) George Simpson, Peter Hammersley, Eddie Wheeler and Don Cregor

Pat and John Hughes

*below* Milton Krever

**Four editors for whom I worked**
(*top left*) Fred Newman (*Publishing News*)
(*top right*) David Whitaker (*The Bookseller*)
(*below left*) Louis Baum (*The Bookseller*)
(*below right*) Gerry Isaaman (*Ham & High*)

**Three who published my books and yet remained friends**

Robin Hyman (*Publishing & Bookselling in the Twentieth Century*) with Inge, his wife

Ronald Whiting (three novels)

Dieter Pevsner (*Hampstead: London Hill Town* and *A Celebration of London*) with Florence, his wife

Window display at Foyles for *The Book of Hampstead*, February–March 1960

Launch party for the book at the King of Bohemia:
Kay Dick, W. G. (Bill) Smith – Editor of *Books & Bookmen* – and Ernest Raymond

Ken Hoare and Joan O'Donovan

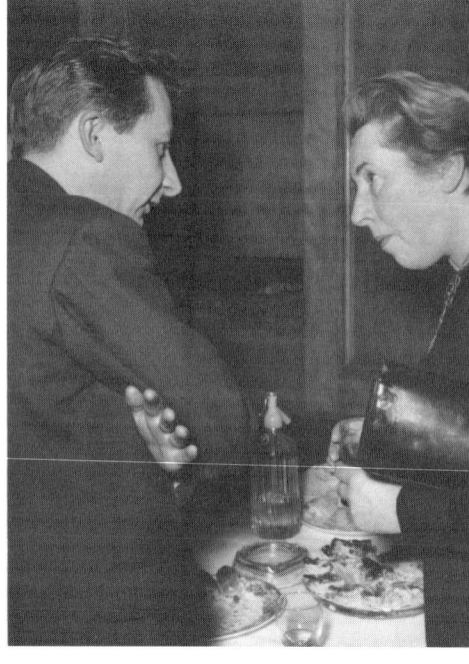

At 6–7 Hampstead High Street, celebrating *The Story of My Days* by Ernest Raymond – the author, Mavis, Diana and Ernest Raymond and Alan Steele, 1968

At 11 Hampstead High Street, October 1960, celebrating twenty-five years of Penguin Books. The author and the penguin (now in Hampstead Museum), with sales director Bruce Hepburn

## Other book-trade gatherings

Retirement lunch for Ivan Chambers, Criterion Restaurant, February 1971.
Mavis with three former chairmen of the Society of Bookmen – Robert Lusty,
Philip Unwin and Ian Parsons

At Claridge's following retirement party for Ainslie Thin of Edinburgh organised by David
Whitaker (*left*) and the author, here seen with Ainslie (*right*) and Eppie, *c.*2001

**Parties at Hadley Wood**

With two friends of sixty years' standing,
George Simpson (*left*) and Martyn Goff (*right*)

Leslie Martin

Jessica with her home-
made mince pies

My niece, Sue D'Arcy, with Jack Cooper at a Boxing Day party

**Holidays**

Mavis (*left*) with Val and George Simpson, setting out for Ireland, 1992

The author with Barbara Scott in Spain, 2001

At Roussillon, in the Vaucluse, with Mavis and Michael Floyd (*centre*), 1989

Mavis at Siena on her seventieth birthday, 1996

At the Pensione Bencista, Fiesole.
Michael Floyd, Mavis, Pat Floyd
and Christopher Wade

On the Adriatic, 2002. Judith Davis and George Simpson

## Favourite places

The Pont du Gard in 1969 when traffic still
crossed it and people were permitted to walk
over the unguarded top.

My two favourite Romanesque churches:
Issoire and Brioude in the Auvergne

Florence: Palazzo Vecchio (1967)

Despite the fellowship he might have been expected to find at chapel he needed male company of a more worldly nature, but I wondered at his acceptance of the bizarre rituals he had to face by being 'on the square'. It was a subject I never discussed with him or with Bill who did not suggest to either Gordon or me that we should join.

Pop was the kindest of landlords, befriending many lonely and often impoverished elderly folk. Often, when one died, the only mourners at the funeral were himself and his wife. My parents-in-law lived modestly but comfortably off the many controlled-rent, leasehold houses they inherited, took package holidays on the Continent and were generous to their children.

Until I acquired a car we saw little of Peggy and Peter who lived at Colchester except when, with Peter John and Julie, they stayed with Alice at St Leonard's for their summer holiday. We were not politically compatible with Peggy and Peter, who were both deep-tied Tories. As adults we tacitly agreed not to discuss the subject. She belonged to Colchester Conservative Party; Mavis was a lifelong member of the Labour Party. Peter and I provoked each other to argument on most subjects but desisted when we realised it upset Alice. We talked about cricket, tennis and other members of the family. I got on very well with their children. Peter John won a scholarship to Cambridge, became a solicitor, married Di, the daughter of another lawyer, and had three handsome sons. The lovely Julie worked for me briefly at the shop and lived with us before going to South Africa where she met Gethin Dalton. She bore him three daughters before dying tragically young from breast cancer, aged only thirty-nine.

It was partly due to Peter John and Julie that we held large Christmas parties after we had moved to Hadley Wood. The ground floor drawing and dining rooms had been made one and the house cried out to be used for festive gatherings. The Scott children, both of whom were working in London, hinted that they would find it congenial to be invited for Christmas so would we kindly ask their parents. Jack and Liz Cooper, Barbara and Don Scott, John and Sylvia Ford and sometimes George and Val, his wife, joined us for increasingly lively celebrations when raucous outbreaks of singing, which Mavis encouraged, drove the neighbours to spend the holiday elsewhere. Few of us had tolerable voices and those who had were drowned except for the year that, during a sudden, unexpected lull, Val Simpson spontaneously sang Vilia from *The Merry Widow*.

In 1973, on the one hundredth anniversary of my grandmother's birth I attempted to arrange a weekend party at a country hotel as a celebration of her life and family. It didn't happen. Some said they couldn't face spending a weekend in the company of so and so; others said they couldn't afford it. The response was dismal. I didn't achieve such a gathering for another thirty years when more than fifty of us had a buffet lunch in my garden in Barnet but by then there were gaps in our ranks. It was an occasion when many met for the first – and possibly in some cases – the last time.

It was ironic that the offspring of my extreme Tory sister and brother-in-law went successfully through the state education system whereas our daughters did not. Amanda did not fit into the grammar school in Finchley and Jessica, at a comprehensive in Southgate, found herself unchallenged. This was a disappointment to Mavis who favoured the comprehensive approach and was also opposed in principle to private education. Because neither of us thought we should sacrifice our children to political theories Amanda was enrolled at the mixed King Alfred's, in Hampstead, (the only school I would really love to have attended myself) while Jessica was placed at a convent on Hadley Common (and I was the one who had to swallow the greater pride over that collective *volte face*). King Alfred's suited Amanda. She had good tuition there from very sympathetic teachers and met her first husband, Simon Clark, also a pupil. The nuns on Hadley Common had a beneficial effect on Jessica without submitting her to religious indoctrination. After a few terms there she took matters into her own hands and transferred to Barnet College to take A-levels. Both girls in due course attended universities, Amanda taking Russian and social anthropology at Manchester (where she met Gerry Leversha, her second husband, a teacher at the celebrated grammar school), Jessica spending several years at Sussex reading European Studies, which gave her the advantage of a year in Paris and another, as an *assistante* in Dijon. Later she went to Sheffield to take a further degree. She then became a teacher and married. Each have two children, Michael and Jonathan (Amanda and Gerry); Rosalyn and Robert (Jessica and Andy). Consistent with the pattern of modern times both couples have separated; I however continue to meet and like both my sons-in-law.

Once the girls had left home Mavis insisted that we must take lodgers for the top floor of our Hadley Wood house which had provided large bedrooms for the girls; she thought it antisocial to have so much space to ourselves. This conferred a huge benefit on us when we took our sabbatical in 1982, leaving the entire residence in the hands of an amiable Anglo-Lebanese couple who took impeccable care of it during our five-month absence.

Mavis never liked living in Hadley Wood, where we moved only because we had been gazumped on houses in Finchley and Woodside Park. When a station was built near Hadley Wood, on the King's Cross to Edinburgh line, an entirely middle class community emerged around it, at first solely in solid Victorian edifices with frontages in red brickwork. By the time of our arrival in 1969 the community had spread into several estates and had a row of shops though not, regrettably, a pharmacy, bank or pub. The majority of residents were car owners who gradually ceased to support any but the CTN-post office because it was essential to drive to Barnet, Enfield or Cockfosters to collect prescriptions or use banking services. There was an infant school, a community hall and a church but it lacked the equivalent of a village green. Within years of our arrival even the railway station had ceased to be manned and had become hazardous for lone passengers to use. It was not a convenient place in which to bring up a family accustomed to urban amenities. It depressed Mavis to such an extent that I agreed we should move.

We looked at a house in East Barnet which on first viewing we were enthusiastic about, but when we returned to clinch the deal and take measurements Mavis grew strangely quiet while I chattered away to the vendor. In the car on the way back to Hadley Wood she had a change of heart; 'I can't live there. It wouldn't do for us. We won't move and I won't mind.' She stood by this and I was lucky to be allowed more than a quarter of a century in the house and garden I loved. I even took to gardening (mostly of a destructive nature although I grew beans and potatoes) under my wife's supervision. It was good for us to share another hobby; by the time we next moved the garden, thanks mainly to her, was perfect. In it, for many years, I had legally indulged a passion for late evening bonfires. There is something utterly tranquil about raking and controlling them, standing alone in the twilight, on a calm evening. I know of few pursuits more relaxing.

When Alice came to stay with us at Highbury or Finchley the visit always began in party mode. A glass of gin and tonic or champagne and she was on top form. However as the visit went on she began to yearn for home even though living alone was not agreeable. There was not enough for her to do at our house although Mavis had no compunction about involving her in any chore which enlivened her, from darning my socks to riddling the terrible, misnamed 'Ideal Boiler' which we had inherited. Alice liked to be busy but her heart condition caused her to tire quickly. Then she began to sigh. She sighed prodigiously. After that she took to yawning. Huge inevitably contagious yawns. It often became a relief to us all when the visit drew to a close. As that prospect neared my mother cheered up visibly and departed in a welter of love and goodwill. The fact was she missed Bill desperately and soon tired of her own company, a trait I have inherited.

Alice developed a heart condition sufficiently acute to necessitate spells in a nursing home in St Leonard's where she became friendly with the owner, known as 'Matron'. When Matron was widowed there arose a strong bond between the two women which was certainly of benefit to my mother. Alice's GP was an arrogant doctor who clearly resented the creation of the NHS. (My father didn't approve either.) NHS patients were, for him, undoubtedly second class citizens, even those, like Alice, who had private health insurance. When I expressed concern about her health he had the audacity to breach confidentiality, instructing Alice to request me not to write to him. A few months later, in his surgery, he explained to Peggy and me that the thinness of her heart walls could – and did – cause instant death. We were treated coldly but civilly.

Shortly before she died I drove Alice to Scotland to visit Bill's relatives and to stay with the delightful Cathie and her less delightful husband. Jim brought out all the sighs and yawns in Alice when Cathie left her with him while she was at work; he was so mean that he wouldn't take her anywhere in case he had to pay, so they stayed at home eating food provided by Cathie. Val and George came with us as far as Lakeland where we picked them up on the return journey. This led to several party evenings. George and I were lucky in knowing each other's families and getting on well with them. This was Alice's last holiday. She died a few months later on our daughter Jessica's tenth birthday, not yet seventy.

Amanda and Jessica were born within thirteen months of each other, an instance of severe lack of planning. Mavis coped well, with assistance from both our mothers. It was hers who insisted that we must continue to take continental holidays, leaving the infants in her care at St Leonard's. We rejoiced in our good fortune which was further boosted by Pop's arranging a bank loan to enable us to buy our first house in Granville Road, Finchley and sustaining a habit of leaving a cheque on the dining table at the end of a trip to see us. Thus, by the time Alice died, in 1968, the house was ours. We then took out our first mortgage, allied to a life policy which, together with the funds from selling Finchley, allowed us to buy the three storey, five bed-room, semi-detached Victorian house, with long garden, in Hadley Wood, on the northern edge of Greater London – priced at £11,750. For the next twenty years Geoff Hill, my accountant and the High Hill auditor, warned me against any impulse to pay off the mortgage. On maturity it brought me in £22,500 which was only a little less than I had paid in interest for two decades. (The other day I heard it had been sold for over a million; in 1995, we received a 'mere' £340,000.) I have always enjoyed good luck with property deals; seldom with literary ventures.

Relations with my brother Gordon improved markedly the moment he became engaged, in 1951, to Joan Sild. Eventually the four of us became friends, despite the embargoes laid down by Gordon as to what were forbidden as suitable subjects of conversation. Politics was not allowed nor was religion. And you must never talk 'shop'. Work was something to be tolerated as a necessity of life but it was bad form to refer to it; equally bad was to even hint at any success one might have enjoyed and all publicity was to be avoided. He hated any mention of me in the media, just as he had abhorred the front page story printed in the *Kent & Sussex Courier* in June 1940 proclaiming him a hero for having helped a friend along the road to Dunkirk. Travel as a topic was permitted because he and Joan, along with Susan their only child, drove on the continent each summer in pursuit of the sun. He also got a kick from cathedral architecture although painting was taboo as well as any attempt at analysis of literature, drama, music. You enjoyed such manifestations of human creativity or you didn't; it was pretentious and worse – boring – to discuss them. And you never, never re-read a book – what would be the point? You already knew the plot. So Joan, who adored him, was not allowed an easel and paint brush until after Gordon's death, but was expected to be either a cricket widow or to attend matches and help with teas. We once almost fell out when I declined his invitation to watch Tunbridge Wells in a club cricket final at Lord's because this took place on a Saturday when I preferred to be at work. He was further affronted when I turned down his club's annual dinner and the added allure of sharing a bedroom with one of his friends whom I didn't know. Joan and Mavis, who got on well together, smoothed this over. They met annually with Peggy for lunch and the exchange of Christmas gifts at the Charing Cross Hotel. No doubt the foibles of their men folk were a subject of comment . . . and if they weren't they should have been.

Had the RAF not posted me to India I would probably never have journeyed outside mainland Europe and the Greek islands. My grandmother scarcely ever left Kent, let alone England; my mother, visiting Paris for her honeymoon, was seasick on the Channel crossing. Thereafter she never travelled outside the UK though I remember her misery aboard a Clyde steamer and on a ferry to the Isle of Wight, which was where for her Abroad began. Rightly, my wife was not prepared to tolerate a stay-at-home husband so, in 1955, we went by train and ferry to Knocke, in Belgium, and from there, by coach or bike, to Bruges and into Holland. In 1957, with Mavis pregnant, we travelled by train, to Port Vendres, on the Mediterranean, close to the Spanish border. George came with us; Peggy Bowyer joined us there.

It was my first experience of a *gîte*. One never learns. I have yet to rent one that has been moderately tolerable. This had a vast room with a fine view of the Pyrenees, furnished with only a double bed, a single bedroom and bathroom, off the kitchen-diner and a long passage posing as a hall. Peg slept in the single bedroom. George was accommodated in an adjoining villa where he felt so remote and gloomy as the sole inhabitant that from night two he slept in the passage/hall. The lighting was vestigial throughout; the apartment was comfortless but there was a garden and there we sunbathed and read on days when the Vent du Nord was not raging.

On some days we explored the coast. Collioure, the next little resort, was more attractive than Port Vendres, with a sandy beach complete with a stall in a small marquee stocking expensive art books. Other towns beside the sea were Argeles, Banyuls and Cerbere, the last place before Spain. Mavis and I ventured up a steep hill but didn't get far. She suggested hiring a car another day, an outing that was to prove memorable. A M. Casanova planned it, taking us to Prades, birthplace of Casals, where we visited the church (gaudy Baroque) before embarking on a long, winding road to an inland pass. Halfway there we stopped at Villefranche to lunch at a restaurant where we invited our driver to join us. The cuisine was superb, the wine flowed. There were hors d'oevres, trout, chicken, dessert, cheese. As one dish followed another I wondered aloud to George, 'How much will this cost?' He shrugged his shoulders. The chef appeared to seek our approval. We toasted him. He brought more wine; he drank with us. When we paid it came to 15*s*. (75p.) each. After, while M. Casanova drove round hairpin bends on the ascent of the Pyrenees, I was euphoric, replete in mind and body.

The sun-drenched terrain was spectacular. A single track railway line weaved above, below, across us, sometimes close, at others like a backdrop, with a small train chuffing along it. There was little traffic on the road, a scarcity of people in the fields and only a few in the tiny villages through which we passed. It was my first lesson in the absence of population in French communities, a phenomenon still apparent today. The occasional beasts in the fields munched contentedly, or dozed, as we ourselves did periodically.

At Puigcerda, the frontier town, M. Casanova said he could go no further; his insurance did not cover driving in Spain, so we walked into the little town at siesta time. Soldiers strutted menacingly about. Most of the shops were closed. We bought postcards and briskly returned to the car. We hadn't liked Spain and commiserated with Peg who had to go on to somewhere near Madrid to be a lady's companion and teach English to her children. During the long journey back to Port Vendres, darkness fell. Once on the plain, M. Casanova sped through the quiet countryside to make up for time spent over that fabulous lunch. I was beginning to like travel.

In 1959 we did holiday by car. It belonged to Martyn Goff and the fourth member of the party was his then partner, Peter Harvey. Martyn was passionate about Italy. Peter shared some of the driving of his Austin Atlantic, registration MG 5 (if you please), a model that had been discontinued. It was a long, semi-sports car with two very wide doors, allowing easy access for back seat passengers and it attracted admiration wherever we went, especially from small boys. The destination was Venice although we were proposing to stay at an up-market resort bordering Jesolo. Our hotel was on the sands at Pineta di Jesolo, well away from the relentless vulgarity of its parent town. Martyn combined a love of Renaissance Italy with the relaxation (as he sees it) of a beach holiday. Peter, who was then a clerical assistant with a firm of undertakers, cared little for the cultural delights ahead but had one principal ambition – to become more deeply suntanned than any of his office colleagues. I was in a mood to get away from it all and happy to lie about reading in the sun for at least part of the time. Mavis enjoyed swimming and needed a rest; Jessica was less than six months old.

Martyn planned the holiday with expertise and enthusiasm, introducing me as a user to *Michelin* guides, which until then had only been items we sold at the shop in the summer. (I became addicted; the *Red* to France would be my Desert Island Discs' book choice, not that I've ever been asked to make one.) We crossed on the car ferry from Dover to Calais, lunching in the restaurant because Martyn believed in two main meals a day; which was as well because it was a long stint until dinner. Journeying through the centre of Brussels, partly by underpasses, we got little impression of a city about to be transformed into the architecturally repellent capital of the EU. Beyond it, we made for Monschau, a small German town in a gorge, renowned for the beauty of its setting. The hotel dining room was empty when we arrived but the instincts of a good innkeeper prevailed and we retired well fed to another new experience – the duvet.

Next morning because formidable mileage lay ahead, the drive down the Rhine to Augsburg was interrupted only by a hearty lunch. I had hoped to see Cologne Cathedral but there wasn't time to make a diversion; instead there were the numerous schlosses to see, high above us, on both sides of the river. We reached Augsburg – at one time a city dominated by the banking dynasties of the Fuggers and the Welsers – in time for a perambulation before dinner, but I cannot remember anything of it and I was not keeping a journal. The only fact I recall is that a second experience of the duvet put me off them for life.

On the following day we passed through Munich. Was it before or after that we saw a chilling sign – 'Dachau'? I was surprised that Peter didn't understand its significance. Martyn, quickly, quietly told him. That was the day we had lunch at Salzburg, where it rained heavily and where Martyn's admirable capacity for keeping everyone happy showed once again. We were all becoming travel weary; the weather was bleak.

This was not why we'd come.

Martyn found a restaurant and approved the menus. Drinks warmed us. Suddenly it was fun, even exciting, with our cheer-leader looking forward to crossing the Alps and wondering if the Grossglockner would be open. (If it weren't, what would we do? Use sledges?) The mountains positively called. Wasn't that, initially, one of the attractions for me of this holiday? But the magic didn't work as we climbed in low mist towards the little town of Fusch, where we booked in for our last night before Venice (Jesolo). It rained even more heavily. I lay awake anticipating certain disaster next day as we went 'over the top'. Mavis lay blissfully asleep. How tragic, I mused, that our little girls would be orphans in less than twenty-four hours. I was so moved I fell into a deep slumber.

We awoke to sunlight. By the time we approached the Grossglockner, which had been declared open, I was enchanted by the snow-laden mountains. Suddenly there was a delay; we were in a traffic snarl-up. Ahead men were clearing snow from the road to let us through. The strong sun was melting high banks of it which had been piled on to the road sides and causing mini-avalanches. We stopped for elevenses at a hotel, un-shuttered only that day, before descending, past Heilingenblut, boasting a church with an exquisitely thin spire, to Lienz which was suddenly spread out on a plain below us. There, seated for lunch at a table without shelter, I felt sunstroke was imminent. I became so 'squiffy' that for more than half a century I have believed we were at the more famous Linz.

As we approached Italy, somewhere near the ski resort of Cortina d'Ampezzo, in the Dolomites, Martyn suffered a personality change. He bellowed words such as '*magnifico*' and '*for-mi-da-bi-le*', with an occasional '*mama mia*', thrown in, assuring us that 'every butcher's boy in Italy whistles arias, mainly from Puccini, most of the time'. (In fact, we did not meet a single butcher's boy during our stay and if we had, I believe he would have been warbling *Ciao, Ciao Bambino*, the comparatively sober 'top of the pops' at the time.)

Martyn's reaction to being once more in his favourite country was exhilarating. He was having a good time; he wished us all to join in. Mavis and I did not totally succumb to the Italian 'experience' on this first trip, but we did later, and how could anyone not be overwhelmed by Venice?

First came Pineta di Jesolo and the Hotel Bellevue, set back from the sands amidst palms and shrubbery. It was modern and comfortable with Venice, according to Martyn, 'just down the road'. Only the cuisine failed it. There was one dinner at which Martyn referred to the excellent veal we'd enjoyed at lunch. Peter, a good foil to his partner, unwilling to accept too much fantasy, said, he hadn't had veal. I seconded him. We both insisted that fish had been served, an anonymous, tasteless white fish, but certainly not veal. Hard to disconcert, Martyn affirmed 'Well, anyhow it was delicious'. Peter and I pulled faces. The actual menu, composed in mangled English was more entertaining. It offered on one occasion, 'Boiled hen with mixte contours'; even Martyn, who didn't like to have 'his' hotel ridiculed, found that endearing. He has an immense capacity for enjoyment and for tolerating what others find lacking in excellence, but he always hopes everything will be marvellous and sometimes doesn't notice when it's not.

The route to Venice, via the appalling Jesolo with its high rise hotels and apartment blocks and 'English Pub', led to the Ponte Sapione (sixteen miles 'just down the road'). There we embarked on a passenger ferry which took us on to Venice (at least two sea miles), allowing us to enter, as all first-time visitors should, from the lagoon. Behind us was the Lido, ahead the dazzling magnificence of the incomparable city . . . the Doge's palace, the Schiavoni water front, with the San Marco Campanile rising over them. It is a sight which has never palled on me.

Sometimes we went to La Serenissima by road, passing through squalid Mestre to park by the entrance to the Grand Canal, where we were joined by Martyn's friends, Teddy and Nada Behrman. Teddy stood at the prow of the vaporetto and behaved in the most charmingly proprietorial manner as he named the various gorgeous palazzi we passed, Nada throwing in, 'That one's supposed to have been Desdemona's', pronouncing the name *a la* Verdi, not Shakespeare. We felt privileged. Then Teddy took us off down narrow streets, over little bridges to a ristorante where the scampi was superb. I had not eaten it before. It has never tasted so good.

On another evening we had seats in San Marco for an open air symphony concert played by a brass band. Beethoven's Seventh was the pièce de résistance; St Mark's is always magic. Every time I visit Venice I insist on having a table outside Quadri's or Florian's, and ordering a bottle of wine to be savoured while listening to the fine musicianship of the small combinations rivalling one another across the piazza.

Although I have come to prefer both Florentine and Sienese painting to Venetian, at the Accademia I took to Tiepolo and, at the Doge's palace, marvelled that each Tintoretto seemed more massive than the last. I was disappointed by the absence of Canalettos which I had supposed would dominate the city, though why should I have needed them when the major theme of his work was all around me?

We walked across the Bridge of Sighs, took a trip on a gondola, did all the correct things apart from going to the other islands for which there would have been time had we actually been staying in Venice. Martyn drove us to Padua where we saw the Scrovegni chapel with its Giotto murals and were allowed (unlike today) all the time we needed to gaze at them. We lunched alfresco on a noisy corner around which every youth in the city rode loudly whining Vespas. (We couldn't hear what they were whistling.)

On the return journey we made for Belfort where we stayed in an inexpensive hotel offering traditional, succulent cuisine and a dining-room we deemed 'vairry Frensh', its walls hung with every sort of clutter from old posters to live cats.

The last night was spent in Montmartre. Martyn drove with habitual skill along fairly traffic-free French roads with many bends – there were no motorways then – and I endured a form of car sickness for the only time in my life, leading me to lie under the car rug all the way to Paris. There during the night the car, parked outside the hotel, was raided and among the items stolen were toys we had bought in Venice for the children. This was sad, though worse damage was done to a small passenger window which had been, not smashed, but wholly removed and left on the pavement. As we drove towards the Channel, I tried to keep it in its correct position to stop a draught but gave up the fight and on arrival for lunch at Nouvion, a small town in Picardie, the usual group of small boys were surprised that, before getting out, I Elastoplasted the window into place. We then had another meal of a lifetime, despite the hostility of the owner's wife who announced that we couldn't have lunch because it was too late – after one-thirty! We persuaded her to serve drinks which she did with a bad grace. Then her husband appeared from the kitchen and greeted us with customary French politesse, asking the inevitable question, 'Vous-êtes Allemagne?' Mavis put him right, adding that it was a pity we couldn't eat at his restaurant.

'Pourquoi, madame?

'La femme a dit . . . .'

'Pouf!' He laughed. (La femme looked daggers.)

He then sat on our table to outline the three course meal he would provide. It was wholly delicious, ending with home-grown raspberries and cream. 'La femme', required to serve, continued her abuse to one and all, but began to enjoy the performance she was giving. She held her act together uncompromisingly right up to the moment we paid and took a warm leave of her husband.

The small boys gathered for our departure. Having taken my seat, and before Martyn turned on the ignition, I solemnly removed the small back window and placed it on my lap. Immediately the engine sprang to life and we drove off leaving behind a firm impression that this was the way to start an Austin Atlantic.

It was Martin Eve, an independent and far from affluent publisher, who suggested Grenoble. When he wasn't issuing far left books such as *The Socialist Register*, Martin indulged his passion for Stendhal, starting with a new translation of *Love*. It was easier for him to sell that to me than *The Socialist Register*, a worthy volume not much coveted by my customers. Grenoble was Stendhal territory, an interesting city in the French Alps, close to the Château of Chartreuse and to the Vercors which had been a centre of the resistance. We travelled by train, spending some time in Paris en route at a cheap and crummy hotel facing the Pantheon and eating well off the St Germaine, at Le Chope Danton recommended by another independent, more prosperous publisher Ernest Hecht. Its décor had evolved and grown mellow over decades, its bric-à-brac, like its cats, undisturbed, undusted but the steak-au-poivre would have seen off any spitefully inclined microbe.

Train travel between Victoria and the Gare du Nord was tolerable. Reservations were not then necessary; there were always available seats. From the Gare de Lyon south it was different. Arrive at the terminus on time and you were all right; boarding somewhere down the line meant standing in the corridors and squeezing against the windows as the food and drinks trolley was shoved past you. Train hopping featured, Ralph Abercrombie having recommended – 'If you like the look of somewhere get off and get another train next day.' We did this at Macon and Dijon, alighting at the first-named because it had been raining when the train stopped at the other. Inevitably, facing the station was a hotel; they are thus placed to trap the unwary. Hours later, after an enjoyable perambulation of Macon, with dinner beside the Saone, we returned for much needed rest only to be disturbed every few minutes of the night by express trains seemingly roaring through our room. I fantasised that northbound ones were rushing the wines of Burgundy to Paris and London while those going south contained the empties. Next day, at Lyon, we joined a Thomas-the-Tank-Engine style locomotive which groaned gently up towards Grenoble from where we spent days in the mountains having a picnic with strawberries on a Vercors hillside, a guided tour of the Chartreuse monastery and a visit to the distillery in Voiron where the monks' heady potions – the green even more highly spirited than the yellow – were concocted from age old secret recipes.

Dijon, where we broke the journey on the return trip, we liked even more than Grenoble, a handsome city with a notably good restaurant – Le Pré aux Clercs et trois Faisans – in the low crescent of buildings facing the palace of the Dukes of Burgundy. Our hotel there was quiet, comfortable and central but the following night we were back to the semi-squalor of the one near the Pantheon. We had balanced staying there with crossing the city to Montmartre and affording the Sanglier Bleu where we had dined so well with Martyn and Peter. It was an expensive meal which we didn't enjoy and, to assuage our guilt, next day we took the Metro to the Gare du Nord instead of piling our luggage into a cab.

The following year we were again in Dijon, having been driven there by George Depotex, then sales director of André Deutsch. Earlier in the year he had called on me at the bookshop. Over lunch I told him how Mavis had developed a yearning to visit Provence. In an unguarded moment he had said, 'Georgie and I will be driving down there to go to our favourite spot on the Riviera. André pays for the petrol, provided I call on customers in Paris on the way back.' 'You wouldn't like to give us a lift?' I suggested cheekily.

George was a very good-natured man and André approved of the trip. His boss looked favourably on High Hill as an outlet for his list. If George had any doubts they were overruled. Mercifully we all got on, although the Depotexes' requirements of a hotel were rather more basic than I would have wished. Mavis who could sleep on a plank did not complain, even at Arras. There in the Grand Place, the cobbled, splendidly restored Flanders-style square which is a delight to the eye but not the feet, we had a narrow bedroom with about three inches between the double bed and an overpowering armoire.

We left early in the morning. The Depotexes did not include sight-seeing en route as part of their holiday. They were anxious to reach the Med as soon as they could, allowing for the speed restriction imposed by Georgie. (Her real name is Georgette but she was always known to friends in the book trade as Georgie, which could be confusing.)

After Arras came Dijon, where we savoured the delights of Le Pré aux Clercs, then Arles where we stayed in the Place Lamartine, arriving in a heatwave. No, not a heatwave; it was normal Provençal weather for the time of the year. The sun shone unremittingly, the mosquitoes had one field night after another, the paving stones were scorched. The city fascinated us and, quite apart from the Roman ruins, gave us the unforgettable experience of waking one morning around 2 a.m. to see the Place swarming with sheep. This was the transhumance in action; the animals were being taken by train to the mountains for their summer pasture.

The Roman arena at Arles is formidable, and still in use for bull-fights, opera, what-have-you; the Roman theatre though vestigial, with two remaining pillars starkly upright and little else, is even more impressive. And there were the Alyscamp, the cathedral, several churches, all of which were to become familiar when I came to write a book about 'my' Provence.

At this time Mavis was the tour leader. It was too hot to remain in Arles all day so we went on coach excursions to the plateau of Les Baux, with its narrow streets and ruined castle, to Daudet's windmill, the abbey of Montmajour and on into the Camargue where the guide pointed to the egrets and other birds and where we lunched at the grotty, fly-blown, little walled town of Aigues-Mortes, the very name of which sounds like a fatal disease. There massive flies could not be prevented from sharing our lunch. On the way home we stopped for a mini bull fight in a corral just off the road. Standing safely behind a sturdy fence, teenagers baited the wretched bulls; it sickened me and I returned to the coach. It was all very well for Hemingway, Ken Tynan and others to intellectualise bull fighting because its crude drama appealed to them; I see it simply as extreme cruelty to animals.

The intense heat at Arles affected us, aggravated by too great an intake of wine. Feeling the need of sea breezes we took a train to the coast where at Bandol we made the dismaying discovery that we had lost our appetites. All I fancied was a lightly boiled egg and thin slices of brown bread and butter – delicacies unheard of in France. We lay low for two or three days, sitting on beaches, taking gentle walks until recovery was achieved by having a supper of well-cooked rump steak and not too much red wine. I have seldom felt more relieved. To be in France and not relish your food is dire.

We went inland again to Aix-en-Provence from where we took buses to Cezanne's Mont St Victoire and to a lakeside where we picnicked while a large French family, who had arrived by car, set up table and chairs for their long Sunday roast lunch. On to Avignon by coach to stay in a rundown hovel close to the Place d'Horloge, taking dinner alfresco while a mistral began to rage. Provence was growing on me. I blessed Mavis for having chosen it. To go by train to Nîmes we needed to cross the Rhone to Villeneuve-les-Avignon, the town on the right bank which was built during the Papal era to provide houses for cardinals and the like. At Nîmes we caught site of the amphitheatre (even larger than that at Arles) but of little else because our rail connection to Clermont Ferrand was imminent. A crowded train, on a narrow gauge, conveyed us on an almost idyllic journey up through the Massif Central. There was sufficient seating for all passengers, plus a smattering of livestock, moving at a gentle pace for about six hours during which the climate changed from the sultry heat of the plain to the fresh warmth of a summer evening. When we walked out to dine at Clermont Ferrand I donned a cardigan; at the restaurant I appreciated fully for the first time the dress code in France. Waiters and waitresses are all smartly, formally clad but the customers can wear whatever they like. There was no nonsense about ties and jackets for men. This welcome fashion had not yet reached Britain.

Come 1964, we set off to France and Italy in our own transport though I was not the driver. The company had bought 'Maud', Bunty Sharp's Ford Escort. It was at least five years old but in reasonable condition, so far as I could tell, but I knew nothing about cars and took her word for it. It never occurred to me to have lessons, take my test and drive it myself. Instead I asked Bunty if she would chauffeur us as part of her duties and we would pay her holiday expenses.

'Where are we going?'

'How about Rome?'

'Christ!' She replied, being a practising C of E worshipper.

I asked: did she think the car could stand up to going twice over the Alps? She supposed so, and it almost did. I planned a route, having rejected Bunty's proposed method of just pointing the car in the correct direction. We made no bookings except at Pisa where Peggy Bowyer was joining us. Otherwise, armed with *Michelin* guides, we set out to 'do' Italy. Probably at the back of my mind was a plan to get it all over with so far as that country was concerned, then I might not have to go there again.

Increasingly Maud, during the course of a three week expedition, began to show her age. In the latter stages keeping her on the road became the motoring equivalent of beating an old sheepdog. She did make it over the Alps, on the outward journey, but only thanks to a Belgian truck driver who towed us up the French side of the Mont Cenis pass when we had run out of petrol. On the return journey she flagged alarmingly. In a heat wave in Burgundy she broke down several times. We didn't attempt Rome, calling a halt in Tuscany. My comments on many of the places I visited are incorporated in *Next Time Round in Tuscany*. The first time began with lunch at Lucca where we drove through one of the narrow gates of the city and parked near the church of San Michèle with its exuberant frontage. Then came Pisa where we had rooms reserved at a hotel overlooked by the leaning tower, rooms of a seedy nature which were antechambers to the hotel office and had little by way of air or ventilation.

Pisa's exquisitely beautiful cathedral complex captured us at once; for me, it remains one of Europe's five-star delights. Asked to name a prime example of perfection I would have to instance this. It is amazing how the grass remains green around the three enchanting buildings. They are above and beyond contamination from the dozens of closely located stalls displaying shoddy merchandise of the lowest possible quality. Nothing can detract from the sheer beauty of cathedral, baptistery and tower. Seeing the tower by night against a starry sky was a magical experience that I have not had since, although I have returned to Pisa many times.

We were all jaded and feeling the heat. We wished to visit Florence but not to stay in the city centre. The management of the forbidding Pisan hotel provided the answer and phoned the Pensione Bencista high on the hillside beneath Fiesole. Nothing could have been better. We were welcomed by a plump lady who, although she was white, strongly reminded me of Ella Fitzgerald. The Signora spoke Italian, French, English and German fluently, changing from one language to another when required. We were given rooms with various views over Florence, or looking on to a semi-farmyard belonging to the hotel, a huge rambling villa managed in a notably individual manner by Signora Simoni and her husband. There were no locks on the doors of the bedrooms, which were not en-suite; dinner was served promptly at 7.30 p.m. every evening with no choice of menu. The proprietors joined the waitresses in serving the guests amid an uproar of gaiety, an incredible din of cutlery and china crashing on to bare tables and much scraping of chairs on stone floors. There was nothing to deaden the sound. Nobody minded. Enjoyment was paramount, with everyone bawling above the uproar. In contrast, anyone staying out late after dinner was requested to drive, not on to the gravel frontage of the pensione, but into an adjoining field and park with a minimum of door slamming.

From the Bencista, we went into Florence, to galleries and churches, up to Fiesole, to the Roman theatre and Franciscan priory and places beyond, to Settignano and names familiar from *A Room With a View*. Maud also chuntered us to Siena and San Gimignano. We didn't think much of Italian cuisine or wine but we were enthralled by most of what we saw.

On the return journey we stayed one night at Parma, with its rose red cathedral, then three on Lake Orta, at one end of a square where the noise increased as the night turned into the small hours. By day we sat beside the lake or went by boat to an island with an abbey exhibiting saintly relics. One evening when Bunty had become irritated by our constant complaints about Italian cuisine she ordered a 'gourmet' meal for us all. It wasn't very good.

Peg left us at Como to take a train home. Then we entered upon Maud's second fall from grace. She became incontinent. High up on a pass leading to Switzerland Bunty chugged into a narrow lay-by, unfenced against a sheer drop down the mountainside. A kindly Englishman stopped to see if he could assist. 'You know what you want?' he said. We didn't. 'White of egg, That will seal the radiator.'

'And do you have white of egg?' I asked witheringly. He had. And it worked.

We then wisely turned back towards Italy, placing the car and ourselves aboard a skeletal train to take us under the mountain and into Switzerland. As we crossed much of France, despite the fact that we were heading north, it became hotter and hotter. We gave up eating before sundown. Even at Dijon, where I had planned we should dine at Le Pré aux Clercs, none of us had an appetite until, at the moment of stepping across the threshold of that marvellous restaurant, the aromas emanating from the kitchen transformed our diminished condition. We ate with relish, savouring every mouthful. All was well with the world. And soon to get even better when, twelve months on, Maud was discarded in favour of a newer, larger vehicle, an estate car to be used for collecting books from publishers and delivering them to libraries and schools. The moment I saw it in the showroom at Vandervell's, Belsize Park, I knew I had to drive it.

Becoming car owners completely transformed our lives. To indulge our new obsession while continuing to earn a living it became necessary to diversify. I was assisted by an invitation, in 1967, from Graham C. Greene, of Jonathan Cape, to update and expand the history of publishing and bookselling, written by the recently deceased Frank A. Mumby, which had borne their imprint since 1930. Graham's initial proposal envisaged little beyond a straight revision encompassing changing ownerships of companies, current trends and correction of errors. I saw it differently. Familiar with a work I admired, I was aware that it almost wholly neglected the history of bookselling in the UK during the twentieth century and omitted mention of most technical, educational and specialist publishers while ignoring purveyors of romantic fiction, notably Mills and Boon. Graham was sympathetic to my view and gave me free rein. I had carte blanche not only to revise the work as I saw fit, rewriting the entire history from 1870 onwards, but also to drive my car around the UK calling on bookshops and publishers, to Frankfurt for the annual book fair and to the Booksellers' Association Conference at whatever venue it was held.

It became difficult to combine running an expanding business with a literary project which as I widened the terms of reference tended to get out of hand. Mavis was not always able to join in my travels. ('Where's Daddy?' Asked one of our daughters.' 'He's gone off on a Mumby', answered my wife.' 'What is a Mumby, Mummy?' . . . .I don't know how she replied but she must sometimes have wondered if it weren't a Bunbury.) What had begun as a highly stimulating second job took me to the edge of a nervous breakdown. I survived but it would have taken a perceptive psychiatrist to disentangle the motivation behind what I was doing. Which took precedence: recording the history of the book trade, managing the business providing our living, or satisfying a desire to drive as far and as often as possible?

During the writing of *Mumby* we went also to the Continent every year – not only to the Frankfurt Book fair which was an extra – but on actual holiday, to France, Benelux and Italy. Our daughters came too, also Mavis's mother, who kept the children entertained in the back of the car, regaling them with family sagas and sometimes singing little known Victorian ballads in a high soprano, while I drove on and on, promising to stop soon for the ritual picnic lunch. ('One-thirty is his drinking time,' Mavis would comment hopefully.)

We visited memorable places, we had lengthy picnics, the children were given the run of several beaches. It wasn't only the driving which absorbed me. I tried to keep my obsession within the limits of enjoyable family holidays and we did visit many entrancing places but in the early days of my new-found freedom we were too much on the road. This made Jessica irritable but she didn't tell us that it was because she felt queasy when being driven. Going over the Alps she sat with a rug over her head; she was frightened and we thought – I thought – she was just being difficult. All was well when we were settled near the sea for ten days on the Franco-Spanish border, then came the long haul back to a Channel port. On the last night when we had booked into a hotel in Normandy she asked to join me on a walk before dinner. We tramped across fields, she held my hand affection-ately, making observations about the countryside. The ordeal by car was almost over.

We developed a habit of spending the first night of the main holiday at The White Cliffs Hotel, Dover, which incorporated my grand-mother's sometime boarding house. This was partly to allow us to get well into France on the first full day's drive but also because it allowed us contact with my Dover relatives. Don, Edie, Aubrey and Jean (his second wife) would dine with us and toast us on our way. One year Don took Mavis for a ride along the sea front in his Rolls. He was the one who was most in touch with us. Once he was so impressed – because I had a book review in *The Daily Telegraph* – that he suggested I write a novel based on his life story; he forecast that it might sell as well as a Jeffrey Archer story. I declined but appreciated the com-pliment. In the same correspondence he enlarged on my grandfather's gnomic sayings, adding one that was inspired by the departure to Australia, from Tilbury, of close relations who emigrated. Apparently the old man would suddenly declaim, 'The women cried – The women howled – The captain bawled.' Possibly it made sense of the one I quoted in the first chapter – 'Three ships went down that very day.'

In the early years our destinations were solely in France. In 1968 student rioting meant we reached the Jura via Benelux, and that allowed us a day in Switzerland. Spain was out of the question because Franco still ruled, likewise Portugal had Salazar in command and Germany didn't appeal because of WWII. Greece, quite apart from the Generals, was just too far.

1966 was the first driving holiday en famille, when we were accompanied to Brittany by George and Valerie, stopping at Bayeux to look at the Tapestry and at Honfleur to visit the Boudin museum. During a week at Beg-Meil we were introduced to the various joys of seafood; the children coping heroically with lobster claws and mussels.

It was the Dordogne the following year. That was when we discovered Queyssac and took that region to our hearts. Then came the Jura (1968) and a trip over the Massif Central down on to the Cote de Roussillon, (1969) where at Canet Plage we almost committed mass murder. The Vent du Nord was the cause. To protect ourselves from wind and sand we hired a large beach umbrella which I thought I had fixed firmly. A sudden gust uprooted it, making it fly, vicious spike over multi-pronged sunshade, up the crowded beach to the promenade. Amazingly, no one was injured. I marched apologetically through the droves of holidaymakers to retrieve, and then return, it to the hire shop. Driving, I reflected, was a much safer pursuit than lying about on a Mediterranean plage.

For three years we travelled in the Vauxhall Victor but by 1969 I had switched to a Volvo and have remained with one ever since. We usually set off at what was then called the Whitsun bank holiday which meant the girls were away from school for only a week. In 1970 when I suggested Venice at the same time of year there were objections. I was appalled. I would have been so grateful to my parents had they taken me from school to go on holiday. Amanda and Jessica complained they would get behind with their work. Mavis took their side. I was distraught. Eventually I persuaded them that Venice was an education in itself; thus – though for the last time – we went at the end of May.

In Italy we again stayed in the Hotel Bellevue at Pineta di Jesolo. By the sea we built Lefratine, a grand sand city. I beachcombed for any item washed up for use in defining or decorating our city. Each evening it was vandalised, then all but washed away by the tide. Rebuilding became so obsessive that it was with some reluctance that we neglected our sand city to go into Venice. We went also to the islands of Burano, Murano and Torcello, the last named of which I would list in my top ten of Europe's most entrancing places. It was the original settlement in the lagoon – possibly by Attila the Hun – and is now little populated. There are a few memorable buildings and ruins, one hotel and restaurant, a farmhouse or two, on a small island which became tyrannised by the mosquito. The church stands starkly across a partly overgrown piazza; within are mosaics and statuary; the detail is infinite. Torcello represents a symbol of the wayward need to establish a centre of civilisation on unlikely terrain, in this case, on a marsh. It is beautiful in its simplicity and isolation, but has been insignificant in the growth of European civilisation over the last one thousand years.

A small motor boat delivered us onto a simple landing stage from which we walked up a narrow path beside an equally narrow canal to the little settlement. It was calmness incarnate. No bird sang, no reed so much as stirred, no butcher's boy would have dared to whistle Puccini. On Torcello you relax into the distant past, although you may, should you so wish, catch up with the present by taking a drink at the restaurant. Even there tranquillity rules. Set down your glass or cup gently. Make no sound; swallow, don't gulp.

Burano (glass), Murano (lace) are quite different. They are suburbs of Venice, reached by water but workmanlike, attractive in a minor key and, like their larger neighbour, car free, as were we for most of our time at Pineta. I was by now able to leave my vehicle for whole days without suffering withdrawal symptoms.

Until 2006 not a year was to go by without booking car ferries across the Channel, the Bay of Biscay or the North Sea. I became the planner with Mavis usually eager to go along with what I proposed, particularly when we envisaged a sabbatical together for five months, taking in many countries we had not previously visited. And I was always the driver. Although she became competent with her own car in the UK, until illness caused her to give up, she never drove abroad. She did though become a skilled navigator/map-reader, despite having so little actual sense of direction that when driving from the south coast, she always entered London via Putney Bridge and took signs to 'Hatfield and the North'.

Our last vacation as a family was, in 1972, to Scandinavia. Going south had for so long been our motivation that heading for the Baltic did not initially appeal to me. The very name Scandinavia was chilling but there were personal reasons for choosing it. Around 1946 Mavis's uncle Harry, serving on a Royal Navy minesweeper, had docked in an Oslo fjord where on a quayside he met a Norwegian who told him his niece wished to perfect her English.

'You need my sister,' advised Harry which was how Kari was put in touch with Louise who soon contrived to visit her in Oslo. Meanwhile my mother-in-law, at her home in St Leonards-on -Sea, had taken as paying guests a Swedish girl with whom she and her family formed a friendship which still continues. Ingrid, by then a student doctor, had returned several time since to the UK and had stayed with us at Hadley Wood for Christmas in 1969. Several times we had been urged to accept hospitality in Stockholm and the prospect of driving in three new countries soon attracted me as did meeting 'foreigners' in their homes. Louise was overjoyed. She was elderly, widowed and almost deaf and had not expected to visit any of her Scandinavian friends again; it offered a way of returning some of her kindness to us. (We crossed the North Sea to Esbjerg and there was relief in some quarters that I accepted an overnight car ferry and did not insist on driving through the Low Countries and Schleswig-Holstein to get there.)

One of the benefits of travelling in Scandinavia is that one does not have to pretend to speak any language but English which is widely spoken by the natives, even the ones who have not been abroad. Even Mavis did not attempt to learn the simplest words in Norwegian, Swedish or Danish. One of the disadvantages was the cost of almost everything. To mitigate this we took a great many tins of food for our picnics. At our first near Odense, I opened a can of pâté. On the label I read – 'Product of Denmark'.

At Odense we visited the Hans Andersen museum which has left little impression on me although I can see its exterior in my mind's eye. When you don't remember you don't but I do recall that Copenhagen, the first overnight stop, proved embarrassing. Our daughters were then aged thirteen and fourteen, my mother-in-law was seventy nine. Walking from our hotel to a restaurant we passed down a street where, in the windows of most buildings, were large signs in English advertising donkey sex and other perversions. Mavis and I exchanged looks; neither of us commented. It was easier to explain *The Little Mermaid*.

Driving in both Sweden and Norway I found tiresome. There were long, wide roads, covering vast distances and carrying little traffic. We had a powerful car but there was a maximum speed limit of 56 mph which it was irksome not to exceed. And, of course, I remained totally abstinent whilst on the road because you are liable to be breaking the law in Scandinavia if you so much as glance at a wine label. Also the scenery was generally unexciting. The saving grace was the warmth and hospitality of those whom we visited. In Stockholm, we stayed in the same block of flats where Ingrid was living. It towered above the city centre of which we had a stupendous view. Sunlight filled our room from about two in the morning onwards. Mavis slept undisturbed by it. In the evenings we took an overland suburban train to the home of Ingrid's parents for dinner. Mary, her mother, drove us around the city in the mornings and evenings, to the zoo, the royal palace etc.; Charles, her father, told us of life during WWII when Sweden was neutral but suffered similar shortages to those we had endured. They were good, kind souls who welcomed us again twelve years later when I reacted more positively to Stockholm.

It was unusually hot that July of 1972 with much better weather than we had experienced in England. On the way to Stockholm we stayed at Jongkoping where by some error (there was no *Michelin*) we had booked at a hotel which was dry without being officially temperance. It was not possible to be served even a bottle of beer. The manager made a pretence of searching for one but clearly disapproved of alcohol. At Karlstad, on the way to Norway, there seemed to be absolutely nothing to do after supper but walk around a vast park with a lake. I remember it as an unnaturally clean and tidy town with so much uninhabited space that each person there seemed to have a whole street to themselves. And Mavis and I were given twin beds head to toe, not side by side, which was unfriendly. Jongkoping and Karlstad were altogether too sanitised for my taste, although they gave me some insight into the plays of Strindberg. (Ho-ho!) Also we were without native company. Ingrid did not rejoin us until we reached the southern, Gulf-Stream stroked coast.

Entering Norway, we encountered the first small signs of tattiness. Many lorries queued at the frontier; there was just a hint of squalor. I tried to imagine, behind prim, curtained windows, Ibsenish interiors wracked with guilt and intrigue, with women screaming to be let out. We passed over a bridge and watched logs being swept along on the current. Somehow I had expected they would have been marshalled into military ranks but they floated chaotically. I liked that.

Kari and Per Owing, with their three children, lived in a light, modern house at a small town in woods outside Oslo. Louise and the girls stayed with them. Mavis and I had student accommodation at the university. Kari fed us lavishly, Per, a solicitor, took time off work to drive us to the ski runs, the fjord where the *Kon-Tiki* was docked and the park where the grotesque Vigeland sculptures dominated all views. (The occupying Germans had liked them enormously, Per told us; so did Louise.) We saw the Munchs in the national gallery and way out contemporary art at the Sonja Heine museum on the outskirts of the city. The Owings shielded us from the high cost of living but we were able to reciprocate in some degree when they subsequently came to London.

We drove back to Sweden to Bastad, a holiday resort on the Kattegat, where we were joined by Ingrid at a homely hotel. At nearby Holmstad, there was a prominent Picasso looking rather out of place. More time was spent by the sea where I immersed myself not in the water but in reading or in talking to Ingrid. Whenever we met she sought advice about which English novelists to read. I, to my shame, knew of no Swedish author but Strindberg and a contemporary dramatist whose name I couldn't recall.

The last full day of that holiday was the most exciting. When we left Bastad there was a distance to Esbjerg and the car ferry of about two hundred and twenty miles. We had nine hours in which to reach the Danish port, all on good roads. But I had not allowed for the ferries. The first from Gothenburg to Helsingbor, close to Elsinore, did not delay us much; the other, in mid-most Denmark, did. There were no reservations. We joined a lengthy queue for the one boat with a small car deck which plied across a short stretch of water. We waited three hours for our turn, leaving us only another two for the final hundred miles. And there was no motorway. I took a salutary doze while on the ferry, then drove westward at a ferocious pace. There was no speed limit in Denmark at that time . . . or so I was told. I found the experience wholly exhilarating. By the time we were halfway to Esbjerg I knew we would make it but dared not say so. We arrived within minutes of the car decks being sealed, then marched into the bar to celebrate as the ferry moved out of the harbour.

We also got to know our own country better, from the rat runs of greater London to the byways of provincial England. I ought to feel repentant, writing in 2008, because of the effects of the motor vehicle on society and for my share in it, but I tend to balance the benefits and disadvantages. We resent attempts by national and local government to curb us but having a car for the last forty plus years has brought me a freedom I did not know before, and one that I have gained without recourse to the airways. About them I can and do have a holier than thou attitude because I never – but never – fly. Nor have I used the London tube for more than three decades because I cannot bear the thought of being trapped in it. Yet I have taken the Eurostar many times – always with a flask of brandy in my pocket – so my argument is irrational. And my objection to air travel is totally personal. It frightens me. So why doesn't exceeding the limit on a French autoroute and letting the needle go beyond a hundred mph have a similar effect? It could have something to do with the fact that, in my car, I am in control but it doesn't explain my relaxed state when being whisked by a TGV train at a 150 mph, or whatever, or why I am not alarmed when the vessel I am aboard, ocean going liner or small craft, is lurching about on the Channel. My argument about always liking to be able to get off or out of a conveyance is spurious. Even so, *I do not fly* and I hate knowing that anyone I care about is flying whereas almost everyone I know is in peril on the roads every day.

In the forty years since I became licensed I have driven 145,000 miles in Europe and many more in the UK. It has enriched my life; I hope it hasn't done irreparable harm to others although I can already see, in my mind's eye, Green Peace and other banners held aloft by those marching against me. (Where have they their parked *their* cars, I'd like to know?)

With the car I am in a similar position to that of the unrepentant cigarette smoker. (In 1976, I gave up smoking; in 2008 I am still enjoying my car.) I approve on the whole of the legislation against smoking although I feel sorry for addicts, of whom I was never one. I accept the restrictions on driving and am law abiding about them. I even approve of them. But I still take my car to wherever I am allowed. And that is why this chapter is a celebration of my forty years of doing so legally . . . for 99% of the time.

## 10

## Trade Associations and the Pretenders' Cricket Club

Despite having correctly democratic leanings I do not find it easy to be on a committee of more than one.

I had attended scarcely more than a couple of meetings of the London branch of the Booksellers' Association before I was co-opted on to the committee; no doubt some person desperate to get off it had seen me as ripe material. Very soon I became Secretary, a role I tolerated for two years before contriving to dispose of it to John Prime of Collet's, the so-called communist chain founded by Eva Reckitt, the daughter of a Hull millionaire. If I had continued as Secretary it would swiftly have become my turn to be Chairman and to run the risk of being elected to the Council of the Association. This met monthly and climaxed in an orgy of resolutions and working parties at the annual conference, an event regarded as the highlight of the year by many booksellers and their wives. Publishers, who were present by invitation only, didn't have a conference of their own but were, with their wives, an important element in ours which lasted from Friday until Monday, plus another two days spent travelling to and from a resort in some far-flung locality of the UK. It was never held in London because most of those attending it worked there. It was particularly useful for publishers' sales directors wishing to encounter their out of town customers socially. The occasion utterly belied the state of penury which most booksellers claimed to endure. They, along with publishers, attended in their ever more luxurious cars, fortunes were spent at the bars and several days of meetings culminated in a black tie banquet which was addressed by an eminent author and by the presidents of both trade associations. The most interesting encounters always seemed to occur late in the evening so that one stayed up half the night drinking and talking. I went to four conferences in a row, enjoyed the company, opted out of the tedious business meetings, during which I might take a publisher's wife out for a tour of the surrounding countryside, and found the extended weekend so exhausting, that I settled instead for longer holidays with Mavis. After 1959 I attended only three others over the next twenty years. The last was at Torquay where my presence was required because I had written a paper for discussion by various 'working' groups. Biographer Philip Ziegler, then an editor at Collins, and I had been asked to provide theses on fiction, with recommendations for improving its saleability. On the third day, when the groups had completed their deliberations, there was a session we had to attend to hear their comments. All of half an hour was allowed for this but at once discussion deteriorated into a squabble about discounts. From this there arose the vexed subject of returns of unsold copies. Philip and I were scarcely noticed on the platform; few questions were addressed to us. When one bookseller delegate complained bitterly that many publishers operated a policy of refusing to take back single copies for credit and asked what could be done about this mean-spiritedness, I caught the Chairman's eye and dived in. 'Simple,' I said, 'You order two more and request to return three.' I got the loudest laugh of my life; André Deutsch, who had been looking anguishedly bored, let out a loud guffaw and all but fell off his chair. There was no further debate. We retired to the bar. And that really sums up my views on conferences.

I felt some guilt about this negative attitude to the Booksellers Association affairs because I liked its director, Gerry Davies, and appreciated that trade associations had a role to play. I attempted to salve my conscience by supporting other worthy bodies, serving on two committees for long periods.

In my first days as a bookseller Martyn Goff had enthused me about the National Book League which enjoyed a renaissance after 1945 under John Hadfield, an editor, anthologist and novelist. It was a part of the brave new post-war world, aiming at bringing more literature to more people and particularly to the young and unwashed. It occupied handsome offices in Albemarle Street, Mayfair, and worked zealously to achieve its objectives. Alan Steele, a firm supporter, sat on its executive committee. He thought I should join him although Mavis warned: 'He'll wreck it. He'll point out all its shortcomings, then it will wither away. He won't mean it to but that's what will happen.' Such was her faith in me.

The finances of the League were chronically unstable. A few

publishers supported it generously; most did not. Scarcely any book-sellers donated more than a paltry annual sum; a dwindling number of private members remained. The restaurant ran at a loss; there was a large overdraft at the bank. I attended meetings over several years, coming away from them feeling that I had been in a fantasy world. By then the Director was Jack Morpurgo, historian, sometime academic and former editor at Penguin. Jack worked hard liaising with government departments, hosting numerous functions at Albemarle Street and generally proselytising on behalf of books but he wasn't a fund raiser, didn't suffer fools and had prickly relations with many publishers. After a while I found attending executive meetings unrewarding and embarrassing. There seemed little point in suggesting new projects because there were no funds. I didn't actually resign but lapsed until the appointment, several years on, of Jack's successor.

I was more enthusiastic about being secretary to the Society of Bookmen which had been formed in 1921 at the instigation of the novelist Hugh Walpole; its objects were, and are, to 'promote and extend the use of books by the cooperation of all concerned in their creation, production and distribution, and to discuss and initiate developments for the good of the book trade.' Election has always been by a simple ballot, rubber stamping the recommendations of the committee. The President, when I joined, was Sir Stanley Unwin, one of the few remaining original members, the Treasurer was Alan Steele, while George Kamm of Pan Books (he who had accosted me about the Alfred Wilson unpaid account) was still Secretary.

The Society attracted as speakers, not only leading book trade luminaries, but writers, politicians, academics and people of achievement in most professions and callings. They did not receive a fee. It was considered as much an honour for them to speak to the Society as for members to have the opportunity of hearing them. This was before television had intruded into every living room and placed us all on one way nodding terms with the famous.

The Bookmen was a sounding board for ideas; at its early meetings, Book Tokens and the National Book Council/League, were first mooted. Since then the Publishers Association and the Booksellers' Association have extended their secretariats and marginalised the raison d'être of the Society, but without affecting its prestige. Well into the seventies at least most of those elected still felt themselves hugely honoured.

The Bookmen was run by its three executive officers, with Sir Stanley giving his seal of approval to anything contentious. In those days members were not asked to join the committee for three year stints, they were detailed to do so. It was rather like going on fatigues in the services. They had to do little more than nod assent to what the officers proposed, a classic *Yes, Minister* situation. When I was press-ganged in 1960, not then understanding the system, I mistakenly felt I had 'arrived'. I didn't know that George Kamm, having been thirteen years as secretary, was looking for a successor. He appointed me his assistant, instructing me in the ways of running the dinners, delegating various duties and observing, eagle-like, to ensure I carried them out to his satisfaction. I had scarcely passed muster when George died suddenly and I became secretary rather sooner than expected to the alarm of the incoming chairman, Robert Lusty. He, now managing director of the Hutchinson group, had noted statements made by me to the trade press and heard my comments at Bookmen dinners. He was inclined, so I heard, to rank me with the then fashionable 'angry young men'. I confided this to a Scottish bookseller friend, Ross Higgins, who deflated me by saying, 'you're too old to be an angry young man' (I was thirty-four). Bob had very willingly agreed to succeed Philip Unwin at a time when he expected to be working with George Kamm. He was unaware that I was equally alarmed, because the great Mr Lusty, much quoted in the national press and said to be one of the highest paid of publishers, with a chauffeur-driven Bentley, was not one of my drinking pals. I thought of him as reserved, even a little arrogant, a very cardinal of the publishing establishment.

This eminent dignitary invited me to lunch at The Garrick, where I had been only about twice in my life. In the bar we took to each other instantly and were soon deep into the business of suggesting likely candidates for the Society. For the next thirty years we exchanged hundreds of letters, occasionally acrimonious, usually packed with comment and gossip, on mutual acquaintances and trade affairs. We worked well together. I correctly deferred to his seniority but also spoke my mind. He, like myself, had started his working life as an unpaid newspaper reporter. Now not only a senior publisher, and a governor of the BBC, he knew everyone. Long before my appointment he had begun planning speakers for his three year stint as Chairman. They included the esteemed American publisher Alfred Knopf, J. B. Priestley, two women speakers (although he opposed women membership) – Christina Foyle, an old friend of his, and Marghanita Laski – Dr Ramsay, Archbishop of Canterbury and the Duke of Edinburgh. I suggested he should go for a young man called Jack Straw, then an extremely rebellious leader of the National Union of Students and invite him to debate with Prince Charles. He rejected that but agreed we should be addressed by publisher's rep, Reg Dignum, of Gollancz, who gave us good value.

What Reg, the Archbishop, the Prince, or anyone else said to the Society I must not reveal because it is a rule, protecting confidentiality, that everything uttered by speaker, or from the floor, goes unreported and unrecorded. I can reveal though that in a private conversation with the Archbishop during dinner we talked of censorship and he said he was against it in principle. 'I wish you would say that in public,' I replied. He smiled benignly, making no comment.

Even if I wished to break the rule I could not set down what else Michael Ramsay said that evening as I don't remember, nor could I quote Prince Philip because I excused myself from that meeting. This was not due to my lifelong republican convictions – I could manage to be civil if I met a member of the royal family – but because Bob went back on what was supposed to be an invitation from the Duke to attend 'an ordinary meeting'. It wasn't. At drinks before the meal at Kettner's, in Soho, where we then held meetings, the royal personage was programmed to meet only the officers and members of the committee (ten of us) while, after dinner, his speech was not to be followed by the customary debate. I could not tolerate the prospect of my friends kowtowing to royalty and preferred to be absent, Alan Steele kindly doing me another service, acting as secretary for the evening.

Robert Lusty was a clear-minded managing director who rationalised the numerous imprints which Walter Hutchinson had acquired over several decades. Hutchinson had been a capricious, often harsh, employer who gave up dating publications and who made no attempt to give his lists their own individuality. Indeed, any two or more might issue a book on the same MCC cricket tour at the same time. Bob changed all that. Sport became the province of Stanley Paul, romance of Hurst & Blackett, what we would now call, mind, body and soul, of Rider, and so forth, with Hutchinson itself retained for major general works and particularly prestigious authors such as Arthur Koestler. I never heard Lusty's praises sung as an editor or as a discoverer of talent; it was not said of him that 'he had a publisher's nose'. Yet, despite apparent bashfulness, he did not deflect the spotlight of publicity when it shone on him. He seemed more inclined to court it and for many years he was the most frequently quoted of publishers. This may have been due partly to his status at the BBC Certainly, even before the death of Stanley Unwin, he had assumed the role of unofficial spokesman for the Book Trade.

Bob Lusty was a tall, black-haired man with a rugged face, which with age came to resemble that of a St Bernard dog. From childhood he was partially deaf and though he spoke in a low, rich choke from the back of his throat, he was not too difficult to understand; he did not mumble. He had a need to be heard in public, composed his speeches with meticulous forethought, many a literary flourish and much humour but, immediately before delivery, suffered severe stage fright, a not unusual manifestation erroneously confused with shyness.

At Michael Joseph's, except during the war when he held the fort, Lusty was editorially overshadowed by the owner; there was also Charles Pick, whom he loved not, in the wings and, as it were, waving at the audience. Bob needed the opportunity provided by Hutchinson's as much as that conglomeration of imprints required someone to organise it.

In more than thirty years of friendship we had a few differences but he having been brought up as a Quaker was always forgiving. When my revision of Mumby's history of the book trade was published in 1974, Bob wrote a long, on the whole favourable review, with one wrong assertion. I had taken trouble to acknowledge everyone who had helped me, listing them alphabetically in the prelims. Bob wrote that he could not recall having given assistance (which he had) and suggested I was seeking reflected glory by thanking so many of the great and the good. I was probably still smarting from this when, reviewing his autobiography, *Bound to be Read*, published the following year, I accused him of name-dropping. He was furious. The charge was the worst I could possibly have made; he would rather have been called anything but that. What, I retorted, worse than murderer, sexual pervert, pyromaniac etc.? As always it blew over. (And I was not a Quaker.) Once I embarrassed him by ghosting the autobiography of an English cricketer for his Stanley Paul imprint. Shortly after publication I asked to have his chauffeur drop him in Hampstead High Street one evening. (By then he was living with Babs, his second wife, in the Suburb.) We went to The King of Bohemia where I told him that earlier in the week, on the Monday of the Lord's test, with the ground full and 'the author' playing for England, his book was not on sale at the bookstalls. Bob took in the complaint and looked mildly embarrassed. This was not due to being told of the incompetence of the Hutchinson distribution machine but because I had revealed myself as a ghost for one of his imprints. Ghosts were below-stairs people. He never thereafter referred to the incident; I returned to the shop feeling I had committed a faux pas.

Robert Lusty, a warm-hearted friendly man, had his detractors. There was a period while he was head of Hutchinson when the company's bottom line was not healthy. He told Alan Steele, 'my masters' (the printer-owners) 'hate me and I don't like them but it would be too expensive for them to fire me. I have a watertight contract.' Matters eased when he was knighted (for services to the BBC, not for publishing), an award which changed the attitude of 'his masters'.

As chairman of the Bookmen, Bob was succeeded by Alan Hill, a brilliantly innovative educational publisher of worldwide renown. (To date my brief life in *M & F* is his only biography.) Alan and Bob, who published for different markets, had in common membership of the Bookmen and the Garrick, and residence in the Hampstead Garden Suburb.

Alan's speakers for the Society, included the fiercely anti-immigration Tory MP, Enoch Powell, who wittily savaged the Net Book Agreement when he spoke to us and, from the opposition benches, Michael Foot who had just become a Hampstead resident. Michael gave a brilliant, but for a politician unusually short, speech. When he sat down Philip Unwin made the inspired suggestion that he should tell us of his experiences of working for Lord Beaverbrook. This led to a fascinating, off-the-cuff, character sketch of the newspaper baron. It was on such occasions that one felt membership of the Bookmen was a privilege.

In the early sixties, my life time interest in theatre flagged. Playgoing, because of the need for child-sitters, became a monthly, even quarterly, pastime and I had given up writing for revue. Mavis and I made occasional visits to Stratford but no longer had direct contact with Mountview, although remaining friendly with some we had known there. And we had moved into a lasting phase of our life of enjoying above all spending many evenings together talking, eating, drinking; we had become closer friends than ever before.

Mavis remained involved with Labour party matters and was studying for a French honours degree; I had two novels published and wrote the above-mentioned life of a test cricketer. This latter came about when Desmond Elliott, agent and publisher, asked Ernest Hecht to recommend someone to ghost the memoirs of an England spin bowler whose talents as an all rounder I much admired. Protocol demands – if it still does – that a ghost goes along with the pretence that the book proclaiming itself an autobiography has actually been written by the person whose name is on the title page. Even forty-five years later I feel restrained from revealing whose life it was although at the time all his colleagues and many of my friends knew. I will call him Ted Somers. I fell into a routine of meeting him at Lord's at the end of a day's play, chatting with him and other county players in a pub in St John's Wood, then driving home with him to have a meal and a recording session. Ted was an amiable man. He did not think cricket or sport all the time and seemed to enjoy meeting Mavis and having supper with the family before we got down to work. After each session during which he talked fluently, airing his opinions lucidly, I turned the tape recording we had made into a chapter. Once I failed to switch on the machine – technology and I habitually have misunderstandings – and needed to remember it all. It didn't make an exciting book. There was little meat because Ted was not permitted, by contract with his county team, to make controversial judgements on those who ruled it, on the MCC or his fellow players. I clung desperately to the view that devoted supporters of cricket are quite accustomed to being bored for days on end and that there were fanatics who bought every cricket book. One reviewer wrote that he had Ted's personal assurance that every single word was his own. Ted may well have believed that; he probably hadn't understood how much editing had been necessary. My idol Denis Compton was supposed to write a foreword. Finished copies proclaimed he had but the actual pages allocated to it were blank. He had promised and really intended to do so but never got around to it. As the copy deadline neared I called him and he assured me it would soon be in the post. I suggested I might write it for him, since I had written the rest of the book, but he wouldn't hear of it. On the only occasion I met him, decades later, he apologised, seeming genuinely upset when Mavis chided him for letting Ted down.

Publisher Ernest Hecht was not only part of a group of truants from work who regularly met at Lord's, he had also become one of the

Pretenders whose pretensions had been enhanced by Jack Cooper organising it into a team with a fixture list. The game was still supposedly played with overall levity but I had noted an attitude of deep seriousness entering more and more into the approach of those participating. Ernest, who was very nearly as unskilled as myself as a cricketer, had for some reason been promoted to become an opening batsman. He, with John Matthews, who was actually a very competent player, set off for the crease with a look of grim determination. He seldom stayed there for long. As for Jack, I knew that the spirit with which we had started the club was passing him by, when one evening in The Rosslyn Arms, he began to explain to me the theory behind his brand of leg spin bowling. Too late I said, 'Jack, I don't think of you as any sort of bowler at all.' He went on imperviously and lo, the very next week, he took several wickets. I put this down to his extraordinary action. Following a brief run up he sent the ball in a high trajectory towards an amazed batsman who became transfixed as it slowly, slowly, slowly descended. And the better the batsman the more likely it was to get him out which, when Jack was accurate, it sometimes did. To further emphasise his devotion to the game, in the winter Jack organised practice evenings at the Middlesex County Cricket School in Finchley. I was being outclassed. I remained captain although I still hadn't acquired boots. When we came to play Harrow Town 2nd XI, on their home ground, I felt ridiculous and resigned my office in mid-game, handing over to Matt Jackson whose bowling had won my team victory in that first match on Parliament Hill.

Soon I ceased playing but occasionally umpired. This didn't work either. When ennui overtook me due to the laborious way the game was going I tended to shout, 'No ball!' or to allow lbw appeals just in order to get a new face at the wicket.

I did stay on as Chairman for the annual committee meeting and the yearly dinner both of which I enjoyed more than any of the actual cricket matches. The committee consisted of seven, later eight, members who evolved as an oligarchy. They were John Ford, who had proposed the name of the club, John Matthews, Matt Jackson, Charles Cregor and I (all of Mountview Theatre Club) who had taken part in the original fixture, Jack Cooper and David Harrison, the publishing friend first encountered when he called as a rep at Jackson's, and later Ernest Hecht. An annual meeting was held in our Finchley house on a winter evening at which the main business was mostly a matter of determining who could raise the loudest laugh. Mavis was often present, when she wasn't making sandwiches for us, and she was appointed chair of the cap subcommittee after we had chosen the official colours of the club – grey and red. Jack made some attempt at keeping to an agenda, there were pauses in the gagging while we agreed subscription fees and other vital matters but overall these meetings provided some of the funniest evenings of my life. They were equalled only by the annual dinner, held at various addresses – Fleet Street, Hampstead, Soho – at which speakers were expected to perform as stand-up comics, being heckled fiercely throughout. It was necessary to raise a laugh once every ten seconds to be allowed to proceed without persistent uproar.

Jack Cooper recruited players from the Hampstead Labour party and from contacts in journalism, who included two Aussies and a future Indian statesman. He arranged an annual fixture against *Tribune*, the left wing weekly edited by Richard Clements, members of whose team sometimes turned out for us. Michael Foot, a founder and former editor of *Tribune*, was once in Dick's side. He appeared on the field immaculately dressed, not in his notorious donkey jacket but wearing brown corduroy trousers and a grey shirt. Dick placed him on the boundary where, while his wife's dog yapped about his ankles, he took a magnificent catch off a ball that was going for six.

On Sunday evenings following a match Mavis, forbearing as ever, often cooked for temporarily wifeless members and for Ernest Hecht, who occasionally employed her as a reader.

Ernest had a true nose for the book which was right for his Souvenir Press, yet the huge success of *The Trachtenberg System of Mathematics* may have surprised even him. He never ceased boasting about it, at every match asking, 'Do you know how many *Trachtenberg* we've sold?' He was made to pay for it; at the next annual dinner of the Pretenders I pressurised him to buy cognac for all those present. I first met him at an annual dinner of the Book Publishers' Representatives Association, a bibulous occasion celebrated at the Freemasons' august headquarters in Great Queen Street, Holborn. It was the custom of reps to invite bookseller-customers, publishing associates and others to the yearly piss-up. Ernest and I were at the same table and from the start exchanged good humoured insults, which has been part of the pattern of our relationship for nearly half a century. Twice a year we lunch one another extravagantly. He calls me 'the two bottle man' because one doesn't satisfy my needs; sometimes we have a third. We savour each other's prejudices, enjoy each other's company. At his offices, a virtual slum, opposite the British Museum, he chooses books which sell. Ernest has flair; Ernest survives. He is not just self-assertive about his achievements, he brags, quoting waterfalls of figures, about the size of reprints and the acclaim given to his enterprise by eminent critics. And every few years, as a sort of Thanksgiving, he hires The Bloomsbury Theatre, and the services of an international star, for a champagne evening which lasts long after the final applause. His survival for over fifty years as an independent general publisher is a remarkable achievement, especially as he still does not admit to being more than forty-nine.

Jack Cooper was the last of us to retire from the field when he was well into his sixties but thereafter the Pretenders became a even more serious contributor to Sunday cricket, though not lacking in humour. The club now has a web site and e-mail, an imposing fixture list and goes on tour. I attended the 50th anniversary dinner at the Royal Commonwealth Society in October 2006, with Leslie Cramphorn, another ex-book trade captain. When I spoke, with John Matthews, and Matt Jackson also present, I wasn't heckled as much as in former times but Mavis would have been very chuffed could she have known that the ragtag and bobtail team for which she had been the inspiration had survived for half a century. Jack Cooper who assured this had died two years after her.

Once Jack Cooper had taken the Pretenders under his care its unofficial home became The Rosslyn Arms in Hampstead where Henry Martin, supported by Sheila, his wife, was landlord. The Rosslyn was Jack's local long before he became official candidate for Labour in the 1964 election; it often seethed with his friends and associates. In a way the pub was so basic that, although there wasn't actually sawdust on the floor, it bore some resemblance to a typical constituency Labour Party headquarters. Jack wrote a profile of it for *The Heathside Book* which I published, praising its down-to-earthness and the friendly, no-nonsense approach of its landlord. Henry had to be heavily provoked before banning anyone from his two bars but when he did so it was for life. He became a Pretender, taking welcome breaks from being a publican which, as a tenant, was a seven day a week task. Sheila often came along to watch, subsequently becoming our scorer.

After the early years of High Hill I was only regularly at the counter on Saturdays, a day which I relished, the busiest of the week when we sold vast quantities of books and when the shop became a popular meeting place, often giving it the same buzz you hear in the interval of a play which the audience is enjoying. Some customers were publishers who were local residents but that didn't stop them from making purchases at full price, when we weren't exchanging the latest trade gossip. Saturday was only ever my day off when we were on holiday or if there was a family wedding. Saturday was fun. A day or, as it became, 'days' off during the week had many advantages; for one thing it meant we didn't have to spend weekends in other people's houses.

The mid-sixties stretched us in terms of staff. It was a time of full employment when retailers requiring rather more than just a pair of hands found it difficult to compete in salary and benefits with black-collar jobs and industry. The situation was not improved by the fact that I was spending much time writing, reviewing, publishing, being secretary of the Society of Bookmen, enjoying my marriage and family and becoming as besotted as Mr Toad by my new motor car.

Monica was a pillar in the shop, taking charge of the children's department and Ralph was splendid, when he wasn't having a break-down. Looking back I can see I was doing too much but until the end of the decade it didn't take its toll of me. By then fortunately we had engaged Doreen Gotch who joined us in 1968. I had known her socially and as a customer for some years. Earlier, when her marriage foundered, I had approached her on the recommendation of Dave Mindline. She had liked the idea but her teenage children begged her not to forego the security of working for Camden Council. When, two years on, Doreen invited us to dinner, along with Barbara Hosking, Mavis's ex-Transport House colleague, she asked if my offer was still open.

Barbara had already told us that Doreen was the kind of person who without actually taking over would make herself indispensable. It was a typically shrewd assessment. Doreen had quiet manners and a beautiful speaking voice that would have been the envy of many actresses in those days before they all had to talk in estuary English. She firmly identified with whatever organisation employed her and eased herself into High Hill, mostly in the office, sometimes in the shop, learning the routine, noting all methods in use, getting to understand our whole function. A few months after her arrival I at last found a deputy managing director in John Ford, my sometime colleague at William Jackson's in the fifties, and fellow Pretender. Doreen worked closely with him to evolve a system which the business urgently required. Until then far too much of what occurred was in my head, or in Monica's. Doreen, with John's backing and authority, created a new order of simple, easily comprehensible efficiency. She became acquainted with publishers. Not the same ones who lunched me or who I met at parties but those in the trade departments who could influence speedy delivery. During the fifteen years she was with us she cemented goodwill while chivvying publishers and wholesalers for urgently needed books. She also became our unofficial Personnel Officer, a natural at providing a shoulder on which to weep. Most of the staff shared their problems with her. She was understanding, realistic, saw their viewpoint but also took into account the needs of the business. After some years, we elected her to the board, not in the casual way in which so many are made directors just to give them a little kudos – like handing out a CBE – but because we knew she would actually direct. She took the appointment seriously, having a natural authority which her new status enhanced and everyone was pleased. One of the tasks she took over from John, who had inherited it from me, was that of engaging the middle rank and junior staff. Neither of us had been effective in this role. I allowed initial judgements to prevail too much while John, if he couldn't see any blatantly obvious reason why an applicant should not be accepted, offered the job out of a spirit of fairness to the first comer. He was very happy for Doreen to assume this portfolio which led to a number of intelligent, personable and eager-to-work young people joining us.

The combination of John and Doreen added stability to the organis-ation. John and I had only one major row in the next twenty years although there were disagreements on minor matters. Doreen and I never exchanged a cross word which did not signify that she bowed down to me all the time; she was just extraordinarily tactful.

John had a particularly useful asset in being 'our man at the Book-sellers' Association'. He was already on the Council when he came to us and it was agreed that he and Sylvia should continue to attend the annual conference. I urged him to become President, which sounds presumptuous but the office was open to almost anyone willing to accept it. He refused to put himself forward but was serious about his membership on the Council, keeping the peace between the

Association and me. John's other duties, apart from administrative, were with the library and school accounts, although he was nominally in charge of paperbacks but we were too small to have a rigid structure and no sleep was lost about this. One appointment though was his and his alone. He was the Fire Officer.

Because we occupied three linked properties only one of which we owned ourselves, and because these properties were rambling nineteenth-century additions to others in part much older, we are talking of buildings with many different levels, passages and staircases, and also of tenants in offices and flats. It took well over twelve years for us to get a Fire Certificate. Permitted to continue trading, we were regularly inspected by officials of the fire brigade who made demands which were amended or countermanded by their successors. John saw the retirement of no less than three of them before we were finally declared fit to receive a certificate. There were those officials, determined to be difficult, who loved to wield power and were quick to take offence. They were 'little Hitlers' and it became essential for our survival that John, easygoing and diplomatic, should deal with them. On one occasion, John, for once blowing his top, demanded, 'How did I get landed with this?' I told him it was all part of the infinite variety implicit with being a bookseller.

Two long term appointments, from c. 1970, were Irene Anderson and Veronica Whatley. Irene, an Ulsterwoman with one daughter, eventually became buyer for the paperback shop and was with us until the end. She made friendly links with the reps and also with Pipeline, the paperback wholesaler for London, on whom we came to depend for almost immediate replacement of stock.

Veronique Whatley, known as 'Nique', came to us from Dillon's where she had been the founder's original assistant in the pre-war Store Street days. She encouraged Una to accept the university's offer of bigger, better premises, financed by them, and herself made a speciality out of books on African Studies by, as she told me, 'just taking note of what was being asked for and what was being published.' She was a natural bookseller.

'Nique' – short for Veronique, but I tended to call her 'Veronica' – felt bruised in her last years at Dillon's because Una appointed a young man from an academic bookshop to be her successor. This was Peter Stockham who, to meet the University's demands and qualify for the post, had to graduate. He could not actually work as a bookseller while he was studying, or so Veronica informed me. She was incensed that Peter had been chosen and after leaving Dillon's and joining High Hill she spread word throughout the London trade of what she thought of him. Una, one weekend, visited Mavis and me to beg that we would ask Veronica to desist. This presented me with a dilemma because, independently of Veronica, I had not been impressed by Peter as an officer of the National Book League. There was a further embarrassment in that Mavis was teaching at a school where Ann, Peter's wife, worked as a lab assistant. Nor did I believe that Veronica was Una's natural successor but I thought she might be right for us because we were branching out into academic bookselling and had taken premises, close to our own, in the High Street.

The High Hill (University) Bookshop was opened partly to serve students of the Open University which I sensed would be a winner for us. DIY graduate courses, for students working from home, were made for Hampstead; we drew custom from East Anglia and Kent as well as north London because we were set book stockists. Veronica, followed by Sheila Judd and later Bridget Clements, ensured that we maintained our reputation in this respect but the rest of 'our' academia was more shadowy. And the new name, The High Hill (University) Bookshop, was a misnomer; the only campus in Hampstead was a department of the University of London at Westfield College, near the crown of the hill.

A greater mistake was to engage Eva Dworetski as number two to Veronica. In the 1930s Fraulein Dworetski had owned her own bookshop in Danzig. Then, on coming to Britain as a refugee, she was placed in charge of foreign books at Bumpus by the great John G. Wilson. When his successor, Tony Godwin, couldn't tolerate 'Dwo', as she was known, Una Dillon took her on. Mavis had found her helpful when she bought French books and Veronica believed that if we employed her she would bring many customers with her. Impressed by what they told me, I became anxious lest she went to another bookseller. I called at her home in West Hampstead where I was instantly repelled by her personality. She was a small, strident woman with a few ugly fangs which were all that were left of her teeth but also serious and formidable. I decided to ignore my first impressions; she joined us.

I soon found that my colleagues didn't like Eva; nor did many of my customers. She wore a fawn overall of the type used by continental booksellers; she was just wrong for High Hill. Even Veronica began to complain, 'Dwo is spoiling my fun.'

The University shop was not a success and we sold the property. 'Dwo' was given sanctuary at a tiny bookshop in the City; she died a few years later. Veronica stayed with us until 1975 and by the time of her retirement dinner she and Una Dillon were friends again.

An unexpected bonus of employing Veronica was to have Austen, her husband, as our erstwhile 'store detective'. He was a retired police-man and looked the part, tall, plump, flat-footed, his face mostly wore that benign expression which is a comfort to old ladies and children. He had entered the force at a time of acute unemployment in the thirties. His beat had been in the Bloomsbury-Soho area and that was, presumably, where he met Veronica who was not evacuated with Dillon's, and spent the war years as a nurse.

Austen shared my basic attitude to shoplifters which was to apprehend them, warn them off, and threaten to prosecute if they ever returned. In that way we did not have to attend police courts. Austen's very presence was a deterrent to rogues. When I confessed this attitude in *The Bookseller* I drew criticism from a former Booksellers' Association President, for not doing my duty as a citizen. In younger days I had done the correct thing and endured sessions with coppers, who were maddeningly ponderous in taking down a statement. When I had written one in advance to save us both time, this was not acceptable. The bobby, in his laborious way, had to spell it out in his own limited jargon . . . 'The accused, when apprehended . . . ' and all that. Then, when the accused came before the beak he would be bound over. Following this travesty of justice the stolen books, often by then rendered unsaleable through rough handling, would be returned.

It was when one noticed an intending miscreant on the premises that so much time was wasted. You couldn't ignore the fact that some-one was bent on ripping you off. So you spent ages watching them, making it clear that you knew what they were up to, followed by a period of pretending to avert your gaze to give them time to restore the books to a shelf. Or you might be diverted by a genuine customer which gave the rogue an opportunity to go on pilfering undisturbed. It was astonishing how persistent some would-be thieves were when hovered over. They knew that you knew but they persisted in their efforts. Some were 'plants' deliberately acting as decoys while their associates got on with the thieving unobserved.

Overall it was better not to spend too much time suspecting customers. One of our most gifted classical pianists was frequently in the shop. I didn't then know who he was. He bore an uncanny resemblance to the Sandemann's Port adverts of my youth, wearing a voluminous cape which could have concealed a whole library. He was however an innocent browser. Similarly Chris Meade, later head of Book Trust, had acquired an ex-RAF greatcoat from Highgate School, and loved to come in on his way home; he was a natural book lover but I had not then identified him as the son of some long standing customers. I thought, 'there ought to be a law against coats like that being worn in bookshops.' The next I knew was that Doreen Gotch had engaged him as a temporary assistant. He returned, during vacations, many times and wrote us a touching 'obit' when we closed down.

Once, returning from lunch, I passed a man on the High Street carrying a stack of Batsford Chess titles which I knew had come from High Hill. I took a chance, reasoning that it was unlikely anyone making such a purchase would have insisted on taking them away unwrapped. I turned and followed the man to a second-hand dealer in Flask Walk, catching up with him as he was about to enter. 'They belong to my bookshop,' I cried, consumed with fury and grabbing the books. 'Now piss off.' He did. But supposing I had been mistaken or he had been wily? I could have been in trouble if I had been unable to prove the books were from our stock. The fact that they bore our mark and we had not recorded sales of them would have been dodgy to prove in a court of law. And, it has to be said, my experience of the law in practice is that it by no means favours the victim.

The most flagrant instance of injustice I endured was when a drugged man driving a Landrover crashed into the University shopfront late on a cold January night. The police took him away but told me, when I had been summoned from home, ten miles away, that they could not be responsible for protecting the badly damaged premises. Friends who had been passing helped me to secure them in an ad hoc fashion. When the driver was charged I hung about the court for a couple of hours waiting for the case to be called.

Peremptorily I was told that it was over even before I was aware it had begun. The man had been let off.

'So I'm not required to give evidence?'

'No, Sir,' a policeman informed me.

I complained bitterly.

'You've got your insurance,' said the officer.

Pathos sometimes intruded on to the shoplifting scene. 'Mrs F', an annoying woman, was a regular customer, but one with whom there was always some niggling altercation of a trivial nature. One day I opened the post to receive an unexpected cheque from her for a book she had stolen while she was cross with me.

Humour could also arise. There was a man named Silas whose face was a permanent scowl. Both shoulders bore sizzling chips. He had written a lit-crit title which had not done well. He raged against me for not selling it, against the publisher likewise and against Hampstead residents for not buying it. He took it out on all of us by stealing books. He was caught for an offence committed at another shop. He was discharged conditionally, the judge requiring only a promise that he would not enter any bookshop again for twelve months. This judgment grieved Silas who was not a poor man and who in his twisted way did actually like buying books. One day I saw him outside the shop beckoning me, baring his teeth beneath a stark upper lip moustache, in his version of a smile. He told me the situation and, handing over a bank note, asked me to bring a particular volume to him on the pavement. We both found the transaction amusing and thereafter there was guarded goodwill between us. This withstood even a party that he gatecrashed when OUP and High Hill were celebrating publication of Margaret Drabble's *Oxford Companion to English Literature*. To prevent the public from wandering in off the street – it was a Sunday when we were normally closed – entrance was by the staff door opening on to the car park. Silas got through. Michael Holroyd ('Mr – now Sir – Drabble') confessed to me, 'We knew he'd come. He was furious he hadn't been asked and badgered us for an invitation. It was simpler to give way.' Silas entered, doing his awful grimace, shook my hand and instantly began to chat-up Mavis who was unaware of his former misdemeanours.

The worst thieves to endure were the professionals, the gangs (always said to emanate from Australia) who made sustained assaults on particular shops. There was little one could do about them because they outnumbered the staff but they had the good sense to move on to another shop once they had given us a thorough going over. They were careful not to ruin a source for the next time round.

One year we employed a well known company of security experts who sent us a series of respectable middle-aged ladies, clutching handbags, to case the shop for criminals. This was useless. Succeeding them, came a tough young woman and her boyfriend both ambitious to join the police. They sussed out several rogues and the girl certainly knew her job but she was so unprepossessing that, on the day before Christmas Eve (our second busiest day of the year) I told her we wouldn't need them any more because the rush was over. This was to avoid inviting them to the staff party. The girl made one useful contribution when she told me in her solemn, hush-hush way that, although it bucked the trend, she was certain that I could trust all my staff. None did she suspect; nor did I.

Many of the people mentioned above were with High Hill in the early years. Some remained or rejoined in the seventies and eighties by which time the problems of full time, middle and junior staff were solving themselves. I no longer had to tolerate the often willowy, sometimes grubby, young men who sought a quiet life in bookselling and were innately lazy. The women, affable but unmotivated, were often more bearable. There was an American girl who wanted to be 'a wrider', remarking to me, 'You're a wrider, too, aren't you?' She wore formidably large sweaters and balanced herself on a stool behind a counter and chattered about 'wriding'. There was a young Yorkshire-man who knew little and wouldn't learn, talked incessantly about the 'Archers' and was indolent. There was another youth who liked to dress well, which placed him rather apart in our establishment, and who rowed with his colleagues. All three came to us because I offered fifteen pounds per week instead of the normal ten.

In the transition period between having to bear with who we could get and choosing those we thought we were lucky to have, there came Kevin and Bernard. (I use pseudonyms). Kevin was an Ulsterman who admitted to playing the social security game on both sides of the Irish Sea. He, handsome with many talents, drank heavily and worked with sporadic energy and occasional enthusiasm and was friendly and popular with his colleagues – especially the women. Bernard was remarkable for having had twenty-six jobs in five years. He worked hard, talked hard, was extremely amusing and very well informed. He stayed with us for three years, then having at last married the girl with whom he'd been living for nearly a decade, he felt he had conformed sufficiently, so he gave in his notice. I liked him, we all liked him, but when I was on the point of re-engaging him, a senior colleague warned me not do so.

If a person were to be dismissed I believed they must be faced personally. It was unpleasant but a duty not to be delegated. Doreen did some of the firing after she became the hirer and took a similar attitude. It still remained my place when it concerned a person of long standing. Dear John was hopeless at it. He was too kind-hearted and could never forget his working class origin. Once when I had to wield the axe on a part-timer whom I had known since I worked with her at Foyles, decades earlier, she, Mona Bonser, went to him for comfort after I had delivered the verdict. He said, soothingly, 'Perhaps it won't be so bad. There may be a way out.' This led Mona to suppose that I might change my mind which, of course, I didn't. Shortly after, the young man with whom she had had a relationship for many years, left her for a woman his own age. I felt a terrible heel especially when, over lunch, she wailed, presumably forgetting her dead husband, 'You are the only two men I have ever cared about.' She was a sweet, intelligent soul but had become too old to carry out her duties efficiently and I had to choose between her and a more valuable colleague. The last time I saw Mona, she was on her death bed at the Marie Curie Hospice in Hampstead. I thought she had already drifted into a coma but she opened her eyes, smiled brightly, and asked after Mavis and the children.

## 11

## Charities and The Booker Prize

In 1971 I became Chairman of The Society of Bookmen, three years after relinquishing my role as Secretary. It was the only position I ever coveted in the book world and I was immensely gratified when Alan Steele said he had been asked to sound me out. It was the year of the golden jubilee of the Society, which meant that I would be in the Chair at the celebratory dinner. I was the first bookseller since 'The Gaffer' (Basil Blackwell) to take the office, only the third ever and I was aged forty-four. Of course, I didn't spoil things by enquiring who had turned it down before they thought of me.

David Whitaker, who had succeeded me as Secretary, was still in office and we worked well together for three years. I discovered, when signing minutes, that he had adopted a habit of assessing my performance at each dinner. Some comments indicated he may well have missed a vocation as a welfare officer, which may surprise those who followed his career to its dramatic conclusion in a family boardroom brawl.

I had some outstanding speakers during my term as Chairman, some supplied by André Deutsch who had a natural inclination for pushing his own authors. I slapped him down a few times but he did get me Kenneth Galbraith and George Mikes, who later became a cherished companion at the Garrick. At book trade level, I had Billy Collins, Fred Warburg and Paul Hamlyn; there were debates about pornography and Public Lending Right. It wasn't too bad a record except for my moronic behaviour with Galbraith. The Society has a rule, then strictly enforced, that no member may bring more than one guest to a meeting. Galbraith at the eleventh hour asked to bring with him the editor of a Parisian magazine. We had already turned away members, not just their guests. I therefore decreed that although the lady would be welcome her presence would not be announced. I acted crassly. Having omitted to mention her when I read out the guest list

Peter du Sautoy, of Faber, who was seated next to the French journalist, supposing I had forgotten, rose and introduced her. She beamed upon one and all and was applauded. Galbraith was understandably cool to me and even mocked my taste when I said his account of his ancestors settling in Canada should be reprinted in paperback.

My chairmanship was not always so disastrous. For me there were two highlights of the three year stint. One was the successful vote – second time of trying – to make women eligible for membership, the other was chairing the fiftieth-anniversary dinner at Stationers' Hall. The question of women's suffrage had first arisen while I was secretary. It had been put to a vote but the necessary two-thirds majority was not met even though women were, by then, playing an increasingly prominent role within the trade. The issue arose again when Kaye Webb, the second outstanding editor of Puffin Books, spoke to us. During dinner – to attend which she had been driven from a sick bed in St Thomas's Hospital – she told me she would not have agreed to address us had she known she was not eligible for membership. I totally sympathised and promised her that I would get the ruling changed during my Chairmanship; if not I would resign from the Society. David Whitaker fully supported me and this time we got the necessary two-thirds majority. The first seven women were elected in 1972. They included Kaye, Margaret Drabble and Judy Taylor, editor of children's books at the Bodley Head and Beatrix Potter expert. Maggie Drabble was apprehensive of attending her first meeting and sought my protection; I was delighted to have her beside me for the occasion. Since then there have been several female chairs.

Rooting out the next chairman was an unofficial task for former incumbents. One day over lunch Colin Eccleshare, of Cambridge University Press, with tongue in cheek summed up the views of those present as, 'What is desirable is a black woman bookseller who is also a member of the Garrick.'

Other extramural activities in which I was involved in the seventies were occasional appearances on Melvyn Bragg's TV book programme *Read All About It*, usually transmitted on BBC2 but for at least one episode on BBC1. Melvyn then lived round the corner from High Hill and had not become a household name. He cast his net widely for panellists for his weekly show, inviting three different ones for each programme. His splendid effort to promote books was, I suspect, most widely viewed when it followed the popular *Esther Rantzen Show* on a

Sunday evening. Once I was recognised by the manageress of an off-licence. 'Saw you on telly last night,' she said excitedly. I asked if she regularly viewed the programme. 'Yes,' she replied, her expression now forlorn. 'You've got to watch something.'

A problem about book programmes is that there is something intrinsically dull in three or four people sitting around a table discussing the written word. It does not make compulsive television unless a good argument is provoked and panellists slang at one another. I have always regretted I didn't pursue my chance when the novelist Angela Carter dismissed Lytton Strachey's *Eminent Victorians* as 'too middle class'. It was a stupid comment. Most books over the last three centuries have been written by and for the middle classes. Successful working-class writers such as Lawrence, Sillitoe and of course Dickens become middle class whether or not they like it.

On another programme I eulogised Helene Hanff's enchanting *84 Charing Cross Road*. The other panellists agreed with me, which didn't make for zestful viewing. The following week Jessica was on a train next to a woman who was reading the book. At some stage their eyes met and my daughter asked, 'Why did you choose that particular one?'

'It was recommended by some bloke on telly.'

'That was my father.'

The woman gave her a hostile look of disbelief and went on reading.

After one show had been transmitted I called on Bob Chris at his bookshop in Cecil Court. 'Ian!' He bawled as I entered the shop. 'What did Melvyn Bragg do to your face?' His attendant cronies, mostly publishers' reps, guffawed. Apparently the make-up artist had not been kind to me. Probably I am not photogenic and, had I been given a screen test, I would have failed it. I wasn't too sorry that Ronald Harwood, who briefly succeeded Melvyn, did not invite me to appear. Presenters like editors tend to choose their own teams.

A feature of my childhood at Southborough was the Old Folks' Dinner. I cannot be certain that it was my father who inaugurated this annual event but he was the prime organiser. It was held at the Royal Victoria Hall which, beside and behind the urban district council offices, was less grand than a town hall but vastly superior to the average village equivalent. Bill cared about the welfare of the elderly and under-privileged, a characteristic which along with impatience I inherited from him. In my case it became manifested in a yearly outing for residents at The Booksellers' Retreat, Kings Langley, where thirty or more former book trade employees along with their partners and dependents were accommodated in a Victorian house lacking many mod cons. or in more suitable, purpose built post-war bungalows. Regrettably the site lies beside a main line rail track between London and Scotland along which express trains roar at frequent intervals, interrupting conversation and sleep. Despite this inconvenience many of those who had earned little as booksellers and publishers, plus some of greater means who opted to be there, found it an agreeable address. Always wary of committees I suggested to Frank Sanders, then President of the Book Trade Benevolent Society, that I should invite a number of fellow booksellers to drive one, two or more residents to a country house, or some other place of interest, stand them tea and return them to the 'Retreat' for a short drinks party in the evening. My position was never official and my only stipulation was that I would handle the entire organisation of these trips. I would name a date to suit the residents and choose a destination; all my friends were required to do was pay for themselves and their particular guests. Whatever do-gooding elements might have seemed inherent in the project faded away because most of us made friends with those we drove. It also had the unexpected effect of giving a boost to an able and youngish member of the community, Margaret Course, whose help I was very happy to accept. Margaret had been a bookseller with some worthy institution with a name like the Church Scripture Mission before marrying Gordon Course, a widower who had no connections with the trade. She had served on the board of the BTBS, the book trade charity, and qualified for a house when Gordon became unfit for employment. She was the librarian at the 'Retreat' and arranged coffee mornings; she longed for more involvement and gladly became my link, feeding me a tally of which residents wished to take part in the outings. After Gordon's death she came on holiday twice with us and Mavis and I often lunched at her bungalow, where we were kept up to date with gossip about the residents and directors.

During the later years of the outing the President of the charity was Tommy Joy, an officer of the Booksellers' Association for many years, author of a textbook about bookselling, Assistant General Manager of the Army & Navy Stores and, following his retirement from that post, Managing Director of Hatchard's, Piccadilly. In that latter capacity he was a bookseller to the Queen and made personal deliveries to

Buckingham Palace, a task he relished, but it didn't earn him a knight-hood. He had to be content with being made a member of the Victorian Order. He wrote an autobiography – *Mostly Joy* – and hosted an annual 'Authors of the Year party'. He was an able businessman, short, bald and pompous. He was married without children to Belle, fancied himself as a womaniser and had an affair with one of the residents at the 'Retreat'. When he delivered edicts, which he did frequently, Tommy tended to rock back on his little heels, thrust his head upwards and commence with an elongated and tortured form of the personal pronoun. 'Ay-ee-ay-ee, would say–ee . . . ' And so forth. Although invariably friendly he did not really approve of my privately organised outings which detracted from his own glory. He made this clear when he wrote once to ask for an assurance that all 'my' drivers were fully insured and could be trusted to convey their guests to and from Whipsnade, Waddesdon, Luton Hoo or wherever. His fellow directors, he said, were very concerned. I replied that they must be similarly worried every time one of the residents, all free citizens and mostly able bodied, left their homes to go shopping or on holiday. That threw him. To retaliate he started his own excursions which soon petered out because his guests didn't like being patronised. Yet he was basically a good hearted man and had been known to defend lowly paid shop assistants accused of having their hands in the till. Twice during his long retirement he hired a private cab to attend funerals far from home. One was that of my colleague John Ford. This took many of us by surprise since John and he had not been close. He arrived late, asked me to introduce him to Sylvia, telling me that he had felt compelled to come because John had been so helpful to him at Hatchard's. I then realised that he was confusing the deceased with another of the same name, a senior salesman for William Collins. Despite the error it proved he was not entirely self-absorbed.

Outings from the 'Retreat' included two visits to Christina Foyle's abbey in Essex, where there was lunch and tea and a tour of the library; to Bob Lusty's Cotswold home in a converted silk mill and a trip to Simon Hornby's estate at Pusey. Many senior dignitaries of the trade generously supported our outings. It was my hope that improved conditions of employment would render the 'Retreat' obsolete but this has not occurred and nowadays some of those living there are young people who otherwise could not afford to work in publishing in London. The answer to that, I feel, should rest with their employers.

From my father I also inherited his abhorrence of being in debt. This did not extend in my case to refusing to take out a mortgage on a property but, combined with my experience of working for Hubert Wilson, made me extremely wary of running a business on an overdraft. The company did take a mortgage on one of our shop units because we were offered a freehold by the Public Trustee at two-thirds of the price that Robert Balyuzi, by now an estate agent, had valued it. Pat Peters, who had become our insurance consultant and arranged pensions for senior staff, obtained a fixed mortgage for most of the sum; the rest we financed from profits. Pat is an unsung hero of my prosperity; another was Stanley Underhill, the accountant who introduced me to her. Stanley was our attentive auditor who on a mid-term visit was impressed by how well we were doing, advising we should have an eighteen month financial 'year'. This was then permissible and gave him time to devise legitimate corporation tax avoidance schemes to enable us to make pension arrangements, all entirely non-contributory, for long serving members of staff. They were index linked too, so that in old age, at least until the world banking system crashes, I have a far greater income than in my salaried years. Having done us this service Stanley gave up accountancy and became a monk. Before taking his vows he enjoyed one last gourmet weekend with his mother at The Imperial, Torquay. Our affairs were then handed over to Geoffrey Hill who is my accountant to this day and a source of impeccable advice.

During the seventies I continued to review books fairly regularly for the *Ham & High* and very occasionally for the *Daily Telegraph* when David Holloway found something that suited me. I began work on another Hampstead book jointly published with Wildwood House, whose three working directors were David Harrison, Dieter Pevsner and Oliver Caldecott. They published a series of books roughly categorised as travel, in an almost square format, with excellent photographs, often by Fay Godwin. Knowing that there was a sale for Hampstead books outside NW3, and wishing to benefit from independent editing, I threw the idea at them. They liked it. It was a shame that their imprint went into the doldrums just prior to publication, but I contrived to divert most of the print run to be delivered to Hampstead where the book sold well. Expected sales through Wildwood were disappointing but when Dieter subsequently moved to André Deutsch he commissioned me to complete a companion volume on central London and the City.

This was the decade when High Hill Press published the series of street surveys, compiled by members of the newly formed Camden History Society. When the Society began the Borough Librarian asked me to become Publications Officer. It would have been tactless to decline because Camden Libraries was our largest single bookshop customer, spending over £50,000 per year, but attending committee meetings in the old St Pancras Town Hall was not an attractive prospect. I was able to pass this role on to Christopher Wade, a senior BBC drama official, who also lived in Hampstead. I undertook, on behalf of the Press, to finance publication, pay the Society a royalty and issue the books under a joint imprint. The first, confined mostly to Hampstead village, was a marked success and was reprinted several times. The second, *More Streets of Hampstead* (actually Belsize Park) did not, in my time, go into a second impression and the third, *The Streets of West Hampstead*, lost money. We launched it at a party at the *Ham & High* offices in Perrin's Court, inviting Nikolaus Pevsner (father of Dieter) to speak because it was he who had written, in the relevant *Buildings of England* volume, 'West Hampstead need be visited only by those in search of Victorian churches. The houses and streets require no notice.' Despite this dismissal we asked him to the party. At the time he was already suffering from Parkinson's Disease but agreed to be driven to the occasion by his daughter-in-law. When asked to speak he struggled up a staircase to face us, turned slowly round and, smiling down, declared, 'Now you see the ruin on the hill.'

Christopher Wade edited the *Streets* books superbly assimilating the vast research done by his team into his own racy prose. Mavis under– took the copy editing, I made the indexes; a further connection was born. Ironically, however, it was Christopher's arrival on the Hamp- stead scene, along with that of John Richardson, a Camden councillor- turned-publisher, who deprived me of my monopoly in local books. Between them they published and republished books of local interest. Christopher and Diana, his wife, also became curators of a new local museum at Burgh House, which the local residents more or less rescued from the grips of the Council, converting it into a centre of local historical activity. As the local bookseller, I was happy to be involved even when Gerald Isaaman, by now editor of the *Ham & High*, began holding literary luncheons in the small music room at the house. My reason for being less than enthusiastic about these events was that attendance was limited to fifty-five people, and sales at literary lunches tend to reflect a small percentage of those present. Despite having star performers such as John Mortimer, Frank Muir, Margaret Forster and Donald Sinden, we never sold more than a dozen copies of any particular book, but the occasions were usually fun and helped further to integrate the shop into the community.

Alan and Joan Steele decided to pass their interest in High Hill Book-shops to Patricia Nunn, known as 'Trisha', who had become their surrogate daughter. Trisha who had been a silent witness of all that had happened between Alan and me (see *Mentors and Friends*) decided to risk becoming my colleague. She gradually took over as manager and buyer of what we called 'the main shop' which housed fiction, biography, reference, travel, art, history, London and poetry. She made her own friends among the reps and customers, expressing her enthusiasm for particular titles, chatting about music, theatre, art exhibitions and becoming 'au fait' with local gossip. She also had an understanding of business and was good with junior staff. She succeeded Doreen as the hirer and firer, making excellent choices, some of whom are now gracing the trade in senior positions.

One is Derek Johns who went first into publishing as Managing Director of Harrap, then crossed the Atlantic to take an appointment with Random House. They returned him to the UK to take charge of The Bodley Head, where he commissioned three books from me which he never published. Fortunately our friendship survived and he is now a highly regarded literary agent as joint Managing Director of A. P. Watt. Others include: John Bond, who became Marketing Director of Penguin, before being head-hunted by HarperCollins to take over both Sales and Marketing; Richard Jewett, later a manager in the Blackwell Group; Ros Wesson – a delightfully scatty child when she came to us – who went into publicity, or maybe PR, at Random House, and Robert Lacey, an incredibly highbrow young man who reached us from Australia, became Irene's erudite and efficient Number Two in paperbacks, then joined HarperCollins, via Chatto & Windus, as an editor, with a sometimes ghostly function.

At the start of the seventies, as the employment levels were improving, I became immersed in revising and updating *Mumby* and returned to the executive committee of The National Book

League as an active member. Jack Morpurgo, impeded by permanent tunnel vision, had moved on to academia. His deputy, Clifford Simmonds, briefly held reign while a successor was sought. Many publishers, including Mark Longman who was due to become Chairman, took the view that if the League were allowed to die it would have to be reinvented. He was backed by, among others, Michael Turner who was keen for Martyn Goff to become Director. This, in 1970, was not everyone's choice because there were still those in the trade who thought of him as an upstart, small bookseller from Banstead, Surrey. Martyn wrote to me at home with the news of his appointment. When I informed the family, saying, 'now, he'll get his knighthood. He's always wanted one.' Amanda observed, 'Then we won't be allowed to know him any more.'

I allowed a year for the dust to settle before exercising what I thought was the Society of Bookmen's right, as 'the only begetter', to be represented on the National Book League Executive. I went to a meeting to show enthusiasm for the new Director, taking Mark Longman, presiding, unaware though he greeting me courteously as 'an observer'. This temporarily crushed me but, correct in my assumption, I was duly welcomed back officially. The finances of the League were still dodgy but Martyn's appointment undoubtedly gave it a new sparkle and I was glad to show solidarity. Within the trade it still had some top supporters and that wise old bird, my benefactor and city accountant, William Balleny, remained the hon. treasurer, yet there still persisted formidable animosity towards the NBL.

Rayner Unwin suggested a levy on all publishers of a tiny percentage of turnover, as a basis for fresh funding, but there was no way this could be implemented. Another reason to raise money was in commemoration of Mark Longman whose Chairmanship coincided with the end of his too short life. Mark suffered from a rare form of cancer with which he coped courageously for several years. He was a tall, lean man, an aristocrat in his bearing, and the last of the Longmans to preside over the imprint, founded in 1724. A literary man at heart, I remember going into an executive meeting with him one day when he said, 'I've had a morning of real publishing. I've been dealing with a new book by Nina Bawden. Do you read her?' In his tone, in his eyes, was the genuine enthusiasm of a publisher who knows he has an outstanding author on his list.

The appeal for funds to transform our dowdy collection of books about books into a library of distinction, on the first floor of the handsome Mayfair offices in Albemarle Street, was linked with a more urgent need to remove the current account out of the red. More was subscribed to the Library fund than to the general one. This was, no doubt, partly out of sympathy for Mark who had been popular among publishers. The hon. treasurer at the time was Peter Stockham, essentially a book person with a leaning towards the second-hand and antiquarian trade, one who probably should have become a librarian. There was no doubt about his commitment to books and reading and to the purposes of the League, but he was not a businessman. As Chairman of a subcommittee brought together to plan The Mark Longman Library he committed us to a costly scheme which we were obliged to rubber stamp. It was a disastrous waste of money because, within a few years, we were forced to leave Albemarle Street, abandoning the new library fittings. (The books are now at Reading University as part of the Publishing Archive.)

A continuing preoccupation of the NBL's executive lay with funding. Martyn assembled a distinguished group which included Alan Hill, Kaye Webb, biographer Michael Holroyd and novelist Margaret Drabble (whose attachment to each other grew closer before our very eyes), Angus Wilson, printer Basil Harley, head teacher Michael Marland, Simon Hornby, chief executive of W. H. Smith and the soldier turned bookseller, Charles Hammick.

There were times when we realised we were so close to disaster – a situation highlighted by the report of an independent group of students from the London Business School who concluded we must soon become unviable – that on one occasion we were led to a course of action which still makes me uneasy. The League had been given the Harriet Weaver/James Joyce Collection of Letters and Manuscripts to keep in safe custody. Such was our desperate financial state in 1977 that the Executive agreed to sell this archive to the University of Tulsa. Some members resigned in protest. We defended our action by claiming that there was no other course for us to take if we were to remain solvent. I don't think any of us was happy about it. Yet whatever the explanation, we betrayed a trust.

It became imperative too to sell our expensive West End premises; we looked at alternatives in Hampstead, Elephant & Castle and elsewhere before settling on a disused town hall at Wandsworth, south east London, a former municipal headquarters rendered obsolete by the provisions of a new Local Government Act. Even then there was gloom because, after disposing of Albemarle Street and clearing our debts, we still didn't have sufficient capital to make the purchase.

At this crucial moment, with Martyn away on some overseas mission, a meeting of the executive was called at the Allen & Unwin offices in Bloomsbury, close to the British Museum. Margaret Drabble was chair at the time; I was treasurer. We met in the dingy light of Sir Stanley Unwin's former sanctum. Part of his fortune had founded the Unwin Trust of which the chairman was his son Rayner. It was a gloomy afternoon, the future of the League looked bleaker than ever before. Suddenly, we heard Rayner calmly announcing that the Unwin Trust would be willing to purchase the former Wandsworth town hall to establish a training centre and provide the National Book League with accommodation to continue its good work, granting it a one quarter share of the freehold. A generous gesture indeed.

After the meeting Maggie Drabble and I walked to nearby Blooms-bury Square where I had parked and drove back to Hampstead in a euphoric mood. I had first met her at a meeting of the judges of The John Llewellyn Rhys Award some years before, and later came to know her as a customer. She had risen to fame with her first novel, becoming a cult figure among the young.

John Llewellyn Rhys was an RAF pilot who was killed early in WWII. His widow funded a prize in his memory for a work by an author under the age of thirty. He had had some success as a short story writer so this was appropriate. The annual prize money was one hundred pounds, a reasonable sum at the time of its inception but, by 1969, it was peanuts. Margaret Drabble said that winning for her was a morale booster. The judges, over the years, certainly seemed to have selected books by young writers who became big names. In my first year the fiction and poetry submitted were not, I thought, worthy of an award but I had read a remarkable account of the experiences of ordinary citizens during WWII,by Angus Calder, and I was allowed to call it in. *The People's War* is a compulsively readable, widely researched, item of recent history. The judges read it and liked it. Maggie, at first, was reluctant to give it her vote because she believed the prize should go to a creative work of fiction or poetry. Then her judgement got the better of her understandable sentiments, so Calder won unopposed.

The following year when the final meeting of the judges was due the staff situation at High Hill was so bad that I couldn't attend. While I sold books at the counter the other judges debated between two novels and became evenly divided. It was decided to phone me to cast 'the chairman's vote'. I complied. Then I resigned.

The task of a John Llewellyn Rhys judge was lightweight compared with those who read for the Booker. We had to consider only about thirty books, many of them slim volumes of verse; the Booker panel had to read up to one hundred or more novels of varying length and often found it necessary to re-read those that were short-listed. It was a daunting task I never had to contend with, but I did serve on the prize management committee.

As replacement to Peter Stockham, as hon. treasurer of the NBL, I was not a success in a role which I had misread. I had supposed it meant no more than being titular head of the League's finances with the deputy director, Stanley Jackson, being day-to-day 'Chancellor'; a set-up similar to that of organisations ranging from the Labour Party to various charities, a device for putting someone on the board to help dictate policy alongside, in this instance, Martyn, Simon Hornby, Michael Holroyd, Margaret Drabble and Graham. C. Greene. I paid weekly visits to Albemarle Street to keep myself 'au fait' with current goings on, wrote letters to booksellers urging them to send us donations and to tell their customers about us and penned an article to *The Bookseller*. I was regularly provided with figures by Stanley Jackson to enable me to report the financial position to meetings of the Council, and for a while I had good news to impart. The move to Wandsworth, closing the restaurant and other cuts, helped to keep us relatively solvent.

Then an unhappy situation arose concerning 'X', a senior member of staff whose work was not thought satisfactory. It was agreed by the officers that Simon Hornby, by now chairman, should interview and dismiss him. The day this was supposed to have occurred coincided with a retirement dinner which Ian Parsons and I organised at the Savile Club for Alan Hill. I was surprised to find 'X' present but, as it was a social occasion, made no reference to his dismissal. Next day I learned from Martyn that Simon had changed his mind at the last moment. Instead of sacking him he had told him to pull up his socks. I immediately wrote to Simon to complain and sent copies of my letter to Martyn, Maggie and Michael. Simon phoned in a fury, resenting the criticism. I stood my ground. We became coldly polite to each other.

Nothing more was said until the next general meeting of the NBL, attended by the executive, the national council and such ordinary members as remained. A question about investments was asked so Simon referred it to me. I was hazy in my answer because I had not actually taken much interest in our investments. I asked Stanley to provide the answer. From the floor, Tim Rix, of Longman said that I had no right to be treasurer if I didn't know about our investments. Simon agreed and the meeting was with them. I was humbled. Thereafter Simon became and remained friendly. About to leave on sabbatical, I thought it a good time to hand over the treasurership but remained associated with the League (by then Book Trust) by writing the official short history published for its diamond jubilee. The title, *Sixty Precarious years*, was nothing if not accurate. It was published in 1985 and celebrated with a party at the Banqueting House, Whitehall, where the rediscovered pre-war film about the League (directed by Paul Rotha) was shown. Another document found at the same time, in a cupboard at Wandsworth, was a diary kept by Maurice Marston, the first secretary of the Council. I used extracts from it to illustrate life at the pre-war offices, complemented by an account of Martyn's monthly routine in the 1980s.

One of Martyn's major commitments at the League was to literary prizes. Early in his directorship he became administrator of the recently founded Booker Prize, a role he retained until 2006, although he retired from Book Trust in 1988.

The Booker management committee included representatives of hardback and paperback publishing, a bookseller, an author and members of the Booker McConnell staff. I succeeded John Sandoe, of Chelsea, as the bookseller, in the late seventies. The duties were not onerous. There were two lunches a year at Booker McConnell's directors' dining room in Cannon Street and the annual award dinner held at Claridge's, Stationers' Hall or Guildhall. At the former aperitifs were served to us in commodious, low armchairs around a marble table but once at the dining table it became a positive working lunch. The food was excellent, the wine flowed, small talk was not encouraged. At my first meeting I planned to stay silent until I had grasped the procedure. Immediately there was a discussion about whether or not the value of the prize should be doubled to £20,000. Michael Caine, chief executive of Booker, looked down the table at me and asked, 'What do you think, Ian?' I said it had to be a good thing . . . 'if you can afford it.' A Booker man next to me whispered, 'We could afford ten times that.'

One of our tasks was to appoint the judges for the ensuing year, another to report on the effect of the prize in the shops. Michael involved each one of us. He was a large, tall men with a serious stutter which he did not allow to impede him. Quite what we had to do at the other lunch I cannot remember but it must have had a purpose; Michael did not waste time. (Once when I asked him to describe his daily routine as chief executive of an international corporation he replied, 'I read balance sheets.')

On the committee, I pressed, as did Michael Holroyd, for a small consolation prize for the five short-listed losers – say, £100. Caine would not have it. 'Winner-takes-all' was his policy. There was no question of a vote.

When after serving for two years I perceived that the prize was attracting less and less publicity – everyone who was interested knew the result long before the award was announced – I invited Michael Caine to lunch to discuss my proposal that the final meeting of the judges should not take place until immediately before the dinner. This would ensure that no one excepting them, and Martyn, as administrator, could know the result until it was too late for leaks. 'Then,' I told Michael, 'it will be news and the TV cameras and the reporters will have to be present.' Agreeing, he warned me that when a similar suggestion had been made it had been turned down by the publishers on the committee who said they would not be able to get a reprint through for the winner in time for Christmas. I approached the current members individually and found there no objections, provided the date of the dinner was brought forward by three-four weeks, except from Carmen Callil. She opposed me but wasn't really against the idea. I think she just felt it necessary to be anti anything proposed by a man whom she hadn't before encountered. The BBC fiercely objected to the new policy and assumed it would not apply in their case. Martyn said it would. Some of the pressmen were more realistic. They knew they couldn't have the result of a sporting event until it had actually happened and were accustomed on such occasions to leave their offices to be on the spot. In the event, as foreseen, the BBC camera team came along with the other television teams because it was news.

Unfortunately for the first award under the new policy the judges couldn't decide between the two main contenders and chose an out-sider, the delightful Penelope Fitzgerald. So the decision didn't have the impact needed to foster a bestseller but the following year, so far as anyone could guess, it was a contest between William Golding and Anthony Burgess. Tremendous interest was generated, no doubt encouraged by a judicious leak, or two, from Martyn. The previous evening I was at a dinner at the Garrick, given by Hutchinson's, for Burgess. I urged him to attend the award, knowing that he had already declined. 'No,' he said, 'I never win prizes.' He was right. Golding won.

The following year when Salman Rushdie won the atmosphere at the Guildhall was electric. Quite different from the occasion at Claridge's, a few years before, when we all knew as we sat down to dinner that Iris Murdoch would be proclaimed the victor. Chatto had had a reprint of *The Sea, The Sea* in hand for weeks. The author wandered happily around after dinner with a glass of white wine in one hand, a glass of red in the other . . . quite Tennysonian.

It was because Michael Caine felt I had made a contribution to the success of the prize that I continued to be invited to the dinner for some time after leaving the committee. The prize (now the Man Booker) to this day has news value. The winner is always announced on radio and the award ceremony is usually televised but, as with *Read All About It*, the preamble featuring authors and critics, can make dull viewing. I am proud to have been associated with what has become an institution, one moreover which annually rewards a deserving novelist with a tax-free bonus, but there can never be 'a best book of the year'; it's an excusable pretence.

# 12

## Italy, Sicily and Spain

In 1973 the Steeles accepted our invitation to join us on a holiday to Rome. They, our seniors by a generation, were perfect companions. Although both were experienced and skilful drivers they submitted to having me at the wheel for the entire three thousand-plus miles to Italy and back from Dover, where they garaged their own vehicle. There were no cross words, they observed and commented on what they saw; they also cherished the silences which should be part of any long journey. The trip was punctuated by expressions of delight and appreciation for the ancient sites visited: (Pompeii, Ostia Antica, the Villa Adriana, the Colosseum etc); for the flora and fauna of the Alps; for the wayside picnics and another on the beach at Nice where there was a book fair deemed a legitimate business expense. We didn't stay long, nor did we contract any business.

We stayed at Frascati on a hillside a few miles east of Rome. This became a base also for other journeys, one to Pompeii and back for Alan's sixty-eighth birthday and another to Ostia Antica, the ancient port of Rome which was a different but memorable experience. Ostia is much smaller than Pompeii and less crowded. What I most remember about it was the silence as we wandered through the low ruins attractively overgrown with lichen and plants. There was a greater pronounced sense of antiquity than at the more famous ruin. This also was true of the Villa Adriana inland from Rome which, on a weekday in May, was almost devoid of visitors. We sat at the Canopus by the long swimming pool, with its crescent-shaped ends, one of them still bearing pillars, and read books. We didn't swim. The pool was for ancient nobility only. One week later, when it was nearly time to head for home I asked the others where they would like to spend our last day. The unanimous verdict was the Villa Adriana.

We did not neglect Rome, travelling there by train from a rail head on the lower slopes of Frascati to the enormous twenties-style terminus.

We followed a time-honoured itinerary – the Colosseum, the Forum, Trajan's column, the Spanish steps, the house where Keats died, the vulgar, unsightly monument to Victor Emmanuele, the Sistine Chapel, plus many – but still only a fraction – of the fountains, churches, galleries and museums on offer. As with Florence, I did not bond at first sight, nor, in contrast with my experience of the Tuscan capital, on two subsequent visits. The antiquities were arresting, awesome even and, yes, it was touching to be in the bedroom where Keats had expired but it was infuriating, after mooching in a slow-moving queue past the Raphaels, to step into the Sistine Chapel and be prevented from standing and gazing at the wondrous ceiling because everyone has to be kept moving on. And the garish baroque interior of St Peter's repelled me. It is my loss. Rome, in its entirety, did not grab me, the spell of the Eternal City failed to work.

Returning to Florence the following year was different. We set out with my mother-in-law, explaining how vital it was that we should visit the Nice Book Fair again, but not telling her it had been cancelled because of presidential elections in France. Having planned to go we went and she was delighted to find herself seated on the sands at Cannes which she had always thought of as far too posh a locality for the likes of her. On the previous day we had taken her to the Matisse chapel at Vence which drew loquacious scorn from her. 'Child art', she dubbed it. Nor did it much appeal to us which, in retrospect, surprises me.

Leslie Martin joined us at Fiesole where we again stayed at the Bencista, and from which we often went independently into Florence, following our particular inclinations and beginning to see some of the less popular glories. And we wallowed in the Tuscan countryside on journeys to Siena, San Gimignano, Pisa and up to Vallombrosa, a name familiar to me from studying *Paradise Lost* at school. There were no autumn leaves but we were touched to find at a small chapel a commemorative plaque to Milton. I wrote to Martyn Goff about this and his reply upstaged me by recalling how the scene always brought Horace – or was it Virgil? – back to him.

Driving home, at Susa, we were entertained by Louise's opinion of Forster's *A Room With a View*. She had reverently read much nineteenth- and twentieth-century fiction in the spirit of her upbringing and expected high moral standards in anything purporting to be great literature. On holiday she permitted herself some relaxation and liked to relate to what we were reading but she could not understand our enthusiasm for *A Room With a View.* The behaviour of Miss Honey-church whilst on the outing to Settignano exasperated her. Was the silly woman kissed or not kissed, she dared to ask, having downed one glass of wine over dinner? And why didn't the author make it clear? The eminent Mr Forster had created a stupid fuss about nothing. And what a pity he hadn't chosen a worthier theme.

Next day, with memories of the Belgian truck which had towed us up the French approach to Mont Cenis a decade earlier, we set off in thick, lingering, morning mist on the Italian ascent with more con-fidence than we had felt when travelling in Maud. The climb should instantly involve hairpin bends and magnificent views, but there was little to be seen that morning. We were required to detour through an ancient dripping tunnel bored out of the rock which had once been the only road. This was disappointing but nature had a French accent that day. Once across the border the fog lifted and we were able to observe the snow-capped peaks and the lake high up on the pass with the modern church on its shores, while I looked for the petrol station which had enabled us to continue our 1964 journey untowed. It had gone. I imagined what it would have been like for Bunty to have been dependent on the truck as it came down the steep, winding road to Susa.

When, with Peg Bowyer, we returned to Susa three years later, it was a glorious August day – Mavis was now teaching at a compre-hensive and our vacation had to coincide with that of the school. We made for Vico Equense, on the Bay of Naples, stopping at Orvieto, in lower Tuscany. There before retiring we had sat, on a hot, still evening, studying the west front of the cathedral with its rich carvings made by craftsmen whose names may somewhere be recorded but were not apparent. Much that adorned sacred and secular architecture in western Europe for several centuries was the skilled work of every-day artisans who could not impose call-out charges; in the perfection they achieved lay the greater part of their reward. Set against the highest examples, Orvieto is run-of-the-mill but gazing at what those anonymous hands had achieved I experienced a moment of adulation. (The Cathedral had closed so we could not view the celebrated Signorelli frescoes.)

At Vico Equense we encountered contemporary working man en masse. Between our hotel and the sea was a road and a path which were rights of way. Along them drove, or walked, many Neapolitans making their way to one of the rare public beaches in Italy. As we woke we heard them tramping towards it; in the evening, on their return, they observed us lying on our deck chairs. We hoped they had found sufficient room on their tiny stretches of beach; ours, too, on the hotel's private shingle plage, was restricted.

From Vico we went, via small boat from Sorrento, to shimmering, exquisite Capri and the Villa San Michele (a hair-raising, yet exhilarating, bus ride up to Anacapri and back); via car to Ravello and the tranquilly sited Villa Cimbrone with its semi-wild gardens and sensational views over the bay; to Pompeii and the smaller but better-preserved Herculaneum. On the way home we almost went to the Villa Adriana again. We passed through its gateway during a cloud-burst and sheltered in its cafeteria, taking a sandwich lunch, washed down with fierce red wine from the campagna. There was no question of revisiting the canopus before returning to the rain-swept autostrada again. Innumerable clouds had burst. Visibility was all but nil. Conditions were alarming. I stayed in the slow lane with giant sprays engulfing the car whenever another vehicle overtook us. It seemed foolhardy to proceed but we had a date with Derek Johns at Figline in Tuscany. At a service station I took a break. The foul weather persisted but by the time we entered Figline Valdarno, the sun was beating down. We had a jolly dinner during which Derek regaled us with tales of life and work in Tuscany. (Inevitably, he was writing a novel.)

Sicily was our longest adventure to date, undertaken with Linda and John Parry as passengers. That stretched a long standing friendship. Linda was a kind, affectionate friend whose moods changed frequently from passionate affirmations of belief in a particular artist to fierce condemnation of leftist politicians and ecstatic appreciation of mountain scenery and greenery, often accompanied by outrageous remarks which made us all laugh. These could also lead to sudden sulks and petty annoyance at not being taken seriously. In retrospect, it is astonishing that she and I did not fall out permanently during our three-and-a-half weeks together. This possibly was due to John, her ever-patient and adoring husband, and to Mavis who injected their own streams of humour into difficult situations.

We covered more than four thousand miles during which, at Palermo, Mavis was robbed, having her handbag grabbed as we returned to the car from a picnic under a huge banyan tree. Fortunately she did not try to resist. Had she done so, the motorcyclist thief might have dragged her along the tarmac and injured or killed her. We lost our passports, currency, traveller cheques. She bore it equably. I knew she was deeply shocked but she scarcely showed it. When Linda and John asked, 'Would you like to go home straightaway?' she replied that she couldn't think of giving up the holiday. There were no hysterics. When we went again to Palermo, to see the British Consul, John insisted on acting as policeman to our parked car. In the Consul's office we sat with an Englishman whose small craft had been ship-wrecked off the coast. He had nothing but the borrowed clothes he wore.

We met our hotel bills from the date of the robbery with the help, we afterwards believed, of a 'Godfather'. My London bank seemed inefficient in getting new funds to us or it may have been the fault of the Sicilian bank in Cefalu where we were staying. On returning from seeing the Consul at Palermo it was mid-afternoon on a Saturday when no self-respecting bank would think of being open. But one was. A Sicilian, who was either staying at our hotel, or who 'cared for it', had ordered the bank not to shut until we arrived. This was vital. In those days we didn't possess credit cards and were still using travel cheques and cash. The money from London had been telegraphed along the north Sicilian coast from bank to bank. Finally it reached Cefalu. Then the 'Godfather' permitted the staff to close.

This distressing incident did not prevent us from experiencing some of the many varied attractions of an island which has been visited or invaded by most of the world's major civilisations. Italian is the con-temporary lingua franca but Sicilians speak so many different dialects that my London neighbour, who was born there, says it can be difficult to understand what is being said by someone from the next village. Carlo Levi, author of that quietly remarkable book *Christ Stopped at Eboli*, in his published essays about Sicily substantiated this, while his English translator added a rider to explain that he did not pretend to achieve an accurate reflection of some of the spoken dialogue, advising the reader that the meaning could often be determined by the slightest emphasis stressed on a single syllable.

The Phoenicians, the Jews and the Greeks were in Sicily, so were Arabs from the middle east and north Africa, the Romans and the Normans. Especially the Normans, one might say, plus the Neapolitans and the Spanish. All races, believers in all creeds, have passed through, colonised or just become domiciled. They have given to this almost triangular island, between the toe of Italy and what was ancient Carthage, a rich heritage. By the twentieth century it had manifested itself in a subtle anarchy known as the Mafia which acts so clandestinely – and without apparent recourse to any overt demands for self-government – that although the majority of the population is aware of to whom it should defer, the holidaymaker might suppose himself to be in just another region of Italy, unless a misfortune such as befell Mavis occurs.

Sicily boasts magnificent Greek temples (Segesta and Agrigento), cathedrals which have evolved in contrasting styles (Palermo), or display Arab influence (Cefalu and Monreale) and a stupendous Roman villa at Casale, where the surface underfoot on the path to superb mosaics was like that of a bouncy castle. At Taormina it has a classical theatre built high on cliffs rising all but sheer from the sea. This now popular resort is overhung by Etna, the active, volcanic mountain from which, it is said, ice was sent to the Vatican kitchens.

Driving presented no problems. The roads showed a marked Italian influence especially in the desolate recently constructed autostradi which in 1978 seemed very little used. There were also older thorough-fares through undulating countryside which we took on journeys to and from Agrigento. In one hamlet we looked unsuccessfully for a picnic spot. A local café was hospitable in allowing us to consume our own food at its outside tables. It lay near the top of a steep hill up which I saw a peasant approaching dragging a cart heavily laden with hay. This was just the photo I wanted as a change from many architectural images. I snapped him without first asking his approval. It was thought-less of me. He said nothing but his look registered my solecism. He was as self-fulfilled as those who had carved cathedral stonework, not an object of tourism.

Near Taormina we stayed in the foothills of Etna at the Madonna degli Ulivi, at Via Grande, a semi-religious settlement where visitors were accommodated in modest two-three room chalets and ate com-munally at long tables in a refectory. We were served by novices; the food was excellent, the wine ordinario. We settled our modest bill for three nights with an old crone wearing the filthiest spectacles ever. It was probably due to their opacity that she made a lengthy fuss of deciding how much we should be charged. Was it two nights we had stayed, or longer; had we had dinner each evening, had we had wine? She relied on our memory and scrawled figures on scraps of paper.

Linda longed for us to drive up Etna as far as the road allowed. She adored the thought of looking into the crater and hopefully seeing churning lava. Mavis, understandably, preferred two days on the beach. It was extremely hot and the volcano could only have made it hotter. I suggested the Parrys should hire a taxi. Linda looked resentful. She retaliated by collecting driftwood, which she intended to use for artistic purposes. Arranging the baggage for four on an extended holiday, requires a certain sense of order if it is not to fall about during transportation and be easily accessible for both one night and longer stays. Linda didn't go along with that. All her baggage was required in their bedroom every night. And there was a lot of it including hat boxes – full of medicaments – and parcels of shoes. To this she added her driftwood which, she said, would be helpful for the class she was teaching. I had to give in but there was no way of preventing it from mingling with the baggage and making the boot resemble a jumble sale.

The other side of Linda was her innate generosity. If we slightly demurred from some suggested extravagance she would insist instantly, 'Let *us* pay.' Sulks were never of long endurance and there was a huge capacity for enjoying much of what we did together. At the very end, back at Hadley Wood and about to depart for their home in Hampshire, she behaved typically. Throughout the holiday she had dismissed any consultation of the routes I had previously planned and rejected the guide books we had to hand (guide books were for tourists). However she had some realisation that her behaviour was sometimes undesirable, and her parting message accompanied by a dazzling smile was, 'Please write it all down and tell me where we've been, won't you?'

Good relations endured. I have several of her paintings on my walls. Mavis and I went to a posthumous exhibition of her work in Bayswater in 1998; the following year I loaned two of her pictures to another retrospective in Salisbury. When John died he bequeathed their library to us. (Never go on holiday with friends?)

In 1976 we headed north, on the 12th August, bound for Scotland. Though not intent on shooting game, we spent the first night close to the Yorkshire moors at Helmsley. It was Mavis's first ever visit and only my third. The date became significant as the day we gave up smoking for good. The decision was made spontaneously as we drove away from London. I have never smoked since (though for a while I dreamed of having the occasional puff), nor, I am certain, did she. It was a habit, not an addiction. On that first evening, in the hotel bar of the Crown at Helmsley, we so very nearly gave way because lighting a fag to accompany the first drink was a ritual. Two weeks later, in Glasgow at my cousin Cathie's, we were able to refuse her offer – she was a chain smoker – with equanimity. We were so lucky.

In England that summer we had enjoyed a long heat wave with drought. We reached Scotland over Carter Bar where the views, I have learned since, are magnificent. That day it rained heavily which was not the most agreeable welcome to receive from 'my ain folk'. I have always been ambivalent about my Scottish ancestry; two long-lingering regrets of my youth and middle age were not having a head of jet black hair and a Scottish accent, but having been born in England I am pleased to be a mongrel. When I am upset by the crass insularity of the English I console myself by reflecting that my mother married an immigrant Scot; when I hear militant, arrogant Scotsmen fulminating about 'the Sassenachs' I think how wise my father was to have spent most of his adult years in England, returning over the border only once during my lifetime.

I was mulling over similar thoughts as we descended from rain-sodden Carter Bar into what definitely resembled Abroad when, at Jedburgh, I had little time to take in the ruins of the abbey before being hailed by Ian and Catherine Aitken, London friends who were staying in a local macgîte. Seeing familiar faces was a comfort, giving me the strength to visit the cramped quarters wherein Mary, Queen of Scots, was held in custody. There I may, or may not have considered that little has changed in the treatment of political adversaries over the centuries. More likely I took sides with Elizabeth because of the cultural glories of her reign and her presumed charisma. But when I recently saw Schiller's *Mary Stuart* I felt divided on that issue.

The English heatwave followed us into Scotland despite the shower at Carter Bar and by the time we reached Denny, an undistinguished small town near Stirling, where my niece Sue and her husband Chris were then living, summer was still 'a-cumen in'. It was a pity Sue and Chris had to live in so drab a location but that was where they could find a house near his work. While we were with them they showed no sign of distress, entertained us lavishly and accompanied us on a trip to

St Andrews where we walked among the ruins, on the sands and everywhere except on the sacred green; some even swam.

On the right day, nowhere I have been in Europe is more beautiful than the Highlands. The colours in the rocks and hillsides, in the heather, in the burns and on the lochs is enrapturing. The buildings fit perfectly into the landscape whether turreted castles, solidly unpretentious homesteads or simple crofts. They seem to grow from it, with dignified presence, among spruce copses of trees. There are vast unpopulated stretches with wildlife, livestock on and off the road, salmon in the rivers and the views are never-ending. Why can't I think of a painter who has done it justice? What have I failed to remember from the excellent art galleries in Edinburgh and Glasgow? We lunched by Loch Insh, passed through Aviemore and Pitlochry, shunned Balmoral and had a picnic at Loch Shin near Tongue. Somewhere surely we had another at Loch Nish?

Tongue, our base for several days, was where we became accustomed to the single track roads with passing places. I had to be instructed in their correct use. When I had failed to stop in a lay-by after being flashed by a driver at my rear, he pulled up and pointed out that for all I knew he might be a doctor en route to an urgent case. I resisted replying that I might be a criminal on the run and accepted the rebuke. We drove past Lock Hope and all round Loch Eriboll, where German U-boats surrendered at the end of WWII. At Durness we had a picnic on the sands and saw and heard seals. (We heard them bark, too!) On another northern shore Mavis swam in peaceful water; the only sound was of keening seabirds floating on the waves, a lamentable eerie sound. Then we were all but deafened by low flying RAF planes on exercise. We walked a great deal on causeways and woodland tracks and inspected a summer crafts camp on the site of a military encampment. Caithness proved more flat and fertile than Sutherland. We pretended we saw the Orkneys in a heat mist while standing on a sandy beach littered with rubbish which, said a local, came not from tourists so much as from passing ships. We wandered over the dunes on to a moon-like surface; one late evening as we walked after dinner around the Kyle of Tongue midges attacked us. We were otherwise lucky to escape that pest which has ruined many an August holiday in these parts.

On the day we left Tongue we went again past Loch Eriboll and to Durness before heading south to Badcall Bay, near Scourie, where we stopped voluntarily to observe the dainty, shimmering small volcanic islands lying off the coast. Of necessity we halted again to await a rickety little car ferry, taking all of four vehicles at a time, which transported us from one river bank to another. It was an idyllic day ending at Fort William where rampant tourism was in full flow at a no-nonsense motel insisting on payment for rooms upfront. In the dining room a New Zealand waiter, when I protested about the excruciating din emanating from an over-amplified nasal pop singer, remarked 'You should be here when the bag pipers come.'

Next morning I pulled aside the bedroom curtains to a superb view of Lock Linnhe. In retrospect all lochs look the same though some are more wooded than others. After breakfast we went to Glen Nevis, parked and walked among the foothills of Scotland's highest peak. Just which one it was of the several to be seen I was never certain, but I do believe I saw Ben Nevis for the first time. When we arrived at Glen Nevis in 1936 it was drizzling and there was a mist. As we drove down to Glencoe we stopped for a doze which almost turned into a disaster. The driver, Reyn Martin, was fortunately woken as the car ran on to the turf. This time round we saw the mountains in sunshine, yet they still had a sinister quality. Glencoe stands for treachery, revenge, slaughter: it's a grim incident of Scottish history. It was almost a relief to be beside Loch Lomond in heavy traffic, on I think 'the high road' rather than 'the low road'. I warbled my Harry Lauder imitation in celebration as we went on to Glasgow for a hectic round of friends and relations, plus sightseeing right across the lowlands. In Glasgow there were the grimy Cathedral and Crypt (with the oldest house in Scotland opposite to it); the imposing red brick art gallery – with a fine collection of Impressionists and a Constable of Hampstead Heath which ought to be at Kenwood – and the RAC club where my cousin Tommy gave us dinner and shocked us by admitting he and Jinty, his wife, had never been further north than the Trossachs. On this visit to the city the Lord Provost did not turn out the fire brigade in my honour; nor did I have an opportunity to examine his dentures.

Then Spain became a possibility because Franco had died and young King Carlos had emerged as head of a democratic state. Instead of creeping over the border at gaps in the Pyrenees just to say we had been there, we could now plan a trip to Madrid, Toledo and a friend's house on the coast at Pensicola. In 1971, while staying at Biriatou, I had driven across the frontier, bolstered by the knowledge that I had a £250 bond against incarceration, if found guilty of some technical motoring offence. On a narrow, minor mountain road marked on the Michelin map as being suitable for 'Chars' I used the Col Ibadin to descend upon Bissadoa where I was halted by a customs official who spoke in a strange croak, either Spanish or Basque. Perhaps sensing the futility of attempting meaningful communication he waved us on. From the small town, where I don't recall so much as a postcard being offered for sale, we admired the view of 'our' hotel at Biriatou, then drove back to it with a feeling of relief.

Having won my driving spurs, next we had walked into Spain over a bridge at Irun, of whose existence I had become aware during the civil war when it featured regularly in the news. We approached it up a wide avenue of imposing houses that had seen better days and a chocolate factory emitting a heavy sickly odour. It was a busy but doleful frontier town with many banks. Pavements were badly maintained, the roads were rutted. Every building needed painting. Saddened, we returned over the bridge into a free society.

Four years later in more daring mood we sought to imitate Roland and sallied forth from St Jean-Pied-de-Port over the pass to Roncevaux, metaphorically blowing our horn. This was a frontier village of some charm where we had a drink, bought cards and returned to France. Such short skirmishes into Spain were the merest of pinpricks. Something closer to total immersion was not to follow until 1980 when we spent slightly more than a fortnight there, accompanied by Leslie Martin who had in-laws in Madrid.

We passed into Spain over the Col de Somport and made for Zaragoza where I had booked us into a modern faceless hotel with a garage. I had by then all but given up relying on finding rooms by chance. At the end of a day's drive it can prove more fatiguing than the actual motoring, and this was Spain where I imagined that to leave the car on the street or in a parking space would be inviting robbers. I had no statistics to prove that the Spanish were more criminally inclined than any other European nation and I was to discover over the next two years that their driving discipline was superior.

We had most of an afternoon in which to study Zaragoza, un-productively as it happened. Next day we enjoyed the wild flowers on the meseta and stopped at the walled city of Daroca en route for Madrid where I abandoned the car for three nights. Traffic choked the city.

Every thoroughfare was packed with slow-moving vehicles whose drivers leaned on their horns, not it seemed in exasperation, but because they enjoyed the cacophony. That was the first main impression. The second was that almost every other building was a bank, the third that this was a human sized city from which you could see the surrounding countryside from the Royal palace.

Our main objective was to visit the Prado, which we achieved three times. Badly laid out, closed for lunch (though not for a full four hours siesta) and with unhelpful staff, it was totally redeemed by having wonderful treasures, chiefly the wide range of Goyas. But, as in so many major galleries, there are not only too many pictures, there are too many indifferent and bad ones. The poor ones, however, fade against the masterpieces and especially the vivid image of Goya's man clad in white facing a firing squad.

Leslie contacted his sister-in-law's family which led her brother Carlos into conducting us of an evening around the bars of Madrid to sample the tapas. In those days it was free and laid out lavishly on all counters, various tasty cocktail snacks to be washed down the with a glass of wine before going to the next establishment to see what was on offer. This passed the time until at least nine o'clock when it became possible to order dinner. During our brief stay, apart from the Prado, we saw little of Madrid. There was a park at its rear where we rested between visits and the impressive Plaza Mayor where it was sheer joy to sit and watch the world go by. We left the city by a northern road making for El Escorial, forty miles away. The grim edifice built for Philip II has an interior more agreeable than its outside. In the church I admired the simplicity of the altar paintings and the dome. Following this we were taken on a lightning guided tour of the state apartments, conducted by a very tall victim of Spanish pride clad in a neck-high buttoned coat and white gloves. Regarding us with utter disdain he led us through chamber after chamber, where walls were weighed down with tapestries and paintings, until we came to the Battle Gallery. Here we were left insufficient time to take in a huge mural twice the length of a cricket pitch.

For the next three nights we stayed at Toledo at a parador overlooking the city across the river Tagus, that is if you were lucky enough to have a room with a balcony on that side of the hotel. Leslie, as a single-room person, had to endure a cell into which the only daylight came from a small window way up near the ceiling. Toledo held many delights – a massive gothic Cathedral with choir stalls intricately carved, numerous churches, the el Trasiton Synagogue, restaurants where we were served excellent gazpacho and lashings of tapas, the Santa Cruz museum holding many El Greco's and rows of houses with typical overhanging storeys and balconies. Also, the Taller del Moro, a Moorish workshop with garden and the Fuensalida Palace housing lovely wood carvings. Toledo was a satisfying experience.

We turned towards the coast, where we were to spend eight nights, passing through austere countryside with brief stops at Cuenca – fascinating houses overhanging a high cliff – and a tiny village with an excellent butcher's where we bought ham for a late lunch. An advantage of Spain over France is that you don't have to get anxious about shops closing at any time from midday onwards. Everything in Spain happens so much later that it amazes me to find people awake and active before ten in the morning. Our picnic was taken in grounds marked *privata* where we spent a long while watching, fascinated, as a colony of ants carried the remains of our repast to their hill, manoeuvring with busy skill massive, to them, chunks of bread, avoiding the hazards presented by twigs and fallen leaves. (Would my father have said I was being idle?)

At Pensicola, between the Costa Brava and the Costa del Sol, on a stretch of the Mediterranean not too extensively vandalised by tourism, Peg Bowyer's friend, Frank Barnett had a villa which he had loaned us. There were so many admonitory notices pasted about the living room and kitchen that we wondered if we dared use anything. Leslie remarked, in a rare lapse from Christian goodwill, 'I don't wonder his wife left him'. But we became happy there. An attractive small garden, with patio, included a large sprawling cherry tree on which the fruit was ripe; we shared it with flocks of birds.

We began the long haul home by making for Barcelona where we had a concentrated afternoon in the city visiting the Catalan-Gothic Cathedral (sombre, dirty), the uncompleted Gaudi cathedral (an extravagant fantasy, macabre and funny), the Picasso Museum (some brilliant early work plus especially enjoyable pastiches of famous forbears), drove up and down the Ramblas and rested in a park.

Andorra, which followed, was a mixed blessing. On one mountainside we stopped briefly to drink from a bubbling spring the most delicious water I have ever tasted; on another, as we approached the eponymously named capital, the clutch cable snapped. It happened at half-one so, before calling help, we decided to have our lunch basking in the sunshine, munching sandwiches and sipping wine as the traffic sped by. Then Leslie and I hitched a lift into Andorra where there was a Volvo garage. Having been towed into town we were on our way again within three hours of the breakdown. Those are my only memories of Andorra, a tiny, one-horse state in the Pyrenees which presumably is a tax haven, or it would not have survived independently.

Back in France we spent a night at Carcassonne within sight of Viollet-le-Duc's restored walled hill town and next day, after an eleven-hour journey on slow winding roads, we arrived at Aubusson, getting there too late to see any tapestries in the making because we had lingered in Albi at the Toulouse-Lautrec Museum. A shorter journey, to Giverny to see Monet's house and garden, ended with a foul meal and a night in a filthy room at a hostelry recommended by the Syndicat d'Initiative. We covered the beds with raincoats to protect us from the linen. At eight the next morning I descended to a silent bar-restaurant littered with unwashed glasses and plates. I shouted and slammed doors until a bleary-eyed manager, so hung-over that he didn't register my insults, rendered a bill.

In the seventies we added to our French experience with extended forays into previously little visited regions such as the Loire and the Vaucluse, seldom in those years making use of the motorway system because we liked to explore the minor roads. Mavis observed that my inclination to stay off main roads took us into actual farmyards and down lengthy cul-de-sacs. Discovering red-rocking-chair hotels in *Michelin* ceased to be as absorbing a winter night's occupation as of yore, because the publishers, ever intent on improving their guide, began to feature maps showing their exact location . . . a pity because it encouraged too many users to do what we were doing.

1980 was a year of decision. We'd long planned a sabbatical for five or six months in Europe. Mavis insisted we must first go away, just the two of us, to ensure we could tolerate each other's company during a long absence from our natural habitat. We chose to go to Bologna, Perugia and Ravenna, then spend a week on the Adriatic coast, close to Venice. I planned to pass the test with honours and scraped through with a superior third. The trip nearly ended in disaster on the second night in France, which was spent near Saone, a small town where at the

Hôtel-Restaurant Les Marais there was one room vacant in the roof. We booked it before asking for dinner. The restaurant was closed because it was Friday, when the youth of Saone would be on fire and using it for a weekly rally, but an agreeable young manager offered to serve us steak and chips in an annexe. The din from the weekly reunion was loud and good humoured although I predicted that, as the wine flowed more freely, it would become rowdy, possibly dangerous. Our wine also flowed. Later we staggered up the many stairs believing we might be murdered in our bed.

We were unjust to those youthful revellers. Next morning, after we had washed and packed, Mavis could not find her handbag. She realised she had left it on the table in the annexe. That was that, I said, with memories of what had happened in Palermo. 'If it's not there, we'll drive straight home. Cancel 1982.' Min looked forlorn. Dolefully, we reported our loss. The young manager smiled. 'I have hidden it beneath the counter.' It had not been opened.

Covered in remorse we set off for Italy, promising each other we would not drink so much that evening. We stopped for breakfast near Pontarlier at the Hostellerie de la Vrine where the proprietress and a man to whom she barked orders were having an extremely early and large lunch washed down with vin rosé. How disgusting, we thought.

We made it this time *over* rather than *under* the Simplon into Italy, but our stay beside Lake Maggiore was not a patch on Les Marais. For once, *Michelin* had not got it right.

Bologna, we forecast, could only be better; it is the gastronomic capital of Italy. Apart from that, its best feature are colonnades, wide, shady covered pavements exactly right for the climate. I also took pleasure in the cracked facades of many apartment blocks with stucco peeling and numerous small holes now used as entrances to birds' nests. Some years on, I was delighted when Michael Floyd gave us one of his drawings of houses on a typical piazza.

We ate well during our brief stay but could not linger. The car park at our hotel was on the ground floor, an extension of the office in an ad hoc way. When we came to leave I asked the manager for directions to the N9 for Forli.

'Turn right out of here and then left at the first junction.'

'But there is no right turn out of your hotel. It's a one-way street.'

'No matter. Do it quickly. Will be OK.'

After Forli we climbed to a desolate mountain pass in uninhabited country. There were no other vehicles moving in either direction. The bare terrain gave way to plantations of woods. Not a soul in sight. Just the place to kidnap a foreigner. Then I looked at the petrol gauge and saw it was registering nil. We made it down the hillside to Stia, a wholesome but small town with a small population. The only service station was closed for an extended lunch break. We sat in a little square eating strawberries while watching the locals disappearing to take their midday meal. By the time we left rain was threatening. At Arezzo it deluged down; we bought umbrellas and started to walk upwards towards the city centre. We got no further than the church of San Francesco, where the Piero della Francesca frescoes were barely visible in the gloom, before turning back and proceeding to Perugia where the National Gallery of Umbria provided evidence of the virgin-and-child syndrome wildly out of control. (How could believers so often portray the son of their god as slightly retarded? Answer: as often as they were commissioned to do so.) We found the cathedral mediocre. The city sprawled away from us and we didn't respond to it as we did to nearby Assisi, which was sheer joy. The sublime aisle of Giottos in the upper basilica was, at that stage, the first real highlight of our holiday. The delicate colouring of the frescoes, the bright, bold buildings like children's bricks and the clear story-line of the life of St Francis are enchanting in their authoritative simplicity. There were also the double cloisters and works by Cimabue and Simone Martini but above all, there was peace. Even the multitude of pilgrims was cowed into near silence. We returned next day before going on to Ravenna.

A factor which had determined our itinerary was having read Edith Templeton's idiosyncratic *The Surprise of Cremona*, in which the reader is also taken to Ravenna. There the dear lady wrote imaginatively and with deep feeling about the churches and mosaics but confused the Basilica of St Apollinaris Nuovo with that of St Apollinaris in Classe, seven miles away. Her description of both churches was vivid yet didn't always tally with what I was looking at; she had muddled the two. At St Apollinare in Nuovo I was struck by the intense individuality of the magi. Caspar, in the lead, is about to bow, Melchior, next, ready to stoop, Balthasar, all but upright. There is wonder in their eyes. The male Saints show more character than the women and two are not strictly in uniform – St Martin has his cloak wrapped around him; St Laurent reveals a vivid red undergarment. All, male and female, are named. Above the processions are more figures, on separate panels, where people and birds are interspersed with formal, abstract motifs. The lighting of them is perfect. There are chairs and benches for visitors. The only jarring note came from the baroque tat assembled in the altar area. At Sant' Apollinaris in Classe, with its grandly lofty interior and three spacious naves, the sublime mosaics are spread over and around the altar to make a sensational impact. Above the apse Christ is represented by only one small hand over a slightly crushed circle surrounding a simple cross. Below him is Sant' Apollinaris bordered by sheep, flowers, trees, standing, both hands upraised, palms outward. The background is gold and green. It is mesmerising.

Ravenna, in the fifth century AD the capital of the Roman Empire, instantly became one of my top ten Italian wonders. At St Vitale, there are more equally exquisite mosaics and in a pleasant shady park is Theodoric's tomb, a sombre pile. Theodoric was an Ostrogoth who converted to Christianity; the mosaics post date him. Dante referred to them as 'a symphony of colour'; *Michelin* rates them higher than those in Venice, Palermo or Constantinople.

From Sottomarina, a *molto ordinario* seaside resort, we paused for a break between two wonderous places before going from there to Venice by car. We revisited favourite places and I attempted to follow routes suggested in J. G. Links, the best of all guides to anywhere. His constant advice is not to hurry, not to worry about what you may be missing, to relax and frequently sit down to take a coffee or a glass of wine. Yes, certainly, there is an amazing painting in that church over yonder but it will still be there when you are ready to visit it. Actually, it may well be shut by then, but no matter.

Once we walked to Chioggia to take a ferry to the southern end of the Lido where we caught a bus which rattled us along the island to the vaporetto stop for Venice. Returning in the evening rush hour the bus carried an excessive, and illegal, number of highly voluble and cheerful workers, none of whom appeared to pay for the ride. Crouched on seats obligingly made vacant for us we could see little but trousered legs.

On the drive home across northern Italy we caught up with Mrs Templeton again at Mantua where, under her guidance, we visited the Palazzo Ducale and made a not entirely successful attempt to enter into her fantasies concerning paintings of horses and nobles.

Two days on, Sunday was good for driving into central Paris where Jessica was living for a year. We lunched with her in an attic high above the Rue Franklin D. Roosevelt, just off the Champs Elysées, where the bathroom, loo and kitchen merged. She phoned various hotels on the road to Boulogne for our last night's stay but, as on the previous evening, they were all full. In Boulogne itself we got a partitioned room, into which had been manoeuvred a double bed and a wardrobe leaving a square centimetre or two of floor space for our shoes and baggage. The en suite was down a narrow passage. It didn't matter. Below in the noisy bistro we had a superb dinner (including snails) and Mavis did not leave her handbag at the table.

# 13

## Sabbaticals and the Trade Press

When academics invented sabbaticals to allow themselves to examine their navels every seven years I do not know but Penguin Books had introduced them in a modest way before I was attracted to the practice. I was already taking longer holidays; it was also something High Hill could afford. When first mooted, someone enquired, 'Will people be paid while they are away?' to which the answer was, 'Of course. Otherwise how will they be able to travel?' It was fair to base eligibility on length of service which meant that Monica would be the first to benefit. John Ford reacted with horror; he didn't object to others taking six months off but he couldn't face it. What, he asked, would he do with himself?

Looking back on my sabbatical it is hard to believe my good luck. We had farewell drinks at the shop on the last day of March 1982 and soon after, Mavis and I set off for five months in Europe, travelling 10,000 miles by road, plus a few hundred by sea, staying at thirty-two places in thirteen countries and being visited by nineteen friends and relatives. (Statistics! Statistics!)

When we arrived home, we fell into each other's arms and drank to our achievement. What simple souls we were. We had not sailed in an open boat across a river let alone an ocean, scaled perilous peaks wearing pitons, plunged into dense jungle, crossed deserts on foot, arid plains by bike, back-packed, island-hopped or flown in a balloon. We had been insular Europeans who had crossed by coach into Asia Minor and returned within half an hour to our own continent. And we had rested for the majority of the hundred odd nights in pre-arranged accommodation, with mod cons. Hardly the stuff of Freya Stark, Dervla Murphy, Colin Thubron or Robert Byron; we were their timid counterparts, intrepid explorers of the beaten track, who completed most of the journey in a comfortable modern car which did not once break down, but for us it was a great adventure. We had also been doubly fortunate in leaving our retail business in the hands of trusted colleagues and our house with two young tenants of short acquaintance. We returned to find shop and home in good order.

How do you make a book out of that kind of self-packaged, low key epic? Well, I did, in spite of my long experience as a bookseller of returning to publishers scores of titles which did not sell. I knew the story of our sabbatical – called just that – with the sub-title *Doing Europe for Pleasure* – was unlikely to be commissioned or accepted, even on the old boy network, which was why I offered it to The High Hill Press – and, lo!, it was accepted. Most copies sold were retailed through High Hill Bookshops; some at a pre-publication reduced price.

I will refer here briefly only to those aspects of our European saga which, twenty-five years on, remain vividly with me. At the top of the list comes our first experience of Greece which for all our long identification with France and French culture, and a later addiction to Italy, took precedence. The month we spent on Aegina, from which we visited Athens, Epidaurus, Hydra and elsewhere (including driving through Metamorphoses and emerging unchanged) added an incomparable dimension to our lives.

Dilys Powell, in both *An Affair of the Heart* and in *The Villa Ariadne*, expressed what many of us feel in our innermost selves about Greece and Crete. It is the sky, the sea, the people, the olive groves, the sun-baked earth, the ruined temples, the white-washed churches, the busy taverna. All these things, but not at all times of the year. The climate can be cruel, so can the people . . . not to mention the cuisine. Powell wrote about herself, those she met, the places where they lived and worked, especially the archaeological sites and the villages close to them; the history, the mythology, the topography, are there incidentally, sometimes as foreground, sometimes background. The people were, and are, real to her as she was, and probably is, to them.

It is unlikely that casual, infrequent visitors will penetrate the true nature of this land which, in return for the wide influence it has had down the centuries, has borrowed from other lifestyles. Bad habits know no frontiers. Many of them, in the case of Greece, are the result of foreign occupation. It endured Turkish domination for centuries and in our time was invaded by Nazi Germany. The British and others pilfered (and preserved) its treasures; it suffered civil war and dictatorship. It remains a beacon of civilisation and a prime symbol of democratic aspirations.

What is felt about Greece and Crete (the latter, back in 1982, still an experience several years ahead for us) can be found in Patrick Leigh Fermor, Osbert Lancaster, Nicholas Gage and both Byrons. (Make your own list.)

These thoughts were not much with us as we sped down what the Greeks were pleased to designate a motorway en route from Istanbul to Athens. Mavis was developing bronchitis. I was anxious for us to reach the island of Aegina and the owners of the house we had rented from, an Anglo-Greek couple. The skies were overcast, the Gods were obviously not pleased with our presence; we were not pleased by the horrid lunch of lukewarm roast lamb served near Thermopylae, a name from the past if ever there was.

Then the rains came. There was no sign of the Acropolis as we passed through Athens which presented itself, from the efficient road leading us to Piraeus, as a rundown, drab city.

Thirty-six hours of Aegina changed everything. Mavis was cured, friends were due from the UK. After a month on the road, we unpacked and made ourselves at home. I have seldom felt more content. Re-reading what I wrote in *Sabbatical* I think this comes through. We did not live in anything approaching luxury . . . the comforts of the simple house were, if anything, appropriately Spartan. We were bitten by thousands of insects to a degree that changed our physiognomy, drank of the wine we named Demestika of which all that could be said in its favour was that it didn't taste like Retsina. It didn't taste much of anything and its alcohol level was low, yet our consumption of it caused a shortage in the little town of Aegina and necessitated our raiding shops elsewhere on the island.

We ate better than we drank, consuming fresh fish and vegetables mainly cooked in our own kitchen; sometimes we treated ourselves to moussaka, invariably cold, at a restaurant, or partook of a Greek salad with feta cheese piled on lumps of undressed lettuce and large inelegant slices of tomato. Against this we cracked thousands of pistachio nuts which are grown on the island and had memorable picnics lying under umbrella pines, beside temples, by the sparkling sea. And we travelled in large ships to Hydra, went by car ferry to visit Epidaurus and Nauplia or took a rowing boat to a deserted island which became part of the setting for Diana Raymond's novel, *The House of the Dolphin*.

Aegina was the highlight, La Concia, in northern Tuscany, the runner-up and contesting for third place, the Alhambra (gardens, history, architecture vying to capture our attention), Delphi (hearing Elgar, on tape, in a giant olive grove), Dubròvnik (walking the ancient walls) and Maratea (making love in the moonlight on a terrace overlooking the Bay of Policastro). We had to forego Venice in favour of crossing the Adriatic to Bari; we didn't omit Paris. It was there George and Val Simpson joined us for the final five nights. You cannot go wrong with Paris.

Soon after returning from our sabbatical Fred Newman of *Publishing News* invited me to write a regular column for his then fortnightly publication. I had first tasted the joys of being a columnist long before on the *Eastbourne Herald*; then, for a short while in the fifties I had had a monthly slot in *British Books* and for part of the seventies an occasional column in *The Bookseller*.

There was a long gap between the demise of *British Books* and the appearance of *Publishing News* in 1977. For too long *The Bookseller* was the only trade paper, which was bad both for it and for the trade. Its veteran Editor, for forty years, was Edmond Segrave, a dapper, short, almost bald man who usually wore a bow tie. He was a devout Roman Catholic who had once felt inclined to become a Jesuit priest. He had a small circle of cronies many of whom contributed pseudonymously to the journal owned by the Whitaker family, (of Almanack fame) whose fortunes he had revived in the early thirties when *The Publishers' Circular* was, briefly, the official trade paper. Before joining *The Bookseller* Segrave worked at Heinemann, playing a part in transforming the various novels which John Galsworthy had written about the Forsyte family into saga form. Until his appointment a 'Whitaker' had always edited *The Bookseller* (originally *Bent's Notes*); Segrave made the journal more readable and authoritative and saw off the supremacy of *The PC*, introducing new features written by his chosen few, encouraging a lively letters page and boosting circulation. He became close to Haddon Whitaker, by then head of the family firm. They often lunched *à deux*, in the small directors' dining room of the house in Bedford Square, which became the post-blitz offices, sometimes joined there, once deemed suitably mature, by son and heir, David Whitaker. He, who learned much about the book trade from them, had a tiny office under the eaves, next to the caretaker's flatlet. On a lower floor was Segrave's personal pad which was a monument to disorder. Books and papers swamped his desk, overflowing on to the floor where more were stacked defensively against the front of it. The walls bore fitted bookshelves. On the desk top one small space was kept clear for work on the next issue of *The Organ of the Book Trade*, as it styled itself. Where today he would have put such essentials as the computer, the screen and keyboard, let alone the printer, is easy to guess . . . out of the window.

Edmond Segrave was revered by the Whitakers, and by his assistant Philothea Thompson, Oshia to her favoured friends. I was honoured to be one, as I was not of the Editor's, who never became 'Edmond' to me. I was in awe of him; his acceptance of a piece of mine seemed to seal my career. He accepted several more while it remained unsealed and published most of the many letters I sent him. I was also invited, by Oshia, to contribute to the Christmas round-up of the bookshops, and what they were selling. Segrave came very occasionally to the Society of Bookmen dinners, where I sat with him a couple of times. The closest contact I had was by telephone, first when I was enduring a lengthy contretemps with the Booksellers' Association because High Hill was not meeting its training commitments by sending an assistant on a course. This was due to my belief that the best way to learn bookselling was by actually practising it on the shop floor. Because I didn't wish us to lose our status as a member of the Charter Group of Booksellers I thought of a compromise. I sent a box advert to *The Bookseller* offering out-of-work actors employment for impersonating booksellers on training courses. To my surprise Segrave himself phoned to discuss the wording. He was concerned that it might be interpreted as an incitement to mislead and deceive. I said that, if so, any actor might be chargeable every time he stepped on a stage. The Editor demurred, reiterating his objections for a long while. We finally reached an agreement. I did what he said and amended the copy to make it unlikely that anyone applying for the job would be acceptable to the BA. On the other occasion the great man unbent and was helpful. I had sent him a copy of the essay I planned to publish in the doomed *Book of Westminster*, which included experiences of Christina Foyle. I asked if there was anything I had written which, if submitted to him, he would reject on grounds of libel. There was not but he was in a mood to chat about it genially.

Segrave was succeeded by the devoted Oshia, who was happy to serve up the mixture as before while being approachable to a wider circle of would-be contributors. The change was beneficial to me because Oshia, who had inherited a family house in Downshire Hill, one of Hampstead's choicest roads, came regularly to High Hill to gossip. This led to one of the booziest lunches of my life. It was a Friday, prelude to the busiest day of my week but to her the day of rest when *The Bookseller* had been put to bed overnight down at Colchester ready for publication on Saturday. We met at a wine bar off Tottenham Court Road before crossing over to St Giles High Street, then still a vibrant trading street on the site of what had been one of London's worst slums. Little of it, towered over by atrocious Centre Point, remains today. Then its many restaurants included one run by three Swiss sisters, two of whom bullied the third unmercifully. Oshia sat out the afternoon, eating, drinking, gossiping. I remember returning to Hampstead – four miles to the north – on foot because it was literally necessary to walk off the effects. It was at such times that I realised how truly dedicated a bookseller I was.

Over lunch I suggested to Oshia that I should have a signed weekly column, not one of their pseudonymous jobs. She pursed her lips, toyed with the idea, subsequently coming up with the proposal that perhaps four contributors might rotate. I clutched at that but it came to nothing. The stumbling block was my aversion to ano- or pseudo-nymity. She accepted other offerings of mine and Michael Geare, who had been recruited by Segrave, was also allowed to commission pieces from me. He took to referring to me in print as 'the sage of Hampstead'. Michael was an ex-sales and publicity manager of J. M. Dent, married to a journalist, drafted in, along with Gerry Davies and Colin Eccleshare, to put *The Organ* together each week. He did not enjoy the easiest of relationships with Oshia. Once, in an endeavour to discover whose name was behind which pseudonym in *The Organ*, I casually referred to him as 'the man who wrote Quentin Oates'. She scoffed, venomously, 'He couldn't write that Column.' (But I think he did.)

When David Whitaker, exercising proprietorial rights, decided to succeed Oshia I had better luck with my aspirations to become a columnist. As editor he did well, having a wide understanding of the trade, been active in the Society of Young Publishers and more gregarious than either his father or Edmond Segrave. David almost conceded me a regular slot, although I was never able to convince him that a columnist, like everyone else, needs security of tenure, even though the quality of the copy is bound to fluctuate. He wouldn't have it, stating a regular column would be bad for me. I knew it would not. A compromise was reached when he invented a feature, named 'From

Occasional Hands', in which he could publish other people's work when he wished. In this way I did get published almost every month for nearly two years, once, to describe the Christmas rush at the bookshop, altering the title to 'On Occasional Knees'. I found him a receptive editor. By which I mean he didn't carve up my copy. He says I didn't notice that he did, but I always know when that has happened. Once, late one night at home, we had a slanging match on the phone when he rejected a poem of mine. Next day I trailed down to *The Bookseller* office, to make a peace offering of champagne.

Almost the first time I met David was when I called at the Bedford Square office to take out a new subscription to *The Organ*. I came across him looming about in the entrance passage, wondering how to occupy himself usefully, his large frame needing exercise, his thoughts demanding expression, aware probably that he was too old by now to behave like a spoilt child and get away with it.

'I've just taken out another subscription,' I said, proudly.

'That'll cost us money,' he replied, mournfully.

'Why?'

'Each extra copy printed means a greater loss.

It sounded like a false argument but he insisted it was so until such a time as there were sufficient extra subscriptions to justify increasing the advertising rates. I told him he was talking rubbish.

When David handed over to Louis Baum I had every hope that I would continue to appear almost regularly in *The Bookseller*, although I should have known by then that a change of editor invariably means a change of contributors.

Louis, the first *Organ* editor who was a trained journalist, I knew from the Society of Bookmen dinners. He had come from South Africa where writing for the press carried the danger of trying to print the truth under an oppressive regime. David recognised in him the man Whitaker's needed, and so, bitten hard by the ISBN bug, he handed over the reins to allow himself time to concentrate on committing the trade to publishing by number.

Louis rejected most of my offerings but invited me to contribute an obituary of Gaffer Blackwell saying 'because you are the book trade historian, we'll pay you. We don't usually for obits.' We lunched. He suggested things I might write for him but dropped David's column. I submitted various pieces which he turned down, while promising to think up a new feature which I might write. I tried; it never worked. I even have a letter from Louis, stating: 'I treated you badly.'

I found a home at *Publishing News*. Then, at the very moment I agreed to a fortnightly column, Louis invited me to cover a series of book programmes on BBC television. I was not under contract to either journal so I accepted. Immediately, Fred Newman, editor for *PN*, offered me the same assignment. It was embarrassing but Fred allowed me to write the one for him under a pseudonym . . . which is what I had always refused to do for Whitaker's.

Fred was a realist. He knew which journal was top dog and adroitly angled *Publishing News* at a different book trade market. He was correct and both publications appeared weekly on the same day until July 2008.

When I first wrote for *PN* it occupied offices high up in number 28 Little Russell Street where Book Tokens was once located. Fred Newman's staff, at that time, included Pat Miller, a bright, dashing woman from the western hemisphere who took the rise out of me if I mentioned how anyone was clothed. 'I just love you being our fashion correspondent.' There was also Jonathan Warner, a gifted young man who was helpful when I couldn't find the pay off I sought. Liz Thomson did not join the paper until it had moved to nearby Museum Street, where she took over Pat Miller's desk. The Editorial four had a corner each in a small first floor front with Fred facing Rodney Burbeck, a colleague from his *Daily Sketch* days, while Roger Tagholm, an ex-W. H. Smith bookseller, sat opposite Liz. There was a total lack of privacy. Everybody overheard what everyone else was saying, often chiming in with their own contributions, although at least two of them were on the phone at any one time. When Rodney was introduced to me, he exclaimed, 'Oh, you're real are you?', having supposed I was someone's nom de plume. It was a cluttered room where a lot of work was accomplished. I had to find space on a filing cabinet to correct my proof.

I wrote the column for eight years. I never had a more under-standing and indulgent editor than Fred. Long after the battle between Fleet Street and Murdoch and Maxwell had been resolved, and *The Times* had returned to the newsstands, I enjoyed a weekly ritual at *Publishing News*. On Monday, en route to the Garrick for lunch, I filed my copy, having climbed the stairs beside the jeweller's shop, passed the loo where there was always a smell of escaping gas, natural or otherwise, and exchanged gossip and quips in the crowded editorial room. On Friday – again en route for 'the Drones' – I called in to correct my proof and decide what cuts or additions were necessary to make it fit the available space. This was not a privilege accorded to many journalists at that stage of transition from Fleet Street to Canary Wharf. I mentioned it to Louis Heren, deputy editor of *The Times*, at the club bar. He was amazed, commenting, 'we never see proofs now.'

This Louis was a genial realist, from a working-class family, and joined *The Times*, where a relative of his worked in the machine room as a messenger boy. He had served in the war and returned an ex-officer, like his colleague Jack Cooper, to reclaim his job. He wound his way up through the intricacies of upper class Printing House Square to become a foreign correspondent. Louis lived in Hampstead, when he wasn't in Bonn or Washington. His book *Growing up Poor in London* was a stock line at the shop. He was medium height, had a slight paunch and was flat-headed with an Aussie-style face in the Danish pastry tradition. He almost chain smoked and loved his wine. He was a natural writer and journalist and, in a fair world, Murdoch should have appointed him editor of the paper he served loyally for so long.

Fred Newman, who was at Oxford with Michael Heseltine and Clive Labovitch, had ranged about Fleet Street, academia and publishing before becoming editor of *Publishing News*. Clive, who owned the paper, had previously been associated with Heseltine at the Corn-market Press. Fred was amiable, tough and at times inarticulate. The words, in his excitement to communicate, did not always come out in the sequence he intended. Attempting to punctuate any run-of-the-mill sentence of Fred's would have been a nightmare. His speeches frequently ended with, 'know what I mean?'; often one didn't. Yet he got results and it was his triumph that *P N*, which he eventually owned, survived for three more decades. Its last years, edited by Liz Thomson, surpassed in readability and trade awareness, the now foreign-owned *The Bookseller*. In the eighties, *PN* was a flimsy broadsheet, somewhat brash in approach, with substandard layout reminiscent of a political handout, cramming words into all available space. It carried a healthy amount of advertising and sponsored the Nibbies Awards, an annual razzmatazz at a Park Lane hotel, now a popular fixture of the trade year.

'What shall we call my column?' I asked.

Fred thought for a moment. ' "Ian Norrie" will do.'

I liked it. Only once, in many years did he say what I'd submitted wouldn't do. Then I quickly wrote another piece. Fred was as authoritative as Arthur Goss, of the *Ham & High*, had been about payment. He decided when my rate should be increased. (No union nonsense.) Once he doubled it without warning. Another time, by some quirk of the administration, I was sent, in France, where I was temporarily living, the cheques for all the other contributors. That was quite an eye opener to me but it didn't seem to embarrass Fred. He still went on paying me what he decided I was worth even though he knew I knew some were on a higher rate.

I regretted when, eighteen months after selling the bookshop, my weekly stint came to an end in 1990, although I remained for over a decade an occasional contributor. For many months I had faxed weekly columns from France but it was thought I was getting out of touch, and no doubt I was. Thus an enjoyable feature of my life came to an end and it took some months before I found a substitute.

I thought I may have found it when Gordon Graham, on retirement from publishing, founded *Logos*, a journal for the English-speaking book world.

Following war service in the Far East, Gordon had been employed by McGraw Hill as a journalist before moving over to book publishing. I was pleased to be invited to contribute to the first issue of *Logos* but less enthusiastic when having asked, 'What do you pay?', I was told, 'Nothing. We're a learned journal.'

'But I'm not learned, Gordon. And, like you, I'm an old hack. Books are different from journalism. I expect to be paid.'

It was not on. I submitted . . . 'but only this once', and wrote a nostalgic piece about bookselling. A wholly agreeable by-product of *Logos* was the annual lunch in their beautifully landscaped Marlow garden given by Gordon and Betty (assisted by daughter Sylvia, some-time assistant to bookseller Bunty McNeil, later a rep for Collins), for one hundred or so contributors, advisory board members and other old chums. It was an event which epitomised that innate friendship within the book trade which is an underlying theme of this memoir.

Gordon is a disarming man, ex-veteran of the Burma campaign, whose approach to life seems to discourage conflict, embodying a preference for the Churchillian precept that jaw-jaw is better than war-war; although, like that statesman, I suspect he is physically fearless. Nobody could live less in a time warp than Gordon, yet he has some endearingly old-fashioned characteristics, one of which is to address other men as 'Old Boy'. And he is almost alone among presidents of the P.A. in not having been a member of the Garrick. This could be because he is not partial to lunch.

Both *Publishing News* and *Logos* gave notice of their final editions in 2008. Fred Newman survived for only four months after the demise of his thirty-year venture. Liz Thomson, editor during the final years, obituarised him affectionately but without pulling her punches in the *Guardian* and elsewhere. By then she had joined Nick Clee, the last of 'my' editors at the *Bookseller*, to launch a web-site named *BookBrunch*. I hope it will support them both for a similar three decades. (*Logos* will be perpetuated on the Internet, along with associated archives.)

On the High Hill front my work pattern did not recover from the sabbatical which unsettled me, instilling a desire to travel for longer periods each year and to spend more time writing. After 1982, I was never totally committed to the bookshop although I continued to enjoy the wider ambience of the London book trade. I did not neglect the business any more than was commensurate with having responsible, intelligent colleagues who were capable, as they had proved, of keeping it going highly successfully in my absence. I continued to take the major decisions, usually in consultation with them, but still got away without having 'bored' meetings. The only time the directors met in concert, apart from many social occasions, was for the annual general meeting at which I put pressure on my good friend Geoff Hill, our auditor, to get through the business rapidly because we were all anxious for lunch. Again I was so lucky to be permitted to run the business my way and yet maintain good relations with my colleagues most of the time. When the shop closed, in 1988, we paid all outstanding debts, gave generous severance pay and came out of it financially enhanced.

Closure was unexpected. Turnover and profit were rising satis-factorily in 1987 when Waterstone's announced their opening in premises on the opposite side of the High Street to us which, a decade earlier, had been Woolworth's. After they closed a remainder bookseller, named Susan Reynolds, had leased it. Although 'she' under-cut us on certain titles which were review copies, or perhaps bankrupt stock, our business went unharmed. When I learned 'she' was selling a Pan gardening title which we regularly turned over at the published price, I became their customer, buying all they had at a larger dis-count than Pan offered us. 'Susan's' presence also bore out my long expressed belief that more bookshops in the area would create a larger overall market. This was why I had not been bothered by competition from other legitimate booksellers. Nevertheless the arrival of a Waterstone's on a better, bigger site was a blow to my amour propre. I had taken my position for granted for too long, having the largest bookshop not just in Hampstead but all of north London. Now it looked as though I might be playing second fiddle. And it was upsetting to have Waterstone's advertising in the *Ham & High* that 'at last Hampstead would have a bookshop worthy of its residents, offering a range of world literature for the first time.' (The *Ham & High* accepted the ad but Gerry Isaaman questioned the wording in editorial comment.) I criticised Tim Waterstone in my column in *Publishing News* and was told by a friend I was whingeing, which was tantamount to not accepting the umpire's decision. I still think it was fair criticism but, of course, I should have 'walked'. Which was precisely what, in the following year, I did.

At the same time that Waterstone's opened, Camden Council, by now spending £60,000 p.a. with us, had a liquidity crisis and ceased buying books. We were also faced with imminent massive rent increases on both our leasehold properties. Had I been ten years younger I would have had to cut my cloth and struggle on. Neither Trisha (forty per cent owner) nor my daughter, Amanda (by then on the board), wished to take over the managing directorship. Instead we sold our valuable freehold after months of abortive negotiations with other booksellers, including Waterstone's. I have never regretted the decision. The ending of the Net Book Agreement and the impact of the internet have created a trade so different from the one I was once a part of that I know it would not have suited me.

Many customers were to say – still do say – how much they miss the bookshop but not all felt that way. About a year after we ceased trading Mavis and I were at a party in the Garden Suburb. In one corner of Robin and Inge Hyman's drawing-room a loyal ex-customer was lamenting to me our passing; in another Mavis was listening to a fellow guest, saying, 'Have you been in that marvellous new Waterstone's we have in Hampstead?'

As I subsequently told Tim Waterstone, I thought he did us a good turn in helping to provoke our closure. There is a time for everything and although for a while I missed the shop, particularly on Saturdays, I revelled more in my new found freedom.

# 14

## Scandinavia and Crete

We had scarcely returned from our sabbatical before I was planning an itinerary for Mavis's childhood friend, Barbara Grantham, who had spent most of her married life in New Zealand. There she had an adoring husband and three children but missed what they called 'Yerp'. For her 'New Zeal' had no history, at least in the European, or more particularly, the English sense. We had met her again a few years before when she came home to wallow in castles and stately homes; now she wanted to visit France and Italy for three weeks. That she believed would prove adequate because she is not actually into looking at paintings. Her method of doing so is to glare at them forbiddingly, then to quickly move on to the next. She found it incomprehensible that I should take us out of our way in Rome to visit a church which has two Caravaggios, especially as I had to find several thousand lira in coins to have them illuminated. But she loved the Roman ruins and enjoyed poking around in the eerie catacombs, outside the main entrance to which we sat on a bench and had a picnic, all the while pretending not to understand gestures being made by an attendant, who thought this somehow improper, to move on. As Barbara didn't and she was the Christian among us, I persuaded the ladies that we should continue with our lunch. There is a snap of Barbara brandishing a wine bottle. She was also thoroughly appreciative of the Forum, the Colosseum, Trajan's column and the various fountains. And it was agreeable for the two old school friends to have time off while I went to ogle an ill-lit masterpiece or two.

We arrived in Rome late afternoon to stroll down Via Cavour which, I advised Barbara, was a boring thoroughfare but led to better things. At that moment shots rang out, sirens blared, blue lights flashed and shopkeepers began to put up their shutters. We never found out the cause but sought sanctuary in the forum where we attempted to understand what it had really been like to live in ancient times and sympathised with the vestal virgins being walled-up alive when they had misbehaved.

In the Piazza Navona we dined near the Bernini fountain while a spastic boy with an accordion lay on his back gallantly playing the same notes repetitively. Next day we drove to the villas Adriana and d'Este at Tivoli, at the latter disciplining ourselves to follow the recommended route, thus seeing every fountain in full flow – and not getting too wet.

At a hotel in Sorrento, where we had a private suite on a cliff edge, we were touched by the gesture of an American woman who, one dinner time, brought us her unfinished bottle of wine as a thank you for having enjoyed herself while in Britain. To reach the sea from the hotel there was a spooky descent of several hundred feet in a lift built into the actual rock. On enchanting Capri we walked from the boat up to the town centre through lanes dense with bougainvillea and bussed up the hair pin bends to Anacapri and the cool, calm, whitewashed Villa San Michele. This elegant residence, after a while, seemed altogether too pristine, becoming strangely sinister. At Ravello, we wandered again in the overgrown gardens of the Villa Cimbrone. These places appealed to Barbara but returning along the steep, winding roads of the Amalfi coast Mavis said firmly she would not be driven on them again. They were too unnerving and, 'you can't see the views anyway because you have to watch the road.' I didn't make things worse by confessing that I sometimes swiftly turned my head to have a look.

Barbara preferred Ravello to Ravenna where we again found our-selves overwhelmed by the mosaics and Venice she embraced with enthusiasm. When I booked a hotel on the Lido this drew a con-temptuous snort from a fellow member at the club, who observed sententiously, 'I would never *think* of staying there.' Why? We were travelling by car, Mavis wished to have a handy beach and the journey into Venice from the Lido by vaporetto offers one of the world's greatest views. Using my Links, when I went off by myself, I was encouraged to discover that even that great guide occasionally got things wrong; I didn't take 'him' to the islands when we went as a threesome though I read his brief comments on Torcello where it is not possible to take a wrong turning.

The journey home was partly by autostrada because Barbara had a plane to catch to New Zeal. In Susa we wilted in intense heat; on Mont Cenis we shivered. Once down into France, at Aiguebelle, we booked into an ancient coaching inn, offering basic accommodation and delectable provincial cooking, starting with concombre à la crème, eaten in a room decorated to the height of bad taste. Indeed, higher; the strident design covered the ceiling as well as walls. There was a repeat experience the next night at Montmirail, in a hotel where floorboards creaked, windows could not be opened and doors didn't fit. We paid our bills before retiring because on Sundays the hotel was *fermé*. Next morning, we let ourselves out, hoping the sound of our baggage being trundled down an ancient staircase wouldn't disturb *le patron*'s lie-in.

En route for Calais we took a break at Amiens where the cathedral was in use for morning service so we had to be content with admiring the magnificent west front. I complained, 'Why is everything always closed?' Barbara politely pointed out that it *was* Sunday. Later, in the restaurant on the cross Channel ferry, there was no wine available because the key of the 'cellar' had been mislaid. There is nothing like travel for souring the mind.

For 1984 it seemed not inappropriate to include Soviet Russia in our travels. We were already committed to Scandinavia from a promise made to Ingvar and Adorée who had joined us at Maratea, Italy, two years earlier. We had so often resisted the suggestion we should return to their homeland. 'We'll come in 1984,' I promised. Down there, 200 kilometres south from Naples in a heatwave, with the prospect of Provence, Spain and the Algarve to come, a Scandinavian summer seemed an ideal contrast. And why not extend this to the Arctic Circle, before crossing back into Norway and following the coast south to Narvik and Bergen? Ingvar strongly advised against this and said we must visit Gotland, the largest island in the Baltic Sea. Adorée had written a book about it; he had taken the colour photographs. We could be there in between doing Stockholm and Helsinki and then go on to Leningrad, as it was then called. As a sop to my conscience I contracted with Fred Newman to write some articles about bookselling in Scandinavia for *Publishing News*. I donned suit and tie to visit booksellers. At Erik Qvist's Your English Bookshop, founded in 1905, his son Harald greeted me clad in open-necked shirt and lightweight slacks. His father was on holiday. He told me his brother was a student living in Hampstead. Next we went to the old established Tanum's where owner Knut Lie was also tieless. (He said he had one in a drawer, 'in case'.) I removed mine. His son was working in England at Hamlyn's with our friend Ronald Whiting. It seemed like a cosy extension of the book trade I knew. Mr Lie took us to lunch where we misguidedly asked for wine which is not usually taken at midday in Oslo partly because it is horrendously expensive, partly from custom. Mr Lie, who forgave us, was untediously informative on all aspects of the book trade in Norway. Mavis asked him to recommend a book, in translation, by a contemporary Norwegian. He pulled a thick paperback from the shelf – one thousand pages at least – saying, 'this is a modern classic'. It cost far more than any bottle of wine I might have bought in England. Which was a nice unintentional touch of *touché*.

Per Owing worked away at soliciting while we visited the bookshops; next day he conducted us on a grand tour of Oslo. At the National Gallery it seemed sensible to concentrate on the native paintings though I had some pangs about not lingering over the Impressionists and Rembrandts. We took the same line in Stockholm and Helsinki. Oslo was especially strong in narrative paintings and had a fine portrait of Ibsen by Erik Werenskiold. At Bygdor we saw *Kon-Tiki* again and Nansen's ship the *Fram*, then proceeded to Vikingskiphuset to see the ancient burial ships. These are housed in a single storey building which has the aura of a religious retreat. Its simplicity reflects the comparable and dignified austerity of the exhibits. Viewing platforms have been constructed along the walls of the museum so that it is possible to look into the bare interiors of the boats which may have been used for ocean voyages before they became mausoleums. If I could visit only one place on a return to Oslo, this would be it.

Following an early supper at the Owings we walked the ridge of Lillhagveien, noting the prosperous villas sensitively placed in the wooded terrain. None was outstandingly beautiful or innovative in design; all looked good to live in and had spacious gardens. Lucky middle class, I thought. When I enquired if there were any poor in Norway, Kari told me that on the other side of Oslo, where their daughter Anna lived, there were indeed. We saw something of the 'poverty' as we drove along the E18 to Stockholm, sometimes beside a fjord, at others through wooded valleys and farmland dotted with spruce houses of all sizes. Whatever Kari maintained, none of it looked poverty stricken in the way that parts of British towns do, only mildly down at heel. A tile was out of place on one roof.

In Stockholm we stayed at the Nordberg's pied-à-terre in the centre of the city. Close by was an excellent French restaurant, La Brochette, with affordable prices and an 'English pub' of dubious credentials. From there we went to Gotland for a week with the Nordbergs, travelling by a car ferry which moved at the pace of an old, tired coal barge. Gotland covers 1200 square miles and has a population of 54,000. Adorée, having the status of scholar and author, was permitted to rent one of the oldest houses in Visby, the capital and there we stayed, in the shadow of the spruce cathedral, for six nights. Visby's intact medieval street plan was a visual delight offering vistas from every angle. There were also eyesores, notably two of the great ruined churches boarded-up, fenced-off, surrounded by barbed wire and fallen masonry, as though recently burned out or bombed. In fact the damage was done centuries ago.

There were many old ruined churches. In the grounds of one – amongst the graves – we watched an opera about the life of a monk who was Sweden's first recorded author, Petrus de Dacia. We saw it late on a fine summer's evening which became so chilly that we were pleased we had brought blankets. When we left we were shepherded out into the streets lit only by candles held aloft by the chorus of monks, their heads bowed and covered by cowls. The performance was regarded as a religious ceremony and we were asked not to applaud.

At Visby's museum we first encountered picture stones, which are peculiar to the island. They are headstones erected close to or above graves. Some date back to the fifth and eighth centuries and have abstract designs, others show ships and objects supposedly connected with the lives of the deceased.

We toured the island for five days, once by municipal coach because the trip included a military zone for which foreigners required escorts. The first stop was at Bro, a village which has one of the 92 churches on Gotland dating from before 1350. It was officially described as part Gothic, part Romanesque. It had a Norman-style doorway, a pleasing squat-shaped tower, a quaint Adam and Eve fresco and a gaudily painted font and box pews. Next we were shown the remains of an iron age defence system, the Bulverk, but the evidence was vestigial. Lena, our guide related an improbable and faintly boring troll tale about it. To reach the military area, on the smaller island of Faro, we took a ferry. If signs of the iron age were minimal at Bulverk, the presence of the military on Faro was totally camouflaged as we were led on to a stony beach at Langhammars where raukar stood. Raukar are limestone shapes eroded by sea and wind, gaunt and impressive, a cross between ecclesiastical ruins and outsize fossils. The bumpy journey over a crudely made road was well worth it, as was the view inland from the beach where juniper, wild strawberries, wild thyme and barley sprouted out of seemingly sheer rock. On the way back to Visby, at the Bunge Folk Museum, we saw more picture stones standing stark and dignified against trees, projecting their simple stories dramatically, one a tale of invasion from over the water with a ship in full sail. Elsewhere we were shown limestone quarries and inland lakes while subjected to whole of volumes of information from Lena. I don't remember any of it.

Another day we drove to see an ancient burial site in the shape of large keels, delineated by boulders standing, evocatively, among conifers. Stones marked the outline and it was not difficult, especially after seeing the huge vessels in Oslo, to imagine oneself in a boat, perhaps approaching Lethe? We saw many more that day as well as a few dozen additional churches and another museum presided over by Maja, an egotistic, elderly peasant woman, wearing a sailor's blue-and-white shirt over wide beige slacks and a peaked cap, who was a mistress of the long conducted tour, with English commentary from herself. The museum occupied a lovely old farmhouse where we were made to inspect the contents of numerous drawers and wardrobes containing junk from down the ages. After that more rauker, more Visby. On the return drive I made the discovery that the cause of my habitual drowsiness in the afternoon cannot be solely due to alcohol because I hadn't touched a drop all day.

Our last trip, while Adorée and Ingvar went to watch sheep farming exercises about which I was unable to arouse any enthusiasm, involved nature more than architecture. We were in search of a little town which had a railway museum and took a wrong turning down a country lane where the woods and wildflowers were captivating. Min, the flower expert, identified orchises, hare bells, campanula, rose bay willow herb, St John's wort and many other species.

Our Swedish hosts, rightly proud of Gotland, ensured we experienced many of its delights. Back in Stockholm they took us to the family home at Bromma for lunch with Ingvar's parents who had been so hospitable to us in 1972. We were treated as old intimates which did not excuse us from the ritual of being offered 'soda water'. This indicates it is time to leave.

Twenty-four hours later it was again time to depart, from Stockholm by car ferry bound for Helsinki. We had spent the intervening time at the Vasararvet Museum and in bookshops. The most popular attraction at the museum was the Wasa warship sunk in 1628 and raised in 1961. No flagship ever had a more inglorious record. It sank here in the harbour soon after embarking on its maiden voyage. There was extensive loss of life purely because the monarch of the time had overruled the advice of experts and insisted on installing so many cannons on its decks that it became top heavy. Had he heeded them it might have sailed into battle, gone down all guns a-blazing with even more casualties and probably been forgotten for ever; now, thanks to skilled marine archaeology, it survives to draw thousands of tourists who inspect its great hulk and many of the artefacts which went down with it. It is a monument to autocratic stupidity.

The apparently purpose-built but not too glaringly modern Akadamien Bok was altogether more functional and less dangerous. Owned by the Students' Union and open to the general public it conveyed a more sensible use of materials. The books were effectively displayed and easily accessible and the layout daring. Those shelved on walls were colour-and-number coded for efficient stock control. Those on the floor were exhibited on gondolas and gustaves, free-standing units with many display levels, which could be lifted on to pallets for conveyance to another part of the floor space. Colour coding was continued on hanging signs which could easily be interpreted by customers searching for particular categories. All stock was appealingly displayed in a happy synthesis of contemporary design adapted to traditional bookselling methods. A sign outside the shop in Latin quoted Thomas à Kempis. The Dutch-born manager, Hans-Willem, insisted the shop was not perfect but hinted that he and his colleagues would make it so.

The liner on which we sailed to Helsinki and another massive vessel weaved their way for three hours through the myriad of water channels beside the skerries which make up the complicated archi-pelago named Skärgården. Skerries are islands, all wooded, some inhabited, twenty-four thousand in all. Some were cultivated and bright with flowers, many had roads leading to smartly painted villas; there were hundreds of jetties for small craft. It was a near-perfect evening for a singular and dreamlike experience. The route was as baffling as that of a mountain pass; there seemed no obvious way through the mass of islands but, just as a road will wind unexpectedly around an apparently impregnable hillside, so there was a deep passage to be found past the thronging islands. And to add perspective to this phenomenon, over there, never far away, was the other huge liner performing the same ballet. There were moments when it looked probable that we would collide with it as the two ships emerged simultaneously into a seemingly too narrow channel.

For two hours we remained on deck absorbed by an event which for us was unique. Then hunger took charge. We found a restaurant where there were seats beside a port hole. From them we watched a spectacular sunset. By the time I came to sign the bill we were into the Baltic with the other ferry only slightly to starboard. In the morning when I looked out upon grey skies and a dark green sea there it was again. Soon we were entering the Helsinki archipelago – a mere 3,000 islands. One cathedral became visible to port, another to starboard. The gaily coloured, uncovered market was operating on the broad quayside as it does every day of the year even in the coldest weather. Nine o'clock is a good hour to arrive in a new city. It gives you the illusion of gaining a whole extra day.

Helsinki presented itself as a gigantic development area. Old buildings were being bulldozed, new horrendously glass and steel ones erected. There were banks everywhere – you might have supposed yourself in Madrid – window displays were stylish; people looked well-nourished and dressed. The layout was hard to grasp because it is a port within an archipelago but a tour on the circular tram route helped to fit the jigsaw of streets into place and despite the ragged coastline many of them were encased in a grid system. Our hotel, the Vaakuna, had become partly a builder's yard – even the vestibule was shrouded in sheets of dark plastic. As we arrived a tour was leaving, with harassed couriers performing sheep dog routines around a nervously braying flock. The receptionist, unperturbed, dealt calmly with us; a smartly liveried young porter whisked my car off to a garage I never saw.

Within an hour of checking in we were at the Athenaeum Art Museum, a dowdy building out of place in this prosperous, flamboyantly contemporary capital. Sandwiched between a bank and a new shopping complex it resembled a nineteenth-century, nonconformist chapel, gaunt and tall, disproportionately high for its shallow interior. Steep, bare steps led to the galleries, the walls needed painting, the lighting was unsubtle, the partly glassed-over roof showed signs of leaking. There was an overall air of parsimonious provinciality. But it is paintings which make a gallery and we were soon captivated. The first to attract me was one of the Luxembourg Gardens during the fin de siècle. Had I come all this way to see a painting of Paris, probably by a Frenchman? Wrong. It is by one Albert Edelfelt to whom there is no reference in the Penguin or Thames and Hudson's *Dictionary of Art and Artists*, or in Gombrich's *The Story of Art*. There were good narrative paintings (e.g. Gunnar Berndtson's *The Bride's Song* and a pointillist *English Coast at Dover* by Alfred William Pinch, 1854–1930), also unremarked upon in the reference books. And, irritatingly, there was a publisher whose name eluded me, not hanging on a wall, as some of my bookselling friends might have thought appropriate, but in person and carrying a baby. I think he had once briefly worked for me but I didn't wish to know him in that place at that time while having my first experience of Helsinki. (Mavis, with a sixth sense acquired over thirty years, moved swiftly away from the threat of trade gossip.)

The city is an architectural hotchpotch, not least in its two cathedrals, one of which claims to be based on the Hagia Sofia in Istanbul, but there is enormous originality in a round church sunk into a vast stony cave, in Aalto's aggressively modern Finlandia Hall where the monotony of too much white marble is broken by the varied shape and, above all, in the Sibelius monument in a park. The latter stands on rock and has four feet, supporting several clusters of pipes of differing length, suggesting a fantastic cinema organ which has grown tentacles. And there is no warning to 'Keep off'. Kids are invited to romp on it and can do so without causing damage. Alongside, on another rock, is a sober bust of the composer placed there as a palliative for those who objected to what they deemed the levity of this free-ranging memorial.

At the National Museum it was free night when we called which in a city as cripplingly expensive as Helsinki was a boon. We looked respectfully at a numbingly comprehensive collection of Lapp antiquities and wandered through numerous rooms of reconstructed wooden dwellings. We saw also the Parliament Building, resembling – perhaps intentionally – an enormous power station and the railway terminus, by Aalto, which a guide book wittily described as 'like a thirties radio set.' The sculpture thereon includes brutalised figures, two each side of the main entrance, with symbolic bodies and thick hands supporting massive stone globes. It was from here that we left on a four-night visit to Leningrad. I dared not, as Colin Thubron had, take my car. We were still in the pre-Gorbachev era. For the seven hour daytime journey we were allotted a sleeping apartment with made-up beds. We shared it – though not the beds – with a party of American law librarians on 'A People to People Tour'.

At Viborg (annexed by the Soviets) customs officials came aboard and armed soldiers ordered us to 'Stand up!'. They looked under the beds, then barked, 'Sit down!'. The customs man asked what our wine cooler was. When told, he didn't attempt to confiscate the contents. After that it was endless birches, silver birches, all the way to the grubby suburbs of Leningrad, where we attained the official status of not being a group. One contemporary writer on Soviet Russia advised that 'wisdom surely dictates a temporary surrender' to the package tour. He was probably correct although, groupless, we came through unharmed and only slightly menaced.

On arrival at 'the Finland station' we bade farewell to the Americans and were confronted by a young man dressed in tee-shirt, jeans, sailing cap and pink-rimmed spectacles.

'Mr Norrie.' He said. This was not a question; it was a statement of fact. Had I disagreed it would have been up to me to prove my case.

'How do you know my name?' (An asinine query since my wanted mugshot was probably already on the wall of every Ogpu station in the USSR.)

'I look at your baggage.' He spoke Berlitz English very clearly. He apologised for the rain – 'it always rains in Leningrad' – and led us to a taxi. Were we visitors in our own right, honoured guests of the regime, or already under open arrest? I chatted to the young man about guide books, daringly referring to Thubron's which was certainly banned, and also to Kelly's *Leningrad*. He didn't know the latter. I resolved to give him my copy when we were released . . . . if we were. We never saw him again. He handed us over to a taxi driver who had an amorous girl friend beside him. She received more attention than the road surface as we skidded our way to the Hotel Yevropeskaya to the accompaniment of raucous western rock on the car radio.

At the hotel the receptionist spoke near perfect English to inform us that the roubles we had acquired would be of little use in purchasing wine or other necessities. For that dollars were preferred, so we got dollars. The floor concierge did not have any English, nor was she an ancient crone dressed in black, seated beside a seething samovar, as described in so many travellers' tales of life in the Soviet Union. At least she was traditionally poker-faced. With sinister, threatening gestures, she demonstrated how to exchange a room key for a pass card without which we could never hope to regain entry into the hotel. It was not required for admission to the dining room where there was a deafening din from amplified music. Mercifully every table was taken so we were led into a room marked reserved. There four Indians ate, cowering, embarrassed by the jovial proceedings in the centre of the room where a wedding breakfast was in full swing. At first we too felt awkward at intruding on a private celebration, but the guests nodded and smiled at us. Speeches were made, there were laughter and song; Mavis restrained me from joining in with 'I'm 'Enery the Eighth I am'.

Dinner in Leningrad was never such fun again; in fact we had it only once more, foregoing it twice because we could not prove ourselves to be part of a group or because uniformed porters refused us entry into other hotels. One evening we ate a box of wafer-thin chocolates and an ice cream. You could always obtain ice cream in Leningrad; that and soda water were sold at every street corner. Yet In Tourist, the official Soviet travel bureau, seemed genuinely to care about us. Its acolytes booked us seats for a performance of Georgian dancing, for a hydrofoil trip to Peter the Great's summer palace and arranged entry to both the Hermitage and the Russian Museum. Taxis were thrown in free of charge for outward journeys but to return we were on our own. This was simple by hydrofoil from the summer palace but, when the Georgians ceased dancing, to find oneself abandoned without transport in outer Leningrad late in the evening was daunting. The driver of a tourist coach took pity and lifted us to the Nevsky Prospeckt; we were less lucky in attempting an evening canal cruise. At a kiosk we were advised to buy tickets on the boat; at the boat we were referred to the kiosk. There was total inflexibility. The kiosk closed; the boat sailed . . . without us.

We went twice to the Hermitage which meant that we just began to scratch the surface of that absurdly cluttered collection. By the second visit we had cottoned on to the need to enter as soon as the palace opened and then go straight to the French paintings on the third floor, (no lift). Had we dallied for even half an hour, enjoyment of the riches on view would have been wrecked by groupomanic guides screeching such messages as 'In this room is Van Gogh who liked to paint in bright colours of his native Arles.' Each milling swarm of people spent all of thirty seconds before selected masterpieces, having previously been dragooned through chambers bulging with antique furniture, jewellery, sculpture, bric-à-brac, candelabra, household equipment, medallions, head gear, weapons, the hallowed junk of ages.

At the Russian Museum we were introduced to Repin, Vasikyev, Shishkina and others who are not to be found in British collections and who are seldom mentioned in art reference books.

Leningrad is noted for the soft yellow wash on many buildings, seen to greatest effect on government offices opposite to the Winter Place and the Admiralty. It cast a glow over others, many drearily grey. At sunset all seemed beautiful but during daylight walking the Nevsky Prospect there was a drabness emphasised by the interiors of the murky little shops and the unkempt department store, Gum, where shoddy goods were badly displayed.

On the day we left In Tourist hired us yet another taxi to the station where we were met by another programmed young man – T shirt, jeans, sailor cap, pink-rimmed specs, all-American boy – who shepherded us to our sleeping quarters on the day express, metaphorically closing our file. At Helsinki no one greeted us as we stepped off the train; no one asked were we a group? We conveyed ourselves to the Hotel Vaakuna, took a lift to the ninth floor and ate an expensive capitalist dinner with a sense of relief at having returned intact. Being in a police state really did induce that effect. In 1982, it had been the same in Prague, though not in Budapest.

So many vivid, contrasting and concentrated experiences inevitably made for cultural indigestion. Much of the next twelve days, after leaving the capital and heading northwards through Finland to arriving home via Esbjerg-Harwich, is unrecorded in the memory. At the time there was pleasure on being reunited with Adorée and Ingvar at their home in Sandviken, at revisiting the tiny apartment in Stockholm, making a brief stop at Uppsala and savouring an extended smogersbjold dinner aboard the North Sea ferry, but we could not absorb all the detail. I felt grateful to Ingvar for advising that we should not attempt the Arctic Circle. The 250 miles from Helsinki to Vaasa through unvaried terrain was often tedious enough; the ferry from Vaasa to Umea in Sweden was tame beside the incomparable skerries journey out of Stockholm; south of Uppsala, at Sigtuna, we attempted to picnic, seeking sufficient unsullied space between the droppings of migrant Canadian geese to relax in comfort; the journey through part of Denmark to Esbjerg is a blank. From our house on the northern edge of London we could not offer visitors the equivalent of the Winter Palace, a voyage through the skerries or sight of picture stones; in Sandviken, a pleasant small town, nor could the Nordbergs. We were glad it was so. We felt at home there, especially after we had overcome their Scandinavian habit of giving us separate bedrooms.

Before and after the Baltic, we went on exploring the beaten track in Europe unceasingly. My observations on the Dordogne and Tuscany are recorded in book form; our Cretan adventures were written only as lengthy aide-memoire captions to photographs. What follows is a reduced version of them.

We went twice to Crete. I felt cocky about driving what was seemingly the sole vehicle on the island bearing a British number plate until, reaching a hotel near the western tip, far from tourist haunts, I pulled up beside some vast American banger bearing a New York registration.

The first visit was planned with the help of Greta, a chain-smoking young woman who managed a travel agency in Barnet.

'How do I get the car to Crete?' I asked her.

'That's a good one.'

She enjoyed a change from booking package deals and cheap flights in old biplanes owned by maverick Irishmen and came up with a proposal to join a cruise at Ancona, leave it at Heraklion, rejoin it two weeks later, go on to Rhodes, repeat the routine, then return to Italy via Piraeus, allowing for a morning in Athens. We had never fancied cruises because of 'the other passengers'; this arrangement, with no more than three nights in succession aboard the ship, was a safeguard. At Ancona we boarded the SS *Atalante* to be greeted by an official, dressed like an admiral, who couldn't find our names on the passenger list. We were shoved aside by impatient Germans but I shoved back which sparked off some international ill will. ('Suppose,' worried Mavis, having done homework on cruise-ship procedures, 'we are placed to sit with them for meals?' We were. They ignored us.)

Our right to be present was confirmed when a genial, receptionist dressed as a mere vice-or maybe rear-admiral, called out 'Your keys, Mister Norri-*ay*'; a pronunciation which amused me each time he repeated it over the next four weeks.

Cruise life is artificial. It is different from ferry life. The latter lasts anything from two to twenty four hours, or more, and is not unlike being on a train that has a bar and a restaurant. It is transitory. Enduring relationships are unlikely to be formed; those who are gathered together today will disperse for ever tomorrow. A cruise is more binding. It throws people together. A table is allocated at which you must sit with the same strangers for every meal. For one session of the broken voyage we were placed with a Swiss family – a charming and beautiful lady with two young, well behaved children, and a husband who was half Greek. He told stories about a Dutchman, a Frenchman and an Italian . . . that sort of thing. On deck, after we had all left the table, I heard him telling the same stories to politely attentive but uncomprehending groups of trapped cruisers. It is astonishing that more people are not thrown overboard.

After thirty-six hours we docked at Katakolon to visit Olympia. The coach ride there and back was a welcome break, marred only slightly by the behaviour of some fellow travellers. Led by a Roman Catholic priest, who told me he brought a group each year, the party included too many young people who were plainly bored at the prospect of seeing, as William Brown might have put it, 'a lot of old ruins'. It also included a haughty grande dame who gave a fair impersonation of Katharine Hepburn. Even after the youthful element had been cajoled on to the coach we were delayed because 'Miss Hepburn' had not yet made her first entrance wearing a large floppy straw hat. She moved languidly towards the coach, where she took over the guide's seat, next to the driver, whom she hectored with endless questions. At Olympia the priest handed me a photographic reconstruction of the site which was helpful because the remains are scanty and inexplicable to the uninitiated. The museum was another matter, with superb exhibits including the Praxiteles statue of Hermes and Dionysus, Apollo on a pediment from the Temple of Zeus and a model of all that which was not apparent on the actual site. The Greeks are second to none at creating live museums from dead material.

Next day we docked at Heraklion and bade farewell to the *Atalante* for two weeks. As we drove towards Elounda I stopped for petrol and contrived to request it in comprehensible Greek. I calculated I had a vocabulary of precisely fifteen words. The attendant of course spoke English.

Elounda brought immediate disappointment. 'The villa with sea view' was a further example of that major stock-in-trade joke of the tourist industry. The view was of a neighbouring building site. In vain,

I complained to the tour operator's agent. She said she would see what could be done tomorrow. We said that was not soon enough and took solace in lunch at a hotel actually facing the bay and the island of Sinalunga. There the proprietor listened to our tale of woe, then offered us a second floor apartment in a block adjacent to his hotel. We had a blissful two weeks therein self-catering much of the time and spending almost every evening on our balcony. During the day we either went to a beach – the only one at Elounda had room for, at the most, three diminutive midgets – or toured the eastern part of the island with ever-increasing reward. We visited the archaeological sites at Knossos, Gournia, Myrtos, Gortinus and Phaestos, the Lesithi plateau with its hundreds of windmills close to the alleged birthplace of Zeus and the hinterland of Elounda, taking track roads to villages largely unchanged for more than a century. Our travels reminded me of George Psychandoukis' wartime memoir, *The Cretan Runner*, describing how the young islander risked his life daily in the Allied cause, although most of his adventures took place on the western half which we did not visit on this trip. We went to the south coast where tourism was making a strident impression and saw the cliffs where hippies and other squatters had been turned out of the caves. On one outing to a southern shore we were joined by the Hymans; Robin and Inge, with their daughter Philippa, were staying along the road at a palatial hotel in Aghios Nikolaus but were happy to slum with us for a few hours. (In a private postcard to *Publishing News* I said they were staying at 'a whites only' hotel. It was printed which was unfortunate; Robin's list sold well in Africa.)

Before seeing Knossos we listened to sensible advice and visited the museum at Heraklion, seeing frescoes and the great sarcophagi which reveal much about Minoan life and enabled those who reconstructed the various murals and pots to guess intelligently. At Knossos we resisted the blandishments of the official guides in order to enjoy the freedom of leading ourselves, stopping to look where, and for as long, we liked. What most took our imagination was the so-called Royal Road, the oldest in Europe, a fact which gripped me. We would never have been permitted to linger so long if we had been amongst a group. After lunch we were readmitted without extra charge, again wandering around as the mood took us, blessing the daring of Evans, who risked offending stuffier colleagues by having walls painted as they might have been. At first sight they seem too garish, probably because one associates ancient ruins with an overall greyness but why shouldn't they be colourful? (In Italy, the fine museum at Paestum, across the road from the temples, has exhibits which supports this view.)

From the rear of our apartment at Elounda there was a view of bare hills starting only two blocks away. It was the same on the approaches to the town although the worst sort of package tourism was already spoiling parts of the island. At night we were invariably woken at intervals by drunken Brits on the way back to their poorly equipped, package-deal apartments. On the southern coasts the beaches were becoming overcrowded. It can only have got worse. We were lucky to be there while so much of Crete remained unspoiled, as was also the case at the western end on our second visit.

Three years later the fact that we had bought a house in France and I was writing a book about Provence didn't mean we had to forego holidays in other countries Abroad. Our French neighbours found it difficult to comprehend why, having come to dwell in the sun, we needed to travel to Italy and Greece where the climate was similar; they rarely, if ever, left their native country, even when it became too hot.

On this visit to Crete we took nearly a week getting there via Brindisi, Patras and Piraeus. We had nothing booked but had it in mind to stay on the north coast at Rethimnon or Hania but the former, proving crowded and too much like any seaside resort anywhere, we moved on to a minor road up through the hills, along a narrow, winding way bordered by olive groves and shrubs . . . oleander in white, light pink and rich pink, bougainvillea in purple and raspberry red, gorse and broom . . . in every direction. We passed through a small village, before descending to a plain by the sea where, at Kalives, we found cheap (and clean) accommodation in a moderately uncomfortable apartment with few amenities. It was attached to a restaurant where on the very first night we were invited to join a party which the landlord was giving. Giving? It wasn't clear who was paying. We sat with a group of cheerful Austrian and German motor cyclists who were spending their holiday roaring along the roads of Europe and watched rather poor dancing. A video was promised but never shown. It was a genial, lackadaisical occasion. I don't think we were charged for the dinner, which scarcely mattered since everything was so inexpensive. Another night the proprietor invited us to an early meal which never materialised; when we asked him in for a drink he made an excuse. He had to go to Hania. Cretans, like Greeks, don't go in for aperitifs. Considering the nature of ouzo and raki, this doesn't surprise me.

One day we drove inland from Kalives and had an experience comparable with that we had relished when exploring the mountainous area above Elounda, except that the roads were better maintained and twentieth century plumbing and lighting had made incursions. At a roadside taverna in the village of Malaxa the owner, quite simply, without a weapon, held me up. 'Stop!' He insisted firmly, 'Drink.' Min asked for white wine; I asked for beer. We were given raki, with small, delicious yellow plums and made to sign a Day Book; also to photograph him. The Day Book bore the signatures of thousands of visiting Europeans, some of whom had drawn quick cartoons of the owner. Beside it was a box of photographs sent by grateful patrons. I promised I would add mine.

At the small town of Kandanos we were flattered into staying for lunch by the voluble patron. 'You English. I love English. No like Germans. Ha. Ha. Ha.' He kissed Min's hands. Later, after a tour of the kitchen, he brought out a framed citation proving he had served with the British military in 1944–5. Then he left us alone to enjoy our wine. Later he emerged to greet newcomers and we overheard him saying, 'You German? I like Germans. Germans good' . . . but he didn't add, 'No like English.' The rogue then served us with souvlaki, cheese pies, dips, a Greek salad and another half-litre of wine, all for about seven pounds.

Kasteli, where we spent the second week and Hania (sometimes Chania), which we often visited, could scarcely have been more contrasting in appearance. Whereas Hania, the capital of the western part of the island, is a handsome city built in classical style around an elegant bay, complete with ancient castle (restored) and all the marks of an often violent history, Kasteli is the product of tourism, a town grown out of a fishing village as development opportunities occurred, with untidy, unfinished streets, broken pavements, sandy beaches moderately unspoiled, a community advertising its ad hoc nature at every point. Hania is more or less contained within its original walls and overlooked by mountainous hills; Kasteli is unplanned and verging on anarchy. There was a restaurant adjacent to our hotel, where we were looked after, albeit slightly haughtily, by the owner. One evening I observed that we had not been offered stuffed vine leaves. 'You shall have them tomorrow,' he said instantly. Next evening I dared to remind him of my request and hoped it would be met. He drew himself up with a pride more Spanish than Greek. 'Of course. It was a promise. We care very much about keeping our word.' He was a little like a figure in Elizabethan drama, tall, perfectly erect, with a slight swagger, as he swept about his domain, directing, waiting, taking orders, dressed in a creased shirt and jeans yet wearing them authoritatively. After dining, we retired to our balcony for red wine and cherries. We sat there well into the small hours. In the balmy night air children, making little noise, were still playing in the street as a new day clocked in. It was magically tranquil.

Kasteli was then all but the last outpost of tourism to the west although there were sandy coves and large beaches beyond it, reached up treacherous, unguarded roads and offering little by way of amenities. We settled for what it had to offer. Mavis immensely enjoyed her bathing. I sat on the sands and began to write a novel. The scribbled first, and only, draft was subsequently thrown away because I couldn't decipher it. When tummies began to rumble, often as late as two or half past, we wandered up the beach to a villa-cum-shed with tables correctly laid and pristine napery, where we usually settled for swordfish or other marine life. We were having, for a few days, the holiday we wanted. We felt no need to 'see' anything; I felt no urge to drive.

We did take an excursion to the Omalos plateau lying at the start of the descent to the Samaria Gorge, one of Crete's most famous land-marks. Gorges were not for us but we thought we should take a look. Getting to Omalos did not make for pleasant driving. Mountain roads without any markings or barriers to protect one from a direct drop are alarming, especially when you have a right hand drive car and the terrain slopes heavily on that side. While approaching Omalos I was constantly aware that this was the only way in or out and I would have to return down the same track-cum-road. I tried to put it out of my mind as we wandered on the plateau, watching sheep safely grazing, their shepherds scarcely aware of them. The scenery was spectacular, the day warm and sunny. We had an excellent ham omelette into which the chips had cleverly been cooked. Had the waitress been less surly I would have congratulated her but there was veiled hostility to our presence for the only time on this holiday. It reminded me of the road I must take back so I ordered another bottle of wine. An hour or so later we set off with Schubert playing on the car stereo. I had clocked and timed the outward journey and did a mental countdown.

It worked perfectly but it probably should not be taken as a textbook prescription for how to overcome vertigo while remaining at the wheel. There was more indifference to our custom where we stopped for tea but that was attributable to the World Cup being on television; most of Europe ceases to work when that is happening.

On our last day we drove gently towards Heraklion and the evening ferry, passing many of the typical, white-painted churches, large and small, which we had admired only from the outside. In Provence, in the course of writing a book, I had visited so many, most of them Romanesque and utterly different from these which were usually based on the Greek cross. Here I felt liberated, there was no compulsion to describe them. Next day, in Greece, we successfully visited Mycenae, whose gates had clanged in our faces mid-afternoon in 1982. We nearly missed it this time round too when, about to make a U-turn on a main road, I failed to judge the speed of an oncoming car. Instinct led me to aim straight on to a wide pavement where, fortunately, there were no pedestrians. The other car, going too fast to break, swerved violently, missed me and sped on. It was entirely my fault.

We sat for a moment in quiet relief. Half an hour later I walked through the Lion Gate and saw the tombs of Clytemnestra and Agamemnon, the former sensitively reconstructed with a domed and cone-shaped brick roof. I clambered up – when I was not slithering down – the steep hillside. There was no shade. The remains of the huge castle are not sign posted which adds to the impressive bareness. There is an overwhelming sense of space, accentuated by the views of rolling countryside. I hope it is never given theme-park treatment.

## 15

## Provence

Our lives changed markedly at the end of July 1988 when High Hill
closed. August was spent in tying up the more protruding ends; final
settlement came only months later. Meanwhile we went on holiday,
with a purpose. Derek Johns, by then managing director of the Bodley
Head, had commissioned a book about Provence, where Mavis wished
us to live for at least a year. We went south by a circuitous route over the
Massif Central to Toulouse and Montpellier, then on to Bedarrides,
a small, semi-dormitory town for Avignon, where our friends, the
Elliotts, had a second home in which we had already stayed twice.

From Bedarrides we combed the Vaucluse in search of accommodation to rent. Discovering that property was comparatively cheap
in France, it seemed sensible to buy. We hit upon the attractive town
of L'Isle-sur-la-Sorgue, railhead for Fontaine de Vaucluse, of Petrarch
and Laure fame. Five strands of the river, giant waterwheels adorning
its banks, ran around and through it. We saw several modest single
storey villas on housing estates within walking distance of the shops,
all for immediate sale, all filling the prime requirement that we would
be living amongst French people, and not with expatriate Brits,
Netherlanders and Germans on a remote hillside. Having time, we
could pick and choose. We drove down to the sea at Mentone to visit
David and Nicky Harrison who were holidaying there, then made a
leisurely journey home, taking our time, as I had always wanted us to.

We returned to L'Isle the following spring and selected one of the
houses we had already seen, paid a deposit and were warned by the
estate agent, a fierce little woman, that once we signed we were committed; this was not a land for the gazumper. Her docile but powerfully built husband was at times employed in the role of chucker-out
when vendors, in a truly French manner, attempted to ignore the law
and stay put. It happened in our case on the very eve of completion.
Monsieur paid them a visit; the deal went through.

The contrast between living in Hadley Wood and L'Isle puzzled those who knew how easily I expanded to occupy all available space and how much I valued my creature comforts. In England we lived in a three-storey house with five bedrooms and three hundred feet of garden. It had central heating, fitted carpets, draught-insulation, several fridges, two bathrooms, two loos, attic, garage etc. There was a view over farmland, little traffic or aircraft noise . . . the ceilings were high, the rooms large, the garden – half lawn – included apple and pear trees and a superb chestnut towering over two houses. In France we had a single storey kind of prefab with one medium-sized living room, three small bedrooms, a smaller kitchen, an adjoining remise (out-house), a garden with a willow tree and a gravel yard for a car park. The interior walls were so thin that I could hear what anyone was saying anywhere in the house, the floors were pseudo-marbled, there were a few wall heaters and a just adequate hot water system. The exterior walls, covered with some kind of pebble dash, were sturdier than they looked; they had to withstand the mistrals which struck at all times of the year. It was, by my standards, a modest bungalow with basic amenities. There were mats beside the beds and a couple of carpets, laid down in winter, for the living room. It suited the climate and had it been our main home we would have made it more cosy, just as our French neighbours had theirs. In London we had three thousand books, dozens of paintings, wardrobes full of clothes, cupboards stacked with crockery, knick-knackery, surplus bed linen, eighty-five photograph albums and the impedimenta of a lifetime; in the Vaucluse the 'library' comprised about one hundred volumes and we acquired one or two paintings. Yet, we lived there so contentedly that we wondered why we needed all the possessions at what we stilled called 'home'. (This became temporarily occupied by a Japanese family who paid us £1,000 per month. The L'Isle property cost £45,000.)

Perhaps the greatest difference between Hadley Wood and L'Isle lay in class structure. Hadley Wood was entirely middle-class; it had never been a hamlet let alone a village, whereas L'Isle embraced people from many social strata – teachers, middle managers, hospital workers, refuse collectors – all living in houses similar to the one I have described. No one thought it odd that the refuse worker brought his 'dust cart' home to park on the pavement while he had lunch. He was frowned upon somewhat because he shouted too much at his wife and children but as Marcelle, our retired physicist friend said of him, 'Il est brave.' Her gracious, genteel, elderly, widowed mama who was his immediate neighbour accepted him without question. Along the road there lived a close knit family with at least two dogs who were certainly not well off but they were as much a part of the community as those who lived opposite to them and had had a swimming pool constructed in their garden. All the children attended the same school.

Although not adapting to native mealtimes we otherwise fitted in with the rhythm of life in a small French town. Most shops and offices closed for two or more hours at midday but stayed open at least until eight p.m. On Sundays, a huge produce market lasted from six a.m. until one o'clock, with stalls obscuring the shop fronts and most roads closed to traffic. There was also the brocante market which went on over an extended weekend until early Sunday evening, offering an incredible variety of junk ranging from mammoth items of solid furniture to dirty old bottles and chipped china. In the years we were there this feature went distinctly up-market. Genuine, or convincingly credible, antiques replaced much of the rubbish and took over many of the shop premises. L'Isle-sur-la-Sorgue became a major centre attracting dealers from all over France. Traffic swarmed in, particularly on Sundays, when we either stayed quietly at home, willing the visitors not to extend the parking area on to our lotissement, or we drove off after breakfast, until nightfall.

We went to Provence with the intention of making friends and dwelling side-by-side with the French. We were proud to achieve our object with almost total success. The fact that we never actually bothered to register with the police in the nine years we owned the house made no difference; we paid our local taxes, made no secret of being foreigners and the neighbours accepted us. Even to the extent – which made me very cocky indeed – of joining us for that high mass of the French culinary week, Sunday lunch. On the morning of the first occasion we provided it, I woke in panic. What madness on our part! The moment of truth came when Nicolas, the fourteen year old son of Marie-France and Frederic, who lived next door, asked for a second portion of my beef casserole. Then his father (himself a masterly chef) quizzed me as to the exact ingredients, nodding approval as I listed them. Mavis's marmalade and apple tart went down a treat as well but for starters we played safe with smoked salmon. A few years later Marie-France's elderly mother came to an alfresco lunch under our willow tree and commented, 'If this is how you eat in England, I will come.' She never did but her remark made us feel we had not lived in vain. (And Frederic never ceased to express his admiration for my ability to drive on the 'wrong' side of the road without causing mayhem.)

We exchanged visits with several families on the lotissement who became our friends. One, who remained only an acquaintance, an Algerian immigrant, did us the inestimable service of seeing-off villains who were attempting to break into our property; on another occasion, in our absence, we were burgled but I have always suspected that the sons of a less friendly neighbour were the culprits. (That does not condemn the French; there was a similar incident in Hadley Wood from resident white Brits.)

We lived at 40 les Pleiades, L'Isle-sur-la-Sorgue, continuously for sixteen months after which we returned two, three times every year until 1997. The house was also used by our children, grandchildren and friends. We were the object of scrutiny from the children on the estate, especially in the early months before we had a fast-growing hedge planted. The kids tended to sit on their bikes and stare into the garden while we ate late lunch. The French take that meal early because they don't eat breakfast; we were more into Spanish hours. For some reason the sight of us sitting on the patio or under the willow having lunch at two, or later, fascinated the kids until it was time, mercifully, for them to return to school for the afternoon session. They were also constantly ringing our bell to ask if they might retrieve their ballon. When we weren't in residence presumably they climbed over the fence.

There was something of a village atmosphere on the lotissement which when we first became residents had only one road leading to it from the town. Strangers greeted each other as they walked or biked of a morning to and from the boulangeries. We were invited to an outdoor performance of a play written by a neighbour's grandson and performed, albeit very poorly, by him and his friends. It was all part of bonding. Only Marie-France, next door, spoke much English. She had been an au pair at 'Sous'am'ton' long before and retained a good knowledge of our language; Marcelle, who came regularly to look after her ancient mother, could read English but spoke it little. We got into a habit of accompanying her to concerts in local churches or on a bank of the river. We also went to chamber recitals organised by The Friends of Music of the Vaucluse in nearby towns. The Friends engaged top artists from all over Europe and got away with paying small fees because the Chairwoman of the society owned a chateau where she gave the musicians and their partners free accommodation. We were introduced to these concerts by Rainer and Priscilla, friends of Ruth and Ken Harman in Hampstead. Rainer, who was multilingual, had grown up in pre-war Germany with Ruth and subsequently worked for most of his life in the UK, the States and Paris; Priscilla had known Olivia Manning and our friend David Abercrombie in Cairo during the war. They lived in Avignon for much of the year but in the Vaucluse hills in the hot season.

From les Pleiades I toured the Vaucluse and the Bouches du Rhone to gather material for my book, *Next Time Round in Provence*. This wasn't published by The Bodley Head because Derek left as the result of an American takeover and his successor cancelled the contract. Giles Gordon, my agent, got compensation for me, and the book became the last High Hill publication in association with Aurum Press, who became sole publishers of two subsequent *Next Time Round* books on the Dordogne and Tuscany. I enjoyed all aspects of writing them. Mavis accompanied me on many of my journeys, but remained at L'Isle for a fortnight while I went to the Dordogne with Christopher Wade as companion. Christopher was also an immense help to me in Italy where he knew the language. He spent several 'holidays' with us 'doing' Tuscany, along with Michael Floyd, whose excellent drawings illustrate all the books, and Pat, his wife. It was something of an idyllic existence for several years, and would have been totally so but for Mavis's increasing frailty from Parkinson's and problems endemic to owning a second home.

Our arrival in the Vaucluse coincided with the publication of Peter Mayle's *A Year in Provence*. I had reviewed it for the *Ham & High*, gently praising a gentle book and commenting, 'if this author is fortunate he may attract as much success as did Lady Winifred Fortescue's *Perfumes from Provence* fifty years ago.' The Mayle book from its modest first printing of three thousand copies became one of the top-selling books of the twentieth century. It sold by word of mouth at the speed of a forest fire spreading through literary Britain and even singeing the fingers of those who seldom read. In recording his experiences of moving to the Vaucluse while still in young middle age, purchasing a semi-derelict farmhouse and settling in the sun in a country renowned for its cuisine and wines, Mayle struck a chord to which millions of readers responded. There is virtually no history in his charming book, nor does it make any pretence of being a travelogue.

Written sparingly, with much humour about funny foreigners, it is an easy, engaging read.

Mayle's massive success with *A Year* and with its sequel, which began to scrape the bottom of the barrel, led to much local bitterness which I could not comprehend. It was alleged – by expatriates especially – that the author had ruined Provence, of which the Vaucluse is but one department out of six. It had led to an invasion of unwanted tourists, particularly from the Far East; it was the cause of property prices rising and had effectively dumbed down the unique cultural level of the region. Which was nonsense. I don't know what effect it may have had on the price of derelict farmhouses but our modest villa increased in value by less than ten per cent in nearly nine years while, far from there being traffic jams of coaches clogging all the roads near Menerbes, where the Mayles lived, I saw no evidence of this as I drove about the Vaucluse or when I visited them. On that occasion mine was the only car on their particular stretch of country road. Fame and acclaim often breed envy. For the media Mayle had been too successful by half and had to be taken down several pegs by the same people who, in the first instance, lauded him. I wrote a piece for *Publishing News* attempting to analyse the reasons for his book becoming top of the bestseller list, suggesting this lay in the author's ability to amuse without either over-taxing the reader's brain or writing down; in his preoccupation with food; and in his descriptions of the shortcomings of the work force employed to refurbish an old property. He was living out everyman's dream of finding a place in the sun and getting away from the rat race. His achievement was harmless; he did not deserve castigation.

I enjoyed showing friends and family the gems of the region scarcely mentioned by Peter Mayle including: the Pont du Gard, the lovely abbey of Senanque, the hill towns of Gordes and Roussillon, the source of the Sorgue at Fontaine de Vaucluse, plus places further afield such as Arles, Nîmes, Aix and the Camargue. Of these and numerous others, I wrote in my book.

When *Next Time Round in Provence* was published I became the local rep, visiting the major towns of the region, placing copies on sale or return in many bookshops. At the most famous one, in Avignon, where Frederic Mistral and his friends had held meetings and which had a fine stock of books on the locality, I had to press for payment. The owner sold many copies of mine but was on the verge of bankruptcy which forced me to employ a solicitor who achieved settlement but did not charge me a fee. (Did he get one from 'them'?) At a small shop in St Remy de Provence I replenished the stock for several years. Had all the booksellers in the area sold as many copies I would not have been into rivalling Mayle but might have required more than the one modest reprint which was needed. As with bookselling in Britain, there seemed neither rhyme nor reason in the pattern of sales. Large shops on the Cours Mirabeau at Aix moved few copies but one hidden on the campus sold dozens leading me to lunch the owner and write about him in *The Bookseller*.

While writing and distributing the Provence book, I drove hundreds of kilometres in the two departments it officially covered. The minor roads became as familiar as the main thoroughfares. On them I had little fault to find with native driving (apart from that dangerous hour when the starving workers were heading home for lunch); the cyclists were another matter, as they have since become in the UK. In France, a major problem was their refusal to use any form of lighting at night; nor did they ring bells or honk. They assumed they had right of way and supposed everyone to be aware of their presence.

Early on during our residence I toyed with having a French registration for my car but dropped the idea when we heard from Joan O'Donovan, who had become permanently domiciled in the Dordogne, of the myriad levels of bureaucracy this entailed. I think by law I was required to have changed it after spending more than six months of any one year in France but no one in authority seemed troubled. Nor did we bother with obtaining planning permission when we altered our drive-in, although we tried to conform. On one very hot July day we called at the planning office where documents were produced indicating that not only the gates but the house were in different positions from those actually pertaining. The clerks at the office could not have been less interested. We withdrew discreetly and carried out the alteration.

During our L'Isle years we drove the length of France many times, often transporting furniture for house and garden from one residence to the other. Provence – our part of it – became very much a second home even when returning to it brought news of some minor disaster at the house or, worse, an outbreak of illness for Mavis. She coped not only with the inexorable advance of Parkinson's but chronic glaucoma attacks, becoming all too familiar with the efficient modern hospital at Avignon where she was expertly treated.

Through the Franco-Brittanique Cultural Association we met ex-patriate Brits and English-speaking French people at weekly evening gatherings at a cafe in the town of Carpentras. Nothing could have been less like dropping into the local in England. Everyone sat at tables in wicker chairs, many of those present drank coffee, no one bought rounds. We played a few desultory games of darts, encouraged by a cockney named Bob who had married a local girl and stayed on. There was a young Frenchman who spoke fluent English with glottal stops, having learned it from his estuary-born wife. There were teachers, retired businessmen, wives and mothers, including Ruth who managed a golf club at Fontaine-de-Vaucluse and whose French husband made cheese on the slopes of Mont Ventoux. Ted Davis, her father, had started the society. He and Peggy his wife ran classes in French, an admirable initiative on the part of the invading residents. Even so dear Ted always treated the French as second class citizens. 'They don't understand . . . ' he would frequently comment, only just remembering not to add, ' . . . poor things, they're foreign.' On his foothill of the Plateau de Vaucluse, he designed and maintained a very English garden with well-kempt lawn.

My French did not improve. During our long married life Mavis often attempted to teach me the language correctly. It never worked, any more than it had at school. Neighbour Marie-France was as en-couraging as my wife, flattering even, but I have never been able to converse even moderately fluently in French, although since Mavis died I have improved. The major difficulty, as Amanda once defined it, was always 'the words in between'. Mercifully neither of my daughters inherited my hang up. Both are bilingual with Jessica, to my ear, having a very impressive accent *Pa–r–is–i–enne, avec un plus-petit morceau de Maurice Chevalier.*

We loved it in L'Isle, but setting up house there coincided with the arrival of the next generation; our four grandchildren were born between September 1989 and January 1994. Often we were able to welcome them in Provence but our roots were in England. When the Japanese occupation ended we didn't re-let Hadley Wood.

While writing Provence much of the fieldwork could be done in daily journeys from L'Isle. A French departement was supposed not to extend beyond any place unreachable in a day by the Prefect travelling, on horseback, from its centre. I was either at the wheel of the car or on foot; Mavis sometimes accompanied me and it was also possible to mix business with pleasure because roughly wherever I, or we, went could be justified as research for the book. As I was not dependent for a living on this pleasant pursuit I had the best of many worlds. When we decamped for a few nights to Marseille, Aix-en-Provence or some distant part of the territory it was like taking a holiday. For the Dordogne book it was necessary to find a hotel or gîte for longer excursions. We rented a small house for a month at a hamlet near Montignac, close to the Lascaux caves and there Michael and Pat Floyd stayed with us. Michael was the most undemanding and good-natured of collaborators, always willing to accept the subjects I suggested, infrequently putting in a polite plea for drawing what had taken his eye though not mine.

I had not intended to write the Dordogne book. Before becoming associated with Bill McCreadie and Piers Burnett at Aurum for the *Next Time Round* series I had had a moment of folie-de-grandeur envisaging a renaissance of the High Hill Press. I asked several authors to consider writing for it but only Joan O'Donovan signed a contract, which was for the Dordogne volume. When she submitted her type-script I saw that she had not attempted to follow the pattern of what was to be a series by putting the text into a framework of routes. Instead she wished to be thematic and all but ignored the *Next Time Round* approach. By then Aurum was the publisher and Piers Burnett agreed with me that her book did not fit the bill. She could not be persuaded to alter her approach so I had to cancel the High Hill contract and compensate her, which led to a semi-rift. The healing began when Christopher Wade accompanied me on another trip to the region. We visited Riberac where Joan lived, finding ourselves unsuspectingly out-side her house from which she emerged with a friend. 'Joan', I called out, hopefully, 'lovely to see you. Are we on speaking terms?' She replied she didn't know and then talked, as could be her wont, for the next ten minutes non stop. When my book was published she told me how bad she thought it was and we became good friends once more.

While writing the Dordogne no satisfactory diagnosis could be found for heavy blood pressure in my left eye. For a month I covered it with a black patch and was surprised to discover that this did not impair my ability to drive; I even found it restful, often wearing it in Italy while I was researching for *Tuscany*, the third book in the series. On my fieldwork for this Christopher was again a boon. One summer, Mavis, he and I stayed for four weeks in a remote farmhouse on the edge of a little town named Loro Cuiffenna before moving to Siena for a fortnight. The following year we stayed in hotels in Florence, Pienza and elsewhere. Tuscany covers a much larger area than either of the subjects of the French books so I began by omitting the coast, the north west sector and the whole of the Maremma region. Even so that left a spread of territory involving travel in excess of prefectorial proscriptions. There could hardly be a more satisfying region. Tuscany has everything from mountains to plains, cities to hamlets, a vast range of architecture and the finest collections of Renaissance painting to be found anywhere; it also has a riviera of its own but I ignored that. I was fortunate to have the means, the time and the inclination to explore it, backed by the indulgence of my wife and friends. Mavis was moderately well for some of the time but the Parkinson's was already causing lack of concentration and fatigue and it was distressing for us both that she had to opt out of much of the fieldwork which she would formerly have enjoyed. Michael Floyd also, by the time we had embarked on Tuscany, was ill – more so than we realised. He was not sufficiently fit to journey about with Christopher and me, completing several of his drawings from photographs. Typically, he did not complain. Pat supported him nobly and he met all my requests; sadly he did not live to see publication. Nor was Mavis able to fill her customary role as copy editor. *Tuscany* was the first of my books which lacked the benefit of her advice and expertise. By the time it was drafted she was reading very little apart from what was essential for her own work on letters to children, the first finished copy of which arrived from the publisher on the day following her death.

Earlier in the decade Mavis had often joined me on my post-*Mumby* journeys around the British Isles. These came about as a result of a lunch I gave in 1992 to the then editor of *The Bookseller*, Louis Baum. I owed him one from a lunch two years before at the Groucho Club, where he had become tipsy and insulting. We went to an Italian restaurant in New Oxford Street where, at the very next table, were seated Fred Newman and Tim Godfray, director of the Booksellers' Association. I was maintaining a certain aloofness towards Fred because he had deprived me of my column so it amused me to make a proposal to Louis which I hoped he would overhear. It was that I should survey the vastly changed status of bookselling since I had revised *Mumby* twenty years earlier. I would visit major cities and regions and report on what I found. Louis liked the idea and asked for a treatment to discuss with his colleagues . . . which meant he would commission it if, on reflection, he still favoured the project. I set off with Mavis for France, unconcerned about whether or not he gave it the go-ahead; I had plenty to do anyway. Three weeks later Louis's secretary, phoned to say his colleagues were keen to do the series and would I make a date to discuss it further when we returned to the UK.

The series lasted for five years, running to thirty nine articles including one on Provence. I was paid two hundred and fifty pounds per piece, then the top rate for *The Bookseller*, plus generous expenses. In 1993 there were eleven monthly surveys, in 1994, ten. Then I went bi-monthly for two years, ending with central London and the Royal boroughs and a summing up in 1997. I covered most of the major cities, apart from Hull, Derby, Wolverhampton and Gloucester and all the regions except Wessex; I went to Ireland and Ulster, to Scotland and Wales. We started with Cambridge which got favourable feed-back. By the third article Louis said, 'Go on as long as you like.' He soon withdrew his demand that I should take photographs to illustrate the pieces. I maintained that I couldn't concentrate on interviewing booksellers effectively and also ask them to pose for me. His office thereafter engaged a local photographer except when Louis himself accompanied me to Belfast. Then he took them. Another exception was the Riviera and Provence when my snaps were used in addition to a black and white version of a drawing for the illustrated *A Year in Provence*. By and large the illustrations and presentation were super, with each feature proclaiming Norrie's Nottingham or English Heart-land, or whatever. I put up a wallchart in the breakfast room for the year ahead, showing my timetable and itineraries; I was really enjoying myself. Mavis often came along, not just for the ride, but to research in libraries for her book. Usually I drove to my venues but occasionally went by train, travelling first class. In Scotland we combined trips with holidays. For Ireland, George and Val came with us taking care of Mavis in Dublin while I drove to Belfast. It was our one and only visit to the emerald isle. We loved it, travelling from Rosslare across to Galway, from where we sailed to the Aran Islands. In Dublin there were not only the bookshops to visit but the Abbey Theatre and the art galleries too. We were shown around and lunched by various book-sellers, one of whom reproved me for supposing that Ireland was still a priest-ridden country.

Wherever we went on those trips we met old friends and made new ones. Inevitably there were downsides. On a dark, wet, cold January morning in Cardiff, having left Mavis warmly tucked into bed and set out by bus to the crowded city centre, I asked myself why was I doing this. There was no economic necessity and it was not as though the nation or the world were waiting upon my words. What I wrote was unlikely to influence trends in the book trade. Would any particular bookseller rearrange his window or interior displays, or buy more or less stock, as a result of my comments? Probably not. So, why was I subjecting us to this ordeal in South Wales in the deep midwinter? Because we liked travelling around the UK, seeing the country, the cities, towns, villages and meeting others who were still doing what I had done for so long to earn a living. It was as simple as that. During the years of holidays abroad we had also taken shorter ones in England or Wales discovering our own country, sometimes even straying, just very slightly, off the beaten track. In younger and healthier days we had walked Hadrian's Wall, as well as Chester's and York's, gone single file along narrow coastal paths in Cornwall and Devonshire and braced ourselves in ferocious winds on the Yorkshire moors.

The series for Louis was a coda to my career as a bookseller and ended only when I felt I was in danger of repeating myself. What new was there to say about a particular Dillon's or Waterstone's branch that I hadn't already recorded about others? And I had long since ceased mentioning most W. H. Smith shops. Jenny Bell, the Deputy Editor, threw out a hint that maybe some new angles should be explored. I thought she was right; also I was becoming arthritic which was affecting the amount I could walk. I told Louis I wanted to end with a flourish in Charing Cross Road (two features) and thanked him for giving me a great opportunity. There was an additional factor in that Mavis was by now finding travel a trial. The last article appeared in the spring of 1997 shortly before our final visit together to Tuscany to finish research for my book. Whilst there, on Mavis's suggestion, we called at the Bencista at Fiesole for tea and were delighted to find the Simonis still running it. Yet even they had had to submit to their insurers' insistence that bedroom doors be provided with locks.

We went twice more that year to L'Isle-sur-la-Sorgue, once to put the house on the market and to spend a lazy September in the garden, again in December to complete on the sale of it. Christopher Wade came with us on the latter trip when we sold some possessions, carted car loads of others to the local Red Cross and had certain items of furniture sent home by Headley's Humpers, an English company which had established itself in the town to meet a growing demand from visitors to the antiques fair. In our denuded second home we had a merry last evening snack with Marie-France, Frederic and other neighbours, setting off sadly next morning under grey skies for the motorway and home.

It was Mavis's last journey abroad. She had dearly loved the Provençal experience. There were times of intense personal happiness at Les Pleiades when each of us relaxed with our books and work, made meals, savoured long sessions on the patio or under the willow, talking, indulging a passion for Scrabble, probably drinking too much wine, counting our blessings.

There was a moment on that final drive back from L'Isle that haunts me. After landing at Dover, we stopped at a Little Chef for tea. Mavis said she fancied a jam pancake, which was duly ordered. She struggled to eat it, with fork and spoon but her muscles couldn't manage the task of lifting the thin portions to her mouth. She resisted offers of help and gave up in annoyance. I believe that was the moment when she knew she had had enough. From then on her condition deteriorated. She coped with Christmas – pleased to see her family – but it was a relief on December 27th when everyone had gone and we were left alone to doze, play Scrabble, talk, hear music. There was no question of theatre going any more. We paid one or two short visits to children and friends and she had weeks of respite care in the loving hands of the dedicated staff of the North London Hospice. She accepted my need for a holiday and did not complain when I arranged two weeks in France with Christopher but on the day before we were due to leave, when she was to be admitted to a nursing home, she had another slight stroke. She was taken to the then antiquated Barnet hospital to a dirty, scruffy ward where she contracted pneumonia. I tried to have her transferred to the Hospice but it was too late.

She died on September 14th, 1998. It is only now that I am able to write about her during those last months. On my tape recording for the British Library's Book Trade Lives Project I did not do her justice for fear of breaking down, but I hate to think that anyone listening to it might suppose I distanced myself from her sufferings. In fact she was my closest, dearest friend and did so much to broaden my experience – not least in introducing me to Europe.

# 16

## After Mavis

My travels recommenced six weeks after Mavis died when Christopher and I set off for the Vaucluse. It was only the second time in my life that I had been abroad without Min. In his address at her cremation service Christopher recalled her 'surrounded by baggage in the back seat of the Volvo, hurtling across France and Italy . . . she always insisted on taking a back seat but literally not figuratively.' Once, at her suggestion, we had composed a sonnet, making up lines in turn. Another time we had chosen our Desert Island Discs . . . We had launched Mavis's book, *Dear Boy, Dear Girl*, the previous weekend.

We took in Arras and Dijon, both familiar to me, before heading to Lyon, a metropolis on two rivers, into which Christopher navigated me expertly. Previously, with Min, I had driven under and through a city we had mistakenly neglected. It lies on the Rhone and its tributary the Saone where, in the vieux-cité, Christopher and I stayed at the foot of a hillside named Fourvière, dominated by a monstrosity of a church rivalled in height by a contiguous imitation Eiffel Tower. After a light lunch (no siesta allowed) we climbed to it through a steeply pathed, wooded park. The nineteenth century imitation-Baroque edifice, as though mocking our elderly efforts to reach it, never seemed to draw closer. Most of the church is built above a spacious crypt which is excruciatingly over-decorated with a mosaic floor and columns rising to figures of saints beneath a garish ceiling. It glitters at you. Not a square centimetre of it is left unpainted. In the body of the church there are numerous classical columns with heavy capitals and an apse-like grotto. As we descended to our hotel for a rest before supper, I felt we had got over the worst that Lyon had to offer.

In the rue St Jean we dined at L'Assiette, in an old-style bistro with marble-topped tables crowded into a small space around a commodious sideboard and a spiral staircase to the loo's. Pictures and old advertisements adorned the walls. It was *très vrai*! The cuisine was delicious and there was good burgundy at plonk prices.

Next morning we promenaded beside the ponderously neoclassical Palais de Justice and across the Saone to the agoraphobic Place Belle-cour, to take a bus tour. Invariably this is a sensible way of becoming acquainted with a city. It took us past a mammoth post office built in the Haussman-Parisian style, branches of Habitat and Old England, then crossed the Rhone to the Part Dieu proclaiming late twentieth century Lyon with a vengeance. This left bank of the river was once a collection of small villages with flourishing pig farms. In 1965 it was torn apart to make a business and shopping complex dominated by a vulgar, bulbous tower dedicated to the Crédit Lyonnais and sur-rounded by mock Venetian shop fronts. It is named Part Dieu because, long ago, a noblewoman's coach overturned in this quartier killing many people. The lady was so distressed that she left a fortune to found the Ville Dieu, of which one of the Louis remarked, 'Only at Lyon do they care for the elderly and the sick in a palace.' We came to it as we headed for the Parc de la Tête d'Or where elaborate green-houses were erected in 1880 for imported tropical plants and the largest rose garden in Europe. In its grounds every known species of tree is represented. Back over the Rhone lies the silk weaving district (Lyon, before the machine age, was pre-eminent as a centre of weaving) and the opera house where the first moving film, shot by the Lumière Bros, was made and shown in 1896.

Towards the Saone, through narrow streets, we came upon one of the trompe l'oeil walls for which the city has become famous thanks to a native architect Tony Garnier who has covered windowless surfaces with murals. The first we saw was a happy conceit, depicting famous citizens from Julius Caesar to Robert Carrier, standing on balconies or at windows.

Having got the feel of the city we set about it on foot. I was eager to visit the Musée des Beaux Arts which, thanks to a bequest of nineteenth- and twentieth-century paintings from the actress Jacqueline Delubac, widow of Sacha Guitry, has become a major gallery. The collection is housed in the Pierre Palace around a courtyard with trees, shrubs, flowers and statuary; it also includes many exhibits pre-dating the Debulac bequest, mostly from the fourteenth and fifteenth centuries. There is a jolly 'Ascension' by Pietro Perugino making a pattern of Christ, angels and cherubs taking off and narrowly missing the upturned heads of watching mortals, and a huge Rubens of voluptuous queen-sized women cavorting about the sky. Then came a feast of Impressionists . . . Degas, (a singer in a deep red dress belting out a cabaret number), Renoir (Coco writing with his head lying on the actual paper next to his pencil), Pissarro (Kew Green) and many near contemporary works . . . Picasso (a grotesque woman, her head shaped like a dinosaur's, picking at her toenails), Chagall (the engaging Le Coq wherein a woman is swooning away from the bird in whose feathers you can just discern a couple kissing) and Bonnards of troubled, diffident women, a threatening air shivering over all three. Also a compelling Matisse . . . the woman in the white dress.

This is an outstanding gallery not only of masterpieces but curiosities such as a nineteenth century narrative painting by one P. J. Dagnan-Bouveret which could be taken as a painter's proud defiance at the dawn of a new age. His subject is a wedding photographer, cameraman hidden beneath a black cloth, taking forever to immortalise the self-conscious bride and groom who are posing for him.

After this memorable experience we sat, bathed in sunshine, in the Place des Terraux where there are sixty-nine small fountains representing the same number of official districts in the department of the Rhone. Next day we chuntered dutifully to the Hotel Gadagne which combines the Historical Museum and the Musée des Marionettes in the many chambers of an ancient Renaissance house. There was much to observe in gloomy surroundings . . . an original monumental fireplace, portraits of aldermen, a tiny piano made in 1777, a marquetry-topped desk, Napoleonic souvenirs, Grand Guignol figures, Far Eastern puppets, crockery, furniture, batons, flags, insignia, whole hoards of offerings . . . . far, far too much of everything.

We were flagging . . . well, I was. Christopher isn't into flagging. I rallied to visit the Croix Rousse district where there is a wall painting which soars dramatically into the heavens although it hides only four storeys of a warehouse. This, in the early nineteenth century, accommodated the looms destined to take over from the manual workers and ultimately depress the once flourishing silk trade. Later we dined at L'Amphytrion where the exquisite cuisine was normal for Lyon. We then moved on to Avignon where Christopher disappeared into galleries and historic monuments while I went to L'Isle-sur-Sorgue to close my bank account and to encounter ex-neighbour, Paul Tenconi, coming across the bridge from the post office, hugging a baguette under his arm. Conversation with Paul was always difficult. He had not one word of English and made no concession to my lack of French but he and Colette had been warmly welcoming to us and were among the group under the willow tree at 39, Les Pleaides for our final lunch when we had been presented with a pewter tankard to mark our nine years occupancy. As headman of the lotissement Paul had occasionally admonished me for not keeping my hedges clipped. Now we gripped hands and understood each other.

A theme which emerged on the outward journey was that we focused on galleries and museums. On the return trip it was, more intentionally, cathedrals and Romanesque churches. We left Avignon bound for the Massif Central, climbing to the plateau as rain cleared to reveal autumn colours, our destination Le Puy and the first of the five cathedrals, reached up many cobbled streets, a steep ascent I recalled from a previous visit. This time it was worse. By the time I reached the high steps to the west front I was muttering imprecations. There were no railings, no hand grips, no ropes. The great church itself, looming sombrely, was uninviting. As I collapsed on to the first available pew a vile wind blew through the open doors. Nor did I discover much in the interior to improve my sour mood. Most of the nave was cordoned off because of workmen. In the sacristy I observed cathedral treasure, which never causes my adrenaline to flow. *The Bible of Theodulf* (800AD) lay under glass. Over the altar was a black virgin, behind it, fifties style wallpaper; in a side chapel were faded paintings. As we left by a side door, we were confronted by a major item of kitsch – a khaki-coloured Mary on a lump of rock, clutching a waving, teenage Christ.

We left Le Puy early next morning for Brioude and Issoire where I wanted Christopher to see two outstanding Romanesque churches. St Julien, at Brioude, has a two-layer octagonal tower with a pointed roof and five chapels protruding from its apse; at the west end is another square tower. The outside wall between apse and nave is roughly hewn. The whole edifice is all the better for having been *maintained* rather than restored. It dates to at least 1080 when building began on a site where a Roman converted to Christianity had been martyred in AD304. The outstanding features of the interior, with its high, narrow nave, are the painted columns.

At Issoire the first sight of the restored church of St Austremoine from the ring road, as you turn a corner, is suddenly a staggering view of a seeming replica of Brioude. The two layer octagonal tower has a less impressively pointed roof, resting on a more elaborate base joining the nave with numerous round arches, some blind. The apse and the chapels surrounding it are more richly decorated and there are signs of the zodiac above the windows. It is more spruce than Brioude, thanks to the restoration work, and I think it has the edge over the other church but both should be relished. They represent something approaching perfection.

We drove on past Clermont Ferrand to reach the Loire at Nevers where Min and I had twice stayed the previous year in a hotel beside the river. High above, as seen on the approach to the city, is one of the most imposing of the French cathedrals; it is also rewarding close to and inside. The mostly Gothic building was badly damaged when the Allies advanced northwards through France in 1944/5. It has been nobly restored with stained glass that does not attempt to replace the original designs but has simple abstract panes in rich colours. The city also boasts the church of St Étienne, off a narrow street, where I had not been the previous year. A coach-load of choir boys tumbled on to the street, charged raucously into the church with their suitcases, dumped them into a side aisle and, under the direction of their master, instantly began to sing. Thanks to their presence at a rehearsal I was able to visit the church, noted for its innovative construction which follows the style of the famous abbey at Cluny.

Next we came to Auxerre where the exterior of the Cathedral has a single tower covered in rich carvings; its twin was never built. What was completed is very fine and stands halfway down the hillside on which the city is built. Christopher was bowled over by the interior but I was so alienated by a blaring organ that I had to leave, thus missing the eleventh century crypt. Even while waiting outside for my companion the dreadful vibrating roar of the organ pursued me. I passed the time admiring the west front and reading a plaque informing me that the present edifice replaced a Romanesque one destroyed in 1215; another stone commemorates Joan of Arc who passed this way on 27 February 1429.

The next stop was at Sens where I thought the west door was superbly carved while the entire frontage had variety . . . twelfth century, early Gothic, and according to one guide, 'overall, a prototype for the style', whatever that means. Fortunately the organ was blissfully, powerfully silent.

The cathedral countdown ended at Amiens, where the magnificent west door is second only to that at Bourges. Some of it was under scaffolding so not all of the three thousand carved figures could be seen but each one I looked at was unique. The decoration is rich but not overdone even though there are outbursts of crocketting on and under the three arches. Approaching the church from the rear, along the rue St Denis, there is a fine view of the apse and south east corner, with a riot of flying buttresses and finials and much criss-crossing of supportive struts. It is an almost perfectly proportioned building (one west tower is slightly larger than the other) and, within, the effect is of sheer space. The aisles are wide, the roof soars, the ambulatory is vast. The stained glass rose windows are shielded on the inside by stone frames with tracery. Golden wrought iron gates prevent entry to the choir and altar but there are guided tours. Scarcely anything in this cathedral jars – only the golden pulpit surmounted by a heavy stone angel and the rather poor Gloria adorning the altar.

It was wet and windy on the Channel next day, less rough than on the outward voyage, although we tossed about as we ate our lunch. At Dover, as always on arriving there, I wondered when, or even if, I would ever 'do' the castle, a familiar sight since early childhood.

Christopher also met me the following year at Nantes on my return from the Dordogne where I had visited Joan O'Donovan, by then permanently domiciled at Riberac. Aurum Press had commissioned another Next Time Round title to cover Brittany and Normandy. I thought this too extensive an area for one book and had opted for the first named region which I hadn't visited since 1966. By the time I reached Nantes I was already having doubts. En route for the Dordogne I did ground work at Dinan and nearby places but found that spreading arthritis made tramping around towns and cities, especially those with cobbled streets, no longer the pleasure it had been. After a week of Nantes, Quimper and the unique parish closes, I realised that I would need several visits, many of them probably undertaken alone, to become sufficiently conversant with Brittany to write about it from the next time round angle. I called a halt to the series.

Eighteen months later I was in Arras again en route for Umbria, with Judith Davis who came into my life when I placed this advert in *The Oldie*:

> Widower, 72, seeks companion on car/motor rail to Brittany &
> Umbria in 2000. Non-smoker, wine lover, trencherperson preferred,
> separate rooms, fax – Quentin 0181 441 6909

I took to the agony column approach because Christopher, six years
my senior, was no longer keen to take long holidays. I needed to find
alternative travel companions. I had had trips with both daughters
and their families but they of necessity had to holiday in August and
preferred, on most occasions, to fly rather than drive.

There were seven replies, all from women. One was a self-confessed
C. of E. vicar which disqualified her; another took against me on the
phone so we never met. I made rendezvous with the other five in
various parts of England and Wales, lunching four of them in London,
staying with two overnight – in separate rooms. After becoming friends
with Judith Davis and travelling with her to Umbria I kept contact
briefly with only one other, then destroyed my file.

Judith is a widow, Anglo-Welsh and part Jewish. She plays the
organ and the cello professionally, sculpts, sails, rides a horse and has
been on parachute jumps. Her husband, Merfyn, was a harpist who
played with many orchestras and often under Beecham. She lived close
to the Brecon Beacons in a forsaken Welsh village, through which
traffic thundered. She has since moved to Porthcawl, a South Wales
equivalent of Bexhill but near to Cardiff, an interesting, lively city. She
bravely agreed to my itinerary for a whole month abroad, during
which time we had only one row, which was highly commendable for
two strangers thrown upon each other's company for so long.

En route for Umbria, thunder and lightning pursued us across part
of France, where we paid brief visits to Reims and Nancy, and on
to Basel, where what was not being rebuilt or demolished was
aggressively new. Many roads were under repair, signposting was
sometimes inadequate and there was an unwelcoming air, perhaps
due to the fact that so many of us use Switzerland as a convenient
passage way to the deep south; for each night I have spent in that
country I have stayed at least sixty in Italy. We stopped at Andermatt,
a typical Swiss mountain town quietly exuding prosperity. Following
dinner Judith and I took a stroll by a gushing stream still carrying
away melted snow. The place had a sinister ambience, emphasised by
a slight drizzle and glaring floodlights illuminating the two churches
whose bells were to dominate my night. Their chimes were not

synchronised, one set clanging shortly after the other. I heard midnight, three, four, five and seven, each struck twice.

The journey over the St Gotthard into Italy was dismal. The mountains, dappled with only patches of unthawed snow, were menacing on a grey June morning. At one time I had gained a tremendous thrill from driving over the Alps; now I experienced slight vertigo as we descended into the valley where Judith declared that she felt much better for being out of Switzerland. We soon reached Lugano where we stopped in a dreary service area at a deserted café. A young man stepped out of a cupboard and served us drinks. When I offered lira in payment he accepted them but gave us change in Swiss francs. We were not yet over the border.

By midday we had reached the outskirts of Milan with expectations of at last seeing the famous Duomo. I had booked us into the Hotel Admiral because it had a garage. To find it took close on two hours, after conflicting advice from numerous citizens and policemen. The first sight of the cathedral was bound to be disappointing. (The camera can and does lie.) It looked tiny compared with the fabulous photographs reproduced to maximise its height and grandeur. Moreover, the buildings on its forecourt had been leased to MacDonald's and other similar enterprises. Even so it did not take long to fall under its spell, first as a whole, then in its infinite detail, from the carvings on the great doors to the statuary adorning every wall and the variety of finials and other architectural stalagmites on the roofscape. The exuberance of the sculpture is enthralling – characters posture, leap about, gesticulate extravagantly. They pose like acrobats atop the finials and pinnacles, daring the elements. They are in niches, in little temples, each one part of a deep forest of monumentalia spreading across the vast roof. Inevitably, some are partly obscured by scaffolding but a dynamic structure has to be maintained and it is all but incredible that this one has survived centuries of wars and bombardments. On the roof there are small shrines bearing a wealth of decoration. At the east end the three high windows of the apse are surrounded by a multiplicity of beasts and humans, shepherd-type creatures with horns, bears acting as gargoyles, all manner of beings, executed with that exemplary skill of the almost always anonymous craftsmen to whom it was part of an underpaid day's work. The so-called white marble of the facing stone is nothing of the sort; it is in variegated pastel shades – pinks, blues, yellows, every nuance of the palette present in masterly array, as the strata of the stone moved according to its innate anarchy in any direction it choose.

The interior, dark and more austere than is usual in Italy, did not grab me. The columns are dizzily high but with clumsy clumps of historiation far above a comfortable distance for study. Some of the statuary actively repelled me, such as the figure of St Bartholomew after being flayed alive. The stained glass is good but requires much attention to detail before it becomes meaningful, unlike that at Chartres and Bourges where one can just revel in the simplicity of the glorious colours.

La Scala was a disappointment. How could such an apparently stunted edifice be the most famous opera house in Europe? Could its massive, high interior, as familiar from photographs as that of the Duomo, be contained in this dumpy building unless much of it was below street level? It was closed; I never found out. In contrast I found Milan's main art gallery, the Brera, situated around the atrium of a grand ex-palace, unexpectedly rewarding. I was much taken with a huge canvas by the Bellini brothers, of St Mark preaching in Alexandria. Many turbanned and hooded figures sit or stand in groups in front of a formalised St Mark's cathedral, listening to the Saint. A giraffe crosses the background, a camel stands before an obelisk; the buildings are a blend of Egyptian and Venetian influence. Elsewhere the usual religious themes recur, inevitable virgins-and-child and St Sebastian frequently copping it. There is a repellent 'Marriage Feast at Cana'. Signorellis' Flagellation is striking but sick. The legs of all the figures, including Christ's, are bent in a camp manner; so are those of a man sculpted on a column above the main action. In a Mantegna truly loathsome cherubs tra-la around the Madonna and Child who seem placidly unaware of them.

The collection was enhanced between 1976 and 1984 with donations of seventy two paintings by Modigliani, Bonnard, Picasso, Braque, Severini, Boccioni and others. I particularly liked a Boccioni apparently depicting dancers in a very high chamber. On closer inspection it became a brawl in a gallery involving vividly coloured figures leaping about. And there is an impressive crowd-on-the-march canvas named Filumena, by Giuseppe Pellizza de Volpeda, in which a large horde is led by a roughly clad, bearded man in a wide-brimmed hat. Beside him walks a woman carrying a baby. The title means The Stream; when recently exhibited at our National Gallery it was named 'The Living Torrent'. It is a formidable, worrying picture.

A motif for this holiday was to look for a villa to rent for future use, as a kind of substitute for Les Pleiades. There was also a slight intention, having rejected Brittany as the subject for another Next Time Round book, of considering Umbria but once again I realised I had insufficient background experience and would also lack company. Spello had superb views from the hotel; Spoleto was more rewarding and provided a hugely varied week, during the course of which Judith discovered that she had been there previously. This highlighted to me the life of an itinerant, professional musician arriving somewhere by air on day one, giving a concert on that day or the next, otherwise having spent all available time in rehearsal, and then flying off on day three. She remembered she had been before to Spoleto only when we stopped in the main piazza to look at a building severely damaged in a recent earthquake. It had been shrouded in black plastic which the restorer had wittily covered with drawings of what it had formerly looked like. She had not registered the cathedral, a fine Romanesque church, or any of the public edifices.

To the Spello period belonged the worst Sunday lunch of my life. Before lunch we visited Bavegna and attended an operatic recital in a charming, small theatre where we occupied a box. The performers were said to be students from a nearby school; one was a man in his late fifties. The tenor shouted to deliver an aria from *Carmen*, and wore a dinner jacket. A mezzo ended the programme with a piece from *Norma* much of which was for solo piano. Most of the students were ill-at-ease facing an audience. I doubted if any of the performers would get to La Scala.

Following this unexpected diversion we found every restaurant in the town closed. Judith seemed to have no idea of the significance of Sunday lunch for me – confessing to a preference for peanut butter sandwiches – but suffered being driven about Umbria in a hopelessly unsuccessful search for what I regard as 'the meal of the week'. I had to settle for a bar where I was served an egg sandwich (good), a spinach sandwich (vile) and a tiny portion of tomato pizza. I remained amazingly cheerful; Judith giggled.

At Spoleto the cathedral, in white marble, is four star; seen in early evening sunshine, the colour changes all the time. There is a central mosaic on the façade of Christ, Mary and St John, against a glittering gold background, several rose windows (none with stained glass), a highly pointed roof with crocketting, a long portal with a frieze of heraldic beasts and birds, and a twelve century bell tower harbouring hundreds of birds' nests. A belfry and spire were under scaffolding balanced by a vast orange-coloured crane rising from undergrowth. There is a steep rise to a café opposite the rear of a Romanesque church. We might have stayed there to sup off 'omeletta fantastique' but for a young Englishman who was eager to discourse on his involvement in the forthcoming music festival (founded by Gian-Carlo Menotti whose birthplace this was). I told him Judith was a musician which led him into autobiographical mode. He claimed to recognise her, to have known her late husband, then rehearsed aloud some of his baritone pieces for the festival. At this point I discovered that the fantastic omelette was a vegetarian dish so we excused ourselves.

Subsequently we returned to the cathedral where the walls and pillars are white or cream and light pours in, as it should, through the clerestory. The fitted wooden and stone pulpit has theatrical tassels and there are superb frescoes behind the altar by Filippo Lippi. They are in pastel shades, delicate yellows, pinks, blues, against a glorious azure background of the 'Coronation of the Virgin'. There are other fine frescoes by lesser masters in two linked chapels. The larger one features pagan friezes of animals, mermen, mermaids, mer-cherubs and one resembling a Viking carrying a wand. Opposite the entrance to these chapels is a crucifix of 1187 in which Christ is depicted as excessively gaunt and wearing Bermuda shorts.

A secular joy of Spoleto was provided by a traditional alimentari in the market square, presided over by two portly brothers. Their shop was stacked high and wide with meats, cheeses, spices, lovingly unwrapped by human hand, to give a lingering, authentic aroma of all that is eminently edible. A Roman arch dating from either 23BC or AD23 (what's forty-six years in 2000?) led to many restaurants at one of which we were persecuted by a North American musician who listened to our conversation about Beecham and aspects of Judith's career. To attract our attention he began to play a dummy keyboard.

Gaining admittance to the city pinacotecca, proved exasperating. After climbing dozens of steps, reminiscent of the Uffizi, we found as many again on a return staircase. At the top we were informed the building was closed that day for a wedding reception. We were more fortunate with the Romanesque church of Santa Euphemia, which is almost entirely undecorated inside, apart from a plain marble altar bearing abstract mosaic designs and a simple 'Assumption of Mary'.

To the rear of the nave, up dangerously steep steps, was a special gallery for women worshippers.

When we made a second attempt to visit the art gallery, at the top of the second flight of steps we were informed that another wedding was about to take place. We persevered and on the next day were successful, even receiving an apology from the doorman. I registered a painted ceiling in a pagan style featuring mermaids with big boobs and pastoral scenes, a contented cow ruminating on the edge of a lake and a centaur on its haunches gazing at a lady suspended in an elegant open work cage. It was not highly rewarding. Our tickets entitled us to visit the Casa Romana as well where, it was said, the emperor Vespasian's mother had lived. As we left an English couple present enquired about the pinacotecca. 'That,' declared the keeper of the Casa Romana, 'is now closed for a wedding.'

Later we celebrated Judith's birthday at a restaurant where the menu included actual toad – not frog. We did not enquire if it was served in or out of a hole.

At evening drinks there was an unexpected encounter. A tall, curly-haired, early middle-aged man came to our table with an elegant lady and asked, 'Are you Ian Norrie?' I rose, faintly recognising him. 'Mike Collins,' he said, 'Gayton Road, Hampstead.' Then I remembered the schoolboy who had come to High Hill long ago with a Book Token and asked to exchange it for cash. I had lectured him on his good fortune in having been given a token which, I said, would introduce him to literature. I expected him to buy a football book; instead he took a Dickens novel. Years later he returned to the shop with his fiancee and proclaimed, 'It all began with that Book Token!' By now he lectured in geography at Southampton. Janice, his wife, a singer, was due to appear at the festival. Their son was with them. I told Mike that when he first came to the bookshop I thought of him as a potential delinquent. The son liked that.

At Citta di Castello, where we stayed three nights, a possible gîte for the future was rejected. From there we popped over to Sansepolcro to see the Piero della Francescas. Aldous Huxley named the outstanding Resurrection, 'The greatest painting in the world', which I find a surprisingly silly statement coming from one of his erudition, yet thanks to a young British army commander who had read his comment it was not harmed during the battle for Italy in 1943. It is one of the most vivid images I know but I doubt if any painting is '*the* greatest'.

We returned to Citta to lunch in a park where we were accosted by gypsy brats demanding, 'mangere'. They looked healthy, well fed and well clad. I shooed them away, after which they concentrated on vandalising trees.

On the journey back to Milan we took in Ravenna and Cremona. At the latter, which hitherto I had passed through too briefly, we arrived as the cathedral was closing; the beggars were packing up for the night. Next morning we returned to concentrate on the campanile of the cathedral, a neck-breaking experience best endured by leaning against a wall. Near the lower end, to one side, is a twenty-four-hour clock with several hands and the signs of the zodiac. Beneath it is an arcade, above is a balcony, rising, past Gothic windows to a thickly crenellated top bearing two octagonal temples surmounted by a spire. The tower is three hundred and sixty-seven feet high. The cathedral frontage has a rose window above a triple-arched temple featuring Mary and child. Above and below are friezes of carved stone. The statuary features saints and cherubs striking bold stances. On the roof are pinnacles clad in marble, crenellations, spires and crosses, all exuberantly expressed. The interior is vast, with marbled halls, a high roof, wide crossing, indifferent frescoes and two fine stone pulpits providing an ideal setting for spirited disputations. The complex of buildings here, though not attaining the dazzling perfection of Pisa, is memorable. Judith also visited the town hall, gaining admittance to an allegedly closed exhibition of violins and cellos by Stradivarius (a native of Cremona) and the Amati family. She, pulling rank because she owns an Amati cello, was duly ushered in.

After Cremona we approached Milan to catch the car-train ferry to an unheard of place in Belgium. It took hours to find the autorail terminus. The Stazione San Cristoforo was seedy, from the tracks covered in weeds, to the WCs, dirty floors, cracked steps and almost total lack of attendants. No one demanded tickets or gave directions. After some while I was invited to drive the car on to a container truck, lying in a siding. I didn't believe I would ever see it again. We dozed away the afternoon until summoned to a platform where there was a bar and a small gathering of other intending passengers. We sipped white wine as we waited and noted, across several tracks, a derelict burnt-out railway carriage apparently permanently on display. We hoped it was not an augury.

Time passed, then some of those who had been drinking with us disappeared only to return wearing uniform. They were our train crew. We were ordered to join them in stationary carriages lying beyond several platforms. There, at first sharing a compartment with a man who attempted to occupy six seats, we were semi-entombed for the next fourteen hours. I had paid for reclining chairs for the night and been informed a buffet would be open. I badgered a passing official; he regretted that neither was to be had.

Around 20.45 the train started. Around eight a.m. the following morning, it reached the little-known, small town of Denderleeuw, in Belgium. When we rejoined the car, the rains came. They went on coming with increasing density all the way to Calais, where suddenly it was exhilarating. We had survived a night on the ghastly autorail, we were unwashed, unshaven, fatigued, but the storm had waned, the sun shone and we were aboard the ferry on which, for the first time in a month, as we crossed the Channel, I ate a traditional Sunday lunch.

# 17

## Travels with Friends

Most of my journeys continued to be by car although I became accustomed to using the Eurostar for Paris and Brussels. In the UK, I drove my car regularly to visit Cornwall where David and Maggie Whitaker kindly invited me to their second home at Boscastle; to Suffolk to stay with Ronald Whiting, to Petworth at Joan Aiken's and elsewhere.

Spain, in the spring of 2001, began the previous autumn in Barbara Scott's flat in Willow Road, Hampstead. Lunch therein had provided gastronomic and social highlights for many of us for several decades but they had been sadly interrupted, first by Don's death, then by Barbara's cancer. Now there was a period of remission when she was determined to resume the life she had enjoyed. During a pause between the fourth and fifth courses – Barbara created wonderous dishes in a minute kitchen – our hostess remarked, nodding at one of her guests, 'Dorothy and I are going to Spain in February.'

Flippantly, I volunteered, 'Shall I drive you there?'

'Yes please,' responded Barbara. (Dorothy, who was meeting me for the first time, maintained an exemplary calm.)

In principle the trip was decided that afternoon, although February became April and Dorothy was replaced by Sheila Tucker, whom I knew slightly. Through Spain-at-Heart, Sheila secured self-catering apartments in Ronda and Seville, each for a week and was warned that accommodation during Easter week might be scarce; the Spanish Tourist Office confirmed this when I visited that odd outpost of national pride near Manchester Square. It had an air of cloistered calm. I did not observe a typewriter, let alone a computer. Piles of brochures gathered dust alongside regional maps and city plans. The sole person on duty assured me that not only over Easter, but also during the May bank holiday, many places would be closed and shuttered, including museums, galleries and even churches. Barbara was keen to stay at paradors; none would have us. In Madrid and Toledo I found hotels and elsewhere settled for a hostelry on a cross-roads in the south, unmentioned in guide books, but referred to briefly and bleakly in the red *Michelin*.

We took the twenty-four hour crossing from Plymouth to Santander where there was a delay in disembarkation because of the foot-and-mouth outbreak in Britain. The car was sprayed with disinfectant. A friend had predicted we might be forced to proceed on to the quay-side with a man leading us, crying, 'Unclean! Unclean!'

The road out of Santander rises steeply on to what becomes the great central plain of Iberia. Barbara went first into flower-spotting mode – there were swathes of cowslips, blue bells, euphorbia – then she switched to bird – buzzards, kestrels and skylarks. On the mountains there are stark escarpments and a huge lake, much uninhabited scrub country and some signs of abandoned industry. Until the plateau is reached there are many ascents and descents with hairpin bends but little wildlife although I think I identified a blue, fin-tailed private jet with dual exhaust trails. Approaching Madrid, we lunched on one of these anonymous trading estates which have look-alikes across all of Europe.

The women had not been to Madrid before. We took a taxi to the Plaza Mayor where the formal architecture is restful on the eye and there is sufficient variety in the detail to warrant prolonged inspection, especially of the southern side. On the upper apartments, where dormer windows open on to roof-top walkways with few railings, washing was hanging. Some residents had opened their shutters to view the great square which was a hive of controlled activity, a meeting place for citizens and their children before and after the paseo. The sun had not set. We sat at a café and gloated on our good fortune.

Early the following morning, to the Prado, where the layout was as baffling as ever. I couldn't find Goya's terrifying Third of May and became convinced it was constantly on the move, either to infuriate me or to avoid theft. It was very much a Goya morning, veering between his *Horrors of War* and too many pastoral canvases featuring elegant folk in fine attire prancing about an idyllic countryside. I tracked down the two Majas, one clothed, the other nude, with the luscious lady looking more relaxed when dressed, a panoramic view of Madrid and a vignette of young ladies tossing a manikin in a sheet.

At last, somewhere in this maze of a gallery, I found the *The Third of May* – the prisoner in the gleaming white shirt about to be shot by a firing squad – with, close by, the painter's most unpleasant work, a wizened old crone devouring its own child, supping ravenously, oblivious of the dead and dying around her. It contrasts startlingly with a Turneresque study of a vivid, golden expanse of sun – or is it moon? – thrown across the top half of the canvas while a dog peers up at it but it is *The Third of May* which haunts one. A terrifying moment of truth; narrative painting at its finest.

I left the gallery and boarded an open-topped bus for a soothing tour of the city, alighting once for a windswept snack lunch on the Plaza Mayor and, again, to visit the museum displaying Picasso's Guernica. On its plain wall, I let it absorb me, the black-grey-and-white emotional outburst which until the end of Franco's regime was housed in the Museum of Modern Art, New York. It has in common with masterpieces of earlier centuries that device of combining a sequence of events on one canvas – the bomber approaching, the bombing, the aftermath of the destruction. It is spellbinding.

There were other paintings, including a Picasso portrait of his mother wearing a tapestry-style dress and haughtily holding aloft her perfectly coiffured head, but cultural indigestion was setting in. I hailed a taxi to return to the hotel. It sped along regally designed triple carriageways, divided by parks with broad paths and landscaped gardens. Some of the latter had been annexed by the destitute who had erected wooden and plastic hovels as shelter. On these were written simple pleas for help; some passed by on the other side in expensive limousines.

We reached Toledo and our hotel in time to walk into the city and take lunch at the hour of high tea. Thereafter we became acclimatised and wandered the crowded, narrow, cobbled, winding streets. Contrary to the warnings of the Spanish tourist office, every single shop in Toledo was open. So were the museums and churches, not least the cathedral where a milling mob seethed in its precincts suggesting there might be a cut price offer on for a preview performance of Good Friday. I preferred Toledo on my previous trip when religion was keeping a low profile. At breakfast next day we wondered how disturbed Ronda would be on Easter Sunday. We ate in the shadow of a notice requesting, do not take items with you – a Good Friday message not to nick the hotel fodder for picnic.

We approached Ronda from the 'wrong' direction. Wrong because this is a city famed for its sensational setting above a deep gorge and coming in from the north-east you enter via a modern suburb beside a railway. Locating our gîte was hampered while Barbara, searching for Las Goyescas, inadvertently studied a map of Seville. When the Ronda map was substituted we discovered I had, unwittingly, stopped outside it.

A disadvantage about booking apartments unseen is that you cannot know what you are getting until you arrive, by which time you have already paid. Las Goyescas at least had a friendly, reasonable owner in Jose-Maria. The apartments were on three sides of a narrow court-yard-come-small garden into which little light, and no sun, penetrated. The women had to demand heaters which were turned off at night and came on, with the hot water, only after the owner had roused. He tended to oversleep and, despite it being a self-catering gîte, he provided breakfast. This made for an inevitably late start to each day for Jose-Maria was not an organised man. Each item for breakfast he carried personally to the candle-lit tables from a kitchen area behind a bulky divider smothered in crockery, house plants, bric-à-brac, general junk and an occasional kitten. To and fro he went, smiling and chattering, mostly in Spanish, sometimes English, occasionally in French, beaming goodwill, scattering sweet and savoury dishes around him along with tea, coffee, fruit juice and, once only, an evil-looking liqueur. He had trained for the Church, then had second thoughts and married. He was a dear man although, at first, I thought he overdid pawing the ladies. Then I read in Gerald Brenan that this is an old Andalusian custom; touching is important to the natives. (Rather like dogs obsessed by sniffing everything.)

We fell for Ronda. On Easter Sunday we hurried across the nineteenth-century Puente Nuova over the gorge to be on time for a procession, the centrepieces of which were two formidably large catafalques, borne by hand, one representing Mary, the other, the Host, both carried by groups of young people. The Virgin was hauled by five rows – seven deep – of girls in white dresses. A contingent of boys, dressed in blue, coped with the Host, which was garlanded with red carnations, roses and gladioli, but had the assistance of a person beneath the float whose legs were the only visible part of him. The floats were preceded by uniformed bandsmen in navy blue jackets and grey trousers and elderly citizens carrying croziers. At the rear were more oldies, swinging medallions, and small boys. It was an orderly and good-humoured ensemble making frequent stops for drinks from water bottles concealed beneath flowing robes.

Perambulating in this ancient hill city was rewarding but hard on the leg muscles. Panting up cobbled alleys we paid many visits to the fourteenth-century Palacia de Mondragon, now a museum, with enchanting, shaded gardens. It was inhabited first by Moorish princes, later by Catholic royalty and nobles who built eighteenth-century walls around the delicate Arab courtyards without destroying their essential qualities. To appreciate the elegance of these inner, open areas it was necessary to climb aloft and admire them from various angles.

Far below medieval Ronda is a Roman bridge (Puente Vieja) open to modern vehicles. From it there is a sensational view of the over-hanging Puente Nuova and the sheer drop into the ravine. Beside a third bridge, lower down the gorge, we found the remains of the Arab baths. Inspection was free but there was no signposting, so we had to guess which chambers were hot or cold, or for changing. The bareness was preferable to a virtual-reality job with simulated tableaux and piped water music.

An ascent took us to the Cathedral, Santa Maria la Mayor, on the site of a mosque most of which was lost in the conversion. It has a massive octagonal stone lantern with low pinnacles, topped by a temple-like structure spawning finials, plus a short metal cross dwarfed by a lightning conductor. The interior is spacious and gloomy, with an assortment of altars and catafalques and the Stations of the Cross in one straight line.

I moved on to the Museo Lara, an uncluttered, well-displayed collection of high-class junk, amongst it 'A Small Lathe for False Pivots', a 'Perrgotic Instrument to prove Vacuum Effect' and stills from *Gone With the Wind* and Chaplin's *Tiempos Moderno*. The archive is not extensive enough to be the prime depository for artefacts representing a specific subject; it is one man's museum, housing whatever he was lucky or rich enough to accumulate in a lifetime, a fun-folly lacking gravitas.

From Ronda we went one day to Cadiz via the National Park with Sheila navigating and Barbara holding binoculars at the ready for the first sighting of a golden eagle. Gorse, cowslips, lilac, shrubs in varying shades of red, all presented themselves. I saw, in my biased way, trees *and* forest and was wallowing in both when Barbara hit several top-Cs. A huge bird had flown down close to the car, then swooped up again, its wingspan low over the vehicle. 'It has to be the golden eagle!', she cried, as though we'd stumbled upon the holy grail. The identity of the bird was established; her day was made. I was glad to be able to close the roof, relieved that the eagle hadn't attempted to treat the car as prey and carried it off supposing it to be an unusual type of sheep. Nature can be intrusive, especially in the country.

Cadiz was founded by the Phoenicians in 1100, sacked by the buccaneering Earl of Essex in 1596 and became, in the eighteenth century, the main Spanish trading port with the Americas. It lies at the northern tip of a thin peninsular, once reached only by road around a wide lagoon. Nowadays this feature has been spoiled by a long, low, ugly bridge from the mainland into the suburbs of what, for about fifty blocks, is a dull, modern city of high-rise, relieved on the western side by a sandy beach. I found a space to park on a windy esplanade facing the Atlantic, opposite a likely-looking fish restaurant which, for all its old-salt, Kitsch décor, was a serious eating house.

Following lunch we boarded an open-topped double-decker for a trip about old Cadiz, guided by a young woman with striking black eyes which she used dramatically, provocatively, to emphasise her dual language commentary in Spanish and Berlitz-English. She discoursed knowledgeably but briefly about the cathedral, churches, palaces and squares, we caught glimpses of terraces of traditional houses and of municipal gardens with banyan trees and palms. When the tour ended the cathedral was open. The ladies dutifully entered. I settled for its drab outer walls, preferring to remember Cadiz for its fish restaurant and the alluring black-eyed Susan of a guide.

In Seville, Señor Garcia, our landlord, although Maltese, seemed markedly British; an amiable, self-sufficient, middle-aged property owner who had recently converted part of a large house, with a central atrium, into apartments. Ours was on three floors with a roof patio leading from the sitting room. It was tastefully furnished, the kitchen was well equipped, the beds comfortable. The drawbacks were that the master bedroom (mine) was part of the sitting room and there was only one loo, which was in the bathroom. The second bedroom did not have the twin beds requested so Barbara elected to sleep in a turret furnished with a single divan and little else. But dear Barbara always relished a touch of martyrdom. The house was situated in the old Jewish quarter, almost beneath the walls of the Alcazar and had a fine view of the cathedral spire. Some evenings we catered for ourselves, taking meals on the roof top patio from which we watched the swifts swooping around the floodlit cathedral in a continuous ballet. Barbara told us they never touch down, performing all functions whilst on the wing.

'All functions?' I queried.

'*All,*' she insisted.

Señor Garcia attended a bull fight on the night of our arrival. Next day he was ecstatic about it and we politely tried to show an interest but I don't think he noticed our lack of enthusiasm. He told us of how he had lived in many parts of London and stayed at every parador in Spain. There was a touch of the old colonial about him. This was noticeable in his treatment of the porter who had carried our baggage from the car. I was told by Garcia I should not tip him; he would give him five hundred pesetas. Next day I encountered the man who literally touched his forelock and asked for money. 'The señor paid you,' I said. 'No', replied the wretch but I knew he was lying. When our paths crossed again he looked at me so reproachfully that I gave him two hundred pesetas. I mentioned this to Garcia who was furious and said he would not use the man's services again. True to his word, when we departed our landlord himself wheeled the trolley holding our baggage. I didn't tip him.

While it was a privilege to live in the heart of the old city there were disadvantages. Tourists blocked the narrow alleys as they listened dutifully to their tour-group leaders; buskers made their monotonous music hour after hour, leaning against walls for support, repeatedly plucking the same few musical phrases from their stringed instruments. The groups were encountered again at the cathedral which is megasized, exceeding in actual floor space all but St Peter's and St Paul's, from both of which it differs in not having a dome. Instead it sports a high, square minaret on to which, in the sixteenth century, were added a belfry and balconies. The minaret, called the Giralda, is twelfth-century and represents most of what remains of the former mosque. Compared with the Gothic and Romanesque cathedrals elsewhere in Western Europe the Spanish ones are crudely made. The quality of the carving is inferior, the pinnacles and finials lack finesse, the buttresses may fly but they do not soar. On the exterior there is grandeur without glory; inside, at Seville and elsewhere, I find them a mixture of gloom and glitter, encumbered by side chapels resembling huge prison cells thanks to the metal grilles protecting the treasures they house. (One resembled a second hand furniture repository.) Also, there is that organ in the centre of what should be the nave. Beneath its array of pipes is a hideously lavatorial marble construction with lift-style doors. The actual paintings in the side chapels were dark, dirty, uncaptioned. There was a fine tomb of Columbus with four regal pall bearers who convinced me they were really taking the terrible weight of the coffin. I concentrated on the spectacularly fine roof vaulting but it was a relief to walk out on to the patio, once part of the mosque, where there were many small trees in neat rows offering shade. (There were also loos in portacabins.) I began to ascend the minaret-tower by ramps but, after turning sixty corners with still no sign of the first balcony, I retreated with aching calves. As a building, I preferred the town hall with exuberant carvings of people, beasts and birds on doors, pillars, windows.

One day's walk took me past a former palace, which had become the King Alfonso Hotel, a cigarette factory now housing the university, elaborate, heavily-shaded gardens, the Lope de Vega theatre all but isolated on a traffic complex linking eight or more highways and the Plaza d'Espana, dominated by a monumental hangover of the 1929 American-Iberian Exhibition. This crescent-shaped brick-and-tile edifice looks on to a canal for small pleasure boats and the spacious Parque de Maria Luisa.

There were dozens of churches and palaces in Seville which we deliberately missed to avoid a surfeit. I did not neglect the Alcazar Gardens which were every bit as ravishing as I remembered them from our 1982 visit, still quietly informal and blissfully tranquil with vistas, a wide variety of trees, flowers, shrubs, a magnificent bougainvillea. And terraces, arbours, fountains, pathways to secluded nooks with many places in which to sit or lie. I ignored the Alcazar Palace, meaning to return on our last day which I spent instead on the terrace, reading, sleeping, eating, admiring the roofscapes and opening the odd bottle or two.

We made one trip from Seville, by fast efficient train, to Cordoba. This eliminated all parking and drink-drive problems, the latter of particular concern to Barbara who didn't believe I should have imbibed even a thimbleful of wine if I was to be behind the wheel. In Cordoba two major religions clashed architecturally to such an extent that, several centuries later, the result still outrages this unbeliever. Yet the famous mosque within a cathedral – cathedral imposed on a mosque – describe it as you will, is utterly intriguing and, in many parts beautiful. The Romans were first on the site with a temple. The Visigoths came next with a Christian church which the Moors transformed into a mosque in the eighth and tenth centuries. Three hundred years on, a modest cathedral was added without seriously disrupting the Islamic building but in the sixteenth century, in the words of the Emperor Charles V, the Christian architects 'destroyed something unique to build something commonplace.' In fact it was a partial act of destruction; one can still appreciate many of the finer points of the various creations. Purist considerations aside, the visual effect is stunning. Once accustomed to the juxtaposition of abstract uniform Islamic decoration and the excesses of Spanish Baroque implanted into the Gothic, the *mezquita* is fascinating and there is little which repels. The incorporation of the minaret into the cathedral tower at Seville is trifling beside the transformation inside the *mezquita* at Cordoba. The simple Moorish columns of identical design remain, spreading in dignified splendour, laterally and diagonally, until they are interrupted by Christian altars, choirs and – this being Spain – heavily protected side chapels. The separate standing minaret, on the edge of the Muslim courtyard, is proud and lofty with an added Baroque tower. Inside the Christianisation has produced fine, vaulted carving above the altar and choir. While I was admiring it I antagonised camera clickers impatient to snap the hideous altar itself. I stood my ground, ignoring their shouts to move out of their line of vision. No lynching took place. It was a small victory.

As we walked away I reflected that the worst in Christian painters has often been brought out in depictions of the Virgin and child; how merciful that we are spared toffee-tin representations of Mohammed's mother. There was time for a wander in some of Cordoba's old streets but for little else apart from lunch. This we enjoyed in an open courtyard behind a souvenir shop where I crossed blunt swords with a waiter. When I asked for dry white wine he said that, by the bottle, they had only medium dry. Was it possible to have just a *glass* of dry? Yes, it was. So I instructed him to bring me one every ten minutes. He complied.

On our last evening in Seville we dined alfresco, watching the ballet of the swifts. Next day we arrived at Merida to begin a search for the

Hotel Roma where Barbara had reserved rooms by phone. Half an hour later we had not found it (in fact we had passed it at least once) and I spotted another hotel which attracted me.

'Let's book in here. Then we can phone the Roma and cancel.'

Barbara wasn't having that and gave me the impression that such behaviour would clearly place me in the same category as football hooligans. After another two circuits of the town, we found ourselves outside the Hotel Nuevo Roma. And there was a parking space. I got out, my shirt clinging to me like a bathing suit, and entered the reception.

'*Habataciones*,' I said hopefully addressing a smart Spaniard who regarded me with distaste. '*Para telefones de Sevilla*', I lithped on. It was surprising I wasn't handed over to the Inquisition. I was told coldly that no booking had been recorded, and there were no available rooms.

We returned to the hotel I had spotted on entering the city and there the reception clerks, who evidently favoured tramps, allocated us lofty, expensive apartments with jacuzzi-plus-sauna bathrooms. We had a quick snack, then took a taxi into the Plaza Mayor where we watched the antics of a stork which had nested on the roof of the town hall. In the square where games were strictly forbidden kids were kicking footballs at all and sundry. The following morning, we did the Roman site where the theatre was better preserved than the arena. At the nearby Casa Antifeatro the majority of the excavated mosaics were protected from visitors. It was not group territory so we were permitted to actually walk on some of them. Barbara was worried about this and trod gently. I was surprised she didn't remove her shoes.

Next came Salamanca where we had scarcely got two statues and a nunnery under our belts when we had to shelter from heavy rain, which turned to sleet and soon became snow. We fled to the nearest bar for cognac before setting off through the bleak afternoon for the cathedrals, one grown monster-like out of the pure Romanesque of its precursor, leaving the older building like a maiden aunt who has sacrificed herself for the overall good of the family. The larger, newer church was a mixture of Gothic and Baroque. It is huge and crude although the red brick common to all major buildings in Salamanca softens it a little. The vile weather did not enhance appreciation; an inspection of the gloomy interior could only have been made worse for me if there had been an outbreak of choral evensong.

Relief was at hand. A door and steps in the shared wall lead down to the plain, undecorated earlier church where the side chapels have delicate carvings but its chief glory is an altarpiece of fifty-three biblical scenes in rich colour, topped by a Last Judgement, largely in white. By itself this justifies a visit to Salamanca. It probably is the work of Nicolas Florentino, who signed the contract in December 1445. Those responsible for the garish daubs in the adjoining building learned little from it. The old cathedral dates from 1152; the sealed-off cloister was partly destroyed by the 'Lisbon' earthquake of 1755.

May Day dawned brighter. No sign of frost though 'people' still insisted it was bitterly cold. En route for the Plaza Mayor, at the tourist office I was recommended two basic routes to take in all the principal sights. The first led me at once to the little church of St Martin and the Casa de las Conchas with its delicate arched courtyard, arcades and balconies. The gold façade is studded with four hundred scallop shells. In every direction there are vistas of palaces, churches, pedestrianised streets with open shops. I made for the university which has a main entrance superbly carved, incorporating saints, sinners, animals, heraldic symbols and abstract patterns, a glorious architectural compote, both Gothic and Renaissance. In Spain they are not afraid of overdoing it. The tracery has been likened to that of wrought-iron work; it reminded me of ivory, which can be even more delicately carved. The noble doorway faces a courtyard built on all sides with a statue (1869) of Fray Luis de Leon, a sixteenth-century humanist who taught here. At the far end is the Museum of Salamanca and a cloister, the Patio de las Escuelas (Schools Square) thought worthy of three stars from *Michelin* for boasting the best examples of Salamancan Plateresque.

Inside the university I admired the carving on the monumental stone staircase leading to the serenely arranged library and peered into various ancient chambers where students and lecturers have spouted, imbibed learning and dozed for nearly eight centuries.

I viewed the Roman bridge from high above on a hillside where I all but fell into the Museo Art Nouveau Y Art Deco occupying about twenty modest galleries of a mansion. It should not be treated too earnestly. But the curator could make more effort to differentiate between nouveau and deco and, always supposing he knows, indicate to visitors where one begins and the other ends.

Back in the grand but unostentatious Plaza Mayor I dropped into a seat as the May Day procession marched about, sporting red banners and balloons. There was sporadic musical accompaniment and a degree of good-natured attention from those imbibing coffee and aperitifs. Occasionally there was an explosion – less, I judged, than a hand grenade, more than a burst balloon. No one seemed bothered. Brass bands erupted and tortured singing was heard from officials on the town hall balcony who, in between numbers, harangued the marchers. At a table in front of mine were two young mothers with three small children, plus male partners. The more positive of the women rarely ceased talking and lecturing, holding her youngest in one arm while she swigged red wine from a glass held in her free hand. The children were fed, cared for intermittently, allowed to roam or thrust upon their fathers. They spent short periods strapped into buggies while being forcibly fed. At times they were released to crawl about the plaza and the café, playing with plastic toys or suddenly discovering items of detritus beneath the tables. There was occasional replenishment of sustenance for young and old. All the while the spirited mum talked on, mostly with good humour.

After the official rally had ended and the red banner had been removed from the town hall balcony, there was an apparently spontaneous performance of flamenco dancing, led by a balding, middle-aged man and a short lady in a black skirt. They were joined by two women in green. The only music came from a drummer left over from the demo and the male dancer's castanets. The small group drew an attentive audience which applauded enthusiastically as each dance sequence ended to be followed, so far as I could discern, by another which was identical. This went on for half an hour or so, ceasing abruptly without any obvious crescendo. There was no collection. The dancers then munched jaw-breaker sandwiches and talked intently with some of the audience, making explanatory gestures, before they all gradually drifted away. This was the Plaza Mayor, Salamanca, 1st May, 2001. I had witnessed something authentic; a vignette of local life.

Next, we drove swiftly to Burgos where Mavis and I had stayed for two nights a few years previously.

You can go off places. I slept away part of the afternoon in a squalid, dark little room without a view, willing queasy stomach rumblings to cease. I felt an event was called for. I would go and gape at the cathedral west front. It wasn't as I remembered; its magic had been washed away by cleaning. Suddenly I had a sick headache. I tried to forget it because Barbara's treat-evening loomed.

We sat in an almost deserted restaurant; none of us found anything cheerful to say. To break the mood I recalled menus presented to us elsewhere. Restaurants in Spain are on a par with other parts of abroad in inspiring gems of broken language. One was, '*Habas Salteas con Jamon*' which, on the English version of the menu, became, 'Broad Bean to Assault'. At another establishment we were offered, 'eggs with earth testicales'. This reminded me of the voyage home and the Brittany ferry, with its excellent French restaurant. Why not postpone the treat until we were crossing Biscay? The others agreed. Immediately I began to recover.

Once aboard the ship, we had a small but savoury lunch with two bottles of white Burgundy which, after Spanish plonk, was delectable. Barbara's treat followed seven hours later. It was a very civilised 'last supper' from the buffet of hot and cold dishes – Bayonne ham and melon, smoked salmon, pate, salads with exquisite dressings, egg mayonnaise, tuna fish, couscous, prawns, cheesecakes – consumed while the ship rolled ever less gently, plunging us towards Plymouth.

Barbara almost survived the year, enduring her final weeks stoically as the disease pursued its inexorable path. She died from cancer on New Year's Eve.

During their long marriage George and Val, despite being devoted to painting, spent most holidays in the UK because Val wouldn't fly and George, who never learned to drive, disliked travel, stop. So he had never been to Florence, Madrid, Barcelona, Amsterdam, Bruges, had spent only one day in Venice and none in any part of Greece. Although I introduced him to many fabulous places about which he was enthusiastic he still abhors travel but submits to it amicably. He and Judith at first shied at my suggestion of spending almost four weeks away from their hearths and cats but in retrospect they speak warmly of our long trip to the south Peloponnese. Val had died earlier in the year (2002) which made George eager for diversions. He had been with me to Paris for five days in June and Judith had accompanied me to Antwerp and Bruges the previous month, so between them they were in training for being Abroad in my company.

We took our time; six nights before boarding the ferry from Trieste to Patras. Wimereux had long since become a favoured first-night stand because of the excellent cuisine at the modest Hotel du Centre.

This is a lesser establishment than that preferred by Hampstead folk of whom it is said, 'half of NW3 weekends at Wimereux while the other half is at Walberswick.' George had never done Reims, and none of us had been to Soave, the well-preserved, mostly pedestrianised walled town dominated by a castle. When we arrived there youths loitered in a bored, Sunday-afternoon manner around bars or desultorily kicked at balls, while old men, slumped on pavements, smoked or dozed. Almost every shop was closed. A young man in a red shirt, standing outside a restaurant, promised it would open in the evening. It did, with the management not only eager for our custom but wishing to serve us speedily. We insisted there was no hurry. Dining was what we were doing that evening; nothing else was scheduled. It made no difference. The young man in the red shirt and a woman colleague became frenzied in their efforts to provide the fastest service ever; their neuroses overcame all other considerations. In their eagerness to be rid of us they offered an umbrella which helped to keep us dry in the torrential downpour which began as we paid the bill. Back at the hotel the large vestibule was a desolation area; even the bar was closed.

At Opicina, on a hill top high over Trieste, I had chosen a hotel with a secure car park, an amenity apparently not on offer at any of the hostelries in the actual port. After dumping our bags we squelched out again on foot into the main street where at an unpretentious bar we lunched off fried meat balls and aubergines, served by cheerful, relaxed young women. We decided to leave Trieste for the next day. George did a sloshabout returning with the gloomy news that there no restaurants open, no shops either, nor any sign of the tram or bus terminus . . . let alone a dove. We were in a deserted shanty town quite unlike that I had envisaged when, reacting positively to Jan Morris's *Trieste, and the Meaning of Nowhere*, I had suggested breaking our journey here.

As the afternoon downpour turned to evening drizzle Opicina came sluggishly to life. The Hotel Valeria served meals in a busy dining-room, a cheerful refuge from nowhereness. An ancient waiter performed prodigious feats of memory while moving at a canter around a large L-shaped area, meeting everyone's demands. This true pro kept his cool; we ate well.

Next day we blazed a trail over cracked paving stones, umbrella engaging umbrella rancorously, towards the terminus for the famous tram which clings to the steep cliff face. I looked half-heartedly for the obelisk which, according to Jan Morris, had been erected on the hill-top in 1829 to celebrate the first navigable land route into Trieste, then the only sea outlet for the entire Austro-Hungarian empire. In the mist the obelisk was not visible, but the tram was there. Aboard it we made the slow descent on mostly single track, the driving rain obscuring most of what might have been visible ... *What were we doing here?* Then the sun shone on the quaysides and on a public garden alive with wild cats which we passed through while climbing towards the cathedral and castle. We trod mean, sloping streets and got almost to the duomo before the rains came again, dripping from a wall plaque recording the wedding of James Joyce to Nora Barnacle. (To rid herself of such a name what woman would not get married, even to a wayward genius?) In Trieste, Joyce wrote all of *Portrait of the Artist* and some of *Ulysses*.

For once, despite moaning piped holy music, I preferred the interior of the cathedral with wide nave, painted columns and clerestory, to its outside. The castle, with attached museum, shrouded in ivy and standing beside a Roman forum, did not appeal much but we could not do justice on such a day to this ancient part of the city. In sunlight we had appreciated the fine squares with palatial buildings now mostly used as banks. The raison d'être of modern Trieste ended to a large extent, along with the Hapsburgs, in 1918; the earlier Roman presence is minimal. We did not visit any of the museums and theatres mentioned by Jan Morris. Drenching rain takes the zest out of sightseeing.

The ferry sailed us gently towards Greece on a voyage which, as the years pass, has become more and more idyllic in our minds. One and a quarter days on the Adriatic and beyond in the company of well-behaved students who unrolled their sleeping bags on to stairs, corridors and all public places yet gave no offence. The food was poor, the wine often vile, the weather mostly dry, the scenery romantic. We loved it.

Some while after a last drink at the only bar on board, where a man with a Sid James visage maintained a service to both waiters and passengers, we made it to our cabins. Outside mine was an occupied sleeping bag which I was careful not to disturb. Its owner had gone when I rose at 9.30. It was too late to be served breakfast in the snack bar. Another, on deck, was manned and offered flaky pastry cheese tart. It tasted like nectar; it had to because we were approaching the land of the gods. During the day I dozed, read or looked out upon a coast of striated cliffs beneath small individual, white clouds bobbing about against a serene blue sky. There were few signs of habitation, just occasional small settlements. Stretches of golden sand alternating with hillsides, black against the sky, merged with the sparkling sea. Which countries did we pass – Serbia? Croatia? Albania? It was all Illyria to me.

At Igoumenitsa, on mainland Greece, opposite Corfu, most of the students disembarked to be replaced by one diminutive priest. A pretty, small town on a hillside rose above the docks where there were derelict sheds and shops selling motorbikes. We stopped gazing at them just in time to take lunch before the kitchen closed at 13.30, more than six hours before we were due at Patras.

In late afternoon we entered the Gulf of Corinth where there are Seven Sisters-type-cliffs curving up and down like a child's drawing. It was 21.00 in the evening before, having docked at Patras, we were permitted to make our uncertain way through gloomy lower decks to the parked car, to find which we had to squeeze past enormous trucks and great shackles of iron. No one supervised; no one advised. A German woman remarked philosophically, 'you're in Greece now.'

The ferry was late. Officials were not interested in passports or other documentation. We drove off into a stream of traffic to find our hotel which did not have a restaurant. No matter, there was one nearby where we had to inspect the food on offer in the kitchen. It did not make it any better. A heavily made-up woman with a complicated hairdo mounted perilously on her small head persisted in calling at our table to seek approval for the meal. We pretended it was delicious.

The Delfini Hotel, Patras, undistinguished architecturally, lay back from the esplanade. Its saving grace was rioting morning glory. Breakfast was served in a room where almost everyone smoked. George appeared tired and wan (he is invariably provided with a cupboard substituting as a bedroom); Judith energetically indulged a new theme, that Greek men treat women offhandedly, instancing how on the ferry the porters had carried my bag and George's but not hers. I had the tact not to comment that this characteristic might be termed 'Men's Lib.'

Once out of Patras we came to what in Greece is laughingly called a motorway, comprising two lanes of traffic moving in opposite directions, lacking a central divider but having narrow hard shoulders on to which one is supposed to move when a vehicle at the rear wishes to overtake. The speed limit, varying from 60 k.p.h. (37 m.p.h.) to 40 k.p.h. (25 m.p.h.), was for the most part ignored. I noted another dominant feature of Greek driving – overtaking on hairpin bends.

It became hot and sunny. Mediterranean weather at last. Once into the countryside we stopped at a taverna nestling below the road in a plantation heavily overshadowed by trees. George and I decided to risk the tea; Judith asked for coffee, 'but without the bits, please.' A young man, tired, perhaps drugged, seemed to comprehend. Some while later an elderly woman appeared, laid the table and spoke pleasantly, so far as we could understand her. When the waiter emerged he laid his tray on another table remote from ours and brought over each item separately. The grey-blue tea tasted sickly, like the Nestle's milk of my childhood. We knew we couldn't drink it. George sauntered non-chalantly into the garden, stopped to admire the flowers and returned with an empty cup. By the time I attempted a similar ploy, aware of being watched, I slipped behind a water butt and disposed of the evil beverage knowing I had been seen by the waiter and the woman. Meanwhile Judith had disposed of her coffee, with or without bits. It was not a promising introduction to Greek country fare.

We drove on, unrefreshed, passing through towns with few ring roads. Between them lay tranquil countryside, with olive groves. There were wild cyclamen on the grass verges, abundant bougain-villea, cypresses and barking dogs jay-walking aggressively. I was delighted I had overestimated the mileage to Pylos of which we had our first view, with the Bay of Navarino spreading beyond it, by 13.00. The Hotel Karalis overlooked the bay from about twenty yards up the hill. Judith had wisely plumped for it rather than the more beautifully situated Karalis Bay Hotel, partly suspended over the sea, just a little too far from the town centre. Months ago I had faxed the management with the message . . . 'Kalamera. Please excuse me for writing in English', to receive a reply, ' . . . I like it that you write in English . . . Yours, Mr Spyros.' I booked us in for twelve nights and was assured of 'private parking with nightwatchman'.

At reception there was a youngish man. 'Mr Spy-ros?'

'*Spear*-os', he replied, evincing some surprise that we had actually arrived and apologising because not all the rooms were ready. No matter, I said, what we would really like immediately was a bottle of cold white wine, preferably not retsina. Not only was this possible but it would be served on the balcony of my room, and would not be charged. Moreover there would also be snacks. This set a pattern of hospitality which overwhelmed us for all of our stay. We lunched, glorying in the view of town and bay.

Mr Spyros – we never knew his first name – spoke excellent English; Vlassos, his younger brother, also fluent in our language, claimed to be an Australian. When he invited us to view the Karalis Bay Hotel he stood us drinks. The brothers interchanged as managers of both hotels although Mr S. was indisputably boss. He was clearly astonished when we stayed the twelve days for which we had reserved, but Pylos was a happy choice. None of us had realised the historic importance of the town, and were ignorant of the fact that it was at the Bay of Navarino, in 1827, that the Royal Navy had sunk the Turkish fleet, thus making a crucial contribution to the Greek War of Independence.

The Turks anchored in the bay knowing that the allied navies had gathered in the open sea but unaware that their enemies had been strictly instructed not to start a fight. It was only when British ships nosed their way into the bay that an encounter began, but who fired the first shot? The result was that the entire Ottoman fleet went to the bottom where, allegedly, its remains can be seen to this day. Classicists will also know that Pylos and the bay featured in the Peloponnesian wars with Sparta, as recorded in Thucydides.

Our first full day began with a surprising breakfast in a noisy, high-ceilinged room about which Mr Spyros speedily roamed ensuring we were content. He was proud of the spread he offered – fried eggs (sometimes hot), frankfurters, small portions of bacon, yoghurt, jelly, cheeses, preserves, melon, other fruits and various breads. There was tea from a samovar, coffee from a pot and the most-diluted-ever orange juice.

We spent the day inspecting the small port in which there was little activity. Out in the bay a tanker named *Olympic Breeze*, belonging to Onassis, awaited refurbishment and swung, anchored, on the tide. Launches conveyed crew and provisions to and from docks. On the northern quay many yachts were moored; elsewhere a smallish freighter, out of Kingstown, looked abandoned. The water close to the shore was filthy with oil slicks and detritus. Above the tiniest of beaches, where Judith was to half-heartedly dangle one foot in the water, stood a thirteen-acre fort built by the Venetians, enlarged by the Turks, and now transformed into a nature reserve, at the entrance to the bay. The fort is called the New Castle; the old one was just visible at the end of Sfaktiria, a volcanic strip of hills protecting the town from the open sea.

The town spreads across the hill, terraces bristling with hotels, cafés, a clumsy modern church in concrete (or plaster of Paris) and houses of little distinction. In the large square are fountains, municipal gardens, huge trees, a monument dated 1927 celebrating a hundred years of independence and a mini-market occupying the ground floor of the police station. I, like George, wondered to myself, if twelve days would not prove too long especially when the rain which had followed us across Europe fell soon after lunch; it worried Mr Spyros too who, like all good hosts took the weather personally. When the rain stopped we toiled up to the New Castle to which admittance was free on a Sunday. Beyond the entrance lay an avenue of elegant, high pines; at the end of which Needles-like rocks made up part of the natural wall of the bay. There was a church-cum-chapel, under restoration, with a garden where a large pink bougainvillea gloried above two small arbours with seats, both covered in vines. Flowers, wild and cultivated, were in profusion – geraniums, roses, a species of South African daisy – and there was a small vegetable plot.

Beneath the trees it was a treat to walk on a thick covering of pine needles. The Athenians fought the Spartans here, the Venetians had been invaders long before the Turks and Greeks. Then had come Russians, French, British. Now among the plants and vegetation cannonballs, cannon barrels and an occasional anchor, merge with wheelbarrows and farm-outhouses in a gentle, peaceful, neglected haven. The site, dominated by an octagonal citadel, has access to ramparts with numerous seats from which to enjoy views and observe insects and butterflies.

That evening we discovered 'Charlie's' and the appeal of Pylos was confirmed. Charlie was the name bestowed on the proprietor, by Judith, because his walk reminded her of Chaplin's; most of his restaurant was alfresco on the quayside, where he served simple meals and dispensed wine in large carafes, wine that was dry and far better than the Greek plonk I knew from 1982. We became daily visitors either at lunchtime or for dinner as we fell into a routine of mostly short outings. A twelve day stay was no longer daunting.

We visited Nestor's Palace, near Hora, first inspecting the Tholos, a sombre, high-domed Mycenean tomb resembling a giant honeycomb.

The vestigial remains of the palace, dating to 1200BC, painstakingly reconstructed on an eminence, were protected from the elements by an ugly iron roof, which at least was preferable to plastic sheeting. Walls at knee height were clearly labelled – Sentry Post, Queen's Room, Throne Room – leaving much to the imagination, which is not easily stimulated by stark grey ruins. I tried to visualise them in the bold colours, daringly imposed by Evans on Knossos. One small item, a bath tub, with some mosaic decoration intact, sent a clearer message. The palace was destroyed by fire. Nestor supported the Greeks against Troy, sending a contingent almost as large as Agamemnon's; he had the luck to survive the war and died, perhaps here, in old age.

On the advice of Vlassos, we hired a launch, navigated by an ancient-looking mariner, probably years younger than any of us, to take us on a round trip of the Bay of Navarino to view the submerged remains of the Turkish fleet. The boat duly anchored at one point where we were encouraged to sprawl on our stomachs and look into the water for items of wrecked warships. I didn't detect any but pretended to be impressed because the ancient mariner informed us that 'naughty people' came at night and dived illegally for souvenirs. He spun a fantasy when we stopped at a tiny island where there was a memorial to the British with an inscription of thanks from the liberated Greeks. The Ancient Mariner followed George and Judith up a rocky stairway, himself carrying two litre bottles of water which he claimed were for the refreshment of rabbits. Judith suspected them of being for parched, illegal immigrants, such as hid on the unpopulated isle of Sfaktiria. (She had seen a person, standing on its heights, signalling.)

We drove over a hill top to Methoni to a massive Venetian castle erected to protect a township where the Turks once beheaded every male over ten years old. It had become a tranquil haven smothered in low plants and flowers busy with butterflies. A determined English matron was attempting to photograph them, a task almost as difficult as trying to teach ravens to fly under water. While doing so she lost contact with her husband about whom she complained loudly that he must 'have gorn to have a pee.' We dubbed the couple Mr and Mrs Clatworthy and were glad when they left us to enjoy the peaceful ruins. Next day we passed through Methoni en route to Koroni where boats bobbed about like toys and there was yet another Venetian fortress high above a modern tourist resort. Parts of the long-disused fortifications have become a benign wilderness.

Our various excursions from Pylos were all in this low key. Once on a mountainside in the hinterland we visited an artist's studio where I would have bought a painting but he wouldn't take a credit card. From all journeys we returned contentedly to have a meal, usually at Charlie's where, dressed in white jacket and bum freezer, he served meat balls, sausages, cheese parcels, smoked meats and other light dishes, more delectable than any I had previously had in Greece. On our last evening, when we bade him farewell, he insisted the meal and the wine was on him which was typical of the hospitality we enjoyed. On paying our final bills, Mr Spyros presented us with a bottle of brandy. Twice Vlassos brought us a carafe of wine to compensate for the bad service he said we had received. (Their stock control certainly failed to keep up with our consumption.) On a third and last visit to another restaurant the Polish proprietor presented us with a bottle of wine.

The return voyage across the Adriatic to Ancona was less than idyllic. On arrival in Italy we had a lengthy delay before disembarking thanks to the asylum-seeker problem. Once ashore, worse was to come in the way of traffic jams around Bologna and a severe instance of 'No Room at the Inn' at Modena, where a conference had taken almost all hotel accommodation. George and I had to share a double at £120 each; Judith paid £100 for hers. Next day we made for the Mont Cenis for what was probably my last crossing of a pass I had driven over many times. (In late March 1860 George Eliot and Mr Lewes took the same trail in a covered sledge pulled by mules, travelling in star-light.) Seen in autumn colours, it enraptured us all. We descended to Lanslebourg by hairpin bends, noting the wondrous shades of brown, orange and yellow in the trees, and all against a background of snow-capped peaks.

On arrival at Dover at last I was able to look up at the Conqueror's fortress and declare, 'I've done that.' (In the spring I had stayed with my cousins Dean and Angela near Canterbury and visited not only the castle but the tunnels in the cliffs from which in May 1940 the evacuation of Dunkirk had been overseen and directed.) The fourteenth of October, the date of our crossing was historic, the 956th anniversary of the Battle of Hastings, except that because of the time 'lost' when the calendar was amended there was an error one way or the other of some eighteen days. It's that kind of consideration which makes recording history so unreliable.

The following year we were back in Italy, George, with Judith's support, having agreed to visit Florence and Tuscany on condition that we were away for only two weeks. This meant travelling by rail but once on the train I began to enjoy it. It is only the hassle associated with big termini and the tenseness of having to make crucial connections that I find unnerving. George is almost as bad. Judith, an experienced tourist-class passenger on aeroplanes as well as trains, was much amused, flaunting a certain superiority over two timid males.

We couldn't have chosen a better year for Florence. Terror of terrorists made Europe unpopular that year with Americans, and the Japanese were undergoing a dip in their economy. For the first time in decades it was possible to enter the Uffizi without queuing or booking ahead and the same was true of the Accademia and San Marco. The hotel where we stayed for a fortnight was sufficiently off centre to be close to good restaurants patronised by residents; from my balcony we could see the cathedral tower of Fiesole and identify the Bencista and its grounds.

The comparative lack of tourists was so marked at the Uffizi that, on leaving the fabulous Botticelli room, when I turned to have a last look it was possible to take in almost all the paintings in one sweep of the eyes. It made no difference at the Medici Riccardi where space is so limited that only a handful of people are allowed in for seven minutes at a time, to gaze at the astounding fresco of the journey of the Magi. Bernardo Gozzoli achieved wonders of perspective on a small high wall in creating that lengthy procession of men and horses down a mountainside. On the last occasion that Mavis and I were here together she was just sufficiently fit to undertake the steep steps to the chapel. The memory evoked again a strong feeling of 'last time round' which I also experienced at the Brancacci Chapel where the frescoes are more difficult to view than at the Medici because of the complicated architecture, although the Masaccio figures, remain vividly with me.

At the Accademia the presence of Michelangelo's *David* is over-whelming but the uncompleted works nearby deserve equal attention. The pieta is superb. You can feel the weight of the body as it is handed down from the cross while the other figures, still emerging from the marble, gain from their unfinished state. On earlier visits I had paid little attention to the paintings in a side gallery where there is an entrancing sequence of 15C. wedding scenes by one Cheggia. These provide a comic contrast to the mighty sculptures. In San Marco I

rested in the tranquil cloister before climbing endless steps to be confronted by Fra Angelico's exquisite Annunciation. He was the most
devout of painters, one who always prayed before taking up his brush,
and no doubt the intensity of his religious convictions inspired him to
the heights he achieved, but unbelievers too revere him for his mastery
of colour and composition and for bringing a sublime freshness to
what was then one of the most hackneyed of subjects.

There was an entire fortnight in which to savour the delights of
Florence but we also fitted in Siena, Lucca, Fiesole and Pisa. At Siena I
had the pleasure of conducting my friends, who were unaware of what
was to come, down the dark alleys leading to the Campo, a formidable
city centre which doubles as a race course for the Palio, and is
dominated by the most magnificent of town halls. (Though I am told
that a dour Yorkshireman once remarked, 'Nay, I'll give you it's a sight
better than Manchester's but not a patch on our Leeds.') At Fiesole, in
the Roman theatre the perfect acoustics were tested by George whom
we heard while seated in the 'Gods'; at Lucca there was the deliciously
extravagant frontage of St Michel in Foro to be enjoyed.

Two years on we took the train again, this time to Venice, where we
stayed two vaporetto stops away from the Accademia, in another district
of excellent unfashionable restaurants. I could do little sightseeing on
foot having stupidly not recalled all those little bridges which make the
city less flat than it is naturally. In compensation I took season tickets for
the vaporetti, roving from the Grand Canal over to the Lido partly for
the sake of the glorious view of the Doge's Palace and surrounds on the
return journey. I made my friends go through the ritual of sharing an
outrageously overpriced bottle of wine at Quadri's for the sheer joy of
sitting in St Mark's, wallowing in the architecture and the music from a
quartet (piano, clarinet, double bass and violin) skilfully transforming
light melodies into great music. Few experiences are more agreeable,
although a meeting with Robin and Inge Hyman who were staying at
the Monaco Hotel where they lunched us on the terrace beside the
Grand Canal was another highlight. Venice should be experienced
not once but often in a lifetime; returning to it never diminishes its
attraction.

The Hymans own a flat in Paris, close to St Germaine-des-Prés. I
have spent three short breaks there and others in Amsterdam and

Brussels in the years since 1998. I also filled in parts of France Mavis and I had not explored, notably the Vosges, and several cities in Benelux and Germany but 2006 signalled something like closure. It was the first year for four decades when I didn't drive on the Continent. That gave me a greater sense of deprivation than the actual arthritis and fatigue due to old age but in the spring of 2007 I rallied when Dean Tapley offered to accompany me on a short trip to Normandy using my car. We shared the driving, stayed three nights at Caen, went over familiar routes by the Seine and revisited the Bayeux Tapestry which I found more rewarding and better displayed than on the first time of seeing it. Dean wished to visit the Normandy beaches and I was happy to go along with him. On the cliffs above Arromanches, looking down on the remains of Mulberry harbour, which I had last seen when flown over it in 1946, I felt humbled. What a crazy idea it must have seemed when first mooted, to tow floating concrete quays over one hundred miles across the Channel in face of the enemy. But it worked, as did the whole invasion. Dean and I reminded ourselves how disagreeable our lives might have been had it not. Were I a few months older I could well have ended mine on one of those beaches. I'm glad I never had the courage nor the deep conviction to become a conscientious objector; I'm equally grateful that I was never called on to go into battle.

We returned to Calais using, for the final twenty miles, the old, winding, coastal road from Boulogne, passing through villages and farmland and dotted with fortifications. Over the sand dunes, the views of Kent and the white cliffs make it by far the most pleasant entry into Calais. An agreeable ending to a short holiday. I was grateful to my cousin.

Despite what I have written, in 2008, George and I went on a Saga cruise from Southampton to the Med. and back, calling at ports in Italy and Iberia. It was worth it for a day spent in Florence and I found Gibraltar unexpectedly interesting but the trouble with cruising is that one spends so much time at sea. The incidence, on the ocean, of Romanesque churches, classical amphitheatres and galleries, proved nil. This was disappointing.

# 18

## Oral History, Written History

During the last months of Mavis's long illness, when I was housebound most days and evenings, I found writing a necessary diversion. She spent much time resting or asleep, invariably retiring early to bed, and it was then that I started a novel. Indulging the creative instinct is effective in temporarily banishing painful mental and physical circumstances. *Brought to Book*, the novel I chose to write in 1998, based loosely though quite deliberately on the life of Christina Foyle, allowed me to escape from the ever-present reality of my dying wife and I feel no shame about that. It helped to sustain me during the hours when she didn't need my attention. After her death I completed it as therapy against grief. What may seem more curious is the fact that the book conveyed much levity within an overall structure that starts with Blanche (or 'Christina', if you like) dying and then deals with the bizarre conditions of her will. She leaves all her fortune to one of her six lovers, although which one has to be determined by a ballot. This bears no relevance to anything I know of the famous bookseller's love life.

After Christina's death, in 1999, I would like to have written a straightforward biography of that extraordinary woman. I had a publisher willing to sign a contract if I obtained permission to research the Foyle archives but Christopher Foyle, who with his cousin Bill Samuel inherited much of that part of Christina's fortune which wasn't left to animal welfare, said I could not have access. He was not unfriendly, just adamant, so I contented myself with writing a brief life to include in a proposed book about distinguished publishers and booksellers I had known. This emerged from a project named The Graveyard Press which I had entered into with David Whitaker, to publish short lives of the book trade great, correcting errors in often hastily written obituaries and assessing the subjects with more objectivity than is often accorded them at the time of death. We even formed a company for the purpose, but each of us became interested in other projects and dropped the idea. As a substitute, starting with Christina Foyle, I embarked on *Mentors and Friends*, a series of brief lives of eminent publishers and booksellers I had known. I chose nine other subjects adding, in a postscript, a note about my foremost benefactor, Alan Steele.

A decade or two earlier I would have found a publisher; public library sales would have accounted for a few hundred copies and the book would probably have broken even on a small print run. To my surprise Ernest Hecht read it, liked it and wrote to me the only really serious letter I have ever received from him. But would he publish it? No way. The demand, he asserted, would be too low. Would he not, if he really thought the book to be of sufficient importance – which he did – risk losing some of his considerable fortune on it? No. 'You're a mean bastard,' I told him, adding 'It isn't right for your list anyway. Now buy me lunch.' 'It's your turn,' he retorted, then suggested the book should be published by subscription. I reported this to Andrew Hewson, literary agent, who had also been generous in his praise. He thought this could be the answer and personally promised to buy six copies. He also recommended I should ask Elliott & Thompson, who had published *Brought to Book*, to take it on. David Elliott readily agreed and sent out a brochure which drew two hundred subscribers, sufficient to go ahead. I felt grateful to my friends and others who paid their £25.00 each for the book unseen, even though a score or more of them had read either the whole typescript or individual chapters.

I received a lot of disinterested, helpful advice, with everyone forecasting a post-publication sale once the rest of the trade knew about it. That didn't happen because the book went unreviewed in the national heavies and also in *The Bookseller*, which was under new ownership and an editor who had come from outside the trade. He had been friendly in lending me photographs from the journal's archive but he could not be persuaded to feature it in his columns as a news item or to review it. I try not to feel bitter but it rankles that, after being a contributor over a period of nearly fifty years under five editors, the 'Organ of the Book Trade' chose to ignore *Mentors and Friends*. Even *Publishing News* gave it only a friendly paragraph in the gossip column. My appeal to Liz Thomson, the editor, who I had known since she joined the journal as a reporter, to send it for review to one of the young bloods of the trade for a truly objective comment, went unheard. It was mentioned favourably in Gordon Graham's *Logos*, in the Penguin Collectors'

Society half-yearly booklet and in the final issue of a magazine for the antiquarian book trade where Brian Alderson, book dealer, expert on children's literature, and long-standing friend, wrote approvingly apart from pointing out that where I referred to Erasmus Darwin I had meant Charles. This boob went unnoticed by the fifteen people who had read the typescript of that particular chapter, as well as by David Elliott and myself who had read it many times. After a lifetime spent in writing, editing and publishing books, as well as selling them, it amazes me still how obvious errors get overlooked.

*Mentors and Friends* was well received by many of its subscribers, even by some without book trade connections. It is a book of which I am proud; at least it exists in various archives and may prove of value to book-trade historians and biographers. Among those who were helpful to me was Christopher Foyle, who not only read my chapter on his aunt and made pertinent comments, but subscribed six copies. I wish he had warmed to my project earlier because it would have fascinated me to have written in greater depth about Christina, who was a remarkable woman, almost certainly more sinning than sinned against. The tape I made with her one morning, in the late nineties, at Beeleigh Abbey, her historic Essex home, forms part of the Book Trade Lives Project in the sound archive of the British Library. This oral history enterprise, formerly named the National Life Story Collection (NLSC), is a record of the lives, in their own words, of thousands of artists, cooks, clerks, business tycoons, middle managers, authors and workers in widely different occupations. I became involved when I mentioned to Martyn Goff that it was a pity the memoirs of publishers and booksellers were, in most cases, no longer published except for occasional volumes paid for by the authors. I felt a lot of potentially valuable trade history had become unrecoverable. He was already Chairman of the NLSC, in which capacity he suggested I should make a list of those whom I thought should be taped, although he warned that each and every project had to find its own backing within the framework of the British Library, which provided only administrative staff and storage.

I compiled an initial list of a hundred and fifty potential inter-viewees, almost all of them publishers or booksellers, and made a start by taping Ronald Whiting. I also went to Beeleigh Abbey, as mentioned above, to place Christina Foyle on record. I found myself in her smallish ground floor study so crammed with books that it was difficult to squeeze myself in. There I attached a microphone to her cleavage which I found embarrassing, though she did not. She offered me champagne which I declined in favour of tea because it was only mid-morning. I spent about one and a half hours asking her questions. She, already well into her eighties, was inclined to repetition and we often proceeded along the did-you-know-old-so-and-so track until I remembered it was her memories we were supposed to be preserving for posterity, not mine. Following the recording, we moved to a gloomy, hexagonal gothic chamber, possibly once a side chapel, where champagne and smoked salmon, followed by chicken, were served.

Even down at Beeleigh, in the remote Essex countryside, where a squad of old retainers fussed around, always addressing her, as 'Miss Foyle', Christina was authoritarian and sharp. 'Margaret!' she would call out, 'Bring more champagne.' 'Denise, why haven't you served the potatoes?' And so on. The ambience of upstairs/downstairs was apparent as the minions scurried about obeying Madam's wishes. I wished I had kept my tape recorder turned on because in the spirit of gossip she uttered indiscretions, asking if I had met a certain senior manager who her nephew Christopher had recently rumbled and sacked for the usual reason. When her will was published, I saw that she had bequeathed this person a five figure sum and, apparently, forgotten to amend it.

I had lengthy recording sessions with Ron Whiting, in my own house, where he complained that they were too detailed. 'Who cares?' he demanded, 'who my father's colleagues were at the jam factory where he worked?' Oral history, I explained to him, had to be as wide-ranging as was practical, it had to include everything to do with a subject and his/her forbears.

My mastery of the technicalities of tape recording was tenuous. Several times I had to phone the office for instruction and Ronald was patient about this, because he was only marginally more capable than I was. At least six sides of Whiting were made before I was quietly transferred to an advisory role. (The archive does have two other interviews of mine, with Alan Hill and Martyn Goff. The former includes Alan's memorable dismissal of Beethoven's music as 'too soupy'.)

By the time I gave up interviewing, Martyn Goff had lunched with Rayner Unwin, chairman of the Unwin Trust, founded by his late father – Sir Stanley. As a result he and his fellow trustees offered

£50,000 and a further similar sum, if matched, pound for pound, by others. This got Book Trade Lives going.

I had already recruited Michael Turner and David Whitaker, both now retired, to join me as advisers and, in so doing, breached protocol although no one at the BL rebuked me openly for taking matters into my own hands. It was obvious for Martyn to invite Rayner to swell our ranks but the appointment, as salaried interviewer, of Sue Bradley was through official channels and my assistance was not called upon. It was an inspired choice. Sue had interviewed professionally before and very soon came to know as much, probably more, about the twentieth century British book trade as anyone alive. At first she had to learn the demarkation line between the retailers of new and second-hand/ antiquarian books, which are two distinct professions although sometimes undertaken by the same person. Sue also had to be instructed in what was, and was not, strictly book trade outside of retailing. Printers and binders were not while production personnel within publishing were. The book trade certainly needed printers and binders but theirs was a separate industry, except that occasionally, they might enter the retail market (e.g. Jarrold's of Norwich). Literary agents were deemed to be in a grey area; literary editors, however friendly, were quite definitely categorised as journalists. Sue came to appreciate these subtleties as she went about to tape the Thins, in Edinburgh, Tony Schmidt, in Aberdeen, and independent booksellers, working or retired in Cumbria, Dorset, Kent and elsewhere. In London and the south east she visited the homes and offices of publishers. In addition to those on my original list and those suggested by members of the advisory board she used her initiative to record others who were recommended by interviewees.

Two years into the project I made a futile attempt to analyse what had already been achieved by breaking down the sixty or so interviewees, first into publishers and booksellers, then into sub-categories of each. I circulated a paper to the committee and made recommendations for obvious gaps to be filled, the idea being to keep the archive balanced. But oral history is not balanced. It is anarchic. It has no structure. This at first perturbed me because as a writer I have always been accustomed to working to a length and a pattern. A book should have a beginning, a middle and an end. It should reach a climax, it shouldn't be repetitive. But oral history doesn't have a shape. It is like psychoanalysis. The interviewee is on a couch; the interviewer probes.

The 'patient' is encouraged to air his thoughts, explain them, describe those people he mentions, take any and every digression which turns up and pursue it relentlessly. It is essentially tedious to the listener and virtually impossible to read as narrative.

When Sue was recording me I made a list of subjects in an effort to maintain some sort of coherent control. I presented it to her at the start of a session. She placed it in front of her, then politely ignored it as she led me to wherever she perceived we might be going. All my life I have written for editors who demanded a specific number of words. The lack of this discipline worried me. The sessions were tense. I always demanded an interval after about two hours because I had a sick headache or needed a drink, or both. We would break off, have lunch, then recommence, recording for perhaps another hour. It was tiring, concentrated work.

Rayner Unwin's problems with the Project were that he could not be persuaded to understand that written and oral history are complementary and that published memoirs do not invalidate an accompanying tape. I instanced Victor Gollancz, as undisciplined a writer as ever made the printed page. Because of his patriarchal status no one at Gollancz dared to suggest to Victor that his own work should be edited. Or, if they did, he overruled them. His immensely long memoirs, commencing with *A Diary for Timothy*, might be supposed to tell all. They do not. Extreme egotists, such as Victor, are unlikely to ask themselves the same pertinent questions as Sue Bradley would. If they had, their answers might have raised Timothy's eyebrows.

Rayner died before we were able to convince him that he should lie on the couch. He had recently written his memoirs, manifesting a self control unknown to Victor, confessing what he saw as his misjudgements when, after a long wait in the wings, he had assumed control of George Allen & Unwin. They are a valuable historical document, not only for trade historians, but for students of J. R. R. Tolkien with whom he had a long writer-editor relationship. I was touched when he sent me a copy affectionately inscribed. I knew Rayner, who had the warmth I found lacking in his father, for over forty years At NLSC meetings he more than once expressed doubts about the length of each tape which was devoted to early life and ancestry. He believed, as I did, that limits should be set according to the funds available, thus requiring interviewees to concentrate on their working careers. The professional oral historians demurred although approving his insistence that we should interview former workers in the industry who carried out the more menial tasks . . . secretaries, packers, those occupying uncarpeted office space.

Diana Murray, widow of Jock, was one 'patient' who firmly refused to make more than one or two tapes. Some of us went on for twenty-thirty sides; later the chore of listening to mine to ensure they included nothing slanderous, or too unkind, became so onerous that I have never made it to the end.

Martyn continued to search for other sponsors. David Whitaker gave a generous sum, others gave smaller amounts and, after Rayner's death, the Unwin Trust indicated that further funds were likely to become available. The project could have been unending but the BL called a halt on the grounds of maintaining a sense of proportion. For them the overall enterprise was becoming unbalanced; possibly book trade folk were more loquacious than painters, city financiers, fashion designers etc. I regretted this because it left too many untaped, who might soon be dead and it seemed foreign to the unending nature of oral history. Sue might well have found herself a job for life but probably, for her sanity, it is better that she has moved on to different work at the University of Newcastle.

In this ultimate (I hope) decade of my life, when looking at paintings is a more enriching experience than playgoing, I am relieved that I didn't become a drama critic. To have endured some minor classics twenty or more times and certain offerings even once would have been life-threatening. Theatre was a vital part of my life for seventy years (although I coped without it during my time in India and Provence) but, in the wrong hands, even favourite plays can let you down in a way that much loved paintings do not. The major art galleries have thus far resisted updating the meaning of masterpieces on their walls. I have yet to come across a Fra Angelico's Annunciation depicting Mary in a blouse with torn jeans receiving an angel landing by helicopter, although I would have no objection to a contemporary canvas which illustrated just that.

Frequently I hear it said, 'I don't understand paintings. I don't know how to look at them.' There is no mystique about it. You have only to go into a gallery, wander around it and wait until a picture grabs you. Then you stand in front of it and let the magic work. It doesn't matter whether or not it is by a great master; all that can come later. Just allow the chemistry between you and what is set before you to weave its spell. In due course you will refine your taste, widen it, learn more about what you see, dare to pronounce judgements, rejecting this and embracing that. You can take your time, move away, return and have another look. Greatly daring, you may acquire paintings/drawings of your own, support a living artist in the way you reward a living writer by buying his books. Then you can get to know them on your own walls.

In the theatre, directors may be justified in cutting some of the more obscure minor scenes in Shakespeare and of the longer speeches in Shaw; where they err is in substituting invented business which can produce longueurs of their own making. In most instances I am against presentations of the classics in contemporary costume or that of a period far removed from the original. It can be patronising, a dumbing-down gesture to emphasis contemporary overtones but, more often, it is an excuse for showing-off. A good working rule would be not to mount a play in costumes and settings later than the time in which it was written. I cannot believe it helps to set Chekhov in any period except the latter part of the nineteenth century in Russia. The time and place are essential to it; the universality lies in the truth of the writing. Please spare us Madame Ranesvsky bewailing her lot beside a crumbling Caribbean planter's bungalow, or a governor's summer palace in the Himalayas during the Raj. And let us not have Goneril and Regan swanning about in gracious Edwardian ballroom gowns while rejecting their father's private army. It is one thing to use the theme of Oedipus in a contemporary play in a modern setting; to place Sophocles' tragedy in twenty-first century Thebes is ridiculous.

A significant element in the current obsession with modernising a classic lies with the necessity felt by directors to be seen by their competitors to be 'doing something new with it'; the other is the elaborate stage equipment now available which make the transformation scenes of the pantos of my youth seem tame. We all know what can be done with the ingenious devices available at the Olivier Theatre. They can add to the enchantment of, say *The Wind in the Willows*, but are not needed to convey the magnificent language of Shakespeare or Congreve. At the Aldwych, in the sixties, Peter Brook's production of *King Lear*, with Paul Scofield, was performed for three hours on an almost empty stage and there was little if any music. Nor was the stage much adorned for that deeply moving second act of *The*

*Cherry Orchard* in a recent revival at the National when Trevor Nunn wisely allowed the author to set the mood which was perfectly caught by the actors lounging about, philosophising, in the merest suggestion of open country. It was simple theatre at its best. The costumes told us the date, c.1890, the dialogue that we were close to Gayev's house. We could not have been anywhere else. And it is possible to present effective theatre at low cost without employing voice coaches and all those other hangers-on listed in current programmes, by using trained actors who have been taught to project their voices and their persons.

There can be no offence in Michael Frayn or David Hare writing their own version of *Twelfth Night*, any more than there was to Shakespeare leaning on *A Spanish Tragedy* to create *Hamlet*. Present day composers score their own sounds and musicians play them but orchestras are not required to perform Beethoven's seventh in the style of Stockhausen. They may take it at varying tempi, omit some repeats and draw the notes from instruments more refined than those available in the composer's day but, by and large, they treat Beethoven with respect, which is more than can be said for the way many directors and actors deal with Shakespeare.

I haven't totally rejected theatre all the while I am able to drive over Waterloo Bridge and park beneath that concrete horror designated the National Theatre to confront what is on offer. There is always a chance that once again disbelief will be suspended despite – or even because of – what directors have done. I will always remember what Tyrone Guthrie in a particularly inspired and exuberant production 'did' for *Tamburlaine* and how Michael Blakemore extended the bounds of simplicity with *Copenhagen*.

One day in late July 2004, on my way to lunch at the Garrick, I resolved to throw a hostage to fortune and book the club for my eightieth birthday three years hence. Previously Michael Rubinstein had done this for a similar celebration at which I was MC. On a Sunday, when the club is not usually open, members may hire it for a private party with dress regulations relaxed, children admitted and no gender taboos about which room or staircase may be used (apart from the Ladies and the Gents). It had been a joyful occasion with many of Michael's family present and even more of his friends. There was no seating plan for lunch. As guests entered the coffee room (as the main members' dining room is known) they were handed a cloakroom

ticket, selected at random from a hat held by Joy Rubinstein, allocating
them a seat at a particular table. This was a dangerous way of over-
coming the horrendous task of placing everyone individually. Because
we were all so well behaved it worked. The only moment of possible
conflict arose when Michael, in replying to the toast, chose to comment that he believed the Israelis owed an overall apology to the
Palestinians. This was not enthusiastically received by some of his
Jewish friends but they bore it well.

Michael did not practice Judaism; he favoured a kind of sufism and
wrote gently amusing stories about a mullah when he wasn't practising
law or involved in more scholarly work, such as a study of the cart
tracks of Gozo or of the Rembrandts in the Hermitage. He came from
a legal family. His uncle wrote the bestselling Pelican publication *John
Citizen and the Law*; he himself had acted for Allen Lane and Penguin
books in the *Lady Chatterley's Lover* case; his father had written plays
published by Victor Gollancz, who was a relation; his brother Hilary
was a publisher turned literary agent and founder of *The Good Hotel
Guide*.

I felt flattered at being appointed MC for the birthday lunch and
became a temporary, honorary Rubinstein to propose Michael's health.
I owed him a lot because he had put me forward for membership of the
Garrick in the seventies, with Alan Steele as seconder. Michael and Joy
lived for a long while in the Vale of Health on Hampstead Heath and
they were frequent visitors to the shop. Once I had been elected, our
friendship bloomed; we both became part of the unofficial fraternity
known as 'the Monday club', which assembles at the round table at the
east end of the coffee room. Formerly it was known as 'the publishers'
table' (and still is by older members) because it was colonised by the
likes of Hamish Hamilton, Robert Lusty, Jack Newth (of A. & C. Black,
which brings out *Who's Who* annually) and other heads of imprints,
many of whom were chauffeured to and from the club in company
Bentleys. By my time, the senior, dominant figure was George Mikes,
the Hungarian-born humorist, who could never bring himself to sit at
any other table and who would have left the coffee room rather than
place himself at the long central table where tradition insists that a
newcomer must occupy a chair next to or opposite one already taken.
Although to describe George as dominating any gathering is slightly
absurd – because he was a small round man with no aggressive
tendencies except towards his childhood friend, and publisher, André

Deutsch. He entertained a suspect notion that he was unable to recognise anyone except by their voice. I caught him out a few times but usually this foible was allowed to go unchallenged; it was a simple conceit which seemed to give him pleasure. George rarely used the first-floor cocktail bar and was thus ensconced in the coffee room before his friends were ready to join him. He would almost crouch there at the far end of the room, alone at the round table (this was permissible by club protocol), awaiting our company. He had made his name with a best-selling satirical assessment of the English entitled *How to be an Alien* which, after sixty years, is still funny. Like many Hungarians he became totally integrated into his adopted country. He lived in what he described as a very tiny house – it became smaller with each repeated description – in south west London close to the Hurlingham Club, of which he was also a member. There, following a divorce, he lived alone although he frequently referred to his mistress, whom I did not meet until his memorial gathering.

There are fewer publishers – most of them retired – frequenting the table nowadays, notably Robin Hyman and David Gadsby (successor to Newth on the *Who's Who* front); there are other booksellers, the antiquarian Anthony Rota, expert dealer in modern first editions and reliable authority on the opera houses of the world; Philip Joseph who 'retired' home from Johannesburg, where he had run a successful shop, to buy a small, ailing remainder chain which he and his son expanded to forty branches before selling to an American group for a vast sum; Bing Taylor, the Anglo-American sometime president of the Booksellers' Association, and former publisher; Andrew Hewson, actor turned literary agent; Michael O'Donnell, doctor and broadcaster; Gerald Isaaman, former editor of the *Ham & High*; Eric de Bellaigue, financial analyst and historian/student of the book trade; cardiologist Michael Oliver, professor emeritus of Edinburgh University; and historian of Spain, Jocelyn Hillgarth, lecturer at Harvard and Toronto. Michael Oliver and Jocelyn are academics who are passionate about painting and theatre. They are a latter day Box and Cox; Michael spends the summer months in Umbria, Jocelyn lives on Majorca in the winter. They seldom meet which cuts down overcrowding at the round table, officially a six-seater, though it has taken eight, even nine at times.

All those named and their partners were invited to, and most attended, my eightieth birthday lunch held, as was Michael

Rubinstein's, on a Sunday. Friendships often formed at the club extend into family life; our wives are or were known to each other; we visit each others homes. Being a member, far from exemplifying exclusivity, has widened close acquaintanceship more than any other experience since National Service, and brought me in touch with many I would not otherwise have known. Despite infrequent outbursts of intolerance there is innate goodwill between members who are in a sense bound into good behaviour by the staff, male and female, who serve us with affectionate dignity, keeping us at the correct distance. On the day of my celebration I dare say there was comment behind the scenes on the way some of those attending were dressed. It happened, although already August, to be the first really hot day of the summer. Gentlemen had been advised on the invitation that the so-called tie rule (in fact, only a convention) would not apply. Smart casual attire, as requested, was interpreted liberally although no man wore shorts. Yet the ceilings did not fall, the structure remained stable and the esteemed subjects of the fine theatrical portraits on the walls were not observed to frown, blush or wink.

Half of those present had book trade and Hampstead connections, twenty were family, including my daughters, grandchildren, sister, four cousins, a niece and a nephew; Mountview Theatre Club was represented, so were The Pretenders. My two closest friends for over sixty years, George Simpson and Martyn Goff, are not members of the Garrick. George, who whether or not he likes it is regarded by my family as an honorary Norrie, was MC; Martyn was absent because he was in hospital. We should have sat down eighty-five but two retired hurt at the reception; a quarter of those invited declined through illness and holiday commitments; some of those I would most like to have been there had died. Sister Peggy's short, restrained, affectionate 'few words' all but stole the show; David Whitaker proposed my health and referred to me as 'a life enhancer', a designation which, one person present commented to me, quite matter-of-factly, 'went too far'.

A few hours later I sat alone on my patio and reflected on my good fortune. In my reply to David I had said I did not believe in a hereafter but that should I be wrong I hoped we might all meet again, glasses charged, around a great table in the sky or possibly beneath it. I do not look forward to a repeat in ten year's time. Too many of us are lingering for too long and, when you consider eternity, what is an extra decade or so beyond three score years and ten? Time spent on earth is infinitesimal. 'We are all used to non-existing,' wrote George Mikes, adding that he had not existed in 500BC, and would not be alive in AD3117.

We come from one black hole and disappear into another. For a brief period in between, supposing you are favoured, you may respond to Michelangelo, Rembrandt, Monet; to Beethoven and Chopin, Shakespeare and Chekhov; you may find yourself humbled by the Himalayas, entranced by the Scottish Highlands, overwhelmed by sight of the Pont du Gard and Gothic cathedrals, beguiled by Romanesque churches or an English spring morning. You may bask in 'a beaker full of the warm south'; sip Chablis in the silence of a balmy summer's night . . .

To have been adult, healthy and middle-class in Western Europe, during the second half of the twentieth century, is probably as privileged a lot as one could have hoped for at any time in history. Born 1927, just missing action in WWII, sufficiently educated to make a moderately prosperous living doing something I found stimulating, having a long, happy marriage, children, grandchildren, hosts of friends, a more than adequate pension – I should be so lucky. What have I to moan about?

Well . . . it will probably see me out but it can't last. The freedom of expression and the comparative safety of West European cities, which I have been able to take for granted all my adult life, are in danger of being seriously eroded by humourless, religious fundamentalists and politically correct legislators who are daily undermined by derisive, power-without-responsibility media commentators. Surely it is likely we shall destroy ourselves either by misuse of the ghastly weapons we have invented or through our abuse of the earth's resources? Or will civilisation once again be saved by the skin of its teeth?

(Yet there are still new experiences to be savoured. On the last day of Wimbledon 2007 I watched players – admittedly in a mixed doubles, not a singles final – enjoying themselves on the centre court and actually *laughing*, even when they had lost a point.)

# Burgh House

New End Square, Hampstead, NW3 1LT.

Tel 01-431 0144.

HAMPSTEAD MILLENNIUM
& HAMPSTEAD MUSEUM

present

an Exhibition

## *Writers and Hampstead*

*Observations on the place and the people*

## 101 COMMENTATORS FROM DOMESDAY TO DRABBLE

JOHN KEATS

Devised by IAN NORRIE

Calligraphy by GEORGE SIMPSON

## March 8 – April 27

Weds – Suns 12 – 5 Admission Free

D.H. LAWRENCE

EXHIBITION
TO BE OPENED BY

## MELVYN BRAGG

at a PREVIEW PARTY on
March 7 at 6 pm

VIRGINIA WOOLF

YOU ARE MOST CORDIALLY
INVITED TO THE PREVIEW PARTY

Poster for Writers and Hampstead Exhibition, 1986

# Postscript
## (originally my Christmas card for 2004)

The Rise and Fall of the British book trade in three imperfect sonnets:

Before fifteen hundred moveable type
Was not in use to set secular hype.
'Solemn and sacred works' were preferred
So Caxton confirmed to Wynkyn de Worde.
'A godly book shall be man's brightest pearl.
'Cry "hymnals and psalters", give both a whirl.'
Next he went on to reissue missals,
Costing no more than penny tin whistles.
Old Testament tales he also reprinted,
Purple prose passages, pure and unstinted.
Asked, 'Surely these are dangerous libels?'
Caxton replied, 'Truth is stranger than bibles.'
    Bulk orders and singles arrived every morn.
    The problem of distribution was born.

Four centuries later, Collins and Hodder
Dealt in both sacred and secular fodder,
While fiction evolved in a three-decker set
Borrowed from Mudie's, sold strictly non-net.
'Til, enter stage right, a hero (not villain),
Thinly disguised as Fred'rick Macmillan.
He told competitors they must support
A Net Book Agreement for retailers caught
In cut-price combat they couldn't afford.
Loss leader arguments must be ignored!
So Murray, Black, Blackie, Longman, et al
Forbade booksellers to under-booksell.
    Deliv'ry was poor, thus shops became partial
    To wholesaler service from Simpkin Marshall.

In the Depression the trade felt the rub,
So someone suggested, 'Start a book club.'
At Park Lane lit luncheons a Foyle became queen,
Then Allen Lane sang, 'Let's beguine the Penguine.'
Books boomed in wartime as never before;
In peacetime came Churchill's *Second World War.*
    Simpkins then foundered; discounts were too low.
    Pound-foolish suppliers bore this body blow.

The paperback challenge made markets wherein
Bare boobs vied with eggheads, both dumped in a bin.
Encouraged by Charter, bookshops came of age
(Yet staff were still paid a derisory wage.)
Publishers, slow to get books out of storage,
Relied, to their cost, on Bertram's of Norwich.
Discounts rose sharply; to such an extent
Some feared they'd reach one hundred per cent.
Trade giants on both sides were forged into chains.
The Net Book Agreement slurped down the drains.
Conglomerates, globally, started a trend
To take over the British. This signalled the end.
    Net became inter-net, Amazon stirred,
    Distributing every blynkyn' de worde.

# Index

(Author's note: A simple key to most persons and places, also to some works of art and literature, mentioned in the text. This is not a scholarly work so there are few cross references. *M&F* refers to *Mentors and Friends*.)